THE CAMBRIDGE HISTORY

OF

ENGLISH LITERATURE

VOLUME VII

CAVALIER AND PURITAN

The Cambridge History
of
English Literature

Edited by

A. W. Ward, Litt.D., F.B.A.
Master of Peterhouse

and

A. R. Waller, M.A.
Peterhouse

Volume VII

Cavalier and Puritan

New York: The Macmillan Company

Cambridge, England: at the University Press

1933

PRINTED IN THE UNITED STATES OF AMERICA
BY THE FERRIS PRINTING COMPANY

CONTENTS

CHAPTER I

CAVALIER LYRISTS

By F. W. MOORMAN, B.A. (Lond.), Ph.D. (Strassburg), Assistant Professor of English Language and Literature in the University of Leeds.

CHAPTER II

THE SACRED POETS

By the REV. F. E. HUTCHINSON, M.A., Trinity College, Oxford, Chaplain of King's College.

Contents

Contents

CHAPTER VI

CAROLINE DIVINES

By the REV. W. H. HUTTON, B.D., St. John's College, Oxford.

CHAPTER VII

JOHN BUNYAN. ANDREW MARVELL

By the REV. JOHN BROWN, D.D.

CHAPTER VIII

HISTORICAL AND POLITICAL WRITINGS

I. STATE PAPERS AND LETTERS

By A. W. WARD, Litt.D., F.B.A., Master of Peterhouse.

Contents

CHAPTER IX

HISTORICAL AND POLITICAL WRITINGS

II. Histories and Memoirs

By A. W. Ward, Litt.D., F.B.A.

PAGE

CHAPTER X

ANTIQUARIES

Sir Thomas Browne. Thomas Fuller. Izaak Walton. Sir Thomas Urquhart

By George Saintsbury, M.A.

CHAPTER XI

JACOBEAN AND CAROLINE CRITICISM

By J. E. Spingarn, Professor of Comparative Literature, Columbia University, New York.

Contents

CHAPTER XII

HOBBES AND CONTEMPORARY PHILOSOPHY

By W. R. SORLEY, Litt.D., LL.D., F.B.A., Fellow of King's College, Knightbridge Professor of Moral Philosophy.

CHAPTER XIII

SCHOLARS AND SCHOLARSHIP, 1600–60

By FOSTER WATSON, M.A., Professor of Education in the University College of Wales, Aberystwyth.

CHAPTER XIV

ENGLISH GRAMMAR SCHOOLS

By J. BASS MULLINGER, M.A., formerly librarian of St. John's College.

Contents

CHAPTER XV

THE BEGINNINGS OF ENGLISH JOURNALISM

By J. B. WILLIAMS.

CHAPTER XVI

THE ADVENT OF MODERN THOUGHT IN POPULAR LITERATURE

THE WITCH CONTROVERSY, PAMPHLETEERS

By HAROLD V. ROUTH, M.A., Peterhouse, Professor of Latin, Trinity College, Toronto.

The Cambridge History of
English Literature

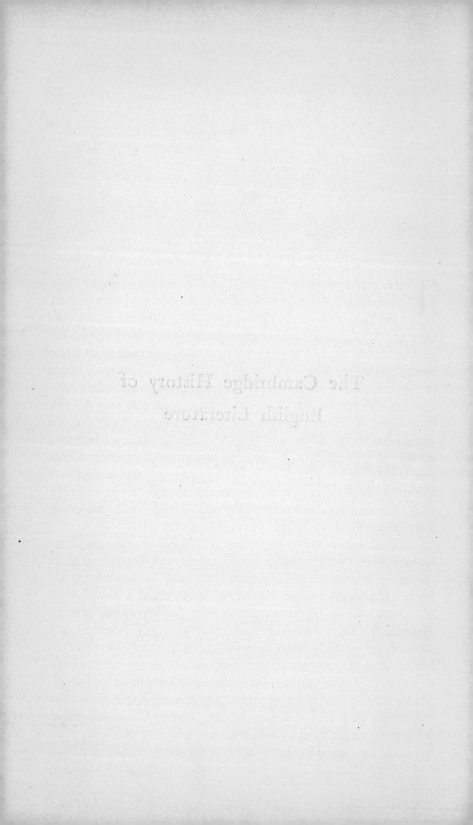

The Cambridge History of
English Literature

CHAPTER I

Cavalier Lyrists

THE early years of the reign of Charles I are made illustrious by a great outburst of song, which is very varied in character, and which suffered no diminution in volume or melody until the sound of the lute was drowned by that of the drum, and love-lyrics to Celia or Anthea gave place to the scurrilous abuse of the *Rump-Songs*. The true home of this lyric, as of the French *Pléiade* song of the preceding generation, was the court, where the pastoral fancies and gallant inventions of cavalier poets were promptly set to music by composers in the royal service, and sung before the monarch at Whitehall. But, in the case of the greatest of these Caroline lyrists, the inspiration spread from court to country, and the most memorable of the *Hesperides* songs are those which sing of hock-carts, country wakes and Devon maidens going a-maying.

The Caroline lyric, again, is a portion of the great renascence lyric which begins with Surrey and Wyatt, includes the great masters of Elizabethan song and, as Swinburne has finely said, "grows fuller if not brighter through a whole chain of constellations till it culminates in the crowning star of Herrick." Yet, if the unity of English song from *Tottel's Miscellany* to *Hesperides* is undeniable, it must be acknowledged that, as we pass from the sixteenth to the seventeenth century, a certain change of form and temper is apparent. Many of the old melodies pass away, and are replaced by something new and different in character. The Petrarchian influence, which made itself felt, not only in the sonnet sequences, but, also, in the song-books and miscellany lyrics, of the Elizabethan age, loses much of its potency after the year

1600; its chivalrous and dreamy idealism ceases to charm, and there is a return to the greater directness and less ethereal temper of the classical lyric of Anacreon, Catullus and Horace.

The swift decline of the sonnet after the close of the sixteenth century is one of the most remarkable events in the history of the English lyric. The decline was due, in part, to exhaustion; in part, too, to the opposition which the sonnet encountered at the hands of two poets—Jonson and Donne— the impress of whose genius is felt in English poetry far into the seventeenth century. Donne's war upon Petrarchianism, and his creation of a love-lyric which, in its individuality and plangent realism, as well as in the "metaphysical" qualities of its style, was directly opposed to the visionary romanticism and Italian grace of the sonnet, has been the theme of a preceding chapter;[1] but the influence of Donne upon the secular lyric of the Caroline age, though apparent enough in Suckling, was less penetrating than that of his contemporary, Jonson, who, if he joined with Donne in cursing Petrarch "for redacting verses to sonnets," would fain have sent the author of *Songs and Sonets* to Tyburn "for not keeping of accent." And, whereas Donne, in the audacity of heady youthfulness, was a law unto himself, in all that pertained to lyric art, Jonson, in poetry as in drama, deliberately set about imitating the best models of the classical muse. In the field of drama, his endeavours met with but partial success; but, in poetry, he was more fortunate, and won for himself, as a reformer of the English lyric, an influence which may even be compared with that of Malherbe in the poetry of seventeenth century France.

The classical lyric, as represented, in particular, by the odes of Anacreon and the songs of Catullus and Horace, had been regarded with due respect already in the early days of the renascence. The Anacreontic temper is seen in such a song as Greene's "Cupid abroad was lated in the night" from *Orpharion* (licensed 1589) and in Lodge's *Barginet of Antimachus* from *England's Helicon*, while translations or imitations of Anacreon find a place in *Canzonets to foure voyces*, set to music and published by Giles Farnaby in 1598. Spenser introduces into his gorgeous painting of the Bower of Bliss the theme of Ausonius's famous lyric, *Collige, virgo, rosas;* and, among

[1] Vol. IV, Chap. XI.

many English renderings of Catullus's famous song to Lesbia, *Vivamus, mea Lesbia, atque amemus*, none comes so near to the spirit of the original as Campion's "My sweetest Lesbia, let us live and love." The influence of Catullus is seen, too, in most of the Elizabethan wedding-odes, while renderings of the famous *Integer vitae* ode of Horace are frequently met with before 1600. But, until the coming of Ben Jonson, the influence of the classical lyric on English poetry was fitful and uncertain. Its supporters, only too often, had followed wandering fires; and, led astray by metrical heresies, their classicism had found expression in the attempt to reproduce in rimeless quantitative verse the Sapphic or Anacreontic measures of antiquity.

Jonson's attitude towards the classical lyric differed widely from that of his predecessors. Caring nothing at all for quantitative measures, he was conscious, in spite of his *Fit of Rhyme against Rhyme*, of the value of rime in English lyric verse; what he admired most of all in the lyric of Rome or Greece was its sense of proportion and structural beauty, its restraint, lucidity and concision of style and its freedom from extravagance and mannerism. It is well known that several of his most famous songs are faithful transcripts of classical models; elsewhere—as, for instance, in the songs from *The Masque of Augures* or from *Mercury Vindicated*—he reproduces much of the atmosphere of the ancient world. And, even where there is neither direct imitation nor the reproduction of a classic atmosphere, his lyrics, in virtue of their style, show a certain classic feeling, which was immediately recognised by his contemporaries and successors, one of whom, contributing his meed of praise to the dead laureate in *Jonsonus Virbius*, speaks of his lyrics as

> Tuned to the highest key of ancient Rome,
> Returning all her music with his own.

Jonson was the first, and, in some ways, the greatest of English literary dictators, and his influence, during the declining years of his life, upon the circle of poets, dramatists and others who gathered about him in the Apollo chamber of the Devil tavern, at Temple Bar, was of the strongest. It is apparent in the lyrics of the dramas and masques of the Jacobean age. In Elizabethan days, the dramatic lyric, thanks to the "wood-notes wild" of Shakespearean song, had, in the main, resisted the influence of the Italian art lyric and remained true to the principles of the old folk-song. But, after the withdrawal of Shakespeare from the stage, the classical lyric, as attuned by Ben Jonson, becomes supreme in drama. The later dramatic songs of Heywood and Fletcher, and those of Ford and Shirley, almost without exception, have a classical ring in them, which brings them very near to the manner of Jonson, and removes them far away from the lyrics of Amiens, Feste, or Ariel. And, when we turn from the lyrics in the dramas to those which were sung in the banqueting chamber at Whitehall, the influence of Jonson is again felt. As we shall see presently, it is everywhere apparent in the lyrics of Herrick and Carew, and its presence is likewise felt in those of Cartwright, Randolph and Waller. We recognise it in the orderly structure and finished grace of their lyrics, and in the substitution of the language of courtly gallantry, which Jonson had caught from the masters of Roman lyric, for the language of prostrate adoration, which dominates the Petrarchian school of poetry.

Yet the Petrarchian influence died hard in England. Habington still clung to the old ideals, and, in many of his lyrics to Castara, we hear the accents of the sonneteers. So, too, in the main, did Thomas Stanley, who, in spite of the fact that he was a good classical scholar, and translated some of Anacreon's odes into English verse, shows, in his best work, more of the spirit of medieval chivalry than of Augustan Rome. And the same may be said, again, of Richard Lovelace: in virtue of his associations, he belongs to the school of cavalier lyrists, whose foremost representatives are Carew and Suckling; but his songs to Lucasta owe little or nothing to Jonson or the lyrists of antiquity. His affected conceits and his sins against what is now held to be good taste are, perhaps, those of his own age; but the chivalrous temper of his songs, and the worship which he pays to her whose beauty enthralls him, are very like what we meet with in Petrarch and in the renascence sonneteers who followed Petrarch's example.

Robert Herrick, who belonged to an old Leicestershire family of Norse extraction, was the son of Nicholas Herrick, a London goldsmith, and was born in Goldsmiths' row, Cheapside, on 24 August, 1591. His father's sudden death, in 1592, led to his mother's removal to the riverside village of Hampton in Middlesex; and here, under the shadow of the proud palace which Wolsey had built, and in which Elizabeth and James held their Christmas revels, the poet's boyhood seems to have been spent. Nothing is known of his school years; but, in 1607, at the age of sixteen, he was apprenticed for a term of ten years to his uncle, Sir William Herrick, jeweller to the king, whose business house was in Wood street, Cheapside. One or two of his poems, including the Horatian *A Country Life: to his Brother, Mr. Tho. Herrick*, date from these 'prentice years; and, very probably, it was the consciousness of poetic power which induced him, in 1613, to abandon the career of a goldsmith, and to enter St. John's college, Cambridge, as a fellow-commoner. Here, or at Trinity hall, the next four years of his life were spent, and to this period belong the letters which he wrote to his guardian and uncle, Sir William. Their persistent "playne-songe" is *mitte pecuniam;* and, except by informing us that, during his last year at Cambridge, he was directing his mind to the legal profession, they throw very little light upon his career as a student.

The ten years which elapse between his graduation at Cambridge, in 1617, and his military chaplaincy under the duke of Buckingham, in 1627, form a somewhat obscure period in Herrick's life. They were probably spent chiefly in London, where, as "the music of a feast," he foregathered with Ben Jonson and his disciples at "the Sun, the Dog, the Triple Tun," and wrote some of his most spirited songs and bacchanalian lyrics. He also numbered among his acquaintance the leading musicians of the court—William and Henry Lawes, Ramsay and Laniere—and wrote songs and pastoral eclogues which were set to music by them; and some of these were sung in the royal presence at Whitehall. There is no evidence that he ever received a court appointment, but he secured the patronage of influential courtiers—Endymion Porter, Mildmay Fane earl of Westmorland and Philip Herbert earl of Pembroke— and he confesses that he owed to them "the oil of maintenance."

In or before 1627, he took orders, and, having been appointed
chaplain to the duke of Buckingham, accompanied him on his
disastrous expedition to the isle of Rhé (1627). Two years
later, he received from the king the living of Dean Prior, on
the southern confines of Dartmoor, and exchanged the festivi-
ties of city taverns and the revels of Whitehall for the sober
duties of a parish priest. This revolution in his career inspired
one of the noblest and most sustained of his poems, *His Farewell unto Poetry*, in which he reluctantly vows to part company
with his muse:

> But unto me be only hoarse, since now
> (Heaven and my soul bear record of my vow)
> I my desires screw from thee, and direct
> Them and my thoughts to that sublim'd respect
> And conscience unto priesthood. 'T is not need,
> The scarecrow unto mankind, that doth breed
> Wiser conclusions in me, since I know
> I 've more to bear my charge than way to go;
> Or had I not, I 'd stop the spreading itch
> Of craving more, so in conceit be rich.
> But 't is the God of Nature who intends
> And shapes my function for more glorious ends.

Except for occasional visits to London—one of which took
place in 1640—Herrick remained at Dean Prior until 1647,
when, having refused to subscribe to the solemn league and
covenant, he was ejected by the Long parliament. The tedium
of "dull Devonshire" oppressed him at times, and then he
broke out into bitter vituperation of the "loathed west," and
experienced an exile's longing for London, "blest place of my
nativity"; but, with an adaptability to circumstance which
is characteristic of him, he seems to have found much that
was congenial in his new surroundings, and took a peculiar
pleasure in the mystic rites and ceremonial rejoicings of village
life. The vow to part company with his muse was, fortunately,
not kept, and he confesses that his country surroundings inspired some of his finest poems. It is natural to associate most
of his courtly lyrics, and such verses as his *Farewell to Sack*,
with the London period of his career; but we are probably
right in connecting his songs

    " of brooks, of blossoms, birds and bowers,
Of April, May, of June and July flowers, "

together with the poems which tell of "may-poles, hock-
carts, wassails, wakes," mainly with the Dean Prior years.
Moreover, the title of his collection of poems—*Hesperides*
—implies that the bulk of them were written in the west
country.   Herrick never married, and it is probable that
the "many dainty mistresses"—stately Julia, smooth Anthea,
sweet Electra, Corinna whom he calls to go a-maying and
Perenna whom he asks to dress his tomb with cypress-
twigs and tears—are but creatures of his imagination.   The
pictures which he gives us, in such poems as *His Content
in the Country* and *A Thanksgiving to God for his House*, of his
life at Dean Prior with his maid, Prudence Baldwin, are
radiantly happy and full of idyllic charm; and, if he sometimes
impaled offending parishioners with an epigram, or flung a
Bible at their heads in church, he won their hearts with the
beauty of his verses, some of which were recited at Dean
Prior a century and a half after they were first written.   A
keen royalist, he followed the progress of the civil war in
alternating moods of hope and misgiving.   He celebrated the
victories of Charles in the western campaigns of 1643–5, wrote
a beautiful dirge on the death of lord Bernard Stuart, slain
at the battle of Rowton heath in 1646, and still clung to hope
when Charles came to reside, a virtual prisoner, at Hampton
court, in 1647.

Eager for fame, Herrick, nevertheless, was in no hurry to
publish his verses.   Many of these circulated in manuscript
among his friends and patrons; and the first to appear in print
was the fairy-poem, *Oberon's Diet*, which, in an imperfect
form, and under the title *A Description of his* [the king of
Faery's] *Diet*, was published in a little volume of fairy-poems
in 1635.   Five years later, three of his poems saw the light:
two of these, "Among the myrtles as I walked," and the lines
on *The Primrose*—"Ask me why I send you here"—were
fathered upon Carew, and appeared in the collected edition
of Carew's poems (1640), while the spirited verses, entitled
The Apparition of his Mistress calling him to Elysium, appeared
under the title *His Mistris Shade* in a volume, published in

1640, also including poems by Shakespeare, Jonson and Francis Beaumont. In the third edition of the famous sixteenth century miscellany *Witts Recreations* (1645) occur *A Farewell to Sack* and *The Description of a Woman;* while, in 1648, soon after his ejection from Dean Prior and return to London, he gave to the press the collection of verses, beautifully entitled *Hesperides*, included among which are not only his "unbaptised rhymes," but, also, the sacred poems, or *Noble Numbers*.

In the following year, Herrick joined with Dryden, Marvell and others in commemorating the untimely death of lord Hastings, but seems to have published no further poetry during the remaining years of his life. He probably spent most of the commonwealth period in London, where he had numerous friends and relations; but, shortly after the restoration, he went back to his living at Dean Prior, where he died in the autumn of 1674.

The twelve hundred short poems which go to form *Hesperides* may fitly be regarded as marking the supreme achievement of renascence song. Herrick is often spoken of as a cavalier lyrist; but it is well to remember that he is much more than this, and that his lyre called into being melodies for which the typical cavalier lyrists—Carew and Suckling—recked little or nothing, but which would have found attentive ears among the contemporaries of Marlowe, Breton and Shakespeare. It is true that he was no Petrarchian, and held in small esteem that union of chivalrous sentiment and Platonic idealism which went to the making of the great English sonnet sequences in the last decade of the sixteenth century; but, while he followed his master, Ben Jonson, in drawing his inspiration from the classical lyrists of Greece and Rome rather than from those of the Italian renascence, he, nevertheless, entered into that heritage of song which had come down from the homelier strains of the Elizabethan song-books and miscellanies, and was ever ready to attune his lyre to the music of Marlowe, Shakespeare and Campion. His fairy-poems closely resemble those queen Mab dreams—

> the children of an idle brain,
> Begot of nothing but vain fantasy—

with which Mercutio attempts to cure the amorous fancies of Romeo, and his *Mad Maid's Song* might very well have fallen from the lips of Ophelia. His *Cherry Ripe* is an echo of Campion's matchless lyric, "There is a garden in her face," and his *Corinna's going a-Maying* reads like a re-creation and expansion of the following little-known song from Thomas Bateson's *First Set of English Madrigals* (1604):

> Sister, awake! close not your eyes!
> The day her light discloses;
> And the bright morning doth arise
> Out of her bed of roses.
>
> See, the clear sun, the world's bright eye,
> In at our window peeping:
> Lo! how she blusheth to espy
> Us idle wenches sleeping.
>
> Therefore, awake! make haste, I say,
> And let us without staying,
> All in our gowns of green so gay
> Into the park a-maying.

Again, we may trace in *Hesperides* the influence of Marlowe. The fame of Marlowe's beautiful lyric, *The Passionate Shepherd to his Love*, reached far into the seventeenth century, but, whereas already in the handling of this theme by "Ignoto" in *The Nymph's Reply* and by Donne in *The Bait* we may detect the inrush of disillusionment, or the hardening of pastoral courtship into gallantry, Herrick's rendering of Marlowe's call to the greenwood in his lyric *To Phyllis to love and live with him* has all the virginal charm and unaffected joyance of the original.

If Herrick enters into the spirit of the idyllic song of Elizabethan days, he has also an ear for that which was still more remote from the sophisticated tastes of cavalier lyrists—the folk-song of the cornfield or the chimney corner. His charms to make the bread rise, to bring in the witch, or to scare away from the stables "the hag that rides the mare," read like the primitive charm-songs of old English poetry, while such lyrics as *The May-pole is up* and *The Tinker's Song* have the verve and melody of the popular song.

But, while there is in Herrick an unmistakable vein of romanticism and a kinship with the untutored melodists of folk-song, it must, at the same time, be remembered that he is one of the most classical of English lyrists. His classicism derives, through Ben Jonson, from the great masters of Latin lyric—Catullus and Horace—as well as from the maenad throng of Alexandrian singers whose songs of love and mirth and wine have been fathered upon the Teian poet, Anacreon. On one occasion, too, he gives us, in *The Cruel Maid*, a free rendering of one of the idylls of Theocritus. Translations, or imitations, of the so-called odes of Anacreon are, as we have seen, to be met with here and there in the later collections of Elizabethan madrigals and miscellany-lyrics; but Herrick, when, in the London taverns, he writes his *Canticles to Bacchus*, or, garlanded with flowers, exclaims—

> This day I'll drown all sorrow;
> Who knows to live to-morrow?

is the most Anacreontic of all English poets. He draws inspiration from Catullus in his epithalamia, and probably wrote his elegy *Upon the Death of his Sparrow* in imitation of Catullus's *Luctus in morte passeris;* moreover, some of his love-lyrics to Julia and Anthea are reminiscent of the famous songs to Lesbia: but he lacks the passion and poignancy of the Veronese lyrist, though he rivals him in the terse precision of his style.

Horace is the inspirer of some of Herrick's most sustained lyrics; and, the more closely the *Hesperides* poems are studied, the more fully do they reveal their author's indebtedness to the odes, epodes and epistles of the Augustan poet. Horace was his first love, and the verses entitled *A Country Life: to his Brother, Mr. Tho. Herrick*, the first draft of which belongs to his 'prentice years, are directly modelled, in thought and expression, upon the famous *Beatus ille* epode. There is not much of Horace in Herrick's love-songs; but, in his more sententious poems, and in those verses in which he promises himself immortality of fame, Horatian echoes abound, while the spirited and highly imaginative poem, *His Age*, which he dedicated to his "peculiar friend" and old Cambridge

acquaintance, John Weekes, is one of the most Horatian
lyrics in English literature.

But the classicism of Herrick extends far beyond the scope
of direct indebtedness to individual Greek or Roman authors.
The atmosphere of his verses may be that of the London tavern
or the Devonshire village, but, often enough, we find, mingled
with all this, the atmosphere of a remote Roman world, clinging
tenaciously to its faith in faun-habited woods, its genii of field
and flood, or its household Lares and Penates. More than
once, too, we are made to feel that there was more of the Roman
flamen than the Christian priest in Herrick, and, even in his
Christian Militant, we discern more of Roman stoicism than
of the sermon on the mount. Herrick, despite his *Noble
Numbers*, is one of the most pagan of English poets, and he
cannot refrain from introducing references to Roman priestcraft
even where, as in his lines, *To the reverend Shade of his religious
Father*, his mood is one of profound seriousness. And, whereas
most of the English poets of the renascence age were content
with borrowing ideas or imagery from the ancient world,
jealously preserving, at the same time, their independence
of mind and their status as Tudor or Stewart Englishmen,
Herrick could be satisfied with nothing less than a full ab-
sorption in the festive life of Rome; he assumes the *toga* as his
daily wear, and lays his offerings of grains of frankincense and
garlic chives before the image of his "peculiar Lar" with a
sincerity which is unmistakable.

His allegiance to the ancient world is likewise manifest
in his poetic art. The Spenserian tradition, with its Italian
grace and slow-moving cadences, made no appeal to him;
and, almost alone of the Caroline lyrists, he refused to bow
the knee to the metaphysic wit and perverse ingenuity of
Donne. In all that pertained to verse and diction, Herrick
was the disciple of Jonson, and, through him, of the great
lyrists of antiquity. The sanity of Jonson's poetic taste, his
love of precision, his fastidious regard for lucidity and ordonnance, are all found again in Herrick, combined with a
delicate charm and spontaneity of utterance which the elder
poet often lacked. Occasionally—as in his *Panegyric to Sir
Lewis Pemberton*, which is obviously modelled on Jonson's
Penshurst, and in his rapturous *Night-Piece to Julia*, which

recalls, in idea and verse-structure, the song of the *patrico*
in the masque *Gipsies Metamorphosed*—we can trace direct
borrowings from Jonson; but what is of far more importance
is the all-pervading sense of discipleship in everything that
pertains to the canons of poetic art.

Most of Herrick's lyrics, as we have just seen, have an
accent of spontaneity in them, but there is abundant evidence
that he was a careful and deliberate artist who practised with
unfailing assiduity the labour of the file. The lines entitled
His Request to Julia indicate very clearly how fastidious was
his artistic consciousness:

> Julia, if I chance to die
> Ere I print my poetry,
> I most humbly thee desire
> To commit it to the fire.
> Better 't were my book were dead,
> Than to live not perfected.

The existence in manuscript form of a few of his poems
furnishes us with abundant evidence of the fact that, during
the long winter evenings which he spent at Dean Prior, he
was engaged in the careful revision of his verses. Early
versions of *A Country Life, His Age, A Nuptial Song on Sir
Clipseby Crew*, together with some of the fairy-poems, are
preserved in the Ashmole, Harley, Egerton and Rawlinson
MSS. and have been collated with the *Hesperides* text by
Grosart and Pollard. The collation shows that, in some
instances, whole stanzas have been deleted and harsh or
obscure lines remodelled, that everything has been sacrificed
to lucidity and precision, and to the perfect adjustment of the
style to the theme. In his lighter lyrics, the language is
simple and even homely; but, in his more sustained odes, and
in verses like the following, it acquires imaginative power,
and becomes rich in metaphor:

> Alas! for me, that I have lost
> E'en all almost;
> Sunk is my sight, set is my sun,
> And all the loom of life undone:

The staff, the elm, the prop, the sheltering wall
    Whereon my vine did crawl,
Now, now blown down; needs must the old stock fall.[1]

The above quotation will also serve to illustrate Herrick's wonderful command of metre. The first half of the seventeenth century was a time of great metric freedom, when poets wrought wonderful melodies through their skilful handling of iambic or trochaic lines of varying length, and through the deft interlacing of their rimes. And, in all this, Herrick is himself a master-spirit. He has left us whole poems—for example, *His Departure Hence*—in which the verses consist of a single accent, and others in which a verse of four accents is followed by one of two accents; while, in such poems as *His Ode for Ben Jonson*, or *To Primroses filled with Morning Dew*, his craftsmanship in the structure of his rhythms, the use of enjambment and the spacing of his rimes calls for the highest praise:

Why do ye weep, sweet babes? can tears
    Speak grief in you,
    Who were but born
    Just as the modest morn
Teem'd her refreshing dew?
Alas! you have not known that shower
    That mars a flower,
    Nor felt the unkind
Breath of a blasting wind;
Nor are ye worn with years,
    Or warp'd as we,
Who think it strange to see
Such pretty flowers, like to orphans young,
To speak by tears before ye have a tongue.[2]

His finest metrical effects are achieved in his iambic and trochaic measures; but, in his more popular songs, he makes skilful use of trisyllabic feet, employing both the dactyl and the anapaest. In a few of his poems, he employs the heroic couplet, and a comparison of his early poems in this measure with those of a later period will show that he shared in the

---

[1] *An Ode to Endymion Porter upon his Brother's Death.*
[2] *To Primroses filled with Morning Dew*

movement of the age towards the Augustan measures of Dryden and Pope.

Herrick's lyric range is very great, and extends from the simple folk-song to the Horatian ode or the Catullian epithalamy. In addition, he has left us epistles addressed to friends and patrons, a large number of epigrams and epitaphs and several pastoral eclogues in amoebean verse, of which the most beautiful is that in which Lycidas Herrick reproaches Endymion Porter for seeking the gilded pleasures of the court and forsaking the Florabell, dainty Amarillis and handsome-handed Drosomell of the hills and dales. Descriptive verse was not altogether to his liking, but his fairy-poems and such verses as those to *The Hock-Cart*, called forth by the contemplation of the festive ceremonial of the country-side, are full of charm and animation. A lover of birds and flowers, and of all the amenities of country life, Herrick can scarcely be called a great nature poet. He rarely attempts to paint a well-ordered landscape, with foreground and background, but prefers to concentrate his thoughts upon some one object in the picture to the exclusion of everything else. His most ambitious attempt at landscape painting is seen in the poem entitled *A Country Life*, addressed to Endymion Porter; in its representation of a day in rural England from cockcrow and sunrise to the evening revelry about the maypole or amid the nut-brown mirth of a Twelfth Night feast, it challenges comparison with *L'Allegro*. But Herrick's command over nature is surest where he can blend descriptions of country scenery and paintings of still life with the outpourings of lyric emotion; or where, as in the verses *To Primroses filled with Morning Dew* or *To Daffodils*, he can turn from the contemplation of the beauty of flowers to reflection on the transience of mortal life.

His poetic genius is best displayed in such lyrics as *Corinna's going a-Maying* or *To Phyllis to love and live with him*. In these poems, a dreamy love-sentiment—which was more to Herrick than intense passion—is introduced to give tone and warmth to the idyllic portrayal of nature and country life, after the manner of the finest lyrics of Spenser's *Shepheards Calender*. In the one poem, all is movement and animation, in the other, a halcyon calm broods over the scene; and, in both, the artistic handling is perfect.

The range of his lyric emotion in his love-songs is considerable. At times, he offends by his gross sensuousness, but, more often, his tone is that of dreamy reverie or, in those love-songs which seem to have been inspired by his associations with the court, that of refined and graceful gallantry. He far surpasses Carew and the other cavalier lyrists in the delicate homage which he renders to those noble ladies who gathered around Henrietta Maria at Whitehall, and is even happier in the pastoral wooing of Mistress Elizabeth Wheeler, the Amarillis of *Hesperides*, who belonged not to the court but the city. In *The Night-Piece to Julia*, and in the famous song *To Anthea*—"Bid me to live"—his lyric emotion becomes intense and spiritualised; the fire of love touches his heart, and he rises to the level of Catullus or Burns:

> Thou art my life, my love, my heart,
>   The very eyes of me;
> And hast command of every part,
>   To live and die for thee.

Next in importance to Herrick's lyrical poems are his epigrams. Included among these, of course, are his scurrilous distichs, which reflect the nastiness of Martial without his wit, and which were discharged against hapless parishioners at Dean Prior, or enemies in town. But his greatness as an epigrammatist consists not in these, but in those *épigrammes à la grecque* which bear a striking likeness to the verses of the Greek anthologists. Some of these take the form of short complimentary poems to his friends and kinsmen, to whom he promises the immortality of reflected fame; others are epitaphs on matrons, little children and maidens dying in the first bloom of womanhood. Here belong, too, his gnomic verses, his quaint dedicatory poems to Juno, Neptune and Vulcan, and to his household gods; and, lastly, his numerous epigrams *Upon Himself* and *To his Book*, in which, in his delightfully frank and ingenuous manner, he disburdens his soul of its hopes or fears.

The epigram had arisen in England under the influence of the revival of learning, and, though at first only the satiric epigram was practised, acquaintance with the Greek epigrams of the Planudean anthology had gradually led to the study of this earlier and nobler form of epigrammatic writing. Jonson has left us several epigrams of this nature, together with others of a satiric kind, and imitations of the poems in the Greek anthology find a place in some of the later song-books, and, above all, in Drummond's collection of *Madrigals and Epigrams*, first published in 1656, but written years before. Herrick surpasses all his contemporaries as an epigrammatist, both in variety of theme and delicacy of finish, and is almost as supreme in the epigrammatic art as in the lyric. In order to compare his workmanship in these two branches of the poetic art, it may be worth while to bring together his song, *To Daffodils*, and his epigram on the same flower. Each, in its kind, touches perfection, and the idea is the same in both:

Fair daffodils, we weep to see
  You haste away so soon;
As yet the early rising sun
  Has not attained his noon.
    Stay, stay,
  Until the hasting day
    Has run
  But to the evensong;
And, having prayed together, we
  Will go with you along.

We have short time to stay, as you,
  We have as short a spring;
As quick a growth to meet decay,
  As you, or anything.
    We die
As your hours do, and dry
    Away,
  Like to the summer's rain,
Or as the pearls of morning's dew,
  Ne'er to be found again.

When a daffodil I see,
Hanging down his head towards me,
Guess I may what I must be:
First, I shall decline my head;
Secondly, I shall be dead;
Lastly, safely buried.

Herrick's sacred verses, or *Noble Numbers*, enlarge our view of his unique personality, but scarcely add to his fame as a poet. He followed the example of Donne in dedicating his powers to religion, when he entered the church; but, unlike Donne, he could not break with the past or change the temper of his mind. His materialistic nature and sensuous fancy are as manifest in many of his religious verses as in his secular, and some of his poetic addresses to God are incongruously like those to his "peculiar Lar." Donne's *Litany* may well have inspired Herrick to write his *Litany to the Holy Spirit;* but the character of the two priests, as revealed in their respective poems, is entirely different. And if his religious verse is unlike that of Donne, it is still more unlike that of his immediate contemporaries, Herbert, Crashaw, Vaughan or Traherne. The symbolism and soul-scrutiny of Herbert, and the seraphic exaltation of Crashaw, were altogether foreign to Herrick, nor could his mundane temperament hold fellowship with the Celtic mysticism of Vaughan and Traherne. But such poems as *His Creed, His Litany to the Holy Spirit* and *His Thanksgiving to God for his House* are a pure delight to us, because of their unaffected *naïveté* and homely charm, while the practical side of his religion is pleasingly set forth in the verses, *To keep a true Lent*, and his lyric emotion and powers of imagination find full expression in his beautiful *Dirge of Jephthah's Daughter.*

The poems of Herrick, in spite of their author's self-assurance of immortality, seem to have been treated with scanty respect in the years which followed the publication of *Hesperides*. Whereas the lyrics of Carew and Suckling passed through several editions in the course of the seventeenth century, no such honour was paid to *Hesperides;* moreover, the references to Herrick in the biographical and critical writings of Anthony à Wood, Phillips and Winstanley are as meagre as they are misleading. The revival of his poetry began in the closing years of the eighteenth century, since which time his fame has grown so steadily that, at last, he has come to take his place among the greatest of English lyric poets. He lacks, it is true, the highest gift of all—that of touching the deepest chords in human nature, and of rousing men to high purposes and high enthusiasms. But this lack of intensity is common to him and to the renascence lyrists as a whole. For the renascence song is that of a nation still in its childhood, unconscious, as yet, of conflicting emotions or complexity of thought, and knowing nothing of the burden of modernity. It is the holiday lyric of men who were content to fleet the time carelessly, in a golden world of their own imagination; whose philosophy was but to seize the day, and gather the rosebuds of life while youth and summer sunshine were still theirs. This is the temper of the songs of Marlowe, Shakespeare and Breton, and—though the horizon of their poetic vision is changed and contracted—of those of Carew and Suckling. And, among all these singers of a day when England was a nest of singing-birds, Herrick reigns as king.

Thomas Carew, who came of the Cornish branch of the Carew family, was the younger son of Sir Matthew Carew, master in Chancery, and of Alice, daughter of Sir John Rivers, a lord mayor of London. The date of his birth is uncertain, but 1598 is the generally accepted year. He was educated at Corpus Christi college, Oxford, but left the university without a degree, and, in 1614, was reading law in the Middle Temple. A little later, he became secretary to Sir Dudley Carleton, British ambassador at Venice. In 1616, Carleton was sent as ambassador to The Hague, and was accompanied by his secretary; but, after a few months' service there, Carew, for reasons not fully known, threw up his post and returned to England. In the October of the same year, he is described by his father as "wandering idly about without employment." In 1619, he was with lord Herbert of Cherbury at the French court, and, soon after the accession of Charles I, he won the king's favour, who made him his sewer in ordinary, and a gentleman of his privy chamber; he also bestowed upon him the royal domain of Sunninghill, near Windsor.

The following years of his life seem to have been spent chiefly among the courtiers of Whitehall and the wits of the town. He was "of the tribe of Ben," and numbered Suckling, D'Avenant, George Sandys and Aurelian Townsend among his friends and acquaintances. Anthony à Wood bears witness to his "delicacy of wit and poetic fancy," and Clarendon describes him as "a person of pleasant and facetious wit"; from Suckling's well-known reference to him in *A Session of the Poets*, it would seem as though he were looked upon as the poet laureate of the court, though the official laureate at this time was Ben Jonson.

In 1634, he wrote his elaborate masque, *Coelum Britannicum;* it was undertaken at the royal command, and was performed at Whitehall on the Shrove Tuesday of that year. Other poems followed, but, in 1638, his life came suddenly to an end. Two years after his death, his poems were collected and published: insufficient care was taken with this edition; for, while some of Carew's poems were omitted from it, other poems which were not his—including Ben Jonson's famous "Come, my Celia, let us prove," and two of Herrick's lyrics[1]—found a place in it.

The right of Carew to stand next to Herrick among the Caroline lyrists can scarcely be questioned, and the two poets have a good deal in common. Had Herrick not been transported, in the year 1629, from the gilded chambers of Whitehall to the thatched cottages of Dean Prior, the resemblance between them, doubtless, would have been still greater. For, up to that date, in spite of a certain inequality in age and breeding, they must have come under very much the same influences, and moved in the same social circles. They never mention one another, but they can hardly have failed to meet, if not in the precincts of the court, then in the society of their tribal lord, Ben Jonson, whose intellectual sovereignty they alike acknowledge. In both, the artistic sense was strong, and the atmosphere of Carew's lyrics to Celia is curiously like that of many of Herrick's to Julia. Finally, both poets render the homage of complimentary verse to the king, to the duke of Buckingham, to John Crofts, the king's cup-bearer, and to Lucy Hay, countess of Carlisle, whose beauty is the theme of many a cavalier lyrist, and who, two centuries after her death, became the heroine of Browning's *Strafford*. But residence in Devonshire widened immeasurably the horizon of Herrick's poetic vision, and enabled him to find, in festooned maypoles and primrose glades, new themes for song of which Carew remained throughout his life wholly ignorant.

Carew resembles Herrick, again, in the fact that his poems

[1] See *supra*, p. 7.

furnish us with an easy transition from the Elizabethan lyric
to that of the seventeenth century; but, whereas Herrick
approaches nearest to the earlier manner in those poems in
which he reproduces the youthfulness and romantic glow of
the best miscellany-lyrics—for example, Marlowe's *The Passionate Shepherd to his Love*—Carew's sympathy is with the
more artificial lyricism of the sonnet.   In his *Elegy upon the
Death of Dr. Donne*, he rightly estimates the achievement of the
great lyric reformer in purging the muses' garden of "pedantic
weeds" and "the lazy seeds of servile imitation"; yet, in such
a poem as the following, he keeps very closely to the Petrarchian manner of the sonneteers, against which Donne declared
open warfare:

> I 'll gaze no more on her bewitching face,
> Since ruin harbours there in every place.
> For my enchanted soul alike she drowns
> With calms and tempests of her smiles and frowns.
> I 'll love no more those cruel eyes of hers
> Which, pleas'd or anger'd, still are murderers.
> For if she dart, like lightning, through the air
> Her beams of wrath, she kills me with despair.
> If she beholds me with a pleasing eye,
> I surfeit with excess of joy and die.[1]

In the main, however, and for evil as well as for good, Carew
belongs to the classical school of seventeenth century lyrists
who followed in the steps of Jonson.   His indebtedness to
Anacreon and the masters of Roman lyric, apparently, was
far less profound than that of Jonson or Herrick, and his
classicism, therefore, is almost entirely confined to those
qualities of style—structural proportion, smoothness and
lucidity of diction and the avoidance of fantastic conceit—
which the author of *The Forest* and *Underwoods* had striven,
and striven successfully, to introduce into English lyric poetry.
Carew's love-poems are not always free from that hyperbole
which was then the fashion; and, in his *Elegy upon the Death
of Dr. Donne*, admiration for his hero leads him to imitate
the *discordia concors* of that masterful genius.   But sanity
of taste is strong in Carew, and it keeps him free from those

---

[1] *Murdering Beauty*

aberrations and excesses which have left their impress upon much of the lyric poetry, both secular and religious, of his day. Above all, he has a fine sense of structure in poetry, and this gives to his verses both shapeliness in the parts and unity in the whole. This structural beauty is attained by methods which are as simple as they are successful. Thus, he is the master of the lyric of two stanzas in which the second stanza is nicely balanced with the first, in much the same way that octave and sestet balance one another in the Petrarchian sonnet:

> Mark how the bashful morn, in vain,
> 　Courts the amorous marigold
> With sighing blasts and weeping rain;
> 　Yet she refuses to unfold.
> But when the planet of the day
> Approacheth, with his powerful ray,
> 　Then she spreads, then she receives
> 　His warmer beams into her virgin leaves.
>
> So shalt thou thrive in love, fond boy!
> 　If thy tears and sighs discover
> Thy grief, thou never shalt enjoy
> 　The just reward of a bold lover.
> But when, with moving accents, thou
> Shalt constant faith and service vow,
> 　Thy Celia shall receive those charms
> 　With open ears, and with unfolded arms. [1]

But if Carew's workmanship is almost always successful, it is very seldom triumphant. In it, as in everything else, he lacks boldness. He never attempts the daring intricacies of rime in which Herrick delights, nor have any of his songs the rhythmic beauty attained, with such apparent ease, by Ben Jonson in his "Slow, slow, fresh fount, keep time with my salt tears," from *Cynthia's Revels*. And this lack of boldness, this unwillingness to reach beyond his grasp, is characteristic of Carew's work throughout. It is true that he has left us at least a dozen songs—such as "Ask me no more where Jove bestows," "Sweetly breathing vernal air," "He that loves a rosy lip," "Fair copy of my Celia's face" and so forth—

---

[1] *Boldness in Love.*

which are wellnigh perfect in their kind; but, when the contents
of his volume of verses are judged as a whole, it must be confessed that, in thought and in feeling, they are somewhat
commonplace and conventional. His imaginative power is
weak, and he has very little intensity of emotion. There is
not much intensity, perhaps, in *Hesperides;* but Herrick possesses a quality which goes far to compensate for its absence—
the charm of personality and self-revelation. This, however,
is almost entirely absent from the poems of Carew. That
decorous and well-disciplined courtier keeps himself, for the
most part, under perfect control, and is only too ready to
barter away sincerity of expression for the mask of gallantry
and conventional compliment. On one occasion, however,
he dares to be himself; and the result is *The Rapture*, a poem
of audacious sensuality, but more fraught with passion and
imaginative vision than anything else he has left us. Elsewhere, the tone of his poetry is studiously moral, and, in his
masque, *Coelum Britannicum*, he is almost puritanical in his
austerity. Here, Mercury banishes Pleasure from the court,
and sets in her place Truth, Wisdom and Religion. Pleasure
is denounced as a "bewitching siren, gilded rottenness," that
has

> With cunning artifice display'd
> Th' enamell'd outside and the honied verge
> Of the fair cup where deadly poison lurks.

In *The Rapture*, all this is changed. Decorum is swept aside,
and Carew, letting his imagination work its will with him,
gives himself up to that orgy of the senses which we meet
with also in some of the elegies of Donne.

Carew has been described as the founder of the school of
courtly amorous poetry; but it seems probable that, if we could
place the *Hesperides* poems in their due chronological order,
the prestige of priority would rightly belong to Herrick. Yet
it seems natural to regard Carew as the leader of that school,
because, unlike Herrick, he is, from first to last, a cavalier,
and rarely strays far from the precincts of Whitehall. Once
or twice, it is true, we find him removed from court, and engaged in praising, after the manner of Jonson's *Penshurst*, and

Martial's verses *To Bassus, on the Country-House of Faustinus*,[1] the lavish hospitality practised by Stewart courtiers while residing at their country-seats; and, on one occasion, too, we find him singing the glories of an English spring. The verses entitled *The Spring* are graceful and harmonious; but the extent of his acquaintance with the ways of nature may be judged by the fact that he represents the "drowsy cuckoo" hibernating, along with the humble-bee, in some hollow tree! Carew's true place of abode is the city and the court, where, polishing and re-polishing his elegant verses, he renders homage to his royal master, pays amorous suit to his Celia, celebrates with wedding-song or epitaph the marriage or decease of noble lords and ladies and wins from his contemporaries the fitting title of the laureate of the court. Invited by his friend, Aurelian Townsend, to commemorate in verse the death of the great Gustavus Adolphus, he finds his laureate muse unfit for the heroic strain which the occasion demanded, and, declaring that he must leave the hero of Leipzig, Wurtzburg and the Rhine to some prose chronicler, he bids his friend join with him in extolling the joys of tourneys, masques and theatres:

> What though the German drum
> Bellow for freedom and revenge, the noise
> Concerns not us, nor should divert our joys.
> Nor ought the thunder of their carabines
> Drown the sweet airs of our tuned violins.[2]

"Easy, natural Suckling" has won for himself, since the days of the restoration and Congreve's Millamant, an assured place in the bead-roll of English poets as the typical cavalier lyrist, the arch-representative of Pope's "mob of gentlemen who wrote with ease" light-hearted songs of courtly gallantry. Considerable in bulk and varied in character as is his literary work, it can only be regarded as the product of certain hours of leisure, snatched from a life of tempestuous mirth, or from the nobler activities of a soldier's career. Suckling, sometimes, has been regarded as a mere reveller of the court, who made

---

[1] *Epigrammata*, III, 58. [2] *Upon the Death of the King of Sweden.*

war upon all that was noblest in love, and substituted songs licentious in spirit and in metric structure for the chaste raptures of Elizabethan love-lyrists. But such an estimate of the man is one-sided and even false. For, while it is true that some of his poems are sensuous and even obscene, there are others which are lofty in thought and full of spiritual exaltation. If he could write the poem: " 'T is now since I sat down before that foolish fort, a heart," in which he vilifies woman's honour, he was also the author of stanzas such as these:

> O, that I were all soul, that I might prove
> > For you as fit a love
> As you are for an angel, for, I know,
> None but pure spirits are fit loves for you.
>
> You are all ethereal, there 's in you no dross,
> > Nor any part that 's gross.
> Your coarsest part is like a curious lawn,
> The vestal relics for a covering drawn.
>
> Your other parts, part of the purest fire
> > That e'er Heaven did inspire,
> Makes every thought that is refined by it
> A quintessence of goodness and of wit. [1]

Moreover, though Suckling's best-known works are those audacious songs which he tossed off in the interval between an afternoon game of bowls and an evening at cribbage, it is well to remember that he was the author of the statesmanlike *Letter to Mr. Henry Jermyn* and the scholarly *An Account of Religion by Reason*—in which he makes war upon Socinian heresies. His plays, too, whatever may be their dramatic value, display a vein of generous romanticism and chivalrous feeling which enable us to understand how it was that the notorious gamester and spendthrift courtier was, at the same time, the close friend of the philosophic Falkland and "the ever memorable" John Hales.

He was born, in the year 1609, at Twickenham, the son of Sir John Suckling, who, belonging to an old Norfolk family, had risen to eminence among the court officials of James I, and,

[1] *Song.*

in the last years of his life, was a secretary of state and comptroller of the royal household.   Nothing certain is known of the poet's school, but, in 1623, he entered Trinity college, Cambridge, and, four years later, passed to Gray's inn.   The death of his father, in 1627, left him an orphan, and the inheritor of great wealth.   The idea of studying law was now abandoned, and, in his twenty-first year, Suckling entered upon his adventurous career as a traveller and soldier of fortune.   He visited France and Italy, returned to England to be knighted, and, in 1631, joined with Charles, marquis of Hamilton, in the campaigns of Gustavus Adolphus.   He is said to have been present at the battle which ended in the defeat of Tilly at Leipzig on 17 September, 1631, and at the sieges of Crossen, Guben, Glogau and Magdeburg; he returned to England in 1632.

The years that followed were spent at court, where his great wealth, his ready wit and command of repartee—to which seventeenth century writers bear abundant witness—and, lastly, the versatility of his literary powers, won him fame and admiration.   He gave magnificent entertainments, wrote plays which he furnished at his own expense with magnificent dresses and gorgeous scenery and, with characteristic ardour, threw himself into all the pleasures of a pleasure-loving court. In 1637 appeared the string of witty, but carelessly written, verses, entitled *A Session of the Poets;* and the following year saw the performance of his plays, *Aglaura* and *The Goblins*. To these years, in all probability, also belong many of his lyrics and occasional verses.   Then, on the outbreak of the Scottish campaign of 1639, Suckling, abandoning poetry and a courtier's life for service in the field, equipped at his own expense a troop of a hundred horse, marched towards the Scottish border and, like his king, suffered defeat at the hands of Leslie.   The Scottish campaign also inspired him to write his tragedy, *The Discontented Colonell*, which was republished in 1646, under the title, *Brennoralt*.

When the Long Parliament was summoned in November, 1640, Suckling sat as member for Bramber (Sussex), and, in the following year, he joined with Henry Jermyn, colonel Goring and others in what was known as "the first army plot," the purpose of which was to win for the king the command of the army. The plot was discovered, and Suckling and Jermyn fled to France. Here, at Rouen or Paris, he spent some months in obscurity and deep dejection, and, according to Aubrey, ended his life by suicide in the year 1642. Four years later, his works were collected and published under the title, *Fragmenta Aurea*, and passed through several editions before the end of the century. In addition to his poems, the volume contained the three plays *Aglaura, The Goblins* and *Brennoralt*, together with his letters and his *Account of Religion by Reason*. In the year 1659 appeared, also, his unfinished tragedy, *The Sad One*.[1]

Suckling's literary fame is now chiefly bound up with his lyrics, some of the most delightful of which first found a place in his dramas. For the most part, they are song-lyrics, and were set to music by Henry Lawes. As a lyric poet, he stands somewhat apart from Herrick and Carew in the fact that he owed little to Ben Jonson: the restraint, classical colour and fastidious workmanship of Jonson made little appeal to Suckling, who censured Carew for "the trouble and pain" expended on his verses, and declared that "a laureate muse should be easy and free." On the other hand, he bows the knee to Donne, whom he acclaims as the great lord of wit. The influence of Donne is most marked in those lyrics which he misnames sonnets, the last of which, "O, for some honest lover's ghost," echoes the famous "I love to talk with some old lover's ghost" of the earlier lyrist. He has little of Donne's intellectuality, but he follows him in the war which he waged upon the unreality and lovelorn fancies of the Petrarchian school of lyrists; while the audacious *bravura* of such songs as "Out upon it! I have loved" or "Why so pale and wan, fair lover," in which he derides constancy in love and boastfully displays an unpledged heart, is directly caught from Donne's "Go and catch a falling star" and "Now thou hast loved me one whole day." And it is this audacious wit, combined with a debonair gaiety of heart, which furnishes the secret of his charm as a song-writer. To these high qualities must, also, be added the impetuous movement of his verse; extraordinarily careless as his poems sometimes are, his best songs have the

[1] As to Suckling's plays, see *ante*, Vol. VI, Chap. IX.

rare seventeenth century quality of tunefulness and the perfect accord of theme and rhythm.

But the finest and most characteristic product of Suckling's genius, after all, lies not in lyric poetry but in narrative. The epithalamium was one of the accepted forms of Elizabethan art-lyric which was handed down to the later age, and Donne, heretic and iconoclast as he was in most that pertained to Elizabethan lyricism, had kept closely to the conventional form of wedding-ode. But when, in 1641, Roger Boyle, lord Broghill, married lady Margaret Howard, Suckling, with daring independence of mind, broke through all conventions, and, instead of a formal epithalamium, wrote his famous *Ballad of a Wedding*. Here we again meet with the directness, light-hearted buoyancy and impetuous movement which characterise his songs; but with these there are associated, what is elsewhere rare in Suckling, the delicate touch and caressing fancy of Herrick.

Our knowledge of Richard Lovelace's career is mainly derived from the account which Anthony à Wood has given of him in his *Athenae Oxonienses*. He belonged to an influential Kentish family, and was the eldest son of Sir William Lovelace, of Woolwich, where he was born in 1618. He was educated at the Charterhouse and at Gloucester hall, Oxford. While at the university, he wrote his lost comedy, *The Scholar*, and, after only two years' residence, he was admitted to the degree of master of arts at the solicitation of a court lady upon whom his "most amiable and beautiful person, innate modesty, virtue and courtly deportment" had made a deep impression. The following years were spent in London, or at his Kentish residence, or as a soldier in the Scottish campaigns of 1639 and 1640. About 1640, he wrote his tragedy *The Soldier*, which seems never to have been acted or published, and which has shared the same fate as his comedy *The Scholar*. In 1642, he was chosen by the cavalier party in Kent to present to the House of Commons the so-called Kentish petition, which asked for "a restoration of the bishops, liturgy and common prayer"; the petition was burnt by the common hangman and, for some seven weeks, Lovelace was a prisoner in the Gatehouse, Westminster. His imprisonment inspired the famous song, *To Althea from Prison.* A promise made to the Long Parliament not to leave London without the permission of the Speaker prevented him from taking a very active part in the civil war, but he contributed horses and arms to the royalist cause, and, after the surrender of Oxford, in 1646, he offered his sword to the French king, Louis XIV, and was wounded at Dunkirk. On his return to England, in 1648, he was imprisoned in Petre house, Aldersgate, where he prepared for the press his volume of poems, entitled *Lucasta: Epodes, Odes, Sonnets, Songs, etc.,* which was published in 1649. Set at liberty after the execution of Charles, he seems to have remained in London, and Anthony à Wood gives us a gloomy picture of his last years:

Having by that time consumed all his estate, he grew very melancholy, . . . became very poor in body and purse, was the object of charity, went in ragged clothes (whereas when he was in his glory he wore cloth of gold and silver) and mostly lodged in obscure and dirty places, more befitting the worst of beggars and poorest of servants.

From the same account, we gather that he died amid miserable surroundings, in Gunpowder alley, London, in 1658. In the following year, his brother, Dudley Posthumus Lovelace, published his remaining verses under the title, *Lucasta: Posthume Poems.* The Lucasta who, after the manner of the heroines of Elizabethan sonnet-sequences, lends her name to his two volumes of poetry, is said to have been Lucy Sacheverell.

Lovelace's standing among English poets is peculiar. He has left us two or three songs which are included in almost every anthology of English verse, and which deserve enduring fame; in addition to these, he wrote a considerable number of lyric, descriptive and complimentary poems, of which it may, without rancour, be said that it would have been better if they had remained in manuscript and perished with his two plays. For, in them, he exhibits most, if not all, of the faults of taste found in Elizabethan sonneteers, together with the fantastic extravagances of the seventeenth century school of lyrists. His love-lyrics to Lucasta are as frigidly rhetorical as the worst poems in Cowley's *Mistress,* while his *Pastoral: to Amarantha* abounds in the otiose conceits of what Ruskin has taught us to call "the pathetic fallacy." To what excesses a labouring fancy, unrestrained by good taste, may run is well illustrated by such poems as *Ellinda's Glove* or *Lucasta's Muff*, by the verses entitled *A Loose Saraband*, in which he declares that love has made a whipping-top of his bleeding heart, or by the opening stanza of the song, *Lucasta Weeping :*

> Lucasta wept, and still the bright
> Enamoured god of day,
> With his soft handkerchief of light,
> Kissed the wet pearls away.

Judged by the bulk of his poems, Lovelace has more in common with Habington than with the typical cavalier lyrists, Suckling and Carew; and, although his addresses entitled *The Grass-hopper* and *The Snail* faintly recall the Anacreontic *Ode to the Cicada*, he cannot well be called a neo-classic or a follower of Jonson.

When compared with his other poems, Lovelace's two songs *To Althea from Prison* and *Going to the Wars* seem nothing less than miracles of art. In them, there is no trace of the pedantry or prolixity, the frigid conceit and the tortured phrase, of his other poems; in their simplicity, their chivalrous feeling and their nobility of thought, they touch perfection. And scarcely inferior to them, though not so well known, is his song, *To Lucasta going beyond the Seas*, the third stanza of which deserves to rank with the most memorable things in English lyric poetry:

> Though seas and land betwixt us both,
> Our faith and troth,
> Like separated souls,
> All time and space controls:
> Above the highest sphere we meet,
> Unseen, unknown, and greet as angels greet.

Had Lovelace always written like this, the comparison which the seventeenth century biographer, William Winstanley, drew between him and Sir Philip Sidney might win our glad approval.

CHAPTER II

The Sacred Poets

IN the history of English sacred verse, there has not been any group of poets like those who wrote in the second quarter of the seventeenth century. Herbert, Crashaw and Vaughan form, not, indeed, a school of poetry, but a group with definite links connecting them. Unlike the Fletchers and Habington, who looked back to "Spenser's art and Sydney's wit," they come under the influence both of the newer literary fashions of Jonson and Donne, and of the revived spirit of cultured devotion in the Anglican church. The welcome given to *The Temple* showed that an age more serious than the Elizabethan was interested in the intimate expression of personal religion. Herbert points the way; but each writer has an individual note and an intensity of feeling which ensure his survival for his own sake. In their development of the religious lyric, which was admirably adapted to the portrayal of subtle emotions, they achieved a modest success, while greater poets triumphed in the ampler fields of allegory and epic.

The fascination of George Herbert is due as much to his character as to his writings. It is true that the reputation of *The Temple* was assured, and nine editions called for, before Izaak Walton's *Life* made Herbert one of the most familiar figures of the century. But *The Temple*, and its prose companion, *A Priest to the Temple* (1652), had already revealed the presence of conflicting traits in their author's character, as, with a rare and almost morbid sensitiveness, he watched his own growth and scrutinised his moods. His personal history, therefore, is of more than ordinary moment for understanding his poems.

The famous Border family of the Herberts had furnished a long line of soldiers, courtiers, judges and men of affairs— an ancestry such as lord Herbert of Cherbury delighted to tell of with a pleasing vanity. The persuasion to a more peaceful calling reached George Herbert, not through his father's line, but through his mother, Magdalen, daughter of Sir Richard Newport of High Ercall, Shropshire. Her husband died in 1596, leaving her with a family of seven sons and three daughters, "Job's number and Job's distribution as she herself would very often remember." George, the fifth son, was born at Montgomery on 3 April, 1593, in the same year as Walton his biographer, and Nicholas Ferrar who stood sponsor to *The Temple*. Magdalen Herbert had all her sons "brought up in learning," but most of them chose the life of the court or the camp. It was natural to a Herbert to "chase brave employments with a naked sword throughout the world," and not even George escaped the "passion and choler" of his race.

At Westminster school, under Richard Ireland, he laid the foundation of his scholarship. His boyish performance in answer to the veteran Andrew Melville's *Anti-Tami-Cami-Categoria* may be lightly dismissed as deserving neither praise nor blame; an injudicious admirer printed it thirty years after Herbert's death. Of greater importance are the two sonnets which he sent to his mother as a New Year's gift, soon after his becoming a scholar of Trinity college, Cambridge. "Doth poetry wear Venus' livery, only serve her turn?" he asks,

> Cannot Thy love
> Heighten a spirit to sound out Thy praise
> As well as any she?

In this sixteen-year-old challenge to the love poetry of the day, he probably reveals the influence of John Donne, who was already his mother's friend, and had written many of his *Divine Poems*, though they first appeared in print in the same year as *The Temple*. If Herbert's early ambition to become a sacred poet never faded from his mind, it hardly held its own during the next fifteen years with academic ambitions of scholarship, and civic ambitions of state employment. Even on the death of his mother in 1627, *Parentalia*, the filial odes which he appended to Donne's funeral sermon, did not include any English poems, and deserved Barnabas Oley's comment, "he made his ink with water of Helicon." His rapid success in the university raised higher hopes. Fellow of Trinity in 1616, and praelector of rhetoric in 1618, he aspired to the office of public orator, "the finest place in the University," as he called it, especially because it brought the orator into relations with the court. The retiring orator, Sir Francis Nethersole, and his predecessor, Sir Robert Naunton, held important political offices. Herbert's high connections, courtly address and knowledge of languages were likely to win him similar promotion. He had made no secret of his intention ultimately to seek the priesthood, and now brushed aside Nethersole's warning that the orator's office might divert him too much from divinity. He canvassed friends and kinsfolk for their support, and sought to "work the Heads to my purpose." He was installed orator on 18 January, 1619, and held the post till his mother's death. As the official mouth-piece of the university, he was expected to use the language of flattery in addressing those whom Cambridge delighted to honour, and he was well qualified to "trade in courtesies and wit"; but, even in an age of adulation, his hyperboles are conspicuous. It is impossible to acquit him of self-seeking in his use of the orator's opportunities. As Walton honestly says, "he enjoyed his gentile humour for cloaths, and courtlike company, and seldom look'd towards Cambridge, unless the King were there, and then he never failed." According to the same witness, "all Mr. Herbert's Court hopes" died with the death in rapid succession of his two most influential friends, and of the king himself in 1625. It is difficult to believe that the chances were all gone for a man of his parts, but the sudden check served to bring once more to the fore that alternative career which he had never put wholly from him. Retiring "to a friend in Kent, where he lived very privately," he debated with himself whether he should return to "the painted pleasures of a Court life," or take orders. Some part of his hesitancy must have been overcome very soon, for he was already a deacon,[1]

---

[1] This fact has been generally overlooked or denied, but the evidence of the Lincoln chapter acts is cited in Daniell's *Life*, p. 103.

when he was instituted by proxy, on 5 July, 1626, to the prebend of Leighton Ecclesia in Lincoln cathedral. How far his entering the diaconate committed him to clerical life cannot easily be gauged. It was one thing to qualify for honorary preferments, it was another to throw in his lot unreservedly with "a despised order" and its professional duties. The parallel case of his friend Ferrar, ordained deacon in this same summer, may throw some light upon the contemporary opinion of the diaconate. Highly as Ferrar regarded it, he protested that "he durst not advance one step higher," and clearly shared that growing regard for the priesthood which the school of Andrewes had encouraged. The point is important, because it indicates that the period of conflict for Herbert was not over, and its long continuance wrung from him poems which bear the marks of mental suffering. The poems of this period have also many references to his agues and failing health. Life was slipping from him, with nothing achieved, when his marriage to Jane Danvers, in 1629, brought a happier state of mind and greater willingness to adopt clerical life. In 1630, Philip, earl of Pembroke, asked king Charles, in whose gift the living was for that turn, to give Bemerton to his kinsman, and, on 26 April, Herbert was instituted to the rectory of Fulston St. Peter's with Bemerton, Wiltshire; on 19 September he was ordained priest. The three years at Bemerton, ending with his burial "in his own church under the altar" on 3 March, 1633, form that part of Walton's *Life*, and of the common tradition about Herbert, which needs least correction. "Holy Mr. Herbert" is no idealised picture of a biographer who saw him but once; it is the estimate of his contemporaries, of Ferrar and Oley, and of lord Herbert, who wrote that "his life was most holy and exemplary; in so much that about Salisbury, where he lived, beneficed for many years, he was little less than sainted." The intensity of the long struggle with himself, which had its echoes even in Bemerton days, saves his life and writings from anything like tameness, though there was peace at the last. The personal note in *The Temple* is an unfailing interest. Herbert himself gave the best description of his unpublished book, when, from his deathbed, he sent it to his "dear brother Ferrar," with the message that he would "find in it a picture of the many spiritual conflicts that have passed betwixt God and my soul, before I could subject mine to the will of Jesus my Master; in whose service I have now found perfect freedom." It is this history of a soul which gives unity to *The Temple*, and makes it a book, in a sense in which *Steps to the Temple* is only a collection.

Herbert was a conscientious worker, continually polishing and resetting his poems. This fact has become clearer since Grosart brought to notice the manuscript, including not quite half of *The Temple*, which had lain, unused by previous editors, in the Williams library. The extensive differences between the Williams MS. and the 1633 edition show that, in revision, Herbert struck out too fantastic conceits, smoothed away roughnesses and replaced unsatisfactory poems by others on the same themes. It remained for a later editor, George Herbert Palmer of Harvard, to turn the Williams MS. to yet greater profit, by using it as a basis for distinguishing between Herbert's earlier and later work. Palmer's order, at some points, is arbitrary and unconvincing; but no greater service has been done towards understanding Herbert than by this attempt to arrange his poems chronologically. Herbert's growth in artistic mastery, as well as in depth of character, is made abundantly clear by this treatment.

In metre, Herbert never goes far afield. He makes no experiments with lines of three-syllabled feet, and even the trochaic measure is seldom used instead of iambic. But, in minor arrangements, as to the length of the lines, the incidence of the rimes and the number of lines to the stanza, Herbert is always looking out to find what will suit each particular poem. Palmer reckons that, of the 169 poems which comprise *The Temple*, "116 are written in metres which are not repeated." The variations run within a narrow circle, but, at least, they show the poet's interest in experiments of form. In *Aaron*, the same sequence of five rimes throughout the five verses is used with consummate success, giving the effect of "one set slow bell." The whole framework, in all its parts, is fashioned exactly to fit the thought of the poem; it is artifice throughout, and yet, within its limits, a masterpiece of art. His constructive ability is one of his best artistic gifts. *The Quip* is a poem of perfect length, its parts are well knit with

a refrain and other correspondences of phrase and it works
to a well-turned close. The same neatness of construction
marks a dozen other short poems, like *The Pulley*, *Justice*, *Decay*
and the two poems oddly called *Jordan*. He has an instinct
for a good ending; not infrequently there is a surprise in store,
as in *The Collar*, where the rebellious mood collapses at the
Master's voice, or in the first sonnet on *Prayer*, where a string
of definitions, both felicitous and preposterous, leads up to
the simplest possible description of prayer as "something
understood." He has also a pretty turn for personification,
which puts life into reflective poems like *The Quip*, *Avarice* and
The Collar. To see how it gives animation to his work, one
has only to compare Herbert's *Decay* with Vaughan's imitation,
Corruption.

Herbert's ingenuity, at times, misleads him into what
can only be called tricks, like the representation of the echo
in *Heaven*, or the intentional failure of the rime at the close
of *Home*. The verses shaped like an altar and the Easter
wings came under Addison's condemnation as "false wit."
They would find no parallel to-day except in *Alice in Wonder-
land*, but many of Herbert's fellow poets—Drummond and
Wither and Quarles—took pleasure in such devices, as well as
in anagrams and acrostics. The number of Herbert's poems
affected by this fashion is very small; but it has most unjustly
told against him with his critics.

A more serious defect of taste he shares with the poets
whom Johnson styled "metaphysical." The fantastic conceits which fashion approved in secular poetry are drawn into
the service of Christian piety; as Chudleigh wrote of Donne's
use of wit in his *Divine Poems:*

He did not banish, but transplanted it.

There is more regard for the quaintness and unexpectedness
of a simile than for its beauty or fitness. Johnson's criticism
is at least sometimes justified in Herbert's case, that "the most
heterogeneous ideas are yoked by violence together." Things
great and small are grouped in incongruous, and even un-
pleasant, association. It was an article of Herbert's creed
that "nothing can be so mean" but that it can be ennobled

to bright and clean uses, and he was justified in his use of illustrations from common life, folk-lore and the medicinal and chemical knowledge which had great fascination for seventeenth century writers. The candle's snuff, the bias of the bowls, the tuning of an instrument, a blunted knife and cold hands that "are angrie with the fire," are successful and popular elucidations of his thought. But the perils of falling into prosiness or bathos beset his path. The fine theme in *Providence* that "man is the world's high priest" cannot recover its dignity after such a playful extravagance as this:

> Most things move th' underjaw; the Crocodile not.
> Most things sleep lying; th' Elephant leans or stands.

The Psalmist is responsible for the saying, "Put Thou my tears into Thy bottle," but Herbert must add, "As we have boxes for the poor." Far worse than mere absurdity or prosiness is the intolerable conceit which ends *The Dawning*, where the "sad heart" is bidden to dry his tears in Christ's burial-linen. Such instances, though they are rare in Herbert, compare with Crashaw's excesses in *The Weeper*. Both poets, too, draw from the senses of smell and taste images which make a modern reader, rightly or wrongly, ill at ease. "This broth of smells, that feeds and fats my minde," in *The Odour*, is nearly as unpleasing as Crashaw's "brisk cherub," that sips of the Magdalene's tears, till

> his song
> Tasts of this Breakfast all day long.

But, despite these temptations to over-daring and tasteless conceits, Herbert got more good than harm from the metaphysical fashion. His interest in thought and in recondite illustration saves him from being thin or facile. He far more often errs by trying to pack too much into small compass, or by being too ingenious, than by working a single thought threadbare, as his successors and imitators often do. A fine instance of his power of concentrated thought is his poem *Man*. And if he is sometimes too artificial, there is no lack of emotional quality in Herbert at his best. There are poems in many different keys like *Throw away thy rod*, *Antiphon* and *The Collar*, which are all tremulous with feeling.

It remains to notice *The Church Porch*, in which Herbert meets the young gallant on his own ground, and avoids the higher arguments that belong to *The Church*. The well-bred, well-informed man of the world, who knows "the ways of learning, honour, pleasure," gives his good-tempered counsels with many a shrewd hit, but without malice. The collector of *Outlandish Proverbs* is the right man to coin these terse maxims of mother-wit. There is no English book of wisdom which holds its own so well; it is kept from cynicism by its humour, and from going out of date by its writer's knowledge of the world.

The anonymous preface to Crashaw's *Steps to the Temple* (1646) introduces the author with the words, "Here's Herbert's second, but equall." In the same volume, Crashaw pays a tribute to his predecessor in the lines which he sent to a gentlewoman with a copy of *The Temple:*

> Know you faire on what you look;
> Divinest love lyes in this booke.

But there is hardly a poem by Crashaw which recalls Herbert, and the two men are widely different in temperament and genius. Crashaw's debt to the older poet is not so much technical as spiritual. The memory of Herbert's self-consecration was still fresh at Cambridge, when *The Temple* was issued from a Cambridge press in Crashaw's second year at Pembroke, and that memory was specially treasured by Crashaw's friends at Little Gidding.[1]

Richard Crashaw was born in 1612 or 1613.[2] He never knew his mother; his step-mother was commended by Ussher for "her singular motherly affection to the child of her predecessor," but she, too, passed quickly out of his life. His father, William Crashaw, was a noted preacher, who spent his substance in buying books and publishing his own contri-

---

[1] Crashaw contributed to Ferrar and Herbert's *Hygiasticon*, 1634.

[2] 1612 is preferable to 1613. His father states in *The Honour of Vertue* (1620), that Ussher had preached at Richard's baptism "eight years afore." His age at the time of his election to Pembroke on 6 July, 1631, is given as 18, which, if it simply implies his age at his last birthday, would, also, allow of the date 1612.

butions to the Roman controversy. The contrast between the father's anti-papal vehemence and the son's ardent Catholicism has often suggested that Richard's change of religion was a reaction from his father's teaching. But, apart from the fact that Richard was only fourteen when his father died, there must also be noticed another strain in the writings and character of the elder Crashaw. The violent controversialist of *The Jesuittes Gospel* concerns us less than the mystically-minded editor of *A Manuall for true Catholickes*. In the *Manuall* (1611), William Crashaw thought fit to gather, out "of the most misty times of Popery," many ancient devotions for the sick and the dying, such as the eloquent "Go forth, o Christian soule." The man who could see the beauty of these prayers through the mists of prejudice, and, in spite of violent disagreement with their doctrines, could translate a Jesuit's hymns to the Virgin, has some share in the authorship of the hymns to St. Teresa and the Magdalene.

From Charterhouse, Richard Crashaw was elected to a scholarship at Pembroke hall, Cambridge, on 6 July, 1631, and, in the following autumn, he commemorated the death of a fellow of his college, William Herrys, in a sheaf of elegies, Latin and English. The English poems, especially the second, *Death, what dost? o hold thy Blow*, show the influence of Jonson, though there is already revealed something of the high colour and passionate note which distinguish Crashaw's later work. In the earlier years of his academic life, as was natural, he gave more attention to Latin than to English verse, and, in the year of taking his first degree, he published *Epigrammatum Sacrorum Liber*, with dedicatory odes to his school and college preceptors. One of the odes, in praise of his tutor, John Tournay, who had recently incurred the vice-chancellor's censure for maintaining the insufficiency of faith alone, shows that Crashaw was passing under high church influences. This sympathy is still more noticeable in the lines *On a Treatise of Charity*, which were prefixed to the *Discourses*, put forth in the following year by "Robert Shelford, of Ringsfield in Suffolk, Priest," a book denounced by Ussher as "rotten stuff." After an eloquent defence of the relation of art to religion, Crashaw ends with ten vigorous lines which were omitted from all subsequent issues of his poems. He attacks

"the zealous ones" who make it "a point of Faith" to call
the pope "Anti-Christ";

> What e're it be,
> I 'm sure it is no point of Charitie.

Crashaw's election to a fellowship at Peterhouse, on 20 November, 1636,[1] caused him to make his home there for the
greater part of the next eight years. There was much that
was congenial to him in that society; another poet, Joseph
Beaumont, was elected in the same year, and Crashaw's
Latin poems show his interest in Cosin's schemes for the
decoration of the new chapel. Of his Cambridge life and
interests, little can be gathered except from his poems and
from the anonymous editor's preface to *Steps to the Temple*.
This preface is not wholly trustworthy evidence;[2] but there
is no reason to doubt its witness to Crashaw's living a recluse
and ascetic life, and imitating the nightly vigils of the Gidding
community. As he afterwards told his friend, Thomas Carre,
he was known in Cambridge days as "the chaplaine of the
Virgine myld." His indifference about food and drink is
noted by both his editors; Carre calls him "a very bird of
paradice" for his unworldliness. For vacant hours, he had
other pursuits besides poetry, but all of them artistic. His
skill in "drawing, limning, graving" is exemplified in the
designs which he prepared for *Carmen Deo Nostro*.

Already, his ardent temperament gave a warmth to his
devotional writing such as has been rarely seen in any English
writer. The canonisation of St. Teresa in 1622 produced much
literature about her, and a wide circulation of her books.
"When the author was yet among the protestantes," as he
shows in *An Apologie*, her writings moved him to impassioned
utterance:

---

[1] Grosart, vol. I, p. xxxi, gives the Latin document of his admission as fellow,
but understands it as referring only to his joining the college, and assigns his
fellowship to 1637, after a year's residence at Peterhouse. Other writers have
followed Grosart.

[2] It can hardly be written by a Cambridge man, because of the evident confusion between "St. Maries Church neere St. Peters Colledge," where the poet
is said to have "lodged under Tertullian's roofe of angels," and the new chapel
of the college with its famous angel roof which the parliamentary agent, William
Dowsing, destroyed in December, 1643. See Walker, T. A., *Peterhouse*, pp.
109, 110.

> Thine own dear bookes are guilty. For from thence
> I learn't to know that love is eloquence.

He was conscious that Englishmen would regard his interest in the Spanish mystic as requiring excuse, but he boldly claims Teresa for his "soul's countryman":

> O 't is not Spanish, but 't is heav'n she speaks.

Crashaw's knowledge of Spanish and Italian affected both the matter and the manner of his poetry. Not only did it bring the writings of the Spanish mystics within his reach, but, also, it infected him with the hyperboles and luscious sweetness of the Neapolitan poet, Marino.

Whether the panegyrist of St. Teresa could have remained content with Laud's "Beauty of Holiness" is doubtful; but the destructive violence of the parliamentary commissioners and the downfall of church and king at Naseby must have made him despair of the Anglican church. On his being deprived of his fellowship on 8 April, [1] 1644, or, perhaps, without waiting for this misfortune, he seems to have gone to Oxford, and cannot be traced again till Cowley found him, in 1646, in Paris. By this time, he had become a Roman Catholic, and the "authour's friend" in the preface to *Steps to the Temple*, which was published in this year, speaks of him as "now dead to us." Crashaw cannot be charged with self-seeking in changing his creed, for he was in sore straits when his brother-poet brought him to the notice of Henrietta Maria, who was then in Paris. With letters of introduction from the queen, and with pecuniary help from others, including, probably, the countess of Denbigh, whose "goodnes and charity" he acknowledges on the title-page of his next volume, Crashaw set out for Rome. There he became secretary to cardinal Palotta, governor of Rome. An English traveller, John Bargrave, who had been ejected with Crashaw from Peterhouse, describes Palotta as "papable and esteemed worthy by all." The same writer gives the last scanty notice of the poet. His delicate conscience was distressed by the laxity of the cardinal's household, and he denounced them to his master, a man of stern morals.

---

[1] Not 11 June, as Grosart and others after him. See Walker, T. A., *Peterhouse*, p. 108.

Palotta recognised that Rome was no longer a safe place for Crashaw after this exposure, and at once procured him a minor office in the church of our Lady of Loretto, of which he was patron. He was instituted on 24 April, 1649, and, by the following August, another had his office, Crashaw having died of a fever, which, perhaps, he had contracted on the journey. There he was buried, the "richest offering of Loretto's shrine." Cowley's elegy on the "Poet and Saint" remains Crashaw's best monument, and is a fit tribute from him whom the elder poet acclaimed, on the strength of his *Poetical Blossoms*, as "young master of the world's maturitie." Crashaw's posthumous volume, *Carmen Deo Nostro* (1652), which contained almost all that was good in the earlier volumes with many valuable additions, had a sympathetic editor, Thomas Carre,[1] "confessor to the English nuns at Paris," but the French printers made sorry work with the English words.

Crashaw sought his earliest inspiration in foreign models rather than in his English predecessors. A curiously high proportion of his work, both early and late, consists of translations. Prominence was given in the volume of 1646 to his translation of the first canto of Marino's *Strage degli Innocenti*. The poem was congenial to the translator, in whose hands it grew even more ornate than the original. A copious use of epithets, which are generally felicitous, a free use of alliteration and an ecstatic emphasis are already characteristic of his style. The eighteenth century, peculiarly disqualified from appreciating Crashaw's religious enthusiasm, retained an interest for *Sospetto*, mainly because of its connection with Milton. Pride of place was given in *The Delights of the Muses* to a translation of a Jesuit schoolmaster's rhetorical exercise, on which Ford also employed his skill in *The Lovers Melancholy*. The nightingale's song has never had such lavish delineation as in *Musicks duell;* but the poem is too ingenious and sophisticated to give the atmosphere of the country. There is far more charm in the dainty song from the Italian, *To thy Lover, Deere, discover*, and in *Come and let us live my Deare*, from Catullus. Translations of Latin hymns occupy a large space, especially in his last volume. They have great merit, but seldom the particular merit of the originals. Thus, his

[1] See *D. of N. B.* for his real name, Miles Pinkney.

Dies Irae has many beauties and fine touches, but it fails to represent the masculine strength of the Latin. Even *Vexilla Regis* cannot escape his favourite phrase, a "full nest of loves." His warm, sensuous imagination kindles with his subject, and he passes only too easily into "a sweet inebriated ecstasy."

Crashaw did better work when he relied upon himself, as in *Loves Horoscope* and *Wishes. To his (supposed) Mistresse.* It is only this last-named example which makes one's faith waver in Crashaw's own judgment that his secular was inferior to his sacred verse. The airy metre of *Wishes*, with its lengthening lines, is exactly fitted to its graceful humour. But, delicate as this poem is, it cannot sustain a comparison with his *Hymne to St. Teresa.* The one is intense with passion, the other is playful and superficial. "The very outgoings of the soule" are in the divine poems; there is grace and dainty trifling, but no more, in the love poems. Nowhere in the secular poems do we find the *élan*, the surrender to an inspiration, the uprush of feeling which carries all before it. Crashaw's passionate outbursts, with their flaming brilliancy, and their quick-moving lines, are hard to parallel in the language, and it is his ardent religious emotion which sets them on fire. He may borrow too freely, for some tastes, from the language of amorous poetry; but it was natural to him to call St. Teresa "my rosy love" or the Virgin a "rosy princess," and he serves them with a noble chivalrous devotion.

There are as serious faults in his sacred, as in his secular, poems. Indeed, the faults are more apparent, because they occur in a finer setting. Crashaw's failures are peculiarly exasperating, because they spoil work which had greater potentialities than that of many poets who have maintained a better level. There are inspired moments, when he outdistances all his rivals, as in the lines which he added to his first version of *The Flaming Heart*, or in the fuller version of the poem *To the Countess of Denbigh.* Vaughan may disappoint by long stretches of flatness, but Crashaw more often gives positive offence by an outrageous conceit, by gaudy colour, by cloying sweetness or by straining of an idea which has been squeezed dry. His defective powers of self-criticism make Crashaw the most unequal of our poets. *The Weeper* contains some of his best and some of his worst lines. That he had no sureness of touch in reviewing his own work, becomes clear when it is noticed that many of the verses in *The Weeper* which have alienated his readers were either additions to the original version, or disastrously misplaced. In the revised form, a verse which few can read without distaste is followed by these perfect lines:

> Not in the evening's eyes
> When they red with weeping are
> For the Sun that dyes,
> Sitts sorrow with a face so fair;
> No where but here did ever meet
> Sweetnesse so sad, sadnesse so sweet.

Within a few months of Crashaw's death, the first part of *Silex Scintillans* had appeared (1650). Henry Vaughan, the elder of twins, was born on 17 April, 1622, at Newton St. Bridget on the Usk, in the parish of Llansantffread near Brecon. His chosen name, Silurist, expresses his intimate love of the Welsh mountains and valleys, with their rocks and streams, woodlands and solitary places, among which he spent his childhood and all the years of his professional life. Both he and his twin-brother Thomas express their debt to Matthew Herbert, rector of Llangattock, who schooled them for six years, before they went up to Jesus college, Oxford, in 1638.[1] He acquired sufficient Latinity to find his chief reading, outside his professional studies and contemporary poetry, in the fathers of the church. He left Oxford for London, with the idea of studying for the law, but, at some date unknown, abandoned it for medicine. The only record of these London days is in the slight little volume of *Poems, with the tenth Satyre of Juvenal Englished*, which he printed in 1646. Except for some feeling for nature, there is nothing that anticipates the distinctive quality of *Silex Scintillans*. The love-songs to Amoret, in which he reveals his kinship with Jonson, Donne and Habington, are not original enough to

[1] So Vaughan wrote to Aubrey in 1673 (Martin's *Vaughan*, vol. II, p. 667), and Wood, probably deriving his information on the point from this letter, states in *Athenae Oxonienses*, s. v. Henry Vaughan, that ' he made his first entry into Jesus Coll. in Mich. Term 1639, aged 17 years.' But in the notice of Henry's twin-brother Thomas, in a later edition of *Ath. Oxon.*, Wood gives 16 as Thomas's age at matriculation in Dec., 1638, and the University Registers confirm this statement (E. K. Chamber's ed., vol. II, p. xxxv).

suggest that he would ever have risen above what half a dozen of the court poets were doing at least as well. More interesting is the literary flavour which he tries to give to the book, in the opening poem, with its homage to "Great Ben" and Randolph, and in the *Rhapsodis* on the Globe tavern. He would have his readers believe that he is of the school of Ben, and seeks inspiration in churchwarden pipes and "royal witty sack, the poet's soul." It may be nothing more than a youthful pose, with its suggestion of duns and debts, full cups and the disorderly Strand, but their author took it seriously when, in his preface of 1654, he "most humbly and earnestly" begged that none would read his early poems.

Before the end of the next year (1647), Vaughan, apparently, had settled down to the life of the country, and wrote from "Newton by Usk" a dedication to *Olor Iscanus*. The book, however, did not appear till 1651, and, even then, only under another's auspices, the author having "long ago condemned these poems to obscurity." The reason for this postponement is the crisis in Vaughan's life, which will be more fitly described in connection with the issue of *Silex*. The poem which gave its name to *Olor Iscanus* sings the praise of the Usk. It has reminiscences of Browne's *Pastorals*. Denham's *Cooper's Hill* had already appeared, but its most famous lines on the Thames were not inserted till after Vaughan's lines were written. The most remarkable, if, also, the strangest, poem in the collection is the Donne-like *Charnel House*. Its forcible epithets—"shoreless thoughts, vast tenter'd hope"—and its array of odd words and similes compel attention in spite of its morbid cast of thought. There are not any love poems, but many memorials of friendship, which had ever a large place in Vaughan's thoughts. The bulk of the work clearly belongs to the period before *Silex* was written, and reflects the atmosphere of the 1646 volume, with its allusions to debts and gay living, and its complimentary verses upon secular writers, D'Avenant, John Fletcher, "the ever-memorable Mr. William Cartwright" and "the matchless Orinda." The poems about his friends who took part in the civil war suggest, but do not clearly settle, the question whether the poet himself took any active part. There are passages where he takes satisfaction in the thought that his hands are clean of "innocent blood." On the other hand, he alludes to a time "when this juggling fate of soldiery first seiz'd me," and also seems to write as an eyewitness of the battle of Rowton heath.[1] There are more signs of his hatred of existing authority than of any active enthusiasm for the royal cause, except that the poem to Thomas Powell, his "loyal fellow-prisoner," and a prayer in adversity, in *The Mount of Olives*, seem to imply that, then or later, he suffered in property and person. The poem that affords the greatest chronological difficulty is called "To his retired friend, an Invitation to Brecknock." The words, "since Charles, his reign," seem to demand a date after the king's execution, but it is difficult to reconcile its flippant, reckless tone with the consistently serious temper of *Silex*, which was published in 1650. Perhaps the poet counted Charles's reign as over with the crushing defeat of 1645, and so the poem may be contemporary with others of its kind and not with the poems of *Silex*. One of the few poems which are certainly late, the epitaph on the little lady Elizabeth, who died of grief at Carisbrooke in September, 1650, is a worthy companion of Vaughan's best work.

The turning point in Vaughan's spiritual and literary history occurs somewhere in the period preceding the publication of the first part of *Silex Scintillans* (1650). There are many indications in this volume, and in the preface which he wrote in 1654 for the second part (1655), that he underwent a prolonged and painful sickness, which nearly cost him his life. Even in 1654, he believes himself to be "at no great distance from death," though he hopes that he is spared to make amends for a misspent youth. In language that appears excessive, at any rate in view of anything that he published, he deplores his share in the "foul and overflowing stream" of corrupting literature, and ascribes his change of view to "the blessed man, Mr. George Herbert, whose holy life and verse gained many pious converts, of whom I am the least."

The nature of Vaughan's obligations to Herbert has been the subject of much controversy. The first and greatest debt is that Herbert directed Vaughan's genius into the channel

---

[1] The tempting solution, that he was present as a surgeon, must be set aside, because his medical studies were probably not begun till later.

where only it achieved notable and lasting success. Vaughan found himself in *Silex Scintillans;* even the few successes outside that volume, like *The Eagle* and the *Epitaph on the lady Elizabeth*, were written after his conversion. What readers have cared to remember are not his poems to Amoret and Etesia, or the occasional verse to friends and literary idols, with its jaunty tone and petulant impatience of "the time's ridiculous misery," but the remote, timeless, mysterious poems of *Silex Scintillans*. It is credit enough to the older poet to have given his disciple "spiritual quickening and the gift of gracious feeling." But the influence of Herbert, for better and for worse, is literary as well as spiritual. Recent editors of Vaughan, by their extensive collections of parallel passages, have placed it beyond dispute that the younger writer, in his new-born enthusiasm for "holy Herbert," modelled himself on the author of *The Temple*. Many of his poems are little more than resettings of Herbert's thought and very words; even the best poems, where Vaughan is most original, have verbal reminiscences, which show how he soaked himself in Herbert's poems. Sometimes, familiar words have received a subtle transmutation; sometimes, they have only enslaved Vaughan to his disadvantage. The little tricks of Herbert's style—the abrupt openings, the questions and ejaculations, the homely words and conceits, the whimsical titles—are employed by Vaughan as his very framework. In the matter of form, Vaughan failed to learn what Herbert had to teach. He knows less well than Herbert when to stop, and, after beginning with lines of such intensity as Herbert could never have written, he is apt to lose his way and forfeit the interest of his readers

The real contributions of Vaughan to literature are, naturally, those poems where he is most himself and calls no man master. His mind and temper are essentially distinct from Herbert's. After the change in his life, he becomes detached in mind from the ordinary interests and ideas of his times, with which he was in any case out of sympathy, and, as with a true mystic, his thoughts move in a rarer, remoter air. He may dutifully follow Herbert in celebrating the festivals of the church; but such concrete themes do not suit him like the more mysterious and abstract themes of eternity, communion with the dead, nature and childhood. The death of a younger brother occasioned a sequence of poems in which the note of personal loss, poignant though it is, is not more prominent than a wistful brooding over man's relations with the unseen and the eternal. This theme receives yet finer treatment in two of his best-known poems, *The World*, and *They are all gone into the world of light*. *The Retreat* combines this theme with another, the innocence of childhood, which recurs in *Corruption* and *Childhood*. In *The Retreat*, which has the added interest of being the germ of Wordsworth's ode,[1] *Intimations of Immortality*, Vaughan achieves a simplicity of expression which is rare with him. Some of his most perfect work occurs where both thought and expression are simple, as in *Peace, the Burial of an Infant*, or *Christ's Nativity*. More often his gift of expression is not sustained and the magic of the opening lines, *e. g.*

> I saw Eternity the other night,
> Like a great Ring of pure and endless light,

soon deserts him. His workmanship becomes defective, his rhythms halting and his expression crabbed.

Another link with Wordsworth is Vaughan's intimate and religious feeling for nature. He has an open-air love for all natural sights and sounds, and a subtle sympathy even with the fallen timber or the stones at his feet. He is happier away from the world of men, and can rejoice equally in

> Dear Night! this world's defeat, the stop to busy fools,

and in the stir that heralds the dawn. It is in his observation of nature that he achieves his most felicitous epithets—"the unthrift sun," "the pursy clouds" and "purling corn." The setting of these natural descriptions is usually religious, as in *The Rainbow* or *The Dawning;* but the lover of nature is as apparent as the mystical thinker.

Into the space of half a dozen years, Vaughan crowded all his best work. His prose translations and original books of devotion belong to the same period. *The Mount of Olives*

---

[1] Trench elicited the interesting fact that Wordsworth owned a copy of *Silex Scintillans*, at that time a rare book. *Household Book of English Poetry*, 2nd ed.

reveals the occasions of many of his poems, and shows that he has been wrongly described as a pantheist. The silence of the forty years that he had yet to live is broken only by *Thalia Rediviva* (1678). For this volume, as for *Olor Iscanus*, the author did not make himself responsible. Most of its contents clearly belong to earlier days. A few poems only appear to have been written after the restoration; for example, *The True Christmas*, which shows Vaughan to be as little in sympathy with the laxity of the monarchy as with the tyranny of the commonwealth. There is an echo of his former successes in *The Retirement* and other numbers of the section, which is called *Pious Thoughts and Ejaculations*. The volume is also interesting because it contains the verse-remains of his brother, "Eugenius Philalethes," who died in 1666. Of Henry Vaughan, there is no further record, except some casual allusions in the correspondence of his cousin, John Aubrey, till the record of his tombstone in Llansantffread churchyard, commemorating his death on 23 April, 1695, at the age of 73.[1] His retired life was in keeping with his small fame as a writer. He knew that his writing was "cross to fashion," and only one of his books reached a second edition; with that exception, nothing was reprinted for nearly two hundred years. He holds his place now, not for the mass of his work, but for a few unforgettable lines, and for a rare vein of thought, which remained almost unworked again till Wordsworth's nature poems and Tennyson's *In Memoriam*.

The religious and mystical literature of the seventeenth century has been recently enriched by Bertram Dobell's discovery of Thomas Traherne, who is specially welcome for his fresh and interesting outlook on life. Like Herbert and Vaughan, he came from the Welsh borders, and had his full share of Celtic fervour. The son of a Hereford shoemaker, he entered Brasenose college, Oxford, in 1653, and graduated in arts and divinity. He was admitted in 1657[2] to the rectory

---

[1] According to the tombstone: but he completed 74 years six days before his death, if his own statement about the year of his birth can be trusted (see above). He composed his own epitaph, probably enough, before he had reached his last birthday.

[2] According to the B.N.C. Register (1909), he was admitted to the college on 1 March 1652/3, aged 15, and was matriculated on the following 2 April. This would give 1637 or 1638 as the year of his birth.

of Credenhill, near Hereford, where he remained for about ten years, until, in 1667, he was made chaplain to Sir Orlando Bridgman, on his appointment as lord keeper, when the Cabal ministry took office. After seven years in this service, Traherne died in his patron's house at Teddington, near Hampton court, and was buried on 10 October, 1674, "in the Church there, under the reading-desk." According to Anthony à Wood, he always led a simple and devout life; his will shows that he possessed little beyond his books, and thought it worth while to bequeath his "old hat."

In his lifetime, he published only *Roman Forgeries* (1673), which might be left to slumber, except for its preface, showing his scholarly love of the Bodleian library, "which is the glory of Oxford, and this nation." Just before his death, he sent to the press *Christian Ethics* (1675), and, a quarter of a century later, the non-juring divine, George Hickes, printed anonymously, with a friend's account of the nameless author, *A serious and patheticall Contemplation of the Mercies of God.* This latter work contained thanksgivings for all the common blessings of life, arranged rhythmically, much in the manner of bishop Andrewes's *Devotions.* The rest of Traherne's works remained in manuscript till the *Poems* were printed in 1903, and *Centuries of Meditations* in 1908. Another octavo volume of meditations and devotions is still extant in manuscript.

All these works, except the controversial volume, reveal an original mind, dominated by certain characteristic thoughts, which are commended to the reader by a glowing rhetoric and a fine conviction of their sufficiency. Like Vaughan, Traherne retains an idyllic remembrance of the innocence and spiritual insight of childhood, and insists that he "must become a child again." The child knew nothing of "churlish proprieties," and rightly regarded himself as "heir of the whole world":

> Long time before
> I in my mother's womb was born,
> A God preparing did this glorious store
> The world for me adorn.
> Into His Eden so divine and fair,
> So wide and bright, I come His son and heir.

Only "with much ado" was the child taught by his elders to prize gew-gaws above the common things of earth and sky; "it was a difficult matter to persuade me that the tinseled ware upon a hobby-horse was a fine thing." But the lesson was successfully taught, and now, for the man who would recover felicity, there was no remedy left but to get free of "the burden and cumber of devised wants," and to recognise again the true wealth of earth's commonest gifts. Man could do God Himself no greater homage than to delight in His creation:

> Our blessedness to see
> Is even to the Deity
> A Beatific Vision! He attains
> His Ends while we enjoy. In us He reigns.

It is a fortunate circumstance that Traherne has given parallel expression to his leading ideas both in verse and in prose, as it affords an opportunity of estimating which medium was the better at his command. His mind was poetic and imaginative rather than philosophic and logical, and yet it may be urged, with some confidence, that he achieved more unquestionable success with his prose than with his verse. Even the opening poems on the thoughts of childhood, beautiful as they are, have nothing so striking as the corresponding prose passage, which begins: "The corn was orient and immortal wheat, which never should be reaped, nor was ever sown. I thought it had stood from everlasting to everlasting." Again, the poems on *Thoughts*, as being every man's "substantial treasures," are less flowing and musical than such lines as these:

I can visit Noah in his ark, and swim upon the waters of the deluge. I can see Moses with his rod, and the children of Israel passing through the sea. . . . I can visit Solomon in his glory, and go into his temple, and view the sitting of his servants, and admire the magnificence and glory of his kingdom. No creature but one like unto the Holy Angels can see into all ages. . . . It is not by going with the feet, but by journeys of the Soul, that we travel thither.

Such writing as this has some of the magical quality and personal note of Sir Thomas Browne's *Religio Medici*.

As a poet, Traherne has not mastered his technique.
His poems are often diffuse and full of repetitions. He is
obsessed with the rime, "treasures" and "pleasures," using
it on page after page; and, even for an age that was not careful
of such things, the proportion of defective rimes is high.
The categorical habit, also, has had disastrous effects, in
unbroken strings of fifteen nouns in one poem, thirteen adjectives in another, fourteen participles in a third. In other
poems, the didactic purpose gets the upper hand, and we hear
the preacher's voice: "This, my dear friends, this was my
blessed case." In spite of such poems as *Wonder*, *News*,
Silence and *The Ways of Wisdom*, he wrote nothing in verse
that is so arresting as his rhetorical prose:

You never enjoy the world aright, till the Sea itself floweth in
your veins, till you are clothed with the heavens, and crowned with
the stars: and perceive yourself to be the sole heir of the whole
world, and more than so, because men are in it who are every one
sole heirs as well as you.

The success of Herbert's *Temple* inevitably produced a
crop of imitations, ranging from Christopher Harvey's *Syna-
gogue*, which, by being bound up with *The Temple* in many
editions from 1640 onwards, achieved a reputation beyond
its deserts, down to the doggerel and wholesale plagiarism
of Samuel Speed's *Prison Pietie* (1677). Vaughan rightly
complained of these facile imitators that "they cared more
for verse than perfection." Those of Herbert's contemporaries who attempted sacred verse without falling under his
influence deserve more consideration. To right and to left
of Herbert stand William Habington and Francis Quarles.
Both belong by birth to the country gentry; but the former
found readers only among his own class, while the latter was
more successful than any writer of his time in gauging the
protestant religious feeling of Englishmen at large. Habington's associations from birth onwards were with the Roman
Catholic minority. He was born at Hindlip hall near Worcester, a house famous for its concealment of priests, on the very
day on which the Gunpowder plot was discovered in consequence (so tradition has said) of his mother's letter to lord
Monteagle. His father was an antiquary, whose *History*

of Edward IV the son completed and published in 1640.
William Habington, after being educated at St. Omer and
Paris with a view to his becoming a priest, returned to England
and, probably in the early months of 1633, married Lucy
Herbert, youngest daughter of the first baron Powis. Her
praises he celebrated in *Castara*, which he published anonymously in 1634. The two parts of which it then consisted
contain poems of courtship and of marriage. A new edition
of *Castara*, a year later, revealed the author's name, and added
to the second part a set of eight elegies on his friend, George
Talbot, which would more properly have constituted a third
part, and three characters of a mistress, a wife and a friend,
introducing the three sections. In 1640, a third edition
included an entirely new third part, consisting of a character
of "A Holy Man," and a collection of sacred poems. The
author recognises that he may be thought "a Precisian" for
his unfashionable praise of chastity, but he would not win
even "the spreadingst laurell" "by writing wanton or profane." In the third part, he leaves the theme of earthly love
"to the soft silken youths at Court," and is full of self-accu-
sation that he should ever have handled the theme, however
purely. There is a sombre and monotonous strain running
through this third part. Advancing death, empty fame and
decay of the tomb itself are its constant subjects. Unlike
Traherne, he hardly finds life worth enjoying, with death
awaiting him:

> And should I farme the proudest state,
> I 'me Tennant to uncertaine fate.

There is grim humour in the description of his deathbed,
where he seems to be a mourner at his own obsequies. He can
put no trust in the predictions of astrologer or doctor:

> They onely practise how to make
> A mistery of each mistake.

In most of the poems there are occasional fine lines, as in the
welcome to death as a safe retreat,

> Where the leane slave, who th' Oare doth plye,
> Soft as his Admirall may lye.

More sustained excellence is found in the poems *Nox nocti
indicat Scientiam*, *Et exultavit Humiles* and *Cupio dissolvi*.
But, in many of these meditative and frigid poems, the thought
is commonplace and uncommended by graceful expression,
or accent of sincerity. Defects of workmanship rather than
of taste mar his work; he judged himself rightly, when he
admitted in his preface that he needed to spend "more sweate
and oyle," if he would aspire to the name of poet. Greater
pains might have eliminated his excessive use of the expletive
"do," many weak rime-endings, clumsy syntax and harsh
elisions (*e. g.* "th' An'chrits prayer," " 'mid th' horrors,"
"sh' admires," "so 'bhors"). In the same year as the complete *Castara*, appeared *The Queene of Arragon. A Tragi-
Comedie*. The author died in 1654 and was buried "where my
forefathers ashes sleepe." His own modest estimate of his
verses will not be challenged, that they are "not so high, as
to be wondred at, nor so low as to be contemned."

Quarles was as little affected as was Habington by the
school of Donne. His chief literary idol was Phineas Fletcher,
"the Spenser of this age." He was born in 1592 at his father's
manor house of Stewards, near Romford in Essex. After
studying at Cambridge and Lincoln's inn, he went abroad,
like his contemporary Ferrar, in the train of the princess
Elizabeth, on her marriage with the elector palatine. After
his return to England, he seems to have lived partly in Essex,
and partly in Ireland as secretary to Ussher. In 1639, he
became chronologer to the city of London. His advocacy
of the king's cause in a series of pamphlets led to his property
being sequestrated, his manuscripts burnt and his character
traduced in a petition to parliament. This last misfortune,
according to his widow, worried him into his grave (1644).
His literary career began in 1620 with *A Feast for Wormes*,
a paraphrase of the book of *Jonah*. He gauged popular taste
accurately in employing a facile, straightforward style, much
familiar wisdom and pious allegory, an abundance of metaphors and similes from common life, but no difficult conceits
of the fashionable kind. *Divine Fancies* (1632) gave a better
taste of his quality, and anticipated, in *The World's a Theater*,
some of the success which attended *Emblemes* (1635), the most
famous English example of a class of writing which began with

the Milanese doctor, Alciati, a century earlier. "Visible poetry . . . catching the eye and fancy at one draught" had a fascination for most religious writers. When Herbert moralised on the speckled church-floor, he was near falling under this influence. Crashaw designed his own emblems for his last volume; while *Silex Scintillans* took its name from the frontispiece of a flinty heart struck with a thunderbolt, and began with a poem, *Authoris de se Emblema*. It is fortunate that these writers, who could do better things, escaped lightly from this misleading fashion. It is as fortunate that Quarles found in it the means of doing his best work. Most of the woodcut illustrations, and much of the moralising, he took straight from the Jesuit Herman Hugo's *Pia Desideria* (1624). But Quarles had something better to give than "wit at the second hand." If his ingenuity and his morality are commonly better than his poetry, at times he rises above his mere task-work to original and forcible writing, as in *False World, thou ly'st*, or in the picturesque comparison of the weary soul with "the haggard, cloister'd in her mew." Sometimes, he reveals an unexpectedly musical quality, as in the skilful use which he makes of the refrain, "Sweet Phosphor, bring the day," and his least attractive pages are brightened by some daring epithet or felicitous turn of expression. His liveliness and good sense, his free use of homely words and notions and his rough humour are enough to account for, and to justify, his popularity.

Of all these writers it may be said that their sacred themes did not lead them to avoid the literary fashions of their day: they and the secular poets trod the same paths. They enjoyed the same delight in ingenuity, the same fearless use of hyperbole, the same passion for finding likenesses and unlikenesses in all manner of unrelated things; and they escaped the commoner faults of religious poetry, its obviousness, its reliance upon stock phrases, its tameness. Nor, with all their artificiality, is their sincerity open to suspicion. They were sacred poets, not from fashion or interest, but from choice and conviction. "The very outgoings of the soule" are to be found alike in Herbert's searching of heart, in Crashaw's ecstasy and in Vaughan's mystical rapture.

CHAPTER III

Writers of the Couplet

NO dogma of Dryden and the critics who were his contemporaries is more familiar than that which gave Edmund Waller the credit of bringing about a revolution in English verse. Dryden wrote, in 1664:

the excellence and dignity of it [*i.e.* rime] were never fully known till Mr. Waller taught it; he first made writing easily an art; first showed us to conclude the sense, most commonly in distichs, which, in the verse of those before him, runs on for so many lines together, that the reader is out of breath to overtake it.[1]

The author of the preface to the second part of Waller's poems (1690) indulged in eulogy without qualification:

The reader needs to be told no more in commendation of these Poems, than that they are Mr. Waller's; a name that carries everything in it that is either great or graceful in poetry. He was, indeed, the parent of English verse, and the first that showed us our tongue had beauty and numbers in it. . . . The tongue came into his hands like a rough diamond: he polished it first, and to that degree, that all artists since him have admired the workmanship, without pretending to mend it.

These words represent the general conviction of an age in which smoothness of rhythm and terseness of language were indispensable conditions of poetry. The self-contained couplet became the universal medium to which these tests were applied; and in Waller's couplets the age found the earliest form of verse which answered them satisfactorily. Waller, during the last thirty years of his life, must have been thor-

---

[1] Dedication of *The Rival Ladies* (*Works*, ed. Scott [Saintsbury's ed.], vol. III, p. 137). See, also, preface to *Fables*, 1700 (*ibid.*, vol. XI, pp. 209, 210).

oughly familiar with the reputation which he enjoyed as the
improver of our numbers; but it would be difficult to discover
any set purpose or novel poetical theory underlying the form
of the poems which made him famous. The decasyllabic
couplet had been employed very generally, among other forms,
by Elizabethan writers; and, in *Englands Heroicall Epistles*,
written before the end of the sixteenth century, Drayton
had given an example of couplet-writing in which there
is as little overlapping of the sense from couplet to couplet as in any of Waller's most admired poems. But the
general tendency of those poets of "the former age" who
used the couplet was to overstep the limits which Drayton
instinctively felt that it imposed. Its bounds were too narrow
for the richness of imagination which distinguished the followers
of Marlowe or of Spenser, and for the elaboration of thought
with which younger poets followed the example of Donne.
Those bounds were better suited to Jonson; but, although
much of his work in this form anticipates the practice of a
later age, his abrupt vigour of language and his natural fluency
were against consistency in his handling of the couplet. In
many cases, where one couplet was allowed to pass into the
next without any break of sense or construction, and where
this continued for many lines together, the demands of melody
prevented the poet from indulging in weak rimes, or ending one
couplet with a conjunction or preposition which bound it to its
successor; but, among the lesser poets of the Stewart epoch,
such tricks became increasingly common, until, in poems like
Chamberlayne's *Pharonnida*, sentences were carried on without
a break through couplet after couplet. The casual beauties
of such passages are hidden by a pedantic neglect of form,
which amounts to a point of honour with the writer. Sir John
Beaumont, in a set of couplets addressed to James I, lamented
the prevailing formlessness of English poetry, demanding, in
place of "halting feet" and defective accents, "ragged rime,"
"fetter'd staves" and obscure language, a type of verse the
requirements of which are most nearly met by the closed
couplet.

The lines *To His Late Majesty, concerning the True Forme of
English Poetry*, not published till 1629, were, probably, written
soon after the publication of the works of James I in 1616. Sir

John Beaumont was a friend of Drayton, and may have had the characteristics of *Englands Heroicall Epistles* before his mind as he wrote. Drayton, also, was the friend, and, in no small degree, the master, of George Sandys, who has some importance in the history of the couplet. Sandys, born on 2 March, 1577/8, was the youngest son of Edwin Sandys, archbishop of York. He entered St. Mary hall, Oxford, in 1589; but nothing further is known of him until, in 1610, he began his travels in the east, the relation of which he published, with a dedication to the prince of Wales, in 1615. In August, 1621, he went to America, as treasurer of the English company for the colony of Virginia, with the governor of the colony, his brother-in-law, Sir Francis Wyatt. There can be no doubt that, before he went, the first five books of his translation of Ovid's *Metamorphoses* had appeared in print. No copy of this publication has been traced; and Sandys, in his preface to the whole translation, published in 1626, implies that the work was done during his residence in Virginia. However, there is an elegy by Drayton addressed to Sandys, which was written very soon after Sandys's departure, and contains historical allusions to events in the Thirty Years' war which show that it was composed in the winter of 1621–2. Drayton praises the first five books of the *Metamorphoses* already translated, and begs his correspondent to "let's see what lines Virginia will produce." Aided by such encouragement, Sandys persevered, dedicating the day, as he tells Charles I, "to the service of your Great Father, and your Selfe," and "that unperfect light, which was snatcht from the houres of night and repose" to the completion of his translation, and, probably, the polishing of its earlier books.

The influence of the study of Ovid upon a more concise and pointed type of couplet had been already a remarkable feature of Drayton's poetry. Sandys endeavoured to translate as literally as possible. In the end, his translation exceeded the original by only some eleven hundred lines. He is sometimes excessively literal. "When auxil'ary brasse resounds in vaine" is an almost too exact rendering of *Cum frustra resonent aera auxiliaria.*[1] "I see the better, I approve it too; The worse I follow" is faithful to its original, without reproducing its real

[1] IV, 372 (Ovid, IV, 333).

force.[1]   Wilful embroidery on the text is sometimes admitted, where a few additional words give a picturesque or dramatic touch to the context.   Thus, in these lines from the tale of Pyramus and Thisbe,

> When Pyramus, who came not forth so soone,
> Perceived *by the glimpses of the Moone*
> The footing of wild Beasts;[2]

and, in this couplet from the tale of Salmacis and Hermaphroditus,

> Her sisters oft would say; *Fie*, Salmacis,
> *Fie lazie sister, what a sloth is this!*[3]

the italicised words are not even implied by Ovid.   More often, probably, Sandys aimed at condensing the sense of the Latin in his English, where an effect was possible.   As a rule, however, he renders Ovid's sense with extraordinary faithfulness, and in verse which is strong and melodious.   Nowhere are his ability and ingenuity so apparent as in passages containing long lists of names of persons or places.   The relish which, as a traveller, he must have found in Ovid's enumeration of the mountains and rivers affected by Phaëthon's experiment with his father's horses is clearly apparent.[4]   A love of outdoor sport, which elsewhere suggests casual words and phrases, led him to find appropriate English equivalents for the names which Ovid gives to Actaeon's hounds:[5] his account of the tragedy gains strength thereby.   In almost every part of the poem we may find passages of vigour and picturesqueness, sustained for many lines together.   Such are the descriptions of the cave of Envy;[6] of the plague;[7] of Pythagoras and his vegetarian counsels;[8] and the comparison of the ages of man to the seasons.[9]   In his rendering of "the good-natured story of Baucis and Philemon," Sandys works with that simplicity of language which the homely subject demands.[10]   He was not habitually superior to what he would have called the "ambages" of his contemporaries.   Richard Hooper, the editor of his poems, has indicated

---

[1] VII, 25, 26 (VII, 20, 21).   [2] IV, 115, 116 (IV, 105, 106).
[3] IV, 339 (IV, 305, 306).   [4] II, 235 ff. (Ovid, II, 216 ff.).
[5] III, 223 ff. (III, 206 ff.).   [6] II, 835 ff. (II, 760 ff.).
[7] VII, 573 ff. (VII, 523 ff.).   [8] XV, 69 ff. (XV, 60 ff.).
[9] XV, 237 ff. (XV, 199 ff.).   [10] VIII, 722 ff. (VIII, 639 ff.).

the obligation under which, in the matter of phrase, he lay to Chapman, not the best model of a perspicuous style. But, on the whole, his style was consistently direct and intelligible; it is even, at times, colloquial. Every one of Ovid's heroes, gods, or monsters assumes, with Sandys, a tendency to "skip" or "caper"; while

> Furious *Medea*, with her haire unbound,
> About the flagrant Altar trots a Round.[1]

However, his directness does not lead to baldness of language, or to avoidance of a sounding word or phrase where it will serve its turn. Similarly, his versification is guided by its opportunities rather than by fixed prejudices in favour of certain rules. A number of couplets, each complete in itself, may quite easily be followed by a series of overlapping couplets. In either case, each couplet will be solid and weighty in texture and content. Sandys was not afraid of double consonants or strong monosyllabic rimes. He frequently allowed himself, and always with good effect, to rime two weak endings. In this freedom and variety of use, Drayton was his master; and it is impossible to say that Sandys did more than continue Drayton's form of couplet versification with great skill and success, and on a larger scale than his master had employed.

Sandys returned from Virginia about 1626, when the first complete edition of his *Ovid* was published. He was appointed a gentleman of the privy chamber to Charles I, and was able to spend the remainder of his life in long intervals of leisure, living at the country houses of his relations and consorting with the poets and wits whom Falkland attracted round him. To a new edition of his *Ovid*, published at Oxford in 1632, Sandys gave

what perfection [his] Pen could bestow; by polishing, altering, or restoring, the harsh, improper, or mistaken, with a nicer exactnesse than perhaps is required in so long a labour.

He added to this edition a translation in couplets of the first book of the *Aeneid*. His mind, however, as he confessed, was "diverted from these studies"; and he forsook "Peneian groves and Cirrha's caves" for Holy Scripture. His *Para-*

[1] VII, 281, 282 (VII, 257, 258).

phrase upon the Psalms of David was published in 1636. Early in 1638, it appeared in a folio edition, with tunes by Henry Lawes, and in company with paraphrases of *Job, Ecclesiastes,* the *Lamentations of Jeremiah* and the various songs of the Old and the New Testament. The decasyllabic couplet was employed in the versions of *Job, Ecclesiastes* and *Lamentations,* in nineteen of the *Psalms* and in two of the miscellaneous songs. Twenty-eight psalms, and three of the miscellaneous songs, are written in octosyllabic couplets. Thirty-six psalms are arrangements of octosyllabic lines, with various rimes, in stanza form. Among these should be noticed five examples of the stanza familiar to us as that of Tennyson's *In Memoriam.* Sixteen psalms are composed of trochaic heptasyllabic couplets, and five of couplets of lines of six syllables. The remaining psalms consist, with nine exceptions, of stanzas in which lines of eight are mingled with lines of six or four syllables, or both. In seven of the exceptions, the stanza is formed by a quatrain of six-syllabled lines with alternate rimes, followed by a quatrain of four-syllabled lines, the rimes in which are formed by the two extreme and two middle lines respectively. The two remaining exceptions are composed of a series of quatrains of decasyllabic lines. The paraphrase of *The Song of Solomon,* published in 1641, is in octosyllabic couplets; the tragedy entitled *Christ's Passion,* an imitation of Grotius's tragedy on the same theme, is in decasyllabic couplets, with occasional incursions into the eight-syllabled measure. In these later works, Sandys's versification, if it does not achieve perfect smoothness, is remarkably regular. The habitual parallelism of sense in single verses of Hebrew poetry supplied natural bounds to the couplet; and only here and there, as in the seventy-eighth psalm, does Sandys show a tendency to run his couplets into one another. He also has abandoned his earlier habit of riming weak endings; and, as a general rule, his rimes are less emphatic and consonantal than in his *Ovid.*

The entry of Sandys's burial (7 March, 1643/4), in the parish register of Boxley, describes him as *poetarum Anglorum sui saeculi facile princeps;* and Dryden's opinion of "the ingenious and learned Sandys" as "the best versifier of the former age,"[1] gives a certain colour, with a necessary qualification, to the

[1] Pref. to *Fables* (1700).

perhaps prejudiced encomium of the Kentish vicar. There cannot be any question that, to the younger generation, Sandys's verse represented a praiseworthy contrast to the straggling licence of the couplet-writers of his day. But, to them, the new age began, not with Sandys, but with Waller; and Waller claimed his own poetical descent from another source. Edmund Waller was born at Coleshill, near Amersham, on 3 March, 1605/6. His earliest known attempt in verse appears to be the poem *Of the Danger His Majesty [Being Prince] Escaped in the Road at St. Andere.* The danger in question was incurred by prince Charles at Santander in September, 1623, as he was returning from his attempt to secure a Spanish bride; but the compliment which the poem contains to Henrietta Maria is so essential to it, that it was probably written retrospectively after the betrothal of Charles to the French princess. In this early essay, Waller certainly did not attain the complete mastery of the self-contained couplet. In one place, four couplets occur together, each of which needs its neighbour to complete its sense.[1] In another, seven couplets run on in close connection, before an appreciable pause is reached; and, even then, an eighth is needed to bring the included comparison to an effective close.[2]

The quantity of Waller's published verse is small in comparison with its fame. He went from a school at High Wycombe to Eton, and from Eton he entered King's college, Cambridge, as a fellow commoner, in March, 1619/20. His parliamentary career seems to have begun about a year later, when, probably, he was returned as member for Amersham. He sat for Ilchester in the last parliament of James I, for Chipping Wycombe in the first parliament of Charles I, for Amersham in the third parliament of Charles I and the Short Parliament and for St. Ives in the Long Parliament. He was a prominent and famous speaker in the house of Commons: when the troubles first broke out, he was on the side of the popular leaders, and took part in the opposition to ship-money. But, by 1642, he was gradually drawn closer to the party of the *via media;* and his parliamentary career was closed, for the time, in 1643, by the discovery of his complicity in the royalist conspiracy which became known as Waller's plot. He was

[1] Ll. 61–68.   [2] Ll. 89–104.

árrested, and, after a trying interval, in which he certainly attempted to save himself by compromising others, was fined and banished. He spent his exile in France, associating with Hobbes and Evelyn. Pardoned at the end of 1651, he returned to England. Cromwell appointed him a commissioner of trade in 1655; and, after the restoration, he once more entered parliament as member for Hastings. He sat for this constituency till his death in 1687, playing the part of Nestor of the house with no little self-consciousness, and using his voice on behalf of that constitutional liberalism which embodied his convictions.

During this long period, he wrote but little. He married twice, and was already a widower when he first met lady Dorothy Sidney, daughter of Robert, earl of Leicester. The lady became the theme of several addresses celebrating her beauty and her cruelty with charming ease and with no more than conventional warmth. In lines written at Penshurst, amid the accompaniments of listening deer, beeches bowing their heads and gods weeping rain in sympathy with the poet, the love of Astrophel for Stella is invoked to rebuke a colder scion of the house of Sidney. As all nature is compassionate to the sighing swain, so is it obsequious to the obdurate nymph. Her presence harmonises and gives order to the park: the trees form a shady arbour for her when she sits, an avenue when she walks. When she comes to London, the delights of the spring are there of set purpose to welcome her. Waller's enthusiasm goes so far as to turn verses nominally addressed to others into compliments to lady Dorothy. Her friend, lady Rich, dies: Waller's elegy is converted into the celebration of the friendship of its subject for Sacharissa. Her father goes abroad: the trees of Penshurst lament his absence, and its deer, grudging to be slain by any hand but his, repine. Not these, nor the regrets of his friends, demand his return so much as the havoc which his daughter is working in the hearts of English youth. It is her portrait which is the occasion of an address to Van Dyck; and the stanzas *To a Very Young Lady* would not have been written had there not been an elder sister to give them their real point. Such indirect approaches may argue a more sincere passion than we are at liberty to discover in the lines *Of the Misreport of her being Painted*, and their companions. But, whether Waller was in love with Sacharissa, or whether she was merely a theme for poetical flattery, her influence over his heart or his verse, or both, was transient. His professed fidelity to Sacharissa did not hinder him from joining the train of poets who celebrated the attractions of Lucy, countess of Carlisle. If he is ready to carve his passion on the beeches of Penshurst for one whose every movement those trees obey, the woods of England are equally admirers of lady Carlisle, and "every tree that's worthy of the wound" bears her name on its bark. Lady Isabella Thynne, and an unidentified Mrs. Arden, received tributes from him, which might be made the foundation, with equal justice, of a tradition of passionate love. Sentimentality may please itself with reading the name of Sacharissa between the lines of *Behold the brand of beauty tossed*, or *Go, lovely Rose!;* but Celia, Flavia, Chloris, or Amoret (who, indeed, is once used as a foil to Sacharissa) may quite as justly claim insertion. Love, indeed, with Waller, as with most of his contemporaries, was the ever fertile theme of verse, on which his art demanded that ceaseless variations should be played. He had much of the old skill in execution, but never reached the climax at which art took on itself the very semblance of genuine passion.

When his poems were first printed, in 1645, Waller himself was an exile, and Sacharissa a widow. She had married Henry, lord Spencer of Wormleighton, in 1639: her husband, created earl of Sunderland, fell at Newbury. The editions of 1645, for which Waller was in no way responsible, contained his love-poems, with a number of occasional verses, and the miniature epic called *The Battle of the Summer Islands*. These poems embrace a number of experiments in lyric metres as well as in the couplet. Very few gallant addresses, and even fewer variations from the couplet form, are to be found in the verses written by Waller after his exile. These, in the main, are complimentary and of historical interest, with the exception of *Divine Poems*, which were published in the year before his death. Waller's most enduring work belongs to this later period: the *Panegyric to my Lord Protector*, the verses *Upon a Late Storm, and of the Death of His Highness ensuing in the same*, the *Instructions to a Painter*, commemorating the battle of Sole bay, and the lines *Of the Last Verses in the Book*, which contain the famous passage "the soul's dark cottage, battered and decayed," are more sustained examples of Waller's poetical gift than any of the pieces published in 1645. Yet, it was upon the earlier pieces that his celebrity as the inaugurator of a new age was founded. Of their contents, something has been said. It is probable that the political misfortunes of the poet, and the early widowhood of Sacharissa, helped to give the poems their vogue. The fame of Waller, however, rested on something less ephemeral. It can hardly be said it was won by exclusive devotion to the work of keeping the couplet within fixed bounds. At no time was he especially careful to limit the construction of his sentences to two lines. The lines *On the Statue of King Charles I at Charing Cross*, written in or after 1674, consist of six couplets: the first three are inseparable, and the next two, joined without a break, contain an antithesis without which the former three could not stand alone. This, however, is an extreme instance; and the habit of expanding a symmetrical sentence over two couplets was Waller's more natural practice. Instances of it may be found, among the earlier poems, in *The Battle of the Summer Islands;* and, among his maturer work, the *Panegyric* to Cromwell is written in compact stanzas of two couplets each.

This method of grouping couplets, with the habit of concentrating the force of a passage in a succinct concluding distich, afforded a noticeable contrast to the paragraphic manner in which the minor Jacobean and Caroline poets handled this form of verse. But felicitous examples of grouping and of single pointed couplets may be found in Drayton and Sandys; and Waller's reputation cannot have been due to these devices alone. Aubrey, referring to Waller as "one of the first refiners of our English language and poetrey," tells the story of him that, "when he was a brisque young sparke, and first studyed poetry, 'Methought,' said he, 'I never sawe a good copie of English verses; they want smoothness; then I began to essay.'"[1] The lines of Sir John Beaumont already mentioned demand for English poetry simplicity of rime and simplicity of language. The avoidance of "fetter'd staves" is a consequence, rather than a necessary accompaniment, of these requirements. Towards these ends, Waller's conscious

[1] Aubrey, *Brief Lives*, vol. II, p. 275.

efforts, probably, were directed from the beginning: the sim-
plification of the couplet could hardly fail to be a result of
their successful attainment. He said, in Dryden's hearing,
that he took Fairfax as his model.[1] Fairfax, in his *Godfrey of
Bulloigne*, invariably concluded his eight-lined stanza with a
couplet, which, by no means always isolated from the rest of
the stanza, led, at any rate, to a full stop. This, of itself,
might not have much effect on couplets pure and simple; but
it is certain that Fairfax's comparative plainness and per-
spicuity of language affected Waller's style, and helped to give
it the purity desiderated by Beaumont. But, to account fully
for Waller's smoothness of rhythm and simplicity of diction,
we must recognise that the spirit of reaction from "ragged
rime" and involved language was very general. It is to be
found, for example, in Suckling and Carew. In neither was it
fully developed, for both were still under the spell of the fantastic verse of their day, and Suckling, in particular, was too
much the amateur to effect a revolution in English poetry.
Waller, on the other hand, stood apart from the characteristic
fashions of his time. He had no taste for elaborate and fantastic metaphors. His invention was small. Not many of
the images of nature were present to him; but he was able to
make creditable use of those of which he was conscious. He
chose highly conventional subjects for his verse, old artificial
themes which allowed scope for graceful classical allusions.
Aiming at a pointed fluency of style, he avoided rough rimes,
and lines loaded with sounding words. And so, without setting
an unalterable limit to the couplet, he played a noticeable part
in lightening its contents, and bringing it one step further in
the direction of systematic coherence and conciseness. There
is in Sandys's translations abundance of proof of the value of
antithesis in restraining the couplet within due bounds. Waller, in his constant endeavour after smoothness, did not take
full advantage of the force which antithesis may give to a line.
His work in English versification was to make his contemporaries familiar with a rimed couplet in which each line was
marked by regular beats and by an observance of caesura; in
which heavy stress on the first syllable of a foot, all redundant
syllables and elisions were the rarest exceptions; in which,

[1] Dryden, Pref. to *Fables, u.s.*

finally, the flow of the verse from couplet to couplet was unbroken by the intrusion of spondaic words or striking, but unmusical, rimes.

To a generation accustomed to a poetical style whose brightness was often concealed by the smoke which enveloped it, the consistent clearness and brightness of Waller's verse must have compensated for its want of that splendour which was frequent, but intermittent, in the writers of the fantastic school. If his polished simplicity was not employed consciously in making the sense and contents of a couplet conterminous, it was bound to exercise an influence in that direction. On his own confession, he did not compose easily;[1] and he seems to have followed up his rare moments of inspiration by a sedulous application of the file to their results. His verse is often, if not always, polished into a state of monotonous elegance. Apart from a phrase here and there, as in the lines on "the soul's dark cottage," there is little which, out of the evenness of his execution, stands forth as a triumph of poetic imagination. The sentiment of the famous lyric *Go, lovely Rose!* fortunate in its opening line, is not above the meritoriously commonplace. His experiments outside the couplet, in many cases, miss that even melody which he usually achieved. There are lines in *Puerperium*, the poem written, probably, to celebrate the birth of Henry, duke of Gloucester, in 1640, and in *Behold the brand of Beauty*, which it needs some discernment to scan correctly; and, in the opening quatrain of *To Amoret*,

> Amoret! the Milky Way
> Framed of many nameless stars!
> The smooth stream where none can say
> He this drop to that prefers!

the third line is an example of a halting accentuation of which, in his couplets, Waller was careful not to be guilty. It was by avoiding the characteristic faults of contemporary English verse, its force which sometimes degenerated into clumsiness, its eloquence which could sink at a moment's notice into garrulity, that Waller achieved his fame, and not by any original experiment of his own. In the imagination and the language

[1] Aubrey, *u.s.*

of men like Sandys, there was still much of "the former age."
The generation which hailed Waller as an innovator and
inventor failed to find in Sandys or Drayton the sense of
relief which Waller gave.

The simplicity of style which Waller achieved was reached,
with the use of somewhat different means, by Sir John Denham. He was born at Dublin in 1615, while his father, Sir
John Denham of Little Horkesley in Essex, was lord chief
justice of the king's bench in Ireland. He was entered at
Trinity college, Oxford, in 1631, and afterwards became a
student of Lincoln's inn. His first written effort seems to have
been *The Destruction of Troy*, a translation of part of the
second book of the *Aeneid* into decasyllabic couplets, made in
1636. This work is hardly a translation so much as a paraphrase, in which Denham succeeded in rendering 558 lines of
Vergil by 544 of his own. His desire to reproduce the effect of
his original was genuine, and went to the length of his using
unfinished lines in places where Vergil had done the same.
However, such brevity, in dealing with an author whose style
notoriously defies reproduction, implies no very close attention
to fine shades of meaning; and the version is somewhat commonplace. Denham's reputation was made by his tragedy
The Sophy, acted at Blackfriars in 1641, and published in 1642.
This prepared the way for the fame of *Cooper's Hill*, the first
edition of which bears date 1642. Aubrey describes the delight which Denham took in the neighbourhood of the house
at Egham, which had come to him by the death of the elder
Sir John, its builder, in 1639.[1] This neighbourhood, as seen
from Cooper's hill, was the subject of a poem which, combining
description with moral reflection in an unfamiliar manner,
was, as an example of that combination, the first of a long
series.

The habit of mind which produced these united elements
of description and sentiment was natural to Denham, and was
expressed by him without difficulty. After the preliminary
argument, addressed to the hill on which he stands, that it is
the poet who makes Parnassus, not Parnassus which makes
the poet, he refers to the distant view of London and old St.
Paul's. He prophesies the eternal security of the cathedral,

[1] Aubrey, *op. cit.*, vol. I, p. 218.

restored by the bounty of Charles I, and celebrated by the lines in which Waller hailed its restoration, and contrasts the tumult of the city with the innocent happiness of private life. The nearer towers of Windsor move him to the praise of the royal line, culminating in Charles I. A contrast is provoked by the memory of a chapel, apparently belonging to Chertsey abbey, which stood on a neighbouring hill: this calls forth reflections on Henry VIII, and on the religious controversies of his own day. The Thames next receives his praise in lines containing the passage which begins "O could I flow like thee"—a passage, however, which is not to be found in the first edition of the poem. The fertile valley, with its wooded banks, suggests old stories of fauns, nymphs and satyrs, and a long description of a stag-hunt, in which the quarry falls at length a victim to the king's shaft. Here, on Runnymede, says Denham, continuing the hunt in metaphor, Liberty, hunted by Power, once stood at bay, and Power laid down arbitrary tyranny. The poem concludes with a comment, appropriate to the times, upon the encroachments of subjects on kingly generosity, and with a warning against provoking the fury of a river, which may be guarded against by embankments, but cannot be confined in time of flood within a narrower channel.

The feature of the style of *Cooper's Hill* is a forcible conciseness, aiming at constant antithesis and occasional epigram. The reflections on the spoliation of the monasteries consist of a string of shrewd observations. Denham knew the value of alliteration in driving a point home:

> May no such storm [he prays]
> Fall on our times, where ruin must reform; [1]

and, a few lines lower down:

> Thus he the church at once protects, and spoils:
> But princes' swords are sharper than their styles. [2]

Repetition of a telling word or phrase is another of his artifices:

> But god-like his unweary'd bounty flows;
> First loves to do, then loves the good he does; [3]

and he is alive to the virtues of an oxymoron:

[1] Ll. 115, 116.   [2] Ll. 131, 132.   [3] Ll. 177, 178.

Finds wealth where 't is, bestows it where it wants,
Cities in deserts, woods in cities plants.[1]

In spite of this studied brevity, he makes no consistent use of
the stopped couplet; and, in *Cooper's Hill*, there is ample
proof that its occurrence in the poetry of this age is the result,
not of a fixed metrical design, but of an effort to be direct and
intelligible in expression.   As descriptive poetry, *Cooper's Hill*
has that tendency to generalise scenery which was already
inherent in English verse.   Local details are subordinated to
subjective musings.   But for the mention by name of Windsor
and the Thames, the woods, the flood and the boldly designated
"airy mountain" might belong to any part of England or even
of Europe.   Denham did not invent the habit of looking on
scenery as composed of certain fixed elements, with conventional equivalents in poetic diction; but *Cooper's Hill* certainly
increased the vogue of this fashion.

Between 1642 and 1648, Denham wrote occasional verses;
and the poem *Of Old Age*, a paraphrase in verse of Cicero's *De
Senectute*, is said to have been published in 1648.[2]   Denham
himself tells us that, on behalf of queen Henrietta Maria, he
gained admittance to Charles I in captivity, and that Charles,
after referring kindly to his lines on Sir Richard Fanshawe's
translation of *Il Pastor Fido*, advised him to write no more,
as verses were well enough for idle young men, but stood in their
way "when they were thought fit for more serious employments."[3]   Denham took the advice, and devoted himself to
the task of transmitting the ciphered correspondence between
Charles and his adherents.   On its discovery, he escaped into
France, and was employed on various missions by Charles II
and Henrietta Maria.   Returning to England in 1652, he
stayed for some time with lord Pembroke at Wilton.   The
translation of Vergil which Aubrey says that he made here
may have been a fragment of the fourth book, *The Passion of
Dido for Aeneas;* but Aubrey, possibly, was thinking merely
of *The Destruction of Troy*, which was published in 1656.[4]   In
1658, Denham obtained leave to live at Bury St. Edmunds.

---

[1] Ll. 185, 186.   [2] Johnson, *Life of Denham.*
[3] Dedication to *Poems*, 1667–8.   [4] Aubrey, *op. cit.*, vol. I, p. 218.

At the restoration, he came into the office, the reversion of which had been promised him by Charles I, of surveyor-general of the royal works, and was made a knight of the Bath at the coronation. His second marriage was unhappy; and to his wife's faithlessness was attributed a strange fit of madness which overtook him on a journey, undertaken in the performance of his duties as supervisor of the king's buildings, to the Portland stone-quarries. He recovered before his death: the poems *Of Prudence* and *Of Justice*, translated from the Italian of Mancini, and the octosyllabic couplets *On Mr. Abraham Cowley's Death*, belong to his latest years. In 1667–8, he published his poems and *The Sophy*, with a dedication to Charles II. His version of *De Senectute* was published by itself in 1669. His last work was *A Version of the Psalms of David*. Denham also wrote a number of verses on current topics in irregular and halting metres, which may have amused his friends, but have little merit in them to-day. Of his shorter couplet pieces, the *Elegy on the Death of Henry Lord Hastings*, written in 1650, treats a subject to which Dryden devoted some of his earliest verse.

Abraham Cowley, whose genius Denham declared to be twin to that of Vergil, occupies a place somewhat outside the main channel of the poetry of his day. He was born in Fleet street in 1618. His essay *Of My Self* tells us what we know of his earliest years, and how the early reading of a copy of Spenser, which lay in his mother's parlour, "filled" his "head first with such Chimes of Verse, as have never since left ringing there." He was sent to Westminster school, and, in 1633, when only in his fifteenth year, published a small volume entitled *Poeticall Blossomes*, dedicated to bishop Williams, then dean of Westminster. In 1636 appeared *Sylva*, a collection of occasional verses and odes; and the composition of the pastoral comedy called *Love's Riddle* also belongs to his Westminster days. His two earliest pieces to which a date can be assigned are the narratives, *Pyramus and Thisbe* and *Constantia and Philetus*, written, on his own showing, in 1628 and 1630. These are in stanzas of six decasyllabic lines: the stanza of *Pyramus and Thisbe* has two rimes, the third and fourth lines forming a couplet riming with the first line, and the concluding couplet riming with the second line; while that of *Constantia and Philetus* consists of a quatrain with alternate rimes, and a final couplet. Spenser's successors, rather than Spenser himself, appear to have been Cowley's model. The two songs in *Constantia and Philetus*, and the epitaph at the end of *Pyramus and Thisbe*, in which the metre is varied by changes from iambic to trochaic lines, and *vice versa*, show that his ear was naturally sensitive to prosody. His delight in Latin poetry, and particularly in Horace, appears in the odes contained in *Sylva*. Of the last three verses of *The Vote*, written when he was thirteen, he was justly not ashamed at a more mature time of life; and, indeed, he did not often excel their heartfelt, if not wholly original, prayer for a moderate estate and a life of quiet study. The opening verses, with their keen and even humorous observation of typical characters, are evidence that, if he sat at the feet of Spenser and the Latin poets, he also had caught the tricks of Donne; and the "two or three sharpe curses" which he flings, in *A Poeticall Revenge*, at the "semi-gentleman of th' Innes of Court" who struck him in Westminster hall are a direct reminiscence of Donne in his satiric mood.

In 1637, Cowley entered Trinity college, Cambridge, as a scholar. He obtained his fellowship in 1640: ejected in 1644, he sought refuge at St. John's college, Oxford. In his first year at Cambridge, he wrote a Latin comedy, *Naufragium Joculare;* and, on 12 March, 1640/1, his English comedy, *The Guardian*, which he brought out in an entirely new form after the restoration as *Cutter of Coleman-Street*, was acted at Trinity before prince Charles. Amid the troubles of the civil war, he acted as secretary in France to the queen and court in their correspondence with Charles I. The discovery of his cipher led to the flight of Denham, already recounted. Cowley's fervent loyalty brought him into a way of life which was little to his taste. For a time, in 1656, he acted as a royalist spy in England. After detection and a narrow escape, he sheltered himself under the profession of a physician, but returned to France before the restoration. Although his detractors cast doubt on his loyalty to his old cause, his *Discourse by way of Vision concerning the Government of Oliver Cromwell* was the work of one who was heartily relieved to see the end of the protectorate. After the restoration, he was refused the mastership of the Savoy, and *Cutter of Coleman-*

Street was a failure on the stage. He found patrons in the earl of St. Albans and the duke of Buckingham, and retired on a fair income to Chertsey, where he died in 1667.

The Mistress first appeared in 1647, and was reprinted in 1656 as part of a four-fold collection of poems. His preface to the collected edition represents him as about to quit the exercise of poetry, and desirous to preserve all his writings which were worth preserving. He excluded his juvenile pieces, and all verses written by him with direct reference to the civil war. Part of a poem on the war in three books "reaching as far as the first *Battle* of *Newbury*," was printed in 1679. The rest he divided into four parts, *Miscellanies*, *The Mistress*, *Pindarique Odes* and *Davideis*, of each of which he gave some explanation in his preface.

The *Miscellanies* and *The Mistress* are composed of lyrics written in a variety of irregular metres. Of the *Miscellanies*, Cowley thought little; yet among these are most of the poems indispensable in any representative selection of his work. In his *Anacreontiques*, he used couplets in which the iambic line of eight, and trochaic line of seven, syllables mingle tunefully and naturally. *The Chronicle*, a great contrast to the tortuous fancies of his love-poems, is one of the best examples of English *vers de société* in any age. The stanzas *On the Death of Mr. William Hervey*, though disfigured by at least one frigid hyperbole, contain admirable lines, and were prompted by genuine affection. The same may be said of the couplets *On the Death of Mr. Crashaw*. Sincere feeling pervades Cowley's excuse to his own church for celebrating a pervert from her doctrines; and, while the conceit in which Crashaw's muse is likened to Mary is expressed tastelessly, nothing could be happier than the wording of the companion conceit. Angels are said to have carried the house of the Virgin to Loreto:

> 'T is surer much they brought thee there, and *They*,
> And *Thou*, their charge, went *singing* all the way.

In *The Mistress*, Cowley was writing set verses on conventional topics, and proved himself capable of endless fluency and ingenuity of fancy. Donne's superficial influence is obvious in the subject of such verses as the stanzas *Written in Juice of Lemmon*, or in *The Prophet*, where the man who proposes to teach the poet to love is given a list of arts and bidden teach them to their chief professors. From Donne are taken the trick of beginning a poem impatiently and abruptly, as though in exasperation, and an extravagant outburst like

> *Love* thou 'rt a *Devil;* if I may call thee *One*,
> For sure in Me thy name is *Legion*.[1]

Equally characteristic of Donne is Cowley's free use of far-fetched and unexpected simile. Love exercises an unbounded tyranny over him, and he calls in the other passions to drive this one out: so do the Indians seek to free themselves from the Spaniard by calling in the states of Holland.[2] His love is so violent that, though his life may be short, he may become "the great *Methusalem* of Love."[3] On parting from his mistress, he recalls the sorrow with which men in Greenland see the sun sink for half a year under the horizon.[4] But, amid these vagaries, he does not give any sign of the capacity for phrases and thoughts of astonishing brilliance which underlies Donne's extravagances. His aim is always to astonish his readers with some new invention of a learned and elaborate fancy. No genuine follower of Donne ever misused his cleverness so woefully as Cowley, when, in presenting his book to the Bodleian library, he called the store of God's wonders "the Beatifick *Bodley* of the Deity." True discipleship does not consist in the imitation of mannerisms; and, in the few poems of *The Mistress* in which Cowley chose to be natural, his manner was far more nearly allied to the level suavity of Waller than to the rugged and cloudy magnificence of Donne. Such are the stanzas called *The Spring*, and the beautiful lines in *The Change*, which begin, "Love in her Sunny Eyes does basking play."

The *Pindarique Odes*, prefaced by paraphrases of Pindar's second Olympian and first Nemean odes, were introduced by Cowley with a little diffidence. He is afraid that even experienced readers will not understand them. Their voluble licence of metre may give the mistaken impression that they are easy to compose. The "sweetness and numerosity" of the irregular lines may be overlooked by a disregard of the necessary cadences in pronunciation. He had little or no insight into Pindar's

---

[1] *The Inconstant*, st. 1.   [2] *The Passions*, st. 4.
[3] *Love and Life*, st. 1.   [4] *The Parting*, st. 1.

metrical schemes: his imitations of the "stile and manner" of
his author follow no fixed system of prosody.　The quality
which he sought to reproduce was the "Enthusiastical manner"
of Pindar, with its digressions and bold figures, clothed in "that
kind of *Stile* which *Dion. Halicarnasseus* calls Μεγαλοφυὲς
καὶ ἡδὺ μετὰ δεινότητος, and which he attributes to *Alcaeus*."
Cowley dsecribes the "Pindarique Pegasus" on which he is
mounted:

> 'T is an unruly, and a *hard-mouth'd Horse*,
> 　　Fierce, and unbroken yet,
> 　　Impatient of the *Spur* or *Bit*,
> Now *praunces* stately, and anon *flies* o're the place,
> Disdains the *servile Law* of any settled *pace*,
> *Conscious* and *proud* of his own *natural force*.
> 　'T will no *unskilful Touch* endure,
> But flings *Writer* and *Reader* too that *sits* not *sure*.[1]

Thus he fortifies himself against charges of unskilful horseman-
ship.　It is possible that he himself remained firm in the saddle
when he wrote the lines:

> Thy task was harder much then his,
> 　For thy learn'd *America* is
> Not onely found out first by *Thee*;[2]

but the reader endures a fall before he makes the discovery
that the last syllable of "America" has to be elided..　Again, the
line, "Which *Father-Sun*, *Mother-Earth* below,"[3] may be made
into eight syllables by eliding the last syllable of "Mother";
but the reader may be excused another stumble.　Cowley's
critical notes on the odes serve unconsciously to set his own
faults in relief.　For the metaphor at the beginning of *The
Muse*, he cites the second strophe of Pindar's sixth Olympian.
But Pindar uses the metaphor merely to introduce what follows, nor does he wear it threadbare.　Cowley, on the other
hand, harnesses to the muse's chariot six abstract qualities
and the suggestion of more; Nature becomes its postilion,
Art its coachman, Figures, Conceits and other qualities its
running footmen; and the whole four stanzas, in lines varying
from two to twelve syllables, describe its progress with a
prodigal use of fancies, which are astonishing merely in their

---

[1] *The Resurrection*, st. 4.　　[2] *To Mr. Hobs*, st. 4.　　[3] *To Dr. Scarborough*, st. 4.

extravagance and want of grace. Amid these things, lines occur in which Cowley's natural melancholy speaks with a note of music—for example, "And *Life*, alas, allows but one ill *winters Day*." But these moments are few and far between. The poet is bent on being clever at the expense of all else besides. Conceits in which the years to come are conceived as eggs within their shell,[1] in which Elijah becomes

> The second Man, who *leapt* the *Ditch* where all
> The rest of Mankind *fall*,
> And went not *downwards* to the *skie*,[2]

are faults of ambition from which Cowley's humour was not capable of saving him.

The fourth part of the volume was occupied by the four books of *Davideis, a Sacred Poem of the Troubles of David*, in decasyllabic couplets. Cowley's deep conviction of religion, though tinged with decided fatalism, prompted him to compose a sacred epic; and David, as the ancestor of Jesus, and as a hero who attained success through sufferings of an epic cast, suggested a possibly fertile subject. Vergil was the model of the poem, which, designed to be in twelve books, like the *Aeneid*, was to conclude with the lament of David over Saul and Jonathan. Whether the subject was suited for epic treatment on this scale is a purely aesthetic question, which Cowley, at any rate, answered in the affirmative. His handling of it was hampered by a passion for digression, and the determination to crowd all his biblical learning into the poem. The first book, after the preliminary invocation, and a description of the opposed councils of hell and heaven, proceeds with the history of Saul's anger, the preservation of David by Michal, his flight to Ramah and the appearance of Saul among the prophets. The charm of David's music suggests a disquisition, containing some staggering analogies on the harmony designed by God in creation. David's visit to Ramah calls for a minute description of the prophets' college, and a less interesting *résumé* of their course of instruction. Balaam's prophecy is applied, happily, to Saul's change of heart. In the second book, a rhapsody on the nature of love introduces us to Jonathan.

[1] *The Muse*, st. 3. [2] *The Extasie*, st. 7

The celebration of the feast of the new moon brings us to the hall of Saul's palace, where we read the story of Abraham portrayed in the tapestry hangings. David, absent from the feast, is regaled by a vision selected by an angel from the miscellaneous treasury of fancy, and sees the history of his royal house unfolded before him until, to his waking ears, Gabriel, an elegant figure clothed in a blue silk mantle cut from the skies, with a scarf formed of the choicest piece of an undimmed rainbow, prophesies the birth of the Messiah. The third book brings us into a labyrinth of retrospect. David escapes to Nob and Gath: his heroes join him at Adullam, and accompany him to Moab. The king of Moab, full of epic curiosity to hear a story of adventure, hears from Joab the tale of David and Goliath and the marriage of David and Michal. With the next morning, the fourth book begins. The last three leagues of the way to "gameful Nebo" are beguiled by David with a sketch of the constitution of Israel under the judges, and a review of the early part of the reign of Saul. Much still remains to be told after the end of the Philistine war; but, with the arrival of the hunters at Nebo, the poem closes.

That Cowley had some narrative art must be admitted: the poem is not dull, and his consistent cleverness stimulates the reader's curiosity, if it does not provoke his admiration. In notes, full of learning, he discusses and defends his embroideries on the sacred story, and explains what may seem to be the novelties of his versification. His couplet has in it more of the weight of Sandys and the older couplet-writers than of the somewhat emasculated melody of Waller or the pointed brevity of Denham. He occasionally allows himself a triplet. Sandys however, in his *Ovid*, had used triplets, though on a very few occasions, and had written several of his *Psalms* in octosyllabic triplets; and, at least once, a triplet is to be found in Waller. Twelve-syllabled lines occur from time to time in *Davideis*, and, in the fourth book, the oracle at Shiloh speaks in this measure. In *Davideis*, such variations are used to express the sense of the passage more thoroughly by the sound. The overflowing of a river, the infinitude of the glory of heaven, the incessant halleluia of the angels—"Halleluia" was a word which led Cowley into strange metrical gymnastics—the hugeness of the appearance of Goliath, the height of Saul, all give occasion to the serviceable alexandrine; and Cowley feels himself bound to call the reader's possibly neglectful attention to this. He indeed refined too greatly on the effect produced by wedding sound to sense. Of the two examples to which he directs us in the second book, one, the line describing the meteor worn instead of hair by Gabriel,[1] is too subtle to make its intended point clear; while the other, describing the doom of the Edomites at the hands of Amaziah,[2] defies all scansion in its effort to be graphic. The fact that Cowley always kept his meaning before him, and sought, with high ideals, for the most effective way of expressing it, is the leading virtue of this, his most ambitious work. Valuing every artifice which may give vivacity to the expression of emotion, he condemns the "putid officiousness" of the grammarians who finished Vergil's incomplete lines;[3] and, where words or description fail him, he himself suppresses the end of his line and the conclusion of his couplet.

Cowley's work, in the development of the couplet form, was neither to smooth its roughnesses nor to disencumber it of superfluous content. He strove to make it an adequate vehicle for narrative verse, and to make its movement responsive to the demands of its subject. His weakness in performance lay in his self-conscious ambitiousness, and the mannerisms in which his thought habitually found expression. Without his example, however, the couplet could hardly have attained that force which, in combination with flexibility and ease, it acquired in Dryden's hands. In many respects, the ease and majesty of Dryden's couplets seem more closely allied to the masculine style of the earlier couplet-writers than to the artifices and not infrequent tameness of Cowley and Waller. Yet it is the case that the intermediary work of each, in its own way, made those qualities in Dryden possible, and that their efforts helped to give his couplets that polish and balance and good sense which, in his case, became a second nature.

After 1656, the poetical work of Cowley was small in volume. In 1643, he had written a bitter, but able, satire in couplets on puritanism, called *The Puritan and the Papist*. His first published work after the restoration was the attack, already alluded to, on the memory of Cromwell, which,

---

[1] Book II, l. 802. [2] Book II, l. 611. [3] Book I, note 14.

although in prose, contains verses, and ends in a set of couplets. The *Verses on Several Occasions*, including the long *Ode upon His Majesties Restoration and Return* and the lively *Ode Sitting and Drinking in the Chair, made out of the Reliques of Sir Francis Drake's Ship*, appeared in 1663. Another ode in the same collection, *To the Royal Society*, recalls the publication, in 1661, of Cowley's brief prose *Proposition for the Advancement of Experimental Philosophy*. The folio edition of his works published in 1668 contained, in addition to the poems of 1656 and 1663, the *Discourse* on Cromwell, and the *Several Discourses by way of Essays, in Verse and Prose*. These later verses include odes and stanzas appropriate to the subjects of the essays, and a number of translations and imitations, chiefly of Horace. The prose *Essays* take their place more fittingly in a discussion of the development of English prose:[1] their value in connection with the poetry of Cowley is that they give us, in language of great refinement and beauty, the key to his scholarly and sensitive nature. While thoroughly conscious of his own art, he obtruded himself but little into the text of his poems. Once, in his later years, disappointed of his hopes of court favour, he blamed himself, "the melancholy Cowley," through the lips of his muse, for his "unlearn'd Apostacy" from poetry, and the devotion to affairs which had left him "gaping . . . upon the naked Beach, upon the Barren Sand," while his fellow-voyagers pressed inland to their reward. He consoled himself by rebuking his mentor, and representing the favour of the king as still possible.[2] This, however, is his one strictly autobiographical poem. The true ambition and devotion of his life was centred in literature. In his own day, his reputation was very high. The influence of Donne, lord of "the universal monarchy of Wit," was still powerful: its finer qualities were hidden by the passion for flights of artificial fancy which it had provoked, and one who surpassed Donne in outlandish variety of conceits might well be hailed as his legitimate successor and even superior. If the reputation of Cowley declined with surprising rapidity, while that of Waller and Denham remained undiminished,[3] it was because, instead of pursuing, with them,

---

[1] See Volume VIII, of the present work.   [2] *The Complaint*, stt. 3, 8.

[3] Contrast, *e.g.*, Pope, *Essay on Criticism*, ll. 360, 361, with *Imitations of Horace*, ep. 1, bk. ii, 75–79.

the natural direction of poetry, he chose to limit his taste within the compass of fashions that were outworn, and to exhaust the last resources with which those fashions could supply their followers. Yet his influence on the verse of the younger generation of poets must not be judged entirely by the eclipse which overtook his fame within half a century of his death. That influence was summed up by Johnson at the end of the searching criticism of the fantastic school of poetry, and of Cowley as "the last of that race, and undoubtedly the best," with which he concluded his *Life of Cowley:*

It may be affirmed, without any encomiastic fervour, that he brought to his poetic labours a mind replete with learning, and that his pages are embellished with all the ornaments which books could supply; that he was the first who imparted to English numbers the enthusiasm of the greater ode, and the gaiety of the less; that he was equally qualified for spritely sallies, and for lofty flights; that he was among those who freed translation from servility, and, instead of following his author at a distance, walked by his side; and that, if he left versification yet improveable, he left likewise from time to time such specimens of excellence, as enabled succeeding poets to improve it.

The general inclination to restrain poetic fluency within definite bounds, which led to the adoption of the self-contained couplet as the standard form of verse after the restoration, prompted Sir William D'Avenant to write his epic poem, *Gondibert*, in a series of quatrains with alternate rimes. The first two books of *Gondibert* were written at Paris, where D'Avenant was the guest of lord Jermyn in his rooms at the Louvre. The whole poem was intended to consist of five books, corresponding to the five acts of a play, each divided into a number of cantos. D'Avenant, according to Aubrey, was much in love with his design; and his preoccupation with it excited the ridicule of Denham and other courtiers then at Paris. In 1650, the two finished books were published, prefaced by a long letter from the author to Hobbes, who had read the work as it advanced, and by a complimentary answer from Hobbes himself. *Gondibert* was never completed. Early in 1650, Sir William left Paris for Virginia: his voyage was intercepted by a parliamentary ship, which took him prisoner. He wrote six cantos of the third book during his imprisonment in Cowes castle, but, finding that the sorrows of his condition begat in him "such a gravity, as diverts the musick of verse," he abandoned the poem, and, during the remaining eighteen years of his life, added to it but one fragment, which was printed in the collected edition of his works in 1673. The unfinished poem, with a postscript dated from Cowes castle, 22 October, 1650, was published in 1651.

In his epistle to Hobbes, D'Avenant elaborately explained his theory of poetry, his choice of the epic form, and his conduct of the various parts of the poem. He was much in earnest in defending the moral value of poetry, and in indicating the salutary influence which "princes and nobles, being reformed and made angelicall by the heroick" form of verse, may exercise on their subjects who, by defect of education, are less capable of feeling its advantages. His aim was to give his readers a perfect picture of virtue, avoiding the snares into which critics had found that previous epic poets, from Homer to Spenser and Tasso, had fallen. His stage was to be filled with characters remarkable for noble birth or greatness of mind, whose schools of morality were courts or camps. The "distempers" chosen as objects of warning were not to be vulgar vices, but the higher passions of love and ambition. As for his "interwoven stanza of four"

I believed [he says] it would be more pleasant to the reader, in a work of length, to give this respite or pause, between every stanza (having endeavoured that each should contain a period) than to run him out of breath with continued couplets. Nor doth alternate rime by any lowliness of cadence make the sound less heroick, but rather adapt it to a plain and stately composing of musick; and the brevity of the stanza renders it less subtle to the composer, and more easie to the singer, which in stilo recitativo, when the story is long, is chiefly requisite.

The stanza itself was no novelty: D'Avenant's innovation consisted in his adaptation of it to an epic poem, and in his attempt to give to each quatrain an individual completeness, to which he felt the couplet unequal. *Gondibert*, even had it been finished, would hardly have achieved the place among epics which its author designed it to fill; and the compliments paid to it by Hobbes, in a letter which contains much sound criticism, flattered it excessively. The characters of Gondibert himself and the virtuous and highly educated Birtha, a Miranda instructed by another Prospero in the shape of her father Astragon, fail to inspire much interest: Rhodalind, the rival of Birtha for the love of Gondibert, is a mere lay figure; and the subtle Hermegild, the haughty Gartha and the rest, merely threaten complications in the plot, the development of which we are spared. The descriptions are long, and the speeches of the characters are intolerably prolix: Gondibert declares his love to Birtha in nine stanzas, and explains his intentions to her father in two speeches, extending over thirty stanzas more. The language, however, is uninvolved, although D'Avenant, who set much store by wit in poetry, indulges constantly in images dear to the fantastic poets, such as those drawn from the mandrake or from the details of alchemy. If he placed too high a hope in the future of his work, he yet strove in it consistently for directness of expression and succinctness of sense. The virtues of his quatrain were proved by the admiration of Dryden, who chose it as the stanza of *Annus Mirabilis;* and the practice, which Dryden, by its use, gained in clear and pointed writing, gives it a place as a link in the development of the couplet form, of which he became the most accomplished master.

CHAPTER IV
Lesser Caroline Poets

WE have to deal in this chapter with a group of poets in regard to the treatment of whom opposite dangers present themselves. Most, if not all of them, from a time immediately succeeding their own, have been very little known, and there are literary histories of repute which contain none, or hardly one, of their names. The school to which, almost without exception, they belong has been constantly attacked and rarely defended. Some of them came in for early ridicule at the hands of the two greatest satirists of their own later years—two of the greatest in English literature —Dryden and Butler. Another generation saw their school as illustrating the "false wit" of Addison; and, in yet another, that school provided subjects for Johnson's dissection of "metaphysical" poetry. They received little, though they did receive some, attention from the greater critics and poets of the romantic revival; and no one has ever bestowed upon their class—very seldom has any one bestowed upon an individual member of it—the somewhat whimsical and excessive, but by no means impotent, and sometimes rather contagious, enthusiasm which, for instance, was bestowed by Charles Lamb upon Wither. Until very recently, none of the group has been easily accessible to the general reader—while some have been absolutely inaccessible, except to those who have time, energy and opportunity to frequent the largest public libraries, or time and means to procure them in the second-hand book-market. Indeed, it is believed that neither the British Museum, nor either of the libraries of the two great English universities, possesses a complete collection of the work which forms the subject of this survey.

There is a certain type of critic who is apt to say, in such circumstances, that neglect proves worthlessness; but this is always a begging of the question, and it can be easily shown that, in the present case, the questions begged are not unimportant. - That the poets here grouped are not worthless can be affirmed with confidence by one who has impartially examined them; indeed, the affirmation is made almost unnecessary, or, from another point of view, is strongly corroborated, by the fact that all anthologists of competence, from Ellis and Campbell downwards, have drawn, to some extent, upon them. That, as a class, they have numerous faults, may be granted without the slightest difficulty. But it so happens that their faults as well as their merits are of the greatest historical value. It may fearlessly be laid down that, without some study of these poets, neither the characteristics of the great Elizabethan period which preceded them and of which, in fact, they were the twelfth hour, nor those of the reaction which, rising with and against them, overcame and stifled their kind, can be fully comprehended. The cast of thought and style and feeling which, when the genius of the man is at its height and the fostering of the hour at its full, produces Spenser and Shakespeare, turns out, when the genius is abated and the hour at its wane, the work of Chamberlayne and Kynaston. The revulsion (sometimes after actual indulgence in them) from the extravagances of Benlowes and of Cleiveland shapes and confirms the orderly theory and practice of Dryden and of Pope.

Nor, though this, of itself, would suffice to warrant treatment of these poets here, is it their only claim thereto. It so happens that they include authors of almost every example (the chief exception being D'Avenant's *Gondibert*) of the English heroic romance in verse. It is impossible, therefore, without taking them into account, to appreciate the effect of the very curious, and far too little studied, heroic influence on our literature. It is further the case that they contribute very largely to the illustration of one form of the great decasyllabic couplet—the form which, partly from its own weakness, but partly, also, from its association with their extravagances of diction and thought and narrative *ordonnance*, succumbed to its rival—the closer knit and robuster distich of Waller and

Dryden. And this leads to yet another point of historical interest about them—the fact, sometimes denied but fairly certain for all that, of their having served as models and teachers to Keats in his revival of their own form. Helots and caricatures of the great poetry of the sixteenth and early seventeenth centuries; gibbeted warnings, who prescribed to the late seventeenth and the eighteenth the ways they should not go; ancestors of some of the most characteristic, and not the least charming, features of the poetry of the nineteenth—these curious persons have woven themselves into the poetic history of the country in a fashion inseparable though not indistinguishable—a fashion that may be ignored, but only at the cost of corresponding ignorance. It will be already evident, perhaps, that, although some of them possess individual interest, their collective interest, both as a group and as practitioners of particular styles and kinds, is superior. Consequently, with a very few exceptions, they may be advantageously treated here in relation to those kinds or styles—romantic narrative, short lyric, overlapping couplet verse, "metaphysical" and "conceited" diction and thought—as well as by a reasoned catalogue of the poets, and a chronological list, accompanied by criticism, of the works.

The group of romantic narratives, or heroic poems, is headed and not inadequately represented by the *Pharonnida* (1659) of William Chamberlayne. Little is known of its author except that he was born, lived (practising as a physician), died and was buried at Shaftesbury on the Wiltshire and Dorset border; and that he served with the royalist army, especially at the second battle of Newbury (1644), when the composition of his poem was interrupted. It did not appear till fifteen years afterwards. Besides *Pharonnida*, he wrote a play, *Love's Victory* (1658), reprinted as *Wits led by the Nose* (1678), and given with the romance by Singer, and a short poem on the restoration, *England's Jubile*, which has been almost unknown until recently. Many years afterwards, and after his death in 1683, a very brief prose romance, disproportionately abstracted from *Pharonnida*, appeared under the title *Eromena*, but nothing is known about its authorship or editorship. The play contains some interesting, and even fine, things, but is chaotic and not of much value as a whole.

England's Jubile, vigorously enough written, is chiefly noticeable for the strong opposition of its style and verse to the verse and style of *Pharonnida*. To this, therefore, we may confine our detailed notice.

When its date, and the circumstances of English and European literature at the time are duly remembered, *Pharonnida* presents itself in a double aspect. On the one hand, it is an evidence of the somewhat groping quest for the novel, and, also, an instance of a particular stage of the long poem. The world-wide popularity of Ariosto and, still more, of Tasso, reinforcing and reinforced by that of the *Amadis* adaptations of medieval romance and of translations of Greek, supplied the principal determinants of this form both in France and in England; but verse romance preserved its attraction longer in England than in France. *Pharonnida*, in fact, may be described as an early attempt at an unhistorical novel, couched in verse instead of in prose. Although Argalia the hero is, in essence, a knight errant, he is, perhaps unconsciously, but considerably, modernised—made much nearer to Stukely and Grenville, Ralegh and Cumberland, than to Lancelot or Gawain, Amadis or Galaor. Pharonnida the heroine has not much character; but she is very prominent in the action, and, if not so real as Malory's Guinevere or the heroine of *Sir Gawayne and the Grene Knight*, is much more so than Oriana or Polisarda. The adventures, on the whole, are free from the sameness which is usually, and not always unjustly, charged against earlier romance; and some of the episodes, especially that of the frail Janusa's passion for Argalia, are remarkably vivid.

Unfortunately, Chamberlayne, regarding him, for the time, as a tale-teller merely, has, as teller of a continuous tale, almost everything to learn. It has been said that the composition of his poem was, apparently, interrupted; and this (with, perhaps, an uncompleted attempt at revision of the earlier part) may, by very charitable persons, be taken as a possible excuse for the incoherence of the story, for the bewildering confusion of names in respect to the same persons and places and for the author's apparent uncertainty whether his action is going on in the Morea or in Sicily. Nevertheless, it seems much more probable that he gave himself no trouble whatever either in original planning or in subsequent revision, but wrote his fourteen thousand lines "overthwart and endlong," as older romances themselves picture the riding of their knights, indulging in battles and sieges and imprisonments and escapes and adventures by land and sea, till, at last, he was tired, and graciously allowed his hero and heroine to marry and be happy ever after.

If this were so, his poetical peculiarities, to which we may now turn, certainly lent themselves—and, indeed, may be said to have tempted him—both to extravagance and to incoherence. His poetical vehicle here is the decasyllabic couplet, excessively overlapped or enjambed—a form which, found, like its definite opposite, and almost all varieties between them, in Chaucer, had been taken up and developed in the generation before Chamberlayne by Browne and others, and was now provoking reaction in the opposite way. Chamberlayne sets at defiance the principles already formulated by Sir John Beaumont, and long afterwards indignantly objected to in Keats by his *Quarterly* reviewer. He will run a sentence on for nearly a page, and that not in the orderly periodic fashion of his contemporary Milton's verse, but in more than the jointed accumulation of Milton's prose, and in a welter of construction which hopelessly defies analysis. Meanwhile, the rime is, as it were, left to take care of itself, or, at most, so arranged as to supply a sort of irregular musical accompaniment to what is, rhetorically speaking, a vast paragraph of prose arranged with great rhythmical, and even metrical, beauty, but observing no kind of necessary correspondence between the rhythm and the sense, and disregarding altogether the "punctuating"—the "warning bell"—office of rime.

It is impossible that such a process as this should not affect —and that prejudicially—the sense itself. It is not merely that grammatical analysis of the meticulous kind is impossible— this often happens, even in the best writers, before the eighteenth century, and, nearly as often, the sense is not a jot the worse for it. The construction justifies itself $\pi\rho\grave{o}s$ $\tau\grave{o}$ $\sigma\eta\mu\alpha\iota\nu\acute{o}\mu\epsilon\nu\sigma\nu$, and there is little or no doubt what that $\sigma\eta\mu\alpha\iota\nu\acute{o}\mu\epsilon\nu\sigma\nu$ is. But, in Chamberlayne, there by no means seldom is doubt. He has allowed a fresh thought, a fresh image, or even a fresh incident, to arise in his mind before he has finished dealing with the last, and he simply does not finish—but drops his old partner's arm and puts his own round the new partner's waist without ceremony, and without stopping the dance movement of verse and phrase. After a time, with tolerable alacrity of mind, some patience and a little goodwill, it is possible to accommodate oneself in reading to what, at first, causes mere bewilderment, and, perhaps, in the majority of readers, mere disgust. That disgust was certainly felt by younger contemporaries, of whom Dryden was to be the most distinguished representative. But it had not been felt by their elders— we have the direct testimony of Izaak Walton as to Chalkhill[1] a minor Chamberlayne in almost every way. And those who, while fully appreciating the faults and their lessons, can prevent these from blinding them to the accompanying beauties, will find not a few such beauties in *Pharonnida*.

However, it is undoubtedly true of Chamberlayne in *Pharonnida*, as Shelley remarked of Chamberlayne's great pupil in *Endymion*, that "the author's intention appears to be that no person shall possibly get to the end of it." The mysterious "Jo. Chalkhill," to whom Walton attributed the poem entitled *Thealma and Clearchus*, published by himself in 1683, though, according to him, written "long since" by a person who was "an acquaintant and friend of Edmund Spenser" (dead eighty years earlier), adopted still surer measures for this purpose by never coming to any end at all. Of the author, nothing is positively known, and some have thought that he was a mere mask for Walton himself, which is not at all probable; but there was a John Chalkhill, who was coroner for Middlesex late in Elizabeth's reign, and this, or another, was grandfather, or, at least, step-grandfather, to Walton's wife. The poem, though very much shorter, is exactly on the same lines as *Pharonnida*—heroic, with a touch of the pastoral; is couched in the same sort of verse, though in somewhat lesser blocks; passes from adventure to adventure with the same bewildering *insouciance;* seems, indeed, to have been written with somewhat more care as to names and places, so far as the author's intention goes; but indulges in a complication of disguises, mistakes of persons and the like, which even Chamberlayne never permitted himself, and which,

[1] See *post*

probably, had something to do with the relinquishment of a recklessly and hopelessly embroiled enterprise. Even in proportion to its length, it has fewer of those "gleams of poetry" which Shelley allowed to be "of the highest and finest" in Keats, and which are not seldom high and fine in Chamberlayne. But it has some extremely pretty passages; and its comparative brevity, helped by Walton's commendations of it and of its author's other work, has secured it some faint approach to popularity.

Yet another short piece of the same kind, revived, like those previously mentioned, though in a small edition, rather less than a century ago by the industry of Singer, is the *Cupid and Psyche* (1637) of Shakerley Marmion the dramatist.[1] Marmion possesses the immense advantage of having the Apuleian narrative to keep him straight and clear; and, though his poem is not a mere paraphrase and, still less, a mere translation, he wisely deviates little from the original in substance or order of telling. This, with the beauty of the story itself, puts it at no small premium in comparison with the others. But Marmion has far less power than Chamberlayne, and not quite so much prettiness as Chalkhill. Metrically, he is very interesting, because he illustrates not merely one but both sides of the "battle of the couplets." He is sometimes inclined to enjambment, but sometimes, also, and, perhaps, more frequently (in a manner which suggests a "son" of Ben Jonson), adopts the opposite form. Nor is he unsuccessful with it, though the looseness of his rimes (which are sometimes mere assonances) is against him. Moreover, that very clue of a ready made and distinct story relieves him of the temptation to discursive extravagance in the literal sense, to which Chamberlayne and Chalkhill succumb. For it is one of the points of interest and importance here, that the characteristics of verse and narrative exercise a constant reflex action on each other. The want of foresight as to what has to be said loosens the bounds of the measure of saying it; and the absence of a sharp "pull-up" in the measure encourages the tendency to divagate.

Pharonnida, Thealma and Clearchus, Cupid and Psyche, have, as has been said, for nearly a century been accessible,

[1] See Vol. VI, Chap. x.

to some extent, without recourse to the very rare originals. This has not been the case, till within the last few years, with a fourth and very curious example of the heroic poem, the *Leoline and Sydanis* (1642) of Sir Francis Kynaston. One or two of Kynaston's lyrics, by the production of which he is distinguished from his compeers, had been noted and quoted by anthologists; and a singular experiment of his in the matter of Chaucer had also been chronicled in the present generation: but his principal poem had been left to curiosity-hunters. Kynaston was a Shropshire gentleman of family, and, apparently, of some means; a member, not merely by incorporation, but by actual residence, of both universities; he was proctor at Cambridge in 1635, and sat for Shropshire in parliament from 1621 onwards. In 1635, he started in London, not without royal patronage, a kind of institute or academy entitled *Museum Minervae*. His enthusiasm for Chaucer led him to execute (in 1635) a version of the first two books of *Troilus and Criseyde* in Latin rime royal—a thing apparently preposterous, but by no means actually contemptible; and he adopted the same measure in his English romance. It holds itself out as embodying some tradition of his Welsh neighbours, and the adventures pass entirely in Wales and Ireland, but are not connected with any of the better-known cycles of either Welsh or Irish literature. They describe the fortunes or (mainly) misfortunes of a king's son and a duke's daughter who are separated by the agency of black magic and reunited by that of white—the heroine, for a time, supporting the personage of page to her rival. In mere poetical value, *Leoline and Sydanis* is the inferior of *Thealma and Clearchus*, and very far the inferior of *Pharonnida;* but, as a story, it is infinitely superior to both, and it shows an important distinction of kind, which is not merley heroic but distinctly heroicomic. Ariosto, rather than Tasso, is the model—if, indeed, Kynaston has not gone beyond Ariosto to patterns still more distinctly satiric or burlesque. Rime royal, which, as a metre, has a decidedly serious complexion, does not lend itself to this use quite so well as the octave. But Kynaston is by no means wholly unsuccessful—and, with some slips into the prosaic (which is the danger of the style, and, in this use, of the metre), presents an early, a fairly original and a very interesting, anticipation of

"Whistlecraft" and *Don Juan*. The Latin *Troilus*, though, of course, only a *tour de force*, is a remarkable counterpart, in its straightforward utilisation of a classical language for modern metre, of earlier and later experiments in classical metre with modern language. And, though the statement may seem rash, it suggests that the rarer and less popular experiment has in it less inherent elements of failure. Something more will be said later of Kynaston's lyrics. But they certainly illustrate that remarkable diffusion of the lyrical spirit which is one of the notes of the age; and, as certainly, they are not the less interesting from being found in company with a long poem of considerable individuality and no small merit, and with a curious experiment of the kind just described —the whole due, not to a professional man of letters or a mere recluse student, but to a person of fortune, of position in politics as well as in academic business and of evidently active tendencies. Their author is not the best poet of this chapter, but he is one of its most notable and typical figures.

The remaining heroic romances of this period are inferior to the four just described in poetical merit; but there are several of them, they are mostly very rare in original editions and they contribute to the importance and interest of the class in the history, both of English poetry and of the English novel. The oldest, the *Sheretine and Mariana* of Patrick Hannay, is not strictly Caroline, as it was published a year or two before Charles came to the throne; but it is essentially of the group. This poem, a tragic legend of love and inconstancy, is based on, or connected with, Hungarian history after the battle of Mohacz (1526), and is recounted by the heroine's ghost in two books and more than two hundred six-lined stanzas of decasyllables. Hannay (of whom next to nothing is known, but who was certainly of the Galloway Hannays, and may, later, have been a master of chancery in Ireland) also wrote a long version of the story of Philomela, in curious lyrical form, which he seems to have thought might be sung throughout (he gives the tune), though it extends to nearly 1700 lines; a poem called *The Happy Husband* (1619); elegies on Anne of Denmark and some smaller pieces. He is no great poet, but has minor historical interests of varied kinds, including that of writing in literary English strongly tinged with Scoticisms.

The Chaste and Lost Lovers or *Arcadius and Sepha* of William
Bosworth or Boxworth is a couplet poem in less than 3000 lines
varied by some other metres, much less enjambed than others
of the period in form, and decidedly less "metaphysical" in
diction; but having a double portion of intricacy and unin-
telligibility of story. It was published, with some minor
poems, a year after its author's death, in 1651; but he seems to
have written it considerably earlier—in fact, when he was not
twenty, in the first or second year of Charles. As might be
expected, these poems lack precision no less than compres-
sion, and they are rather promise than performance; but their
promise is considerable and the circumstances of their production noteworthy. Bosworth, of whom, again, next to nothing
is known, but who, apparently, was a country gentleman
in Cambridgeshire, is, perhaps, best seen in his shorter piece
Hinc Lachrimae or *To Aurora*, which is not so much a single
poem as a sequence of dixains; but there are many good things
in *Arcadius and Sepha* itself.

Besides these, we have further, of the same kind, the *Albino
and Bellama* (1637) of Nathaniel Whiting, a poem of more than
four thousand lines in sixains, with strong inclination to the
heroicomic, and with something of the greater clearness of
tale-telling which the comic element often brings with it, but
with a more vulgar tone than Kynaston's; the *Arnalte and
Lucenda* (1639) of Leonard Lawrence, a piece of little merit, and
one or two others not worth mentioning. The last-named
poem (which is worth mentioning if only for this reason)
pretends to be adapted "from the Greek of an unknown author," and this is an indirect testimony, much stronger than
the direct assertion, to the influence of the late Greek romances
on the whole class.

As will have been seen, they even follow, with the single
exception of *Pharonnida*, the double title, by hero's and
heroine's name, which is usual in those romances; and they
follow them, less superficially, in the predominance of love-
interest as a central motive, and in the working out of the
story by an endless series of mostly episodic adventures.
This may appropriately bring us round to some consideration
of the general character of the class itself. That character
may be put afresh as showing vividly the persistence of the

appetite for poetry, the disposition to couch fiction in verse and the decay of concentrated poetical power in the average writer, despite a strange general diffusion of some share of it; with, on the other side, the strong, blind groping after fiction itself. All these writers want to tell a story; but, for the most part, they do not in the very least know how to do it. Even if they were not perpetually neglecting their main business in order to scatter poetical flowers, which (except in the case of Chamberlayne conspicuously and of others more or less) they, again, do not know how to produce of the true colour and sweetness, their mere notion of novel arrangement is (except, perhaps, with Kynaston) hopelessly inadequate. Their confusion in this way infects, and, in its turn, is aggravated by, the disorder of their grammar, their style and their versification. It is true that, in almost all of them—as, for instance, in such an utterly forgotten person as Bosworth—there is a something, a suggestion, a reminiscence, of a kind of poetry not to be met again for a hundred and fifty years. But it rarely comes—save in Chamberlayne—to much more than a suggestion of poetry; and, everywhere, there is much more than a suggestion of the imperative necessity of an interval of "prose and sense."

Some, however, of these poets also devoted themselves, and a larger number of others devoted themselves more or less, to kinds of poetry which, though certainly not less exacting in respect of purely poetical characteristics, are much less so in respect of the characteristics which poetry shares with prose. In the first chapter of this volume, something has been said concerning the differences derived from, or first exemplified by, Jonson and Donne, of later, as compared with earlier, lyric. But these differences, though exhibited on a larger scale, in greater variety and with more sustained perfection, by Herrick, Carew and others already mentioned, are nowhere more characteristically shown than by some of the lesser people who provide the subject of this chapter. Chalkhill's verse, in this kind—more generally known than anything else here owing to its inclusion by Walton in *The Compleat Angler*—is good; but by far the best lyrist of the poets already mentioned is Kynaston, whose *Cynthiades or Amorous Sonnets* (1642) long ago furnished anthologists of taste with one or two specimens, and might have been much more largely drawn upon. The pieces which begin "Look not upon me with those lovely eyes"; "Do not conceal those radiant eyes"; "When I behold the heaven of thy face"; "Dear Cynthia, though thou bear'st the name" and "April is past: then do not shed" display, in all but the highest degree, though with some inequality, the impassioned quaintness of thought and expression, with the mellifluous variety of accompanying sound, which form the combined charm of this department of verse.

Of lyrists proper, the one writer of whose work at least one piece is almost universally known, is Henry King, bishop of Chichester. King—who was a Westminster boy and Christ Church man, and who successively held all the lesser dignities of the Anglican church as prebendary of St. Paul's, archdeacon of Colchester, canon of Christ Church and dean of Rochester, before his elevation to the bench—was a friend of Donne, Jonson and Walton, and was acquainted with many other men of letters. But his own literary fortunes have been rather unlucky. For, when, nearly seventy years ago, Hannah undertook the republication of King's *Poems* (1657 and later), he at first limited his design to religious pieces, then intended to do the whole, but, finding his biographical and bibliographical material too great for that whole in one volume, promised a second, which he never found time to publish. It therefore happens, by a most singular chance, that the only poem by King which everyone knows will be looked for in vain in the only extant edition, properly so called, of his works. This piece, "Tell me no more how fair she is," cannot, indeed, claim to be of the most absolutely exquisite among the many exquisite lyrics of this period. But there are few pieces which unite a sufficient dose of this peculiar exquisiteness with so complete an absence of all the faultier characteristics—obscurity, preciousness, conceit, excessive sensuousness, "metaphysical" diction, metrical inequality; and, consequently, there is hardly one which can be more fitly put before the average reader as a sample of the style. His other pieces are inferior relatively, but do not deserve the positive sense which is sometimes given to the word. His elegies are sometimes fine; and *The Legacy, The Exequy, Silence, The Dirge*, have caught almost more of the quieter spirit and manner of Donne than has the work of any other poet, though they have not Donne's intensity, or his magic.

There is, however, yet another piece attributed to King which has considerable interest both in itself and as illustrating a peculiarity of the time. There was still, on the one hand, a certain shyness in regard to the formal publication of poetry, and, on the other, the inveterate habit of handing about MS. copies of verses, with the result that ill-informed persons entered them in their albums, and piratical, or, at least, enterprising, publishers issued them in collections, under different names. The instance at present referred to is the curious batch of similes for the shortness and instability of life sometimes entitled *Sic Vita* and, in its best form, beginning

> Like to the falling of a star.

They are, in the same form, attributed, also, to Francis Beaumont; and they either served as models to, or were continued by, some half-score similar pieces—some of them attributed to well-known persons like Browne and Quarles, some anonymous or belonging to a schoolmaster named Simon Wastell. There can be no doubt that King was quite equal to composing the best of them; but his authorship is a question of less interest than the way in which the circumstances illustrate the manners and tastes of the time.

Much more various and extensive, and of more diffused excellence, though no one piece of it may be so generally known as "Tell me no more," is the work of Thomas Stanley, who, again, is a typical figure of the time. His great-grandfather was a natural son of the third earl of Derby; but his descendants had maintained position and wealth. Stanley's father was a knight, and his mother Mary was one of the Kentish Hammonds whom we shall meet again in this chapter, and who were to be of continued literary distinction. The poet first had, as private tutor, a son of Fairfax, translator of Tasso, and then went to Pembroke college, Cambridge, which he left for the grand tour. Coming home just at the beginning of the civil war, he did not take any active part in politics or fighting, but settled himself in the Temple, married soon, used his not inconsiderable wealth for the benefit of numerous literary friends and died in 1678. He holds no small place in English literary history on more grounds than one, as editor of Aeschylus, as author of the first serious English *History of Philosophy*, which was long a standard, and (our present concern) as a poet both original and in translation as well as a copious translator in prose. His original poetical work is mainly comprised in two volumes, issued, respectively, in 1647 and 1651; but, five years later than the last date, he allowed a musician, John Gamble, to "set" a large number of his poems and gave him some not yet printed. The two volumes also contain numerous translations from poets ancient and modern, while Stanley also Englished the whole or part of prose and poetical work by Theocritus Ausonius, the pseudo-Anacreon, Bion, Moschus, Johannes Secundus, Preti, Marino, Boscan, Gongora, Montalvan and others.

The mere list of Stanley's works may suggest an industrious pedant, curiously combined with a butterfly poet. But his work actually possesses very considerable charm. It is possible to lay too much stress on his selection of classical poets for translation, as indicating a decadent character; but, undoubtedly, "the favour and the prettiness" of such things as *Cupida Cruci Affixus*, and *Basia*, the rather uncanny grace of *Pervigilium*, were much akin to the general tendency of Caroline poetry. He has transferred them all well, though not, perhaps, with sufficient discrimination of the original styles: and he has certainly succeeded in maintaining throughout his original verse a very high level of favour and of prettiness themselves. Anthony à Wood called him "smooth and genteel"; but, if one compares his work with that of smooth and genteel poets in the eighteenth century or with the Jerninghams and Spencers and Haynes Baylys of the early nineteenth, there will be found a notable, though, perhaps, not easily definable, difference. Such lines as these, taken at an absolutely haphazard first opening:

> Chide, chide no more away
> The fleeting daughters of the day—
> Nor with impatient thoughts outrun
> The lazy sun

have an *aura* of poetry about them which is something more than smooth and genteel; and this will be found pretty evenly suffused.   And, when Sir Egerton Brydges, who (among other good deeds to this group) reprinted Stanley nearly a hundred years ago, commended one of his songs as "very elegant" with "all the harmony of modern rhythm," he might have told us where modern rhythm had attained the peculiar harmony of this time, which Stanley attains throughout.   Excluding translations and mere commendatory epistles, there are, perhaps, fifty or sixty pieces with the characteristic titles of the time—*The Blush*, *The Kiss*, *To Clarissa*, *To Celia* and so on.   The subjects or objects matter little; but the poetry deals with them (to exaggerate a little) in the way described by Orsino in the opening lines of *Twelfth Night*, as "breath stealing and giving odour."   In fact, these Caroline poets are as the bank of violets spoken of by the duke, and Stanley is not the least sweet patch of it.

Perhaps, however, a still more typical example of these curious writers is to be found in one who dedicated his poems, enthusiastically, to Stanley himself, a year before Stanley published his own.   John Hall, born at Durham in 1627, and educated at the grammar school there, entered St. John's college, Cambridge, in February, 1645/6, and, in little more than a twelvemonth, had published a volume of prose essays, *Horae Vacivae* (1646) and one of poems in two books, profane and divine (1647).   Both received extraordinary praise, among the praisers being Hobbes, Howell and, for the verse, Henry More and Stanley himself.   These four names would indicate that, at the time, Hall, if not a definite royalist, was, at any rate, *persona grata* to the royalist party.   In 1648, he issued a *Satire against the Presbyterians*.   But this, in the changed circumstances of Cambridge and of the country, was not incompatible with his being an adherent of Cromwell, on whose side he wrote pamphlets, besides translating variously. His version of Longinus—*The Height of Eloquence*—has, at any rate, no bad title.   But he did not follow up his promise of original work, he lived hard and he died before he was thirty, in 1656.

Hall's poems exhibit the minor verse of the period, if not in a complete, at any rate in a new and peculiar, microcosm.   Unlike Kynaston, he has no long poem; and, though a professional translator, he does not, like Stanley, mix translations of short poems freely with his originals. But, unlike both of them, he is a "divine" poet; and, unlike Stanley, he has a large portion of light and trivial pieces tending towards the epigram—in fact, he approximates to Cleiveland in this respect, and there is a considerable tangle of attributions between the two as to some pieces. In such verse, however, he has no poetical interest: though a crowd of allusions to persons and things will reward the hunter after game of this nature. His gift in the poetical direction lies wholly in pure lyric, and especially in the employment for it of the abruptly broken metres, with constant very short lines alternated with long, that had come into favour, of strongly "metaphysical" diction and of no small portion of the undefinable atmosphere of poetic suggestion referred to above. The process results in not a very few poems of remarkable beauty: *The Call*, *The Lure*, *The Morning Star*, *Julia Weeping*, *The Crystal*, *An Epicurean Ode*, *Of Beauty*, *The Epilogue* and the curious *Ode* from an undergraduate "to his tutor" Pawson, among the profane poems; *A Dithyramb*, the *Ode* "Descend O Lord," *Self* and the other *Ode* "Lord send Thine hand," among the divine. It is, no doubt, easy to say that, but for Donne and Jonson, these things had never been; yet, after all, we cannot deny to the actual author the credit of the fact that these things are; Jonson and Donne eminently, with others beside them, provided, no doubt, the examples of form; the dying renascence gave its colours of mixed enjoyment and regret; the rich tradition of two full generations in England supplied word and phrase and conceit. Still, in the case of the particular things, "John Hall *fecit*."

On the other side of politics from that which Hall finally adopted, resembling him in precocity and early death and the praise of great men (here, once more, including Hobbes but, also, Clarendon, who is not likely to have thought much of Hall), was Sidney Godolphin. He was a son of Sir William Godolphin of Godolphin in Cornwall, and of Thomasine Sidney; he was born in January, 1610, went to Exeter college, Oxford, in 1624, became member for Helston when only eighteen, joined Hopton at once when the war broke out and was shot at Chagford on 10 February, 1643. But Godolphin, though always regarded with interest by the few who mentioned him, and, though holding the exceptional position of having perished in actual fight at the opening of the rebellion, was, in the stormy times of his death, neglected so far as publication of his poems was concerned. A few pieces—a commendatory poem to Sandys on the latter's *Paraphrases*, one or two others in other books and the beginning of a translation of the fourth book of the *Aeneid*, continued by Waller, and published in the fourth volume of Dryden's *Miscellany*—did, indeed, appear in or near his time. Ellis gave one of his most charming things, "Or love me less or love me more," in his *Specimens;* and Scott another in the so-called *Tixall Poetry*. But the first attempt to collect his work from these sources and from the two MSS., no. 39 of Malone's in the Bodleian and Harl. 1917 in the British Museum, was made by the present writer three or four years ago. The Vergilian piece is an early and interesting document of the heroic couplet on its regular side; but the lyrics are his real title to fame.

These lyrics, few as they are, have the strongly miscellaneous and occasional character which belongs to almost the entire group—there are paraphrases of the *Psalms*, hymns, epistles (with some curious and, as yet, unexplained sporting references) and so forth. But, as usual, the charm lies in the love-lyrics: that given by Ellis and referred to above; the perhaps even better "No more unto my thoughts appear," which is in common measure of the special Caroline stamp, while the other is in long; some fine pieces—a *Chorus*, a *Meditation* in octosyllabic couplets, some lighter attempts, as the song "'T is Affection but dissembled"; one very curious compound, perhaps intended to be detached, of common and long measure; and so forth. Once, in some triplets, he has a piece where almost the whole appeal lies in "metaphysical" thought and word-play on the difficulty of knowing his mistress from Virtue herself—

> Conceits of one must into the other flow . . .
> You are in it, as it is all in you—

and such like puerilities, unsublimated by the strangeness of touch which Donne would have given them, and emphasised by the stopped antithetic couplet. But this is almost Godolphin's only slip into the pitfalls of the period. Of its graces and merits, he has much; and it is difficult not to think that, in a different station and circumstances, he would have had much more.

There are few more curious instances of the chances of books and authors than the fact that, while Godolphin remained in MS., while Kynaston was never reprinted till recently, nor Hall and Stanley till nearly a century and a half after their dates, and then in small editions only, the poems of Sir Edward Sherborne, Stanley's cousin, found their way into the standard collections of English poetry and, therefore, have long been easily accessible. Sherborne lived a rather more public life than his relative, though, as a Roman Catholic, he was debarred from public education. Born in 1618, he obtained the post of clerk of the ordnance, earlier held by his father; but in an evil hour (1642), just at the opening of the civil war. He was not only deprived but imprisoned for a time, after which he joined the king's forces, was appointed commissary general of artillery and made Oxford his headquarters till its surrender in 1646. After this, he suffered severely from confiscation, but was helped by Stanley, and employed by the Savile and Coventry families. He recovered his post in the ordnance at the restoration, and was unscathed by the popish plot; but he became a non-juror at the revolution and again fell into indigence. He died at a great age in 1702, the last of his poetic tribe. But, not at any time had he been of their strongest. Like Stanley, he has left a few original pieces and a great many translations; but Stanley's unfailing elegance is wanting. Most of his translations from a miscellaneous set of authors, Coluthus and Preti, Theocritus and Casimir, are in undistinguished couplets; his original pieces are more lyrical and better; the best being religious. The love-poems are more like those of an inferior Carew than those of Stanley, Godolphin, Kynaston or Hall. But "Chloris! on thine eyes I gaze," *The Vow*, "Love once love ever" and one or two others are not unworthy of a place in a full anthology of the kind at the time.

We have not as yet mentioned a poetess in this chapter, yet there is one belonging to it; one of the first women, indeed, to obtain the position in modern English literature. Very popular and highly esteemed in her own day, complimentarily referred to by Dryden and others and not seldom reprinted for a generation or so later, "the matchless Orinda," as she was called in the coterie language of the time, has, perhaps, been better known to most readers by her nickname than by her works for nearly two centuries past. Her real maiden name was Katherine Fowler; she was born in London on New Year's day, 1631; married at sixteen a Welshman named Philips and began to be known as a writer of verse about 1651; but, though a pirated edition of her poems appeared in 1664, shortly before her death, the first authorised one was published posthumously in 1667. She translated Corneille's *Pompée*, and part of his *Horace*. But her poetical interest lies in a considerable number of miscellaneous poems, the best of which are in the unmistakable style of the group and mainly addressed to her women friends of the coterie—"Rosania" (Mary Aubrey), "Lucasia," "Regina" (this, apparently, a real name) and the rest. There is no very great power in any of them, but the curious "magic music" of sound and echo and atmosphere survives in the pieces beginning, "Come my Lucasia, let us see," "I did not love until this time," "As men that are with visions graced," "I have examined and do find"; nor, perhaps, in these only.

Others of the lyrists must be more cursorily despatched. Patrick Cary, brother of the famous lord Falkland, and author (about 1651) of a pleasant volume of *Trivial Poems and Triolets*, which Scott printed in 1819; William Hammond, again a relation of Stanley and already referred to, a mild but not ungraceful amorist; Robert Heath, author of *Clarastella* (1650), a sort of average representative of style and time who, sometimes, a little transcends the mediocre; Thomas Beedome, a friend of the dramatist Glapthorne and author of some pretty things; the too-celebrated Richard Flecknoe, in whose work it is but too easy to discover general, if not particular, justification for Dryden's posthumous maltreatment of him; Henry Hawkins, a Jesuit, whose *Partheneia Sacra* contains verse-pieces of merit; and, towards the end of the period, the poet-painter Thomas Flatman, whose unlucky name by no means expresses his poetic quality, and Philip Ayres, a copious translator, emblem-writer and so forth, in whom the peculiarities of the first Caroline school are prolonged into the time of the second. Diligent and conscientious students may push their researches further still, and by no means without profit of this or that kind, among the work, sometimes a *satura* of verse and prose, of Robert Baron (who seems to have paid distinct attention to Milton's 1645 volume), Patheryke or Patrick Jenkyns, Robert Gomersal, Henry Bold, John Collop. But there are two writers who must have more particular treatment —Edward Benlowes and John Cleiveland.[1]

In different ways, though with a certain overlapping of community, these two poets are characteristic examples of the defects of the group. One of the two never enjoyed anything but a costly, personal, very limited and fleeting popularity; and, despite (rather than in consequence of) the flouts of certain persons of distinction, despite the additional fact that his principal book has attractions dear to bibliographers and collectors, he has been, until recently, quite forgotten. The other, a man of varied and practical, as well as poetical, genius, immensely popular for not so very short a time, dropped almost wholly out of general knowledge, and, by most of those who have known him at all, has been known either because he made some figure politically, or as the victim of a passing gibe of Dryden and as furnishing Johnson with typical extracts for his important life of Cowley, with its criticism of the metaphysical poets. Benlowes, the elder and by much the longer lived, was born *c.* 1603, probably at the paternal seat of Brent hall, Essex, which he inherited. He entered St. John's college, Cambridge, in 1620, afterwards making the grand tour. At one time of his life, he was a Roman Catholic, but died an English churchman: and it is not certain whether his Romanism was merely an episode or not. So, also, we have only Butler's indirect testimony to the fact of Benlowes's having actually served in the civil war: but he was certainly a strong royalist. It is also certain that he lost his fortune, the main cause assigned being overlavishness to friends and flatterers. Latterly, he lived at Oxford and died there (it is said from privation) in 1676. Butler had already selected him as the subject for his character *A Small poet*, which is full of the bitterest

---

[1] Birth and death dates, where known, are given in the index, but both the birth and death dates and the life circumstances of most of the poets mentioned in this paragraph are quite unknown; and even their *floruit* is usually determined only by the dates of the rare volumes of their work.

ridicule. Long afterwards, Pope wrote, but did not finally print, in the prologue to his *Satires*, the couplet

> How pleased I see some patron to each scrub,
> Quarles had his Benlowes, Tibbald has his Bubb,

with the note "A gentleman of Oxford who patronised all bad poets of that reign." He left these lines out, but, in the *Dunciad* (III, 21), he returned to the subject in the line

> Benlowes, propitious still to blockheads, bows,

with an enlarged note on Benlowes's own bad poetry which Warburton amplified with ridicule of his titles.

Some ten or a dozen different publications are attributed to Benlowes—the use of initials instead of the full name causing doubt—but all of them, except one, are short, most are unimportant and several are in Latin. His title to fame—if any—and the head and front of his offending, lie in a long and singular poem entitled *Theophila or Love's Sacrifice*, published in 1652 in a folio volume of 268 pages, illustrated rather lavishly, but with such differences in different copies as to make the book something of a bibliographical *crux*. This, however, matters little to us. The title, to those acquainted with the literature of the time and group, but not with the book itself, might naturally suggest a romance of the kind discussed in the beginning of this chapter. It is, however, nothing of the kind. Theophila is merely a name for the soul: and the titles of the several cantos—"Praelibation," "Inamoration," "Disincantation," and so on—will at once suggest the vein of theological mysticism which is worked here, though there are large digressions of various kinds, especially in satiric denunciation of fleshly vices. Had there not been a bee in Benlowes's bonnet, the poem might have ranked as a third to those of More and Beaumont—not, perhaps, much more read than it has been, but respected. Unfortunately, that bonnet was a mere hive. In the first place, he selected for his main (not quite his exclusive) medium the exceedingly peculiar stanza of which an example is given below, a triplet of ten, eight and twelve syllables. This combination, which, at the end of others, and so concluding a longer stave, is sometimes successful enough, is, by itself, when constantly repeated, curiously ugly.

In the second, the lack of clear arrangement which, as we have seen, is common to almost all the group, becomes more intolerable than ever in a half psychological, half theological disquisition. But his sins become more flagrant still in respect of composition of phrase as distinguished from arrangement of matter; and they rise to their very highest in the selection and construction of phrase itself.

It would sometimes appear as if his sole concern was to be wilfully and preposterously odd. He wishes to denounce drunkenness:

> Cheeks dyed in claret seem o' the quorum
> When our nose-carbuncles like link-boys blaze before 'em.

He has a mind to hit at the inconsistency of the extreme reformed sects, so he calls them "Proteustants." Butler was particularly wroth with the extraordinary coinage *hypocondruncieus*. In a long description of a bedizened courtezan, there occurs this wonderful stanza:

> She 'd coach affection on her cheek: but why?
> Would Cupids horses climb so high
> Over her alpine nose t' o'erthrow it in her eye?

In short, there is no extravagance of conceit or word-play at which he blenches.

And yet, Benlowes is not a mere madman or a mere mountebank. He has occasionally, and not very seldom, beautiful poetic phrase; and he manages to suffuse long passages, if not whole cantos, with a glow of devotional atmosphere and imagery which is not very far inferior to Crashaw's. He seems, sometimes, to have a dim and confused notion of the mixture and contrast of passion and humour which makes the triumph of Carlyle and Browning; but he never can bring it off, for want, no doubt, of absolutely transcendent genius, but, still more, for want of moderate and moderating self-criticism. He only partially knows what to attempt; and he does not in the least know what *not* to attempt.

In many ways (even beyond those already mentioned), John Cleiveland was a striking contrast to Benlowes. Born in 1613 at Loughborough, where his father was a curate, Cleiveland was entered at Christ's college, Cambridge (where Milton was still in residence), in 1627, and became fellow of St. John's in 1634. He took a strong line as a royalist, was expelled from his fellowship in 1645, was made judge advocate at Newark in the same year, is said to have been in some danger at the surrender of the place, but passes out of knowledge for nearly ten years till, in 1655, we find him imprisoned as a royalist at Yarmouth. He addressed a dignified petition to Cromwell, who released him; but his health seems to have been broken, and he died in London on 29 April, 1658.

Yet, though we have but little detail of his life, he was almost a celebrated person, and quite a celebrated poet. Even Cowley was hardly so popular, and the welter of confusion which besets his bibliography is due mainly to this popularity—the booksellers "sharking up" every scrap that could with any plausibility, and a great deal that could not with any, be attributed to him. He had published as early as 1640; and, for thirty years after his death his poems continued to be reprinted, till, in 1687, what is sometimes called the most complete edition appeared. Winstanley described him in that year as "an eminent poet, and *the* wit of our age." Winstanley was no critic and the age was the age of Butler and Dryden; but he is all the more valuable as witness to the opinion of the average man. If confirmation be wanted, it is hardly necessary to go further than the fact that, of the half-score or dozen editions which had appeared in the forty years or so before this date, hardly one failed to be reprinted or revised, and some were reissued many times over.

The work by which this reputation was obtained, even when bolstered out with spurious additions, is not large; the certainly, or probably, genuine part of it does not extend to more than two or three thousand lines. But Cleveland had a double, in fact a treble, appeal. In the first place, a large proportion of his work was "straight-from-the-shoulder" political satire, sure to be received rapturously by those who agreed with it, and perforce interesting, though unpleasantly interesting, to its victims. In the second, it was couched in the very extravagance of the metaphysical fashion, yet with an avoidance of the intolerable prolixity and promiscuousness, or the sometimes merely foolish quaintness, of men like Benlowes. In the third (though this is not likely to have been consciously noticed), Cleiveland, evidently, is feeling for new melodies in verse; he is not merely a master of the stopped antithetic couplet, but is one of the earliest writers who shake off the literary timidity of the Elizabethans and Jacobeans as to trisyllabic measures, and boldly attempt anapaestic swing.

To appreciate Cleiveland's political pieces, it must be remembered that, as has been pointed out elsewhere, there was not only a deep though half unconscious thirst for the novel, but, also, a similar *nisus* towards the newspaper. When, quite early in the conflict, he lampooned the puritan objection to "&c," in the oath of 1640, and when, shortly afterwards, he poured contempt on *Smectymnuus*, he was simply a journalist of the acutest type in verse—a poetical leader-writer. These things should be compared with the prose writings, on the other side, of his senior at Christ's. There is nothing to choose in bitterness; Cleiveland has the advantage in point. But the shorter compass and less serious form carry with them a danger which has weighed on all journalism since. The packed allusion, and the rapid searching comment, become almost unintelligible to any but contemporaries. Even Cleiveland's most famous, and, on the whole, most successful, piece, *The Rebel Scot*, requires more minute acquaintance with detail than can be readily expected or found. *The Mixed Assembly*, a piece of less than a hundred verses, would scarcely be overcommented on the margins of a hundred pages with a verse of text to each. The force and fire are still admirable when realised; but the smoke of the explosion has solidified itself, as it were, and obscures both.

So, again, in non-political pieces, the same accretion of allusive conceit besets the poetry. Men rejoiced, then, frankly and sincerely, in such an image as this, that, when a bee crawls over Fuscara's hand,

> He tipples palmistry, and dines
> On all her fortune-telling lines.

It can be rejoiced in still, but not by everybody. Yet it should be impossible for anyone with some native alacrity of mind, some literary sympathy and some acquired knowledge, not to derive frequent enjoyment from Cleiveland, even in his altitudes of conceit; and his verse is a real *point de repère*. In 1643, at latest, we get from him such a couplet as this, which Dryden could hardly have beaten forty years later still:

> Such was the painters brief for Venus' face—
> *Item*, an eye from Jane, a lip from Grace.

And, perhaps earlier, certainly not much later, in the semi-serious *Mark Antony* and the avowed burlesque on this his own piece, he attempts, and nearly achieves, anapaestic measure of a kind hardly yet tried. A most imperfect poet he must be called; a poet of extraordinary gifts he should be allowed to be.

Sufficient stress has been laid on beauties, throughout this chapter, to make it, though with some general reiteration, fair to draw attention chiefly, in conclusion, to the warning which the whole group more or less, and these last two members of it especially, supply, and which makes the study of it almost indispensable in order to a thorough comprehension of English literature. There are beauties in almost all these writers; charming and poignant beauty in some parts of some of them; and specially characteristic beauty—beauty that you do not find in other periods; nor can it be denied that both their merits and their faults arose from a striving after that daring and headstrong vein which had made the fortune of the great Elizabethans. But there is one power to whom, almost without exception, they neglected to pay attention: and she avenges herself with prompt severity. Now this power was criticism.

In some respects, they were very excusable. They could hardly yet know that prose was a far more suitable medium for novel and romance writing than verse; the discovery was not fully made till nearly a century after their time. But most of them, from Chamberlayne downwards, might surely have known that, whether you tell a story in verse or prose, you should tell it intelligibly and clearly; with, at any rate, distinct sequence, if not with elaborate plot; and in language arranged so as to convey thought, not to conceal it. They were not to blame for adopting the overlapped form of couplet: they were to blame for letting reasonable and musical variety overflow into loquacious disorder. Although there may be more difference of opinion here, they were not to blame for adopting the "metaphysical" style, inasmuch as that style lends itself to the sublimest poetic beauty; but they were to blame for neglecting to observe that, when it is not sublime, it is nearly certain to be ridiculous. So, again, their practice of fantastically cut and broken lyric, and their fingering of the common and long measures, were wholly admirable things in themselves; but, at the same time, they were apt to make their verse "not inevitable enough"—to multiply its examples in a mote-like and unimportant fashion. To take the two capital examples just dwelt upon: in another age, Benlowes would probably either not have written at all or have been a religious and satiric poet of real importance; while it may be taken as certain that Cleiveland's satiric, if not his lyrical, powers would have been developed far more perfectly if he had been born a generation or two generations later. And those later generations, though they lost something that both Benlowes and Cleiveland had fitfully, and that shows far better in Chamberlayne and Stanley and Hall, benefited, both consciously and unconsciously, by the faults of the school we have been studying.

CHAPTER V

Milton

THE "overdated ceremony," as Milton himself might
have called it, of protesting that the best record of a
great writer's life is in his works can, at least, plead
this in its favour, that it applies to hardly any two persons in
quite the same way. In Milton's case, especially, its application has a peculiarity partaking of that strong separation
from ordinary folk which is one of the great Miltonic notes.
We are not, in his case, without a fairly large amount of
positive biographical information; and that information was
worked up and supplemented by David Masson with heroic
diligence, with lavish provision of commentary and without
that undue expatiation into "may-have-beens" and "prob-
ablys" and "perhapses" which, despite the temptation to it
which exists in some cases, is irritating to the critically minded
and dangerously misleading to the uncritical. But, in order
to understand the external information, we need unusually
constant and careful recurrence to the internal, and, on the
other hand, we are likely to misread not a little of the work
if we do not know the life. Nor is this double process one
requiring mere care. The ordinary conception of Milton,
among people more than fairly educated, may be fairly uniform and reasonably clear; but it does not follow that it is
either correct or complete. He may not so absolutely "evade
our question" as does Shakespeare. The contradictions or
inconsistencies in him may not be trivial and exoteric as in
Bacon. But, like Dante, whom, of all other writers of the
highest class, he most resembles, Milton gives us his life and
his work, to explain each other, it may be, but offering not a
few puzzles and pitfalls in the course of the explanation. Al-

though, therefore, the immense mass of detail which has been accumulated about Milton defies distillation and condensation in such a chapter as this, it has been thought important to give all the principal points, while excluding those proper to a full "life," or a critical edition of the "works" *in extenso*.

The life itself was not extraordinarily eventful, but it was unusually so when compared with the average lives of men of letters; and, though the unusualness was partly due to the times, it was largely increased by Milton's own attitude towards those times, during the last forty years of his life. In the circumstances of his birth and origin, he reflected the peculiar ecclesiastical—which meant, also, the political—history of England for the past three generations. He was born on 9 December, 1608, in the city of London, at The Spread Eagle, Bread street, Cheapside, where his father (and namesake) carried on the business of a scrivener—that is to say, a lawyer of the inferior branch, who had specially to do with the raising, lending and repayment of money on landed or other security. The sign of the office or shop was the crest of the family—an Oxfordshire one of the upper yeomanry; and the reason of the elder John's taking to business was that he had been disinherited by his father for abandoning Roman Catholicism and conforming to the church of England. The poet's younger brother Christopher reversed the process, became a judge and a knight under James II and (probably on that account, for we know very little else about him) has been generally spoken of in a depreciatory manner by biographers and historians. But the brothers seem always to have been on good terms. There was also an elder sister, Anne, who married, and became the mother of John and Edward Phillips, both men of letters, in their way, the latter our chief original source of information about his uncle. Of the poet's mother, we hear but little, and it is by inference rather than on direct evidence that her name is supposed to have been Sarah Jeffrey or Jeffreys.

Milton's father, however, was not only a prosperous man of business, but one of rather unusual culture. His son derived from him his interest in music; and that the father was not indifferent to poetry—perhaps not to romance—is evident from his connection with a contemporary version of *Guy of Warwick*,

which exists in MS. and to which he contributed a sonnet.   He
sent his son to St. Paul's school, giving him, also, a private tutor,
Thomas Young, who was a good scholar but an acrid presbyterian and, later, the "ty" of *Smectymnuus*.   And Milton
seems to have had no objection to being "brought on" in the
Blimberian sense—working by himself when a boy of twelve,
till the small hours.   Although it is impossible to deny the
indebtedness of some of the good qualities of his work to this
"overpressure," it must have had bad results in various directions, moral and physical.   And, though his blindness cannot
have been actually caused by this over-exertion of his eyes, it
was certainly not staved off by the process.   For the time,
however, all went well.   Alexander Gill, high master of St.
Paul's, was an excellent teacher, and his son continued to be
a great friend of Milton when Gill went to Oxford and Milton
to Cambridge.   There, he was admitted at Christ's on 12
February, 1625, when he had just entered his seventeenth
year; and he began to keep terms at Easter.   His college
sojourn begins the Milton legend and controversy—tedious
and idle like all controversial legends and to be kept down as
much as possible.   He certainly did not get on with his tutor
Chappell, and was sent away from college; though not tech-
nically "sent down" or rusticated, inasmuch as he did not
lose a term.   And his transference to another tutor has been
held (though the fact is not quite conclusive) as proof that
there were faults on both sides.   He himself admits "indo-
cility" and grumbles that he was not allowed to choose his
own studies.   That he was unpopular with his fellow undergraduates is not certain, though it is not improbable.   The
celebrated nickname "the lady of Christ's" admits of—and has
been fitted with—both interpretations—that of a compliment
to his beauty and that of a sneer at him as a milksop.   He
certainly must have been as different as possible from the
"Square-Cap" of his contemporary Cleiveland's lively glorifi-
cation of the graduates and undergraduates of Cambridge.
But he protested, later, that the Fellows treated him "with
more than ordinary respect" and wished him to stay up at
the end of his seven years, when, in 1632, he took the M.A.
degree.   The upshot of the whole seems to be that he was
studious, reserved and not quite like other people—once, at

least, and, probably, more than once, becoming definitely "refractory." He was always to be studious, reserved and not like other people; and, in his nearly seventy years, the times of truce were not very common and the times of war very frequent.

It is impossible to say what he would have done if his father had not been unusually, though by no means unwisely, indulgent, and of means sufficient to exercise indulgence. That Milton could work hard at mere routine when it suited him, the disastrous secretaryship afterwards showed; but it is impossible to imagine him in any ordinary profession. He had been "destined of a child" to the church. But, though there is no positive evidence of anti-Anglican feeling in his work before *Lycidas*, and, though *Lycidas* itself might have been written, in a quite possible construction, by an orthodox and even high Anglican who was an ardent church reformer, Milton's discipleship to Young and the Gills, his difficulties with Chappell, who was a Laudian, and his whole subsequent conduct and utterance, explain his abandonment of orders.

No (or only the slightest) obstacles were put in his way, and no force was used to urge him out of it. His father had given up business, and settled at Horton in the south of Bucks, less than twenty miles from London, on the river Colne, within sight of Windsor, and in a pretty, though not wildly romantic, neighbourhood. Here Milton lived, and read, and thought, and annotated, and wrote, for five years, directing his attention chiefly to linguistic, literary and historical study, but, at last, setting seriously to work at poetry itself. Besides smaller pieces, *Comus* (1634) and *Lycidas* (1637) certainly date from this time; and the ingenious attempts of Mrs. Byse[1] can hardly be allowed to carry *L'Allegro* and *Il Penseroso* on to the period that followed. In 1635, he was admitted *ad eundem* as M.A. at Oxford.

Milton had thus twelve years—counting together his Cambridge and his Horton sojourn—of literary concentration; in the first seven, he was somewhat, but probably not much, interfered with: in the second five, he was completely undisturbed. It is quite clear from various passages of his works and letters, earlier and later, that these years were definitely

[1] See bibliography.

and deliberately employed on "getting his wedding garment ready"—on preparing himself for the great career in poetry upon which he actually entered in the last of these years, but which was subsequently interrupted. In a sense, nothing could be more fortunate. Solitude, and the power of working as one pleases and when one pleases only, are among the greatest of intellectual luxuries; they are, perhaps, more than luxuries—positive necessities—to exceptional poetic temperaments. The moral effect of both may be more disputable. It certainly did not, in Milton's case, lead to dissipation, in any sense, even to that respectable but deplorable and not uncommon form of literary dissipation which consists in always beginning and never finishing. In such a temperament as his, it may have fostered the peculiar arrogance—too dignified and too well suited to the performance to offend, but only not to be regretted by idle partisans—the morose determination to be different, the singular want of adaptability in politics and social matters generally, which has been admitted even by sympathisers with his political and religious views.

But the elder John "was for Thorough" in regard to his son's education. He had given him the best English training of public school and university. He had allowed him a full lustrum of private study to "ripen the wine." He now completed the process, at what must have been a very considerable expense, by sending him to the continent—the recognised finishing of the time, but usually open only to men of considerable station and means like Evelyn, to those who had special professional training to acquire like Browne, or to travellers on definite business like Howell. The father was not left alone: for, though his wife died in April, 1637, and his daughter had long been married, Christopher and his wife established themselves at Horton. Milton left home just a twelvemonth after his mother's death, with good letters of introduction, including one from Sir Henry Wotton. He travelled by Paris (where he met Grotius), Nice and Genoa to Florence, where he spent August and September, 1638, frequented the Florentine academies, and enjoyed, with what, no doubt, was a perfectly genuine enjoyment, the curious *manège* of learned and literary compliment and exercise which formed the routine of those societies. We shall not understand Milton if we do not realise his intense appreciation of *form*—an appreciation which, in all non-ecclesiastical matters, was probably intensified further by his violent rejection of ceremonial in religion. He next spent another two months at Rome, made various friends, heard and admired the famous singer Leonora Baroni, celebrated another lady, who may have been real or not, aired his protestantism with impunity and then went on to Naples. Here (through an "eremite friar," whose good offices, on this occasion, might have saved a future association[1] with "trumpery"), he made the acquaintance of a very old and very distinguished nobleman of letters, the marquis of Villa, Giovanni Baptista Manso. He did not go further than Naples, though he had thought not only of Sicily but of Greece. The reason he gave for relinquishing this scheme was the threatening state of home politics and the impropriety of enjoying himself abroad while his countrymen were striking for freedom.

It was inevitable that this deliverance, after Milton had exhausted the vocabulary of personal vituperation and sarcasm against his own antagonists, should be turned against himself. The phrase "what you say will be used against you" is not only a decent police warning but a universal—and universally useless—phylactery of life. But there was no hypocrisy in him; and the saying is as illuminative as his appreciation of the Florentine academies. He did not hurry home, but repeated his two months' sojourns at Rome and at Florence, meeting Galileo (with memorable poetical results) at the latter place, and then travelling by Ferrara and Venice to Geneva. Here, he was at home in faith, if an exile in taste; here, he seems to have heard of the death of his friend Charles Diodati, whose uncle was a minister there; here, he left one of the most personal touches we have of him;[2] and here, or on the way home, or after reaching it, he wrote *Epitaphium Damonis*. He reached England in August, 1639, being then in his thirty-first year; and, at this point, the first period in his life and work closed. The curtain, in fact, fell on more than an act:

---

[1] *P. L.* III, 474, 475.

[2] His autograph in the album of a Neapolitan named Camillo Cerdogni—a refugee in religion—with the addition of the last two lines of *Comus* and the *Coelum non animum* of Horace.

it practically closes the first play of a trilogy, the second of which had hardly anything to do with the first, though the third was to resume and complete it.

The next twenty years saw the practical fulfilment of Milton's unluckily worded resolve to break off his continental tour. He was still not in a hurry, establishing himself first in lodgings, then in a "pretty garden house" outside Aldersgate, with books to which he had added largely in Italy. Here he took as pupils first his two nephews, and then others. To his adoption of this occupation was, in part, due the famous little letter or tractate *Of Education: to Master Samuel Hartlib*. Another result seems to have been the exercise of that "over-pressure" on his pupils which, in his own case, had been largely voluntary. "Can't you let him alone?" was a counsel of perfection in this matter which Milton, like others, never realised.

It is less inconceivable than it may seem to some that, circumstances aiding, Milton might have taken to teaching as a regular profession. For he liked domineering, and he was passionately fond of study in almost any form. But deities other than Pallas found other things for him to do. He struck, not as a soldier, but as a controversialist, into the combat for which he had long been preparing, with the treatise *Of Reformation touching Church-Discipline in England*, before much more than a year had passed since his return, in 1641. It was in less than a year after the actual opening of the struggle that he married. Of the series of pamphlets dealing with matters ecclesiastical, political and conjugal which now began, notice will be taken in the proper place: the marriage must come here.

In what has usually been written of this thrice unfortunate adventure—tragical in all its aspects if tragicomical in some—there has, perhaps, been a little unfairness to Milton: there has certainly been much to his wife. The main lines of fact are remorselessly clear: the necessary elucidations of detail are almost wholly wanting. In June, 1643, John Milton married Mary Powell, the eldest daughter of an Oxfordshire gentleman, whose family were neighbours to the Miltons and who had had with them both friendship and business relations. She was seventeen. He brought her home in June; she went

back, at her family's request, but with his consent, in July,
and refused to come to him at Michaelmas as had been arranged. For two years, he saw nothing of her. These are
the bare facts, and almost all the facts certainly known,
though there are a few slight, and, in some cases, doubtful,
addenda.

On such a brief, an advocate may say almost what he
pleases. What may fairly be said for and against Milton
will come presently: what has been said against his wife may
almost rouse indignation and certainly justify contempt. We
have been told that she was a "dull and common girl," of
which there is just as much and just as little evidence as that
she was as wise as Diotima and as queenly as Helen; that she
had flirted with royalist officers from Oxford (no evidence
again); finally, that "there is no evidence that she was handsome." As for this last, from passage after passage in the
poems it is almost inconceivable that Milton should have been
attracted by any one who was not good-looking.

Whether, however, she was pretty, or whether she was
plain, the reasons of her leaving her husband are not hard to
guess. For the fact is that Milton's attitude to women is
peculiar and not wholly pleasant. It is not merely, as is
often said, that he disdained them and held the doctrine of
their subjection—"there 's example for 't," as Malvolio says
of the same subject in another connection. It is not merely
that he was unreasonable in his expectations of them—there 's
much more example for that. It is that, as was often the
case with him, he was utterly unpractical, and his theoretical
notions were a conglomerate—and not a happy one. Mark
Pattison—an interesting witness, some of whose other expressions have just been cited—chose Adam's ecstatic description
of Eve to Raphael as Milton's real mind on the subject. He
forgot that we must take with it the angel's prompt, severe
and (if one may say such things of angels) hopelessly coarse
snub and rebuke. The fact seems to be that Milton—as
elsewhere, sharply opposed to Shakespeare, and here almost
as sharply opposed to Dante—blended an excessive and eclectic
draft on books and on fancy with an insufficient experience of
life. He accepted the common disdainful estimate of the
ancients; the very peculiar, but by no means wholly disdainful,

estimate of the Hebrews; and he tried to blend both with something of the sensuous passion of the Middle Ages and the renascence, stripping from this the transcendental element which had been infused in the Middle Ages by Mariolatry and chivalry, in the renascence by a sort of poetical convention. An Aspasia-Hypatia-Lucretia-Griselda, with any naughtiness in the first left out and certain points in Solomon's pattern woman added, might have met Milton's views. But this blend has not been commonly quoted in the marriage market. His friend Marvell, in a passage of rare poetic beauty, described his love as begotten by Despair upon Impossibility. Milton's seems to have been begotten upon another kind of Impossibility by Unreasonable Expectation. The exact circumstances of his first marriage we shall never know; those of his second take it out of argument; his third seems to have been simply the investing of a *gouvernante* with permanent rank extraordinary and plenipotentiary. But passage after passage in his works remains to speak; and the terrible anecdote of his obliging his daughters, and elaborately teaching them, to read to him languages which they did not understand, remains for comment. The taste of the seventeenth century in torture was not only, as was said of the knowledge of Sam Weller in another matter, "extensive and peculiar," but, as was said of the emperor Frederick II in the same, "humorous and lingering." But it rarely can have gone further than this.

Once more, the remarkable blends of Milton's character which are important to the comprehension of his work require notice. His immediate conduct seems to have been perfectly correct—he repeatedly solicited her to return, until (according to a perhaps not quite trustworthy account) his requests were not only disregarded but rejected with contempt.[1] But, thenceforward, he allowed his self-centredness, his curious anarchism and his entirely unpractical temper to carry him off in a quite different direction. Indissolubility of marriage,

[1] It may be observed that these overtures, if made, dispose almost finally of what has been called by an advocate of Milton the "horrible" suggestion, based on a written date, that the first divorce pamphlet was actually composed before Mary left him. In that case he would have been an utter hypocrite in his requests to her to come back; and it has been said that hypocrisy and Milton are simply two "incompossible" ideas, to use Sir W. Hamilton's useful word.

except for positive unfaithfulness, was inconvenient to John Milton; John Milton was not a person to console himself illicitly; therefore, indissolubility of marriage must go. The series of divorce pamphlets, accordingly, followed; and, having proved to his own satisfaction that he was entitled to marry again, he sought the hand of a certain Miss Davis, whom some have identified (quite gratuitously) with the "virtuous young lady" of *Sonnet IX*. She, at any rate, had virtue and common sense enough to decline an arrangement of elective affinity.

In any one else than Milton, the proposal would have argued little virtue; in any virtuous person, it could but argue no common sense. And, indeed, the absence of that contemned property is conspicuous everywhere in these unfortunate transactions. Milton was not only (in the straight vernacular) making an utter fool of himself—aggravating the ridicule of a situation the distress of which arises in part from the very fact that it is ridiculous—but, just after he had come forward as a public man, he was playing into the hands of his enemies, and scandalising his friends. There was no point on which the more moderate and clear-sighted of the puritan party can have been more sensitive than this. The very word "divorce"—thanks to Henry VIII and some of the German reforming princes—made the ears of better protestants burn; and, from the days of the lampoons on Luther's marriage to those of the Family of Love, licensed libertinage had been one of the reproaches most constantly cast in the teeth of "hot gospellers." Next to nothing seems to be known of Miss Davis except that she had good looks (as we could guess) and good wits (which is evident). But it was certainly thanks to her, and to time's revenges, that the situation (after Milton had made himself at once a stumbling-block[1] and a laughing-stock for two years) was at last saved, before anything irreparable had happened. The ruin of the royal cause carried the Powell family with it; and, with more common sense than magnanimity, they resolved to throw themselves on Milton's mercy. A sort of ambush was laid— and reason coincides with romance in suggesting that the famous forgiveness scene of *Paradise Lost* had been actually

---

[1] "Miltonist" was actually used in print as a synonym for an opponent of the sacredness of marriage.

rehearsed on this occasion. At any rate, Milton—who, on his side, had very much more magnanimity than common sense—took his wife back in the summer of 1645; and, when Oxford fell, a year later, received her whole family into his new house in Barbican. Of the rest, we know nothing except the birth of three children—daughters—who appear later. At the birth of a fourth, in 1652, Mary died, not yet twenty-seven. Otherwise, there is no record of her married life. Milton is not in the least likely to have visited her early fractiousness by any petty persecution: he is as little likely to have "killed her with kindness." The whole thing was a mistake—a common one, no doubt; but, somehow, "the pity of it" remains rather specially.

What Milton thought or felt on the death of his first wife we have no means of knowing. He did not write a sonnet on it, as he did on that of his second; and, so far as memory serves, there is not any passage in his entire work which can be taken as even glancing at it. But the year in which it occurred was a black one for him in another way. He had now, for a full decade, occupied himself in violent and constant pamphleteering, writing nothing else but a few sonnets and some psalm-paraphrases. He had, indeed, published his early *Poems* in 1645, but he had added nothing to them; and, in 1649, he had undertaken the duties of Latin secretary to the new parliamentary committee for foreign affairs with a salary of £288. 13s. 6d., worth between three and four times the amount to-day. We know a little of his private affairs during this decade, besides the marriage troubles. His wife's father had died in 1646, and a complicated series of transactions in relation to the marriage settlements, and to old loans, left Milton in possession of property at Wheatley, between Oxford and Thame, worth, with charges off it, perhaps £50 a year. His own father died shortly afterwards; and, late in 1647, Milton gave up his pupils and moved to Holborn, with Lincoln's inn fields behind him. On his appointment, he had, for a time (some two years), rooms at Whitehall; but in 1651, he moved to "Petty France"—later, York street. The house, till some thirty years ago, was well known, and, after his time, it belonged to Bentham and was occupied by Hazlitt.

Although Milton's regular official duties of translation and writing seem to have been rather multifarious than hard, they were, in themselves, not good for a man with very weak eyesight; and his unfortunate aptitude for pamphleteering marked him out for overtime work, which was still worse. The last stroke was believed by himself, as a famous boast records, to have been given by his reply to Salmasius's *Defensio Regia*.[1] This appeared in the spring of 1651, and, a year later, he was totally blind. No scientific account of the case exists.

The personal calamity could hardly have been severer; but, as regards the poet, not the man, it was, perhaps, rather a gain than a loss, though it required outward circumstances of a different kind to replace Milton in his true office. His blindness does not seem to have been regarded as a disablement from his official employment, though it led to the appointment of coadjutors and a division of salary; and it was not until later that he engaged in the last and most discreditable of his angry and undignified controversies. Those with Ussher and Hall had, at least, the excuse, in matter if not in manner, of religious convictions; the divorce tracts, of intense personal interest; *Eikonoklastes*, of political consistency; and *Defensio pro Populo Anglicano*, of the same, and of official commission. No one of these excuses really applies to the supplementary wrangle with Alexander Morus or Moir. This Franco-Scot had published and prefaced a strong royalist declamation, *Regii Sanguinis Clamor*, directed against regicides in general and Milton in particular, and written, but not signed, by Peter du Moulin. Milton cooked his spleen for two whole years, rummaged the continent for scandal against Morus, refused to believe the latter's true assertion that he was only the editor of the book and, in May, 1654, published a *Defensio Secunda* which is simply a long, clumsy, would-be satiric invective against his enemy.

Of his private life, during this time, we again know very little. His nephews, like "nine tenths of the people of England," turned royalists, and wrote light and ungodly literature. He seems to have had a fair number of friends—though they hardly included any men of literary distinction except Marvell, all such, as a rule, being in the opposite camp. D'Avenant

[1] See *post*.

may have been another exception, if the agreeable, but not quite proved, legend that each protected the other in turn be true; and, as Dryden's relatives, the Pickerings, were close friends of Cromwell, the younger poet's acquaintance with the elder may have begun before the restoration. He married a second time on 12 November, 1656. His wife, daughter of a captain Woodcock, was named Catherine, and lived but fifteen months after the marriage, dying (as the twenty-third sonnet records pathetically) in childbirth on 10 February, 1657/8. The child was another daughter, but survived her mother only a few weeks. Attention has often been drawn to the "veiled face" of the sonnet as implying that Milton had never seen this wife. It should, however, be remembered, that the Alcestis parallel almost requires the veil. We know nothing more of Catherine Milton, but our state of knowledge might be more ungracious.

Except for the sonnets, of which this appears to be the last, Milton was still "miching" from poetry and indulging no muse: for the inspirers of his pamphlets were furies rather than muses. But he was to be brought back to the latter by major force. Characteristically, as always, but in a fashion so extreme that it would seem as if some "dim suffusion" had come upon his mental, as well as upon his bodily, sight, he not only would not accept, but would not believe in, the restoration. In the last twelvemonth or so of the commonwealth, he addressed two of his stately academic harangues to parliament, on toleration and the payment of ministers. He wrote, in the late autumn of 1659 and later, though he did not publish, *A Letter to a Friend* and another to Monck (which he did publish), gravely ignoring every symptom of contemporary feeling, and gravely prescribing the very doses with which the patient was nauseated. And, on the eve of the restoration itself, in February, 1660, he issued, and would have reissued (had not the king been actually restored), *The Ready and Easy Way to Establish a Free Commonwealth*, which he supplemented by some hectoring notes in his old style on a sermon by Matthew Griffith, formerly chaplain to Charles I, with the obvious text "Fear God *and the king*."

Such extravagant insensibility to the signs of the times, in such a time as the mid-seventeenth century, and in the case of a person of Milton's antecedents, could, ordinarily, have had but one awakening. How Milton escaped this has been accounted for in different ways. Intercession of Marvell or of D'Avenant or of others is one; insignificance is another—though the latter explanation cannot be said to fit in very well with the assertions of Milton's continental renown as a defender of regicide, nor with the fact that all the more prominent cavaliers had been exiles on the continent. The soundest explanation is that given by no friend of the restoration—that the restoration "was not bloodthirsty." Milton did not, indeed, escape quite scotfree. He left his house and lay hid for three months till the Act of Oblivion. His books, or some of them, were, indeed, burnt by the hangman; and, exactly on what charge is unknown, in the early winter he was in the custody of the sergeant-at-arms. It is characteristic again, no doubt, that he exacted a reduction of the fees (as exorbitant) on his liberation (15 December) by an order of the House.

The rest of his life is infinitely important to literature; less so to biography. His circumstances necessarily became straitened. His office, of course, went; and the story that he was offered continuance of it and urged by his wife to accept the offer is absurd, for he had no wife till 1663. He lost £2000, which he had lent to the republican government; something more in forfeited property which he had bought; and a considerable sum by malversation. The great fire destroyed his father's house in Bread street. But it does not appear that he was ever in positive discomfort; and, at his death, he left what would be equal to about £5000 to-day. His third marriage, just referred to, was with Elizabeth Minshull, a young woman of twenty-four, and a relation of his friend and doctor, Paget. Most of the stories of his life date from these days, as is natural, seeing that they were the days of the *Paradises* and of *Samson*. Those as to his harshness to his daughters, and their undutifulness to him, are not improbable, but rather contradictory to one another, and, quite obviously, what would have been told whether true or not. There is not much more consistency or certainty in those about his third wife—though it is generally agreed that he had no fault to find with her. As to residences, he moved from place to place, till he settled in Artillery row on the way to Bunhill fields, where he lived for the last twelve years of his life. His dress, hours, ways of occupying his sightless day, diet, partiality for tobacco and abstinence from total abstinence as regards wine, have been recorded with the strenuous inertia of persons such as Aubrey and Phillips. Like other people, he left London in the plague year, going to his old county of Bucks, but to Chalfont St. Giles, not Horton. He had no lack of friends and visitors—Marvell; the quaker Ellwood, who flattered himself that he had suggested *Paradise Regained;* Dryden, of whom he seems to have spoken with his usual disdainfulness, but who always spoke nobly of him. Nor does he seem ever to have quarrelled with his brother, or with his nephews, however much their principles differed from his own. In 1669, any domestic dissensions which may have prevailed were terminated by the daughters' going out to apprenticeship or superior service. But, in his later years, he suffered more and more from gout, and he died of it on 8 November, 1674. He was buried in St. Giles's, Cripplegate, the resting place of his father.

His widow died at Nantwich in 1727, more than half a century after Milton. Her youngest step-daughter, Deborah, died in the same year. She had married a silk-weaver, Abraham Clarke, and had many children, of whom two lived, and themselves left issue. So far as is known, the last direct descendant of Milton was Elizabeth Foster or Clarke, Deborah's youngest daughter, who died in 1754, and whose seven children had all died young. Anne Milton, the poet's eldest daughter, had married, but died in childbirth. Mary, the second, died unmarried within the seventeenth century. His brother, Sir Christopher, did not continue the name beyond another generation; but there are living representatives of the family on the female side, deriving from the elder Anne Milton, the poet's sister, especially by her second marriage with a man named Agar.

It must not be supposed, from anything that has been said that Milton's temperament was essentially or uniformly morose. His youngest daughter Deborah—an unexceptionable witness, whatever tales are true—described him as excellent company, especially with young people. His very asceticism has been much exaggerated. One anecdote speaks of his special gratitude to his last wife for providing "such dishes as pleased him"; and, while the Lawrence sonnet cannot be interpreted in any sense but that of cheerful enjoyment of festivity, the common limitation of "spare to interpose" is almost certainly wrong, while the other interpretation is supported by the companion piece to Cyriack Skinner. The personal beauty of his youth naturally yielded to age and gout; but he seems always, despite his blindness, to have been careful of his dress and appearance. His delight in gardens was life-long, even when he could not appreciate their trimness. He was a smoker—the austerest puritan had no objection to the Indian weed—and a wine drinker, though a moderate one. Study, in spite of fate and of the harm it had done him, he never abandoned. He was as little of a Nazarite as of a Stylites, and not more of either than of the kind of bacchanalian-amorist poet whom he despised. In fact, if it were not for the testimony of the works, it would not be quite irrational to reject most of this gossip about him; and, as it is, reason, no less than charity, may reject a good deal of it. Nothing but amiable paralogism can give Milton an amiable character, inasmuch as the intensity of his convictions, and the peculiar complexion of these, almost necessitated a certain asperity. But the other testimony which the works bear makes unamiableness a very minor matter.

Nor was this other testimony rejected. It is so easy to get a falsehood into currency, and so hard to stop it by nailing to any counter, that most people still talk about the unworthy reception of *Paradise Lost*—the £15 of which Milton only received £10; the coming of Addison to the rescue some fifty years afterwards; and the rest of it. It must be sufficient here to say that 1300 copies of this long poem, in a most unfashionable style and on a subject which the profane would probably shun altogether and the pious would probably think unsuitable for poetry, were sold in eighteen months; that, apparently, at least 3000 were sold in ten years; that six editions appeared before the close of the century and nine before Addison wrote. Turning from statistics to *belles lettres*, Dryden, the greatest by an infinite distance of the younger generation of men of letters, did it the heartiest justice from the first and always.

Roscommon, who died in 1685, had praised and imitated it.
Samuel Woodford, the paraphrast of the *Psalms* and *Canticles*,
had criticised its versification very soon after its appearance.
And though, even after blank verse had recovered the stage
from intrusive heroics, the extension of its use was slow, that
use came in gradually before Addison took up the matter at
all; and the style was regularly called "the manner of Milton."
Piety, good taste and, perhaps, a slight fellow feeling in
Whiggery, no doubt induced Addison to stamp Milton's
passport with the *visé* of a criticism which retained its importance throughout the eighteenth century. But that passport,
from the first, had been recognised by all whose opinion was
of value and even, in a vague way, by the general. A
considerable commentary had been appended to the sixth
edition by Patrick Hume, in 1695; fifty years later, Lauder's
calumnies and forgeries, curious, and not quite intelligible
(for it was impossible that they should survive examination), started afresh the commentatorial zeal which
had been displayed, not according to knowledge, by Bentley,
and, not altogether according to wits, by bishop Newton.
There was, and still is, plenty of room for comment, inasmuch as Milton could only seem "not a learned man" to
one who, like Mark Pattison, took his standard of learning
from the Casaubons. But such a calculus stands outside
pure poetical-critical appreciation. This has never failed
Milton, and can never fail him. If the spirit of poetry is
not in him, it is nowhere.

It did not, however, show itself *prodigialiter*. The parallel
contrast between the precocity of Cowley and the comparatively slow development of Milton, but a few years
earlier, must have often suggested itself; but it may be doubted
whether it has much real validity as anything more than accident. Indeed, the lesson of another pair of contemporaries—
Shelley and Keats—practically denies it any. The carefully
dated *primitiae*—"at fifteen yeers old," "*Anno aetatis* 17,"
"*Anno Aetatis* 19"—exhibited nothing that almost any good
versifier of that fertile time might not have written. Of the
two boyish Psalm-paraphrases, 114 has absolutely nothing
distinctive; the other, a good metre, but nothing more. The
poem entitled *On the Death of a fair Infant* (his little niece)

can bear its two years further weight for age; but there is, perhaps, only one line—

> Or that crown'd Matron sage white-robed Truth—

which one would pronounce distinctly Miltonic, and even this is not exclusively so. *At a Vacation Exercise*—yet another two years younger or older—makes, perhaps, a slight further advance in more than metre (this will be dealt with separately). But it is only in the summoning of the rivers at the close that approach to individuality is suggested, and, even then, there is a strong suggestion of Spenser.

But if Milton obeyed a common, though not quite universal, law in treading the mere high-road for some time, a parting of the ways came in the most striking fashion with *On the Morning of Christ's Nativity*, composed in the year of his majority. Most striking—for the opening stanzas of the proem, though much finer than anything he had done, were still not quite Milton. Not merely Spenser, but the greater Davies, either Fletcher, several other poets actually or nearly contemporary, might have written them. *The Hymn* itself, in its very first lines, not merely in metre but in diction, in arrangement, in quality of phrase and thought alike, strikes a new note—almost a new gamut of notes. The peculiar stateliness which redeems even conceit from frivolity or frigidity; the unique combination of mass and weight with easy flow; the largeness of conception, imagery, scene; above all, perhaps, the inimitable stamp of phrase and style—attained, chiefly, by cunning selection and collocation of epithet—give the true Milton. "Gaudy" is not an out-of-the-way word, and it may have been suggested to him by the fine Marlowesque line of *Henry VI*—

> The *gaudy*, blabbing and remorseful day,

or by fifty other passages. But, placed exactly where it is in the first stanza, it colours, values, composes the whole. The greater beauties of the piece that follow—the "reign of peace"; the music of the spheres; the silencing of the oracles; and the flight of the dethroned idols—are well known. The piece gives us all its author's poetry *in nuce*—his union of majesty and grace, his unique and all-compelling style, his command of "solemn music" such as had never before been known.

We cannot, of course, go through all the minor poems in detail; but *The Passion* or, rather, the note at its fragmentary close, deserves notice because it completes the testimony of *The Nativity*. That showed us the poet: this shows us the critic whom, as has been well remarked, every great poet must contain. "This Subject the Author, finding to be above the years he had when he wrote it, and nothing satisfied with what was begun, left it unfinished." There have not been many poets who would have been "nothing satisfied" with such lines as

> He sov'ran Priest stooping his regall head
>
> . . . .
>
> His starry front low-rooft beneath the skies;

or, best of all,

> See see the Chariot, and those rushing wheels,
> That whirl'd the Prophet up at *Chebar* flood.

But Milton felt this dissatisfaction: and Milton was right. His hand was still uncertain. It had slipped from the helm as he burst into the hitherto silent sea of the style of the *Nativity*, and he had drifted into mere respectable Fletcherian *pastiche* with some better touches. And he knew this: as, doubtless, he had known the other. There could be no doubt about him after the acquisition and demonstration of the double knowledge.

The recognition of this is the most important thing in the study of the first stage of Milton's poetical career. It was a few years before the executive mastery rendered the critical control regulative rather than prohibitive or suspensory; but very few. The famous Shakespeare lines are probably a little, and even not a very little, earlier than the date of the second folio, in which they appeared, and, if not perfect intrinsically, are admirable as from a young disciple to a dead master. The Hobson pieces, though quite out of Milton's line and much less well done in their own than they would have been by Cleiveland or John Hall, are, at least, curious. *An Epitaph on the Marchioness of Winchester* is a notable study for the verse of *L'Allegro;* and its companion *Arcades*, of which more presently, is a more notable study for *Comus*. A hint from Peele—not the last—and a suggestion from Shakespeare, matter nothing: Milton was to be always a literary poet. These things mark the full initiation, the final winning of the spurs.

From *L'Allegro* itself to *Samson Agonistes*, we have to do with the adept and the knight. The comparative valuation of the various poems of these forty years may be left to others, for it depends partly upon personal preferences, partly upon considerations of scale and subject and other things that can never be brought to a satisfactory common denominator of criticism. But the positive quality of poetry is in and over them all, from first to last, unmistakable by those who have been born or taught to recognise it. And it is this positive quality, in its various individual manifestations, and in its relations to the general history and development of English poetry at large, that we have now to disengage and study in chronological order, only neglecting this latter in the case of the *Sonnets*, so as to group them together, as is usually done, in what is the actual place of most of them,—the gap between *Lycidas* and *Paradise Lost*.

The twin studies of cheerfulness and melancholy will, of course, come first, for it is impossible to admit the ingenious attempt (above referred to) to postdate them. Their extraordinary felicity has not met any important gainsayings. That some of the details are not quite accurate, as natural history, would matter extremely little in any case, and has even a certain interest in connection with the peculiarity (to be noticed later) of Milton's poetic painting. Another interesting point is the skill with which the full or shortened octosyllabic couplet, with iambic or trochaic cadence at pleasure, is handled. This famous old measure, handed down from *The Owl and the Nightingale*, if not earlier, had been fingered into new beauty by Shakespeare and others in the last years of the sixteenth century and had been specially cultivated by Fletcher, Browne, Wither and others in the earlier seventeenth. Its capabilities have never been so perfectly and variously shown as in these two charming poems, which are also, as it were, diploma-pieces, exhibiting Milton's almost unsurpassable combination of bookishness and natural imagination, the art of phrase which still has all the gracefulness of youth, the power over imagery and association, the whole suffused with a temper which is soft even when sad, and which never jars or thorn-crackles even at its most mirthful.

When the beautiful fragment *Arcades* (to return to it for a special purpose) was written is not known; it must have come before *Comus*, but may be of any year between 1630 and 1634. It was addressed to Alice, countess dowager of Derby—the same lady who, as lady Strange (she was by birth lady Alice Spencer) had been the recipient of Spenser's *Teares of the Muses* forty years before, and who, after the death of her first husband (Strange, it must be remembered, was then the second title of the earls of Derby), had married lord keeper Egerton, afterward lord chancellor viscount Brackley. The masque was performed at Harefield in Middlesex, not far from Horton, and it is supposed, though not known, that the music was by Milton's friend Lawes. Fragment as the libretto is, the songs, especially the second, "On the smooth enamelled green" are perfection; and the decasyllabic couplets of the Genius's speech have deep interest as being Milton's most considerable serious attempt in this form. He takes, as was natural, the enjambed variety, but carefully avoids the breathless overlapping of his seniors Browne and Marmion and Chalkhill and his younger contemporary Chamberlayne.

The connection of *Comus* with *Arcades* is so close in all ways that it is scarcely improper to regard it as deliberate. The earl of Bridgewater, for whom it was written, was lady Derby's stepson through her second husband, and his wife was her daughter by her first. He was president of Wales, and, in virtue of his office, lived at Ludlow castle, where *Comus* was acted. His daughter Alice, who acted the Lady, must have been named after her double grandmother. Lawes here certainly wrote the music, and he acted the Attendant Spirit. As

for the story, it was partly supplied (beyond all question) by
Peele's *Old Wives Tale*, largely supplemented from Milton's
classical and modern reading (especially the *Comus* of the
Dutchman Puteanus (1608)) and his own imagination; partly
derived, at least according to tradition, from an actual adventure of lady Alice and her two brothers. But it has not
always been sufficiently noticed that the whole, as it were,
is a filling up of *Arcades*—the Genius of the Wood dividing
himself into good and evil parts as Thyrsis and Comus, the
merely accidental songs being adapted and multiplied to
suit the action, and that action itself being devised, in full
colour and body, to take the place of a mere occasional situation, like that of the earlier piece.

The amplification was more than justified, and in a surprisingly large number of ways. The actual dramatic effect
of the piece is not great; and, on the other side, it has been
pronounced too much of a fully equipped drama to be a masque.
But, putting questions of words and names apart, it is a most
admirable poem; and there have even not been wanting
those who put it, for length and poetic quality combined, first
of all its author's works, while admitting the superiority of
Lycidas in the latter respect and the three great later pieces
in the first. One special point of interest is that Milton here
discards for his "tragedy," as Sir Henry Wotton called it
(*i. e.* the body of his dialogue), the couplet which he had used
in *Arcades*, and adopts blank verse; while the rest of the piece
is in octosyllabic couplet or lyrical measures which are almost
an improvement on *L'Allegro*, *Il Penseroso* and *Arcades* itself.
Something more will be said of the form later: the substance
is amply worthy of it and, like it, duplex in character—an
ethical height and weight which the poet had never reached
before being matched with unimpaired grace in the lighter
parts. It would be difficult to find a poem where profit and
delight are more perfectly blended.

In *Lycidas*, the delight reaches an even higher pitch. For
once, there is no need to quarrel even with such an apparent
hyperbole as Pattison's "high-water mark of English poetry"
—especially as high-water mark is not a thing that can only
once be reached. The circumstances, form and character
of this exquisite poem have been the subject of a great deal

of writing. It formed part of a collection of epicedes on Edward King, a slightly younger contemporary of Milton at Christ's who had become fellow and tutor, and had intended to take orders, but was drowned on a voyage to Ireland in the summer of 1637. Milton's contribution is signed "J. M." only. The general scheme is that of a classical pastoral elegy; the verse form is a very peculiar, in fact, up to its date, unique, arrangement of stanzas and lines of unequal length, for the most part irregularly, and not entirely, rimed, but terminating in a regular octave. To what extent the poem expresses personal sorrow has been largely, but very unnecessarily, questioned; as an elegy, it has, poetically speaking, no superior even in a language which contains the various laments on Sidney before, and *Adonais* and *Thyrsis* after. The whole poem is a tissue of splendid passages, not unconnected, but sewn cunningly together rather than woven in one piece as regards subject. One, however, of these passages contains, for the first time, a note "prophesying war." Up to this date, Milton's verse, though abstaining alike from the passionately amorist tone of contemporary profane lyric, and from the almost erotically mystical tone of contemporary sacred poetry, had contained nothing polemical; and, even in the frequent eulogies of chastity in *Comus*, nothing positively austere. Here, St. Peter, coming among other symbolical figures to bewail the dead, is made to deliver a tremendous denunciation of what Milton later directly entitled "the corrupt clergy" of the time, and a prophecy of their ruin. The strict propriety of this has been questioned, even by some who agree with Milton's views on the subject: the force and fire of the expression (not injured by a little obscurity, which, perhaps, was a necessary precaution) may be admitted by the most thorough admirer of Laud. And all the rest (except from the point of view of an objection to pedantry which is itself ultra-pedantic) is absolutely proof against criticism. There cannot be better verse than *Lycidas*.

The few, but extremely interesting, *Sonnets* derive their interest from various sources. Except the earliest two, and the batch of Italian pieces which follows, they bridge the interval between Milton's first poetical period and his last— dotting the twenty dark years with spots of light. It is true that the evil spirit of the prose pamphlets retains some influence here, that his footing is seen in the *Tetrachordon* sonnets, in the tail-sonnet (twenty lines, the fifteenth and eighteenth of six syllables only) *On the new forcers of Conscience* and, to some, though less, extent, in the political sonnets to Fairfax, Cromwell and Vane. It is true, also, that one (xiv) *On the Religious Memory of Mrs. Catherine Thomson* is the most commonplace thing that Milton ever wrote. But, even were the best and the most of them less good, they would be interesting as resuming (with little following for more than another century) the Elizabethan practice of this great form, and as bringing it nearer to the commoner Italian model. Individually and intrinsically, they do not need any allowance. Wordsworth's hackneyed praise is not very specially applicable to most of them; and Johnson's contempt of the form itself, no doubt slightly accentuated by dislike of the author. Taken dispassionately, Milton's sonnets are examples, curiously various considering their small number, at once of the adaptability of the kind to "occasional" purposes, and of the absence of any necessity that this adaptability should be abused, as Wordsworth himself certainly abused it, and as lesser men have abused it still more. Nowhere, moreover, and this is natural, is the poet's tendency to be autobiographical shown in a more interesting way. The pretty overture to the nightingale not only shows the true Miltonic style very early, but gives us a Miltonic person who might have developed very differently. The other side—the side which did develop— appears in the "three and twentieth year" (vii), and at once foretells the compensations for the loss of the less austere personage. And all the better later examples give that compensation, with lighter touches here and there in the sonnets to Lawes, Lawrence and Cyriack Skinner. The grace of these; the splendour of *On the late Massacher in Piemont* and the sonnet on his blindness; the dignity, even in partisanship, of the three political addresses; the idealised tenderness of the finale on his dead wife—give us not merely great poetry, but invaluable comment on the other great poetry which was to follow them.

The year 1645, however, saw a more important event in Milton's literary biography and in the history of English

literature than the move to Barbican, or the reconciliation
with his wife, or even the downfall of the royal cause. Hitherto
—in this respect following a considerable and respectable,
though inconvenient and dangerous, Elizabethan tradition—
he had been very shy of printing his poems. The Shakespeare
lines were merely a trimming to the edition of Shakespeare
in which they appeared, and we do not know exactly how they
came there. *Lycidas* had formed part of a collection containing other men's work; Lawes's edition of *Comus* was
anonymous. But now, at a time when his mind was occupied
with things very different from the composition of poetry,
Milton consented to the publication of his earlier poetical
work (by, and at the instance of, the bookseller Humphrey
Moseley) as *Poems of Mr. John Milton, both English and Latin,
Compos'd at several times* . . . 1645. It has been supposed
that this publication, with its accompanying commendatory
poems, was intended as a sort of self-vindication, or counter-
sally, in respect of his polemical, and, in parts, highly unpopular, prose pamphlets. This seems very doubtful; for
anything like excuse, or plea in mitigation, was absolutely
alien from Milton's undoubting self-confidence and his positive
contumacy of spirit. Nor does the motto

*Baccare frontem
Cingite, ne vati noceat mala lingua futuro*

necessarily involve any such intention. "Good luck and
escape from the evil eye and the evil tongue to the poems" is
all it invokes. Probably, there was nothing more behind the
matter than the fact that, since Milton returned from Italy,
he had had other things to think about; and that Moseley's
direct solicitation (a fact recorded in the preface) was the main,
if not the sole, occasional cause of the appearance. The book
had a bad portrait, with a Greek inscription, by Milton himself,
stigmatising the badness. For twenty years and more after
this he did not publish any poetry.

On the origin, date and circumstances of the great poem
that broke his silence, a very great deal has been written.
That *Paradise Lost* was entered at Stationers' Hall (that is to
say, that it was printed and ready for sale) on 20 August,

1667, is the main documentary fact. Four months earlier, on 27 April, Milton had executed with Samuel Simmons the famous agreement for four payments of five pounds each, one down, the second when 1300 copies should have been sold, the third when a second edition on the same scale should have been absorbed and the fourth at the exhaustion of a third. But, in each, Simmons was allowed an extra 200 copies on which he was to pay nothing. The MS., of course, had been submitted for licensing;[1] and the actual censor—a chaplain of the archbishop of Canterbury named Tomkyns—had made slight objections but had not persisted in them. The volume, a small quarto, with the poem in ten books, not twelve, was published at 3*s*., and the second payment fell in about a year and a half (26 April, 1669) after the first. Further, the variations of title-page, and, in a less degree, of text, usual in the same edition of books at the time, are unusually great here, and have been carefully tabulated, so far as possible, by Masson. The most important is the notable addition on "The Verse," which did not appear till 1668.

These things, in their various degrees, are certainties; and it is a further certainty that, after Milton's death, his widow compounded for the third five pounds (already due) and the fourth which was accruing, for the present payment, in December, 1680, of eight pounds. The popular version of the matter seldom gets the total—£18—right; but that is not the most important blunder or fallacy connected with it. It is as certain that the offer of £18,000 will not produce a *Paradise Lost*, as that the actual fee or guerdon of £18 did not prevent its production.

With regard to the actual time occupied in composition, and the sources, as they are vaguely called, of the poem, we know very little—practically nothing. There is no doubt that, just before his energies were diverted into pamphleteering, Milton had planned a great epic; and, as his Latin poems show, had thought of something from the legends of the *Bruts*, or stories of Britain, to match the *Iliad* and the *Aeneid*. It is further certain that, about 1640, or a little later, he wrote

---

[1] The actual MS. of bk. 1 which was submitted passed into the possession of Tonson and thence to his descendants, who sold it a short time ago. It was, of course, in the hand of an amanuensis, not in Milton's (see remarks below).

out a long list (actually existing at Trinity college, Cambridge)
of subjects from British and Scriptural history for dramatic
treatment.   Not only is *Paradise Lost* among these, *eo nomine*,
but four successive drafts, each more elaborate than the preceding, exist of the persons and the distribution of subject—
the last and fullest, however, having its title changed to
"Adam Unparadized" [*sic*].   Edward Phillips says that the
opening lines of Satan's speech[1] ("O thou that with surpassing
glory crowned") were originally written and shown to him
and others "several years before the poem was begun," as
the overture of the tragedy.   On Phillips's authority, Aubrey
gives "15 or 16" years for "several"; while the same vouchers
assign the actual date of beginning the epic to 1658 or there-
abouts.   If we believe the quaker Ellwood, it was actually
finished by 1665; but plague and fire stopped the way to the
press.   Aubrey antedates the finishing by two years or so.
On the whole, this is gossip.   What is certain is that Milton
had had the subject before his mind, either for epic or dramatic
treatment, quite a quarter of a century when it was published.
The present writer has always, from internal evidence of a
vague but not unsatisfying kind, been inclined to believe
that the poem was actually begun not long after his blindness
had become a settled fact to him, which would coincide with
the 15 or 16 years above mentioned.   The gossip has one more
interesting item, whatever may be its positive value, that he
wrote, or, rather, composed, it and his other poems by dictation during half the year only, "from the Autumnal Equinox
to the Vernal."

Again, fact assures us that the matter of the poem was
largely the result of general reading.   Fancy, which has sometimes deserved a harsher name, goes further and tries to
assign particular sources.   The lies of Lauder—who actually
took portions of Hog's Latin translations of Milton, garbled
them into divers more or less obscure writers and put them
forth as Milton's originals, plagiarised by him—stand by
themselves here; though, from another point of view, they have
an ungoodly fellowship of literary mystifications and forgeries
to keep them company.   But the parallel-hunters and the
plagiarism-hunters and the source-hunters have spent im-

[1] *P. L.* IV, 32.

mense pains—by no means always or often with malicious
intent—to show that Milton imitated, borrowed from, or, in
this way and that, followed, the *Adamo* of the Italian dramatist
Giambattista Andreini (1613), the *Lucifer*, also a drama, of
the Dutch poet Vondel (1654), the *Adamus Exul* of Grotius
(1601), Sylvester's *Du Bartas* (1605) and even Caedmon, whose
Genesis was published by Milton's friend Junius, in 1655.
Even more than most such things, these suggestions, if they
insinuate what is properly called plagiarism, deserve simple
contempt; and, if they only infer acquaintance, are matter of
simple curiosity at most. Supposing Milton to have read
all these books, *Paradise Lost* remains Milton's; and it is
perfectly certain, not merely that nobody else could have
constructed it out of them, but that a syndicate composed
of their authors, each in his happiest vein and working together
as never collaborators worked, could not have come within
measurable distance of it, or of him.

For, after all the detraction and all the adulation (the latter,
in some cases, as damaging as the former or more so) which
Paradise Lost has received, it remains unique. It is not, as
it has been foolishly called, "the only great poem" in existence;
but it is the only poem as great in a particular way, or, rather,
it is quite alone in its kind of greatness. It will be found that
all objections to it, when examined, involve a sort, or different
sorts, of *petitio principii*. "It has no hero (for Adam is
hardly such and Christ's victory does not come till later)
or a bad and unsuccessful hero in Satan." Why should it
have one? "The story is known beforehand." This applies
practically to all classical epic and drama. "It, or part of
it, is dull." That is a matter of taste. "Its religious ideas
are exploded." That is a matter of opinion. The list of
thrust and parry might be largely extended; but this may
suffice.

On the other hand, it can show a sustained magnificence
of poetic conception, and of poetic treatment in the solemn
and serious way, which has practically never been denied by
any competent critic. It would be difficult to find any two
persons who differed from each other more than Voltaire and
Johnson, or any two who, for different reasons, disliked Milton
more. Yet Johnson practically admits, though without

enthusiasm, the magnificence above claimed, and Voltaire is only enabled to shrug it off—he hardly denies it—by the aid of a certain incompetence to appreciate it if he would. It has been pronounced not delightful by persons not incompetent: it can never, by any such, be pronounced not great. That the whole is not quite at the height of the first two books may be granted; but, even the lower level would be a mountain top in other poetry. It matters little whether it be approached from the side of form, or from that of spirit. As regards form, it practically endowed English with a new medium for great non-dramatic poetry: what, at the very time of its completion, was being pronounced "too mean for a copy of verses," was made great enough for the greatest poem. As regards spirit, we find the loftiest height of argument, the most gorgeous description, action not extremely varied but nobly managed, character not much individualised but sufficiently adapted to the action, above all, a suffused imaginative dignity, not merely unsurpassed, but unparalleled elsewhere.

The exact relations of *Paradise Lost* and its sequel or pendant are rather uncertain. It is so perfectly natural that Milton should have written this sequel that, perhaps, some people may hardly look further; and it is equally natural that some time should be allowed to pass between the successive publications. It has, however, been customary to accept the statement of the aforementioned quaker Ellwood to the effect that he, visiting Milton at Chalfont during his retreat before the plague, "pleasantly" said to the poet, "Thou hast said much here of 'Paradise Lost,' but what hast thou to say of 'Paradise Found'?" Whereupon Milton answered nothing and "sat some time in a muse"; but, next year, in London, showed Ellwood the poem. Of course, if this be true, it was finished considerably before the publication of *Paradise Lost*. There is, however, a good deal that is suspicious about this statement; it is not confirmed or supported by Phillips or any other contemporary authority; and there is against it strong evidence of a kind which receives too little general attention—the evidence of prosody. Critics who take very different views of Milton's versification admit equally that there is a difference between that of the two poems— a difference specially suggesting some interval between their composition; but less between that of *Paradise Regained* and its companion in publication *Samson Agonistes*.

At any rate, these two were published together in 1671[1] by one John Starkey, who lived at the prelatical sign of The Mitre in Fleet street. They had been licensed (again by Tomkyns) on 2 July, 1670. Of the details—copies printed, terms of publication and so forth—we do not, in this instance, know anything; but, as the book is said to be "Printed by J. M.," it has been supposed that it was an independent venture of the poet's own. The sale was less rapid than that of *Paradise Lost*, or (which is improbable) the edition was much larger—at any rate, it was not exhausted for nine years, and the tradition of the comparative unpopularity of the poem is early. Phillips says that it was "generally censured to be [*i. e.* criticised as being] much inferior to the other, though *he* [his uncle] could not hear with patience any such thing." He would have had more than his usual uniqueness if he could have heard it with patience; but an author's partiality need not bear all the blame of his impatience. The inferiority which the "general censure" of *Paradise Regained* has continued to ascribe, though it may be admitted to some extent, is an accidental, and, so to speak, artificial, inferiority. The subject is certainly less interesting: partly because it allows of less addition, traditional or original, to the scriptural narrative, and, partly, because the conclusion is even more foregone. It is probable that, to Milton, with his semi-Arian views, the succumbing of Christ to temptation was a sufficiently epical contingency: to the orthodox and the infidel alike, it lacks that element. The poem is rather long for the actual action and yet rather short in itself—a mere episode in the real "Regaining of Paradise." And there are other objections which may be made, some from what may be called the point of view of the professional critic, some from more popular approaches.

But, in purely poetic value, *Paradise Regained* is little inferior to its predecessor. There may be nothing in the poem

---

[1] Observe that, if Ellwood be right, *Paradise Regained* must have been kept complete and unprinted for five years, by a poet who was in bad health and advancing age, in spite of what has been shown to have been a rather flattering reception, so far as sale went, of the earlier poem.

that can quite touch the first two books of *Paradise Lost* for magnificence; but there are several things that may fairly be set beside almost anything in the last ten. The splendid "stand at bay" of the discovered tempter—"'T is true I am that spirit unfortunate"—in the first book; his rebuke of Belial in the second, and the picture of the magic banquet (it must be remembered that, though it is customary to extol Milton's asceticism, the story of his remark to his third wife, and the Lawrence and Skinner sonnets, go the other way); above all, the panoramas from the mountain-top in the third and fourth; the terrors of the night of storm; the crisis on the pinnacle of the temple—are quite of the best Milton, which is equivalent to saying that they are of the best of one kind of poetry.

Our diminishing acquaintance with the circumstances of *Paradise Regained* as compared with those of *Paradise Lost* dwindles to almost nothing when we come to *Paradise Regained*'s companion in print. No Ellwood boasts its suggestion; although there are two Samson subjects for dramas in the Cambridge list neither of these has any detail appended to it, and one refers to an early episode (the fox tails and fire brands) of the hero's life. And, though the other, *Dagonalia*, is concerned with the catastrophe, it does not follow that the subject would have been treated in the actual way of *Agonistes*. Nor is much to be learnt from the short preface "Of that sort of Dramatic Poem called Tragedy." Although longer and less defiant than the afterthought on "The Verse" of *Paradise Lost*, it is mainly explanatory of differences from the accepted English form, the poet specially objecting to tragicomic admixture, disclaiming stage intention and maintaining the unities of action and time, without mentioning that of place, which, however is, in fact, observed. His comment on his choric metres is less enigmatical than that on the Rous ode in Latin[1] which, however, should be taken with it. It merely disclaims regular strophic arrangement.

The poem itself is of the very highest interest, and does not need any doubtful—hardly any certain—external support. There is scarcely anything, in poetry—Dante again excepted—which combines poetical and personal appeal in so striking

[1] See *post*.

a fashion. The parallel of Samson and Milton himself is extraordinary, even at first blush, and the poet, with his strong autobiographical tendency, has brought it out still further. The blindness, the triumph of political enemies, the failing strength and closing life (see, especially the poignant lines[1] "So much I feel my genial spirits droop . . . And I shall shortly be with them that rest"), the unbroken and undaunted resolution—all are in both. And there are less certain, but most suggestive, added touches. There is no need to make the story of the first marriage worse by confounding Mary Powell with Dalila, nor can the cases be made to cover each other by the utmost violence or the most perverted ingenuity. But, in the Dalila passages of *Samson*, there certainly is that combination of susceptibility to feminine charms and distrustful revolt against them which is thoroughly Miltonic. One cannot but see in the altercation with Harapha what Milton would have liked to say—if he never said it— to an "over-crowing" malignant; and the whole tissue of situations is worked into similarity, now actual, now allegoric.

But, quite independently of this, *Samson Agonistes*, from the purely literary point of view, is a poem of the highest interest and of the greatest beauty. An acting play, we are told, it was never meant to be; but, even of the acting quality, it has probably as much as any English play on the strict classical model can have. It has certainly more than either *Cornelia* or *Philotas*, than either *Merope* or *Erechtheus*. As a poem, dramatised in a given form, it needs no allowance and no apology. Both the style and the versification, to some extent, show that "drooping of the genial spirits" which has been quoted: they are harder and stiffer. But there is even more art, if less "bloomy flush of life"; and the art is almost more imposing than ever, if less graceful. When Mark Pattison thought that, to critics who maintain that beauty is the only characteristic of poetry, *Samson* "will seem tame, flat, meaningless and artificial," he showed clearly that he did not understand the point of view to which he was referring.

Above all, the choruses give us not only much splendid verse, but an extraordinary abundance of special points of interest. To begin with, there is—and this point is not

[1] Ll. 594-8.

Samsonic—the submission to the once loved, then slighted, enchantress rime. The first two or three choruses or choric scenes are blank; rime, not regular, but on a sort of further unregularised *Lycidas* scheme, reappears with the striking *epiphonema* "God of our Fathers, what is man"[1] and is never wholly abandoned afterwards. Nevertheless, the poet continues his ceaseless experimentation in the mere forms of verse, putting rime out of the question—varying the assortment of his lengths, associating different feet on an extension of the same bold principle which had underlain the versification of *Paradise Lost* and, in places, venturing on entirely new rhythms, his intention in which is not yet quite certain, as in the famous "O how comely it is and how reviving" and "When their hearts were jocund and sublime."

And all this art is used for the presentation of a picture of really great action and high passion, a picture which, if we were ignorant of, and insusceptible to, all Biblical associations, if we knew nothing about Milton's personal history, would appeal to the eternal human interests. It may be that, in his central and, as the phrase goes, greatest, works, Milton had sometimes forgotten this appeal. He had not done so in his earlier and happier period; and though the time was late and hardly happy, he had returned to it now.[2]

The subject of Milton's prose work is not a very easy one, and it has often been neglected — comparatively, at least—in general surveys of his work. So long, indeed, as criticism was mainly coloured by the critic's agreement or disagreement with the author's views, it was almost impossible that anything valuable should be said on the subject. There could not be any critical edification in discourse which tended, on the one side, towards a sermon on the 30th of January

---

[1] L. 667.

[2] Later than *Paradise Regained* and *Samson*, and in the year before his death, Milton published (adding the tractate *Of Education*) a second edition of his minor poems (*Poems, etc. upon Several Occasions*) with Thomas Dring. He omitted the English prefatory matter not his own to *Comus*, but added *On the Death of a fair Infant* and *At a Vacation Exercise*, and all his later minor verse except the Fairfax, Vane, Cromwell and Cyriack Skinner II sonnets. Some, but not all, copies of this included a new portrait instead of the old libel. And it is of rather more than merely bibliographical importance to remember that here, also, as in the 1645 issue, and as in Lawes's *editio princeps*, *Comus* is not called *Comus* but simply *A Mask*.

and, on the other, towards a Calf's Head club harangue. But, even if the king be kept as entirely as possible out of the matter, many difficulties, not merely troublesome but, as Milton's own time would have said, "disgustful," remain. That poets have usually been good prose-writers is a commonplace; and that some of Milton's prose passages are among the finest in English is hardly denied by anybody. Yet, even here, there have been gainsayers who were not political partisans, and whose competence was not to be questioned; while, if we stop short of absolute gainsaying, there has been hardly anybody, whose competence and impartiality are not questionable, to praise without abundant and uncomfortable allowance and exception.

The difficulty arises mainly from the fact that, except in the *Education* tractate, and in the curious *Histories*, Milton was always "fighting a prize" in his prose compositions; and that, hardly ever, except in *Areopagitica*, had he a prize before him which was worth the fight in a literary sense. This, to some extent, might have been compensated if he had been a born "Swiss of Heaven" in his controversies—if he had known how to make the most of his case without positive passion. But he did not. One would suppose that no one, unless entirely carried away by sympathy with Milton's causes, could approve Milton's controversial methods. His capital fault is that he never succeeds in bringing, or, apparently, attempts to bring, the matter under any consideration, or upon any ground, which his opponents can be imagined as sharing, or reasonably invited to share. To convict your adversary on your own statement of case is quite idle: and this is what Milton is constantly doing. Even if his manner were less offensive than it is admitted to be, this peculiarity would be nearly fatal. His arguments against Ussher and Hall are not merely indecent in form towards one of the most learned men in Europe and one of the leaders of English literature, both of them aged divines of unblemished reputation: they have the further drawback of constantly taking for granted premises which Hall and Ussher would utterly, and on strong reason, deny. In his divorce tracts, when he is not (with a curious mixture of the pathetic and the ludicrous) urging (under whatever general shield) his own painful situa-

tion, he has recourse to such arguments as the opinion of
Lutheran divines on Henry VIII's conduct—which is about
as valuable as the opinion of Amphitryon's guests as to the
identity of Amphitryon. In the Salmasius and Morus controversies and in the minor political or ecclesiastical pamphlets, it is even worse. Cut the abuse out, and there is not
much left of them: cut out subsequently what cannot be
admitted by the *communis sensus* as real argument, and there
is almost nothing left.

Even so, however, it would have been possible for Milton—
if he had been a cool-headed person with a dominant rhetorical
faculty, or even a strong sense of prose art, mastering his
personal convictions, as his poetic faculty and his sense of
poetical art mastered them in the other division—to make
his prose work, unpromising as is most of it in subject, a
success in treatment. But Milton was never cool-headed;
and when he was out of his singing robes, the poetic warmth
was exchanged for a less genial variety. Hypocrisy—even
of that modified sort which makes every rhetorician (if not,
indeed, every artist) a ὑποκριτής of a kind—was impossible
to him. And it so happened that some of his special characteristics of style, which were harmless and even beneficial in verse,
were dangerous, more especially at the time, in prose. He
was very fond of long sentences—the very first of *Paradise
Lost* contains sixteen lines, and, perhaps, six score words,
while there are others longer. In verse, this did no harm, and
much good—indeed, without it, he could hardly have
achieved, as will be duly pointed out elsewhere, his famous
"verse-paragraph." His unerring sense of verse-form prevented these sentences from being in any way formless.
But, in prose, it was different. Destitute of the girth and
band of the line, enabled to expand and expatiate, to indulge
in parenthesis, and epexegesis, and additional relative clause,
by the treacherous confusion of English and Latin grammar
which prevailed, his sentences too frequently become a mere
welter; and, in citing some of the finest, it is customary to
commit the minor fraud of stopping short where he ought to
have stopped, but did not.

If there had been—as it was practically impossible that
there should be then—an accomplished critic who, at the

same time, was not a political or ecclesiastical partisan, he must have been genuinely distressed by *Of Reformation touching Church-Discipline in England*, when it appeared in 1641. It is impossible to read a page or two without seeing that here was a writer who united the gifts of striking phrase and of rhythmical adjustment as, even in that age of marvellous achievement in these respects, few had done; but who exaggerated the defects of composition, usual after Hooker's time, in an almost unbelievable way. The second sentence, not without premonition of the great flights later, is almost a pattern of Milton's style when not at its best—that style, even at its best, retaining a general likeness in composition, and (as Dryden says) *ordonnance*, to it:

Sad it is to think how that doctrine of the gospel, planted by teachers divinely inspired, and by them winnowed and sifted from the chaff of overdated ceremonies, and refined to such a spiritual height and temper of purity, and knowledge of the Creator, that the body, with all the circumstances of time and place, were purified by the affections of the regenerate soul, and nothing left impure but sin; faith needing not the weak and fallible office of the senses, to be either the ushers or interpreters of heavenly mysteries, save where our Lord himself in his sacraments ordained; that such a doctrine should, through the grossness and blindness of her professors, and the fraud of deceivable traditions, drag so downwards, as to backslide one way into the Jewish beggary of old cast rudiments, and stumble forward another way into the new-vomited paganism of sensual idolatry, attributing purity or impurity to things indifferent, that they might bring the inward acts of the spirit to the outward and customary eye-service of the body, as if they would make God earthly and fleshly, because they could not make themselves heavenly and spiritual; they began to draw down all the divine intercourse between God and the soul, yea the very shape of God himself, into an external bodily form urgently pretending a necessity and obligement of joining the body in a formal reverence and worship circumscribed; they hallowed it, they fumed up, they sprinkled it, they bedecked it, not in robes of pure innocency, but of pure linen, with other deformed and fantastic dresses, in palls and mitres, gold, and gewgaws fetched from Aaron's old wardrobe, or the flamins vestry: then was the priest set to con his motions and his postures, his liturgies and his lurries, till the soul by this means of overbodying herself, given up justly to fleshly delights, bated her wing apace downward: and finding the ease she had from her visible and sensuous colleague, the body, in performance of religious duties, her pinions now broken, and flagging, shifted off from herself the labour of high soaring any more, forgot her heavenly flight, and left the dull and droiling carcase to plod on in the old road, and drudging trade of outward conformity.

Now the reader of this, struggling like Robinson Crusoe with the waves that, though they washed him ashore, all but strangled and crushed him in the process, may naturally protest with all the breath he has left on his deliverance. And he certainly would not lack sound critical objections. There is no necessary harm in the long cumulative sentence: it may be found (for instance in Ruskin) of something like double the above length, but building up a picture whose every stroke is a clear and congruous addition. Milton's, at first sight and not at first sight only, is a daub of plastered touches. One or two of the sections (if they can be called sections) could, indeed, be kept clear by punctuation. But, for the most part, they are not hinged and jointed together; they are thrust bodily into each other's substance so far as composition goes, while the actual words could be thinned out, with, in many cases, almost infinite advantage.

But, a little further thought will discover no small "condolences and vails" of the kind indicated above. In the first place, the reader's sufferings would be considerably mitigated in the case of the hearer, if the thing were cunningly declaimed. Now the ancients never could rid themselves of the idea that poetry and oratory were very close together: and Milton was largely an ancient. Secondly, let it be considered how little it would take to turn the passage into a blank verse tirade, not quite of *Paradise Lost* quality, but of good *Comus* type. And, thirdly, let the positive excellencies be noted. If the word-selection be sometimes bad, it is not always so. How much better is "overdated" than our "out of date"; how fine the kindred "overbodying herself"; how happy the reversal of epithet order (always a favourite device of Milton) in "a formal reverence and worship circumscribed"! While, all through, even if half whelmed by the over-sentencing, there rings the wonderful prose cadence which we never find in English—not even in Malory—till the early translators of the Bible got it somehow from their originals and infused it into our literature for ever.

This passionate, voluminous, eloquent, unequal medium served Milton, when he did not use Latin (in which his manner was not very different), throughout his life, and on almost all occasions. An intenser passion, with a nobler subject, elevated it into the noble, but even then not always faultless, style of the great *Areopagitica* passages; of the fine prayers at the close of *Reformation touching Church-Discipline in England;* of the enthusiastic autobiography of *An Apology [for] Smectymnuus;* of some parts even of the unfortunate divorce tracts. Less fortunate occasions and a lower mood degrade it into the "rude railing and insolent swagger" of *Eikonoklastes*, which Mark Pattison, for all his liberalism and his Milton-worship, describes as "grossly indecent"; or into the inconceivably dreary horseplay—or worse—of the *Animadversions upon the Remonstrant's defence*. With passion and "interest" (in the doubtful sense) almost entirely absent, it composes itself into the sober, businesslike, yet very far from inelegant, vehicle of the *Education* tractate. It is really curious to see how, for the most part, the sentences shorten themselves, how the composition is clarified, the epithets are thinned and carefully sifted, in this tract. And it is still more curious to note the exceptions to this—as in the sentence of the third paragraph beginning, "And for the usual method of teaching arts," where the unblessed memory of his tutor occurs to him, where he loses his temper, his head, his command of the rudder of style, and once more welters and wallows through clause after clause of ill-jointed afterthought and ill-selected abuse.

Lastly, it finds its way into channels again different— those of the two *Histories;* and has something of surprise for us still. Most people who have read it have been more or less fascinated by the little *History of Moscovia*. The oddity of it is, of course, less than it may seem to the modern reader. The seventeenth century was, perhaps, the most learned of all centuries; but—some might say because—it was not largely provided with ready-digested learning. Men, therefore, had to make their digests, their conspectus, their abstracts for themselves: and this is a specimen. It is singularly well done—quite a model of *précis*, with a little expatiation and ornament betraying the poet's hand. The sentences are mostly quite short, but not in the least snip-snappy. The touches that had struck the writer's own attention are selected and composed admirably to catch the reader's. Manners, incidents, local colour—all are used to relieve the mere gazetteer- or chronicle-effect; and, where the piece becomes more dramatic and less summary (as in the rather well known interview between Ivan the Terrible and Sir Jerome Bowes), the style is perfectly equal to the occasion. The reason, of course, is that there is nothing in the subject which is *cinis dolosus;* and so the foot never breaks through the crust, and no "curling tempests" of wrath and incoherence burst out.

This is not quite the case with the much longer and very much odder *History of England*, where Milton gives himself the trouble to tell over again what he well knew (and admits that he knew) to be merely "modern fable." His reason is frankly given and it makes us like him all the better—"be it for nothing else but in favour of our English poets and rhetoricians, who by their art will know how to use them judiciously" as (let us say, though he does not) Shakespeare had done in *King Lear* and Milton himself in *Comus*.

Here, there was certainly "miching mallecho" if wanted—monks and popes and painted images and other dangerous things. But either the "kind calm years" (he revised it in 1670), or the distance of time, or the blessed influence of romance, though under the mask of history, kept the coals from blazing; and the curious power of dramatic recitative, little associated, as a rule, with Milton, reappears. In the story of Edwin and Paulinus, he passes slightly over the famous incidents of the bird flying through the hall, and the violent apostasy of the high priest, to dwell on the sign of the imposition of the right hand. It is to be feared that we can account for his slighting the heroism of Boadicea "as if in Britain women were men and men women." But the Caesarean invasions are told with remarkable spirit; and the use of the historic present in the account of the war between Brutus and the Greeks is excellently vivid. Even the curious parallel introduced (in later editions) at the beginning of the third book as to "the late troubles," though, of course, one-sided,

never lapses into the feverish incoherence of the earlier treatises; and it remains a strange Epimethean criticism of the
actual facts.

In these later years, too, he composed the longest of his
prose works, the Latin *De Doctrina Christiana*, which, after
lying unnoticed in the State Paper office for a century and a
half, was printed in 1825 by Sumner, and served as peg,
though hardly as subject, to Macaulay's essay. It is a curious
document of its author's tendency to "ray out" nonconformity
in almost all directions and on almost all subjects: being
pantheistic in philosophy, Arian in theology, millenarian in
eschatology, semi-Antinomian in ethics (with advocacy of
polygamy) and individualist as regards church government, the
whole, of course, being professedly Biblical in origin. The
recent attempt to attribute to Milton a Latin religious romance
entitled *Nova Solyma* will hardly commend itself either to
any impartial judge of evidence or to any competent literary
critic.

A complete list of Milton's prose will be subjoined; and it
seems better to deal with it here in the manner adopted in the
foregoing pages than to tag more or less slight critical *aperçus*
to the several titles. More emphatically, perhaps, than is
the case with any portion of the work of an author of equal
eminence, it is a by-work. Except *Areopagitica*, there is
hardly a piece of it that can be said to be, in the common
phrase, worthy of its author, as a piece of literature; and there
is much in it that is painful, much that is even offensive, to
read. Yet it may be questioned whether, from any literary
point of view, one can wish that it had not been written.

In the first place, it tells us a great deal about the author's
literary, as well as even more about his personal, character;
and it explains to us at once how the strong pleasure which he
found in form and the strong constraint which it imposes were
needed to produce the perfection of his poetic style, and how
the volcanic quality of his genius forced even that constraint
to permit the variety, the pulse, the fluctuation, which made
English blank verse of the non-dramatic type.

In the second, it has given us passages—the longer of them
well known by quotation and selection, the shorter constantly,
as has been said, to be found in all the welter and confusion

of the mass—of extraordinary beauty, passages without which the crown of English prose writing would show miserable gaps and empty socket-holes.

In the third, it is the strongest possible historical document as to the necessity of an alteration—for a time, at any rate—in the dominant character of English prose style. In the other greatest pre-restoration prose writers—in Donne, in Taylor, in Browne—the solace is altogether above the sin. In Milton, it is not. Take them, and you may say "Well, under this dispensation, a great writer may slip, but look what he can do constantly without slipping!" Take Milton, and the most that can be said is "Such a writer could never have written so ill so often under the other dispensation; but, at any rate, there are some passages, and those very precious ones, which he would only have been likely to produce under this."

Glances have already been made, for special reasons, at some of Milton's Latin works, but, when they are taken as a whole, their interest is very considerable; and it is unfortunate —with a misfortune not likely now to be decreased—that few people know them at first hand. Here, also, there is no comparison between the verse and the prose—in fact, the latter is worse off even than its English companion. A Latin *Areopagitica* would have given opportunity for that stateliness, which is almost as characteristic of Milton's prose as of his verse, to show itself almost unhindered. There are flashes and glimmerings of it in the Latin pamphlets as it is. Even the dull and discreditable Billingsgate against Morus is relieved, so far as literary relief goes, by the passage on the consolations of Milton's blindness and by the encomia on Christina and on Cromwell. But these things are almost perforce drowned in matter of a very different quality. The most enthusiastic devotee of the classics, if he retains any critical faculty, must pronounce the usual controversial style, even of Greek, but, much more, of Latin, to be deplorable; and the comparatively few people who have studied technical classical rhetoric know why it was so. The whole thing was conducted on more or less cut-and-dried rules, which were only neglected—and that not always—by irrepressible genius like that of Demosthenes, or by eccentric individualities of late date like that of Lucian. With Lucian, Milton had nothing in common: with Demosthenes, he had something, but not enough for the purpose. His models were Latin; and not so much the terser and more austere phrases of Tacitus or the vivid cleverness of Sallust, as the academic and parliamentary volubility of Cicero, largely adulterated with the ditch water of many of the renascence Ciceronians. The consequence is that the compositions are merely large themes, patched together with commonplaces of the stalest kind. With a perfect command of such Latin as he chose to use, Milton rarely, if ever, lets himself go into a sublime or eloquent passage such as those which lighten the darkness of the English polemic. The inability to carry the actual argument into any equal court is the same, or greater; but the purple patches of declamation are rarely present. There is a good deal of bandying of authority and of wearisome rebutting on particular points. But, on the whole, the two sentences "Salmasius is an old fool" and "Morus is a rascally and vulgar libertine," represent the whole gist of the two *Defensiones* and their supplements, watered out into hundreds of pages, with floods of bad jokes, trivial minutiae and verbose vituperation.

The verse, for the most part, is free from this great drawback:[1] and, though it has something of the same quality of *pastiche*, stock diction is more tolerable in poetry than in prose. Moreover, these pieces have the distinction of belonging to a body of composition which was the favourite literary exercise of good wits, and was cultivated all over Europe for at least three centuries, if not more, besides that of being written by the greatest poet who ever indulged in this exercise. Many of them are only schoolboy or undergraduate taskwork; but some, even of these, especially that entitled *In quintum Novembris*, *Anno ætatis* 17, have interest; and three of the later, *Ad Patrem*, *Mansus*, a graceful tribute to his old Neapolitan friend, and *Epitaphium Damonis*, an elegy on the companion of his youth Charles Diodati, have much more. Perhaps the unusual opportunity of comparison with *Lycidas* has somewhat enhanced the appreciation with

---

[1] One or two epigrams on the abhorred Salmasius and Morus are not important enough to form substantial exceptions; indeed, a broad, but rather neat, Martialesque distich on Morus seems to be not Milton's at all, but some Dutchman's.

which *Epitaphium* has been sometimes received; and one may not be quite sure that, if we did not know that Diodati was really a friend, and King but an acquaintance, we could discover it from impartial reading of the poems. Perhaps, the extreme rarity of acquaintance with the voluminous *deliciae* of the sixteenth and seventeenth centuries has also enhanced opinion of this piece among those who are competent to read it, but do not know much of the *corpus* to which it belongs. But it certainly has both elegance and pathos.

What seems to have been Milton's last Latin[1] verse of importance, though it is not exactly a success in itself, has extraordinary, and generally overlooked, interest of form.[2] *Ad Joannem Rousium* is an attempt (explained carefully in scheme by Milton himself) at a Latin strophic ode, in which the most singular liberties are taken with the construction and correspondence of the lines and, indeed, with the whole arrangement. His explanation leaves us a good deal in the dark, and, whereas he says that he has "looked rather at a method of convenient *reading* than at one of *singing* on old modes" it seems more like a sort of musical chase of a chain of motives through variations of metre. But it is very valuable for purposes of comparison with the choruses of *Samson;* and it could hardly be more so as an indication of Milton's own interest in metrical experiment.

At this point, we may naturally pass to a general considera- tion of Milton's literary form, which, in his case, is almost more important than in that of any other very great English writer. In general style, Milton's peculiarity appears, as has been pointed out, so early as the poem *On the Morning of Christ's Nativity:* and it perseveres until *Samson.* Even the furious welter of the prose cannot prevent the calm and stately phraseology from emerging—at least occasionally— the mighty rhythm from subjugating the chaotic throng of words, now and then. In the verse, the phenomena go all the other way. It is only on the rarest occasions—when he attempts humour, or when he becomes simply didactic—that the style is other than consummate in its own way. To that

---

[1] He has left us a few Greek pieces of no value.

[2] There is a MS. copy of this in the Bodleian which has been sometimes thought to be autograph.

way, hardly more than one epithet of praise, in the wider and
higher range, can be denied. Milton's style is never exactly
natural; it never has even the quaint eccentric nature which
the conceit of the time sometimes takes on, as, for instance,
eminently in Browne. It is always confessed and almost
ostentatious art: art attained, to some extent, by definite
and obvious rhetorical devices, such as apposition; the old
Chaucerian posing of the substantive between two epithets
for the special purpose of drawing attention to some connection
or opposition between the two; the reversal of the order of
noun and adjective in the same line, or clause. In his poetry,
he particularly affects proper names of resonance and colour—
scattering them over his verse paragraphs with an effect that
is almost pyrotechnical.

But these verse paragraphs themselves are almost the
central secret and peculiarity of the Miltonic manner—serving
as a bridge between his style proper and his versification.
It is perfectly clear that he was dimly aiming at something
of the same kind in prose; and he sometimes came near it.
In verse, he attained it very early, and perfected it more and
more. The thing is not, of course, of his own invention:
it is an inspiration from drama and, especially, from the
soliloquies of Shakespeare. But non-dramatic blank verse
had been little practised by anyone, and the first and chief
example of it, Surrey's translation of the *Aeneid*, though
Vergil gives excellent opportunity, was not likely to arrive at
any such mastery. The early blank verse writer was too glad
to get safely to the end of his line to think about playing
tricks with that line, so as to put it in concatenation with
others. But the dramatist had to do this; and, in doing it,
he discovered—in Shakespeare's case perfectly, in others less
so—the various secrets of the mystery. And the average
dramatist had not only discovered them, but, about the time
when Milton entered upon serious verse writing, had begun
to abuse and degrade the art—making his lines battered de-
formities and his verse sentences ruinous heaps.

To Milton's sense of stately order, such things must have
been abhorrent; and his musical training, no doubt, strength-
ened his aversion. His first finished poems are in tight, not
loose, verse—the sonnet, the solemn stanzas of *On the Morning*

of Christ's Nativity, the easy, but fairly regular and uniform, as well as uncomplicated, sevens and eights of *L'Allegro* and its companion. When he makes a serious attempt with blank verse in *Comus*, there is even noticeable a tendency to fall back on the single-moulded line of Marlowe, accurately constructed in itself and correctly accumulated, but not jointed, and continued, and twined into a contrasted pattern of various but homogeneous design. Yet, even here, the power of his own genius for verse, and his matchless daring in experiment, introduced variety. And when, some twenty years after, he perhaps began, and some thirty years after definitely set to work on and completed, *Paradise Lost*, he had become an absolute master of the blank verse line, single and combined.

The exact principles of Miltonic versification, in the epics and *Samson*, have been matters of sharp controversy; and, in such a *History* as this, it is the duty of a writer to be an expositor and not an advocate. The various opinions on the subject may be reduced, with less violence than in some other cases, to the usual three. The older opinion—long considered the orthodox one and still held by some, though chiefly by foreign, critics—is that Milton's blank verse lines are strictly decasyllabic, apparent exceptions being due to actual elision or running together of syllables; and that, though it cannot be said that they are all strictly iambic or arranged in rising stress, variations from this are due only to wrenched accent, "impure" construction for the sake of preventing monotony and so forth. The opposite view is that Milton, not more from his study of the classics than from that of English poets and, especially, Shakespeare, was fully conversant with the practice, if not the theory, of substitution of equivalent feet—disyllabic or trisyllabic, trochee, spondee, dactyl, anapaest—for the iambic; and that he used this deliberately for the purpose of obtaining varied and concerted music. This opinion, which is that of the present writer, grew up slowly during the eighteenth century, but has been increasingly common in the nineteenth, though not often thoroughly worked out. Between the two, and held by some critics of great distinction, is a theory (or, perhaps, more than one) according to which Milton always intended the strict five-foot ten-syllabled line, but gave himself certain intricate dispensations, capable of being more or less rigidly systematised, by which a larger number of syllables than ten could be written in the line; could (in some cases, though not in all) be actually pronounced in it; but could be metrically elided. To put the thing, per- haps, more intelligibly by examples: according to theory (i) "ominous," when the *i* makes an eleventh syllable, and "the Eternal," when *the* is in the same case, should be pronounced "om'nous" and "th' Eternal" and, in at least the latter case, printed so. According to (ii) "ominous" and "the Eternal" should be written in full, pronounced in full, and reckoned metrically as trisyllabic feet, or (in another notation) as combinations of two unaccented syllables and one accented. According to (iii) they should be written and pronounced in full, but the *i* and the first *e* should be regarded as metrically "vanished."

Putting aside this capital point, on which the student must make up his mind after full consideration of the subject, there are not a few lines of Milton where unusual combinations of foot or arrangements of stress give rise to difficulty. On another great general feature, there is not, nor can there be, any difference of opinion as to fact; and this is that Milton pays no attention to the supposed necessity, or, at least, propriety, of putting a pause near the middle of the line, and that his freedom of handling here is vital to his versification. On the propriety, as distinguished from the fact, of the varia- tion, such unanimity has not prevailed. The more rigid eighteenth century critics regarded the central or centripetal pause as an absolute law, the breach of which was to be justified by no success of result. Johnson was not quite so strait-laced as this; but as, with him, regularity of corre- spondence was the main article of poetry, he objected to such confusions of "the methods of the poet and the declaimer"; and, consistently enough, disliked blank verse altogether. It is, at any rate, certain, that it is by variety of line material (attained by whatever means), and by further variation of pause, that Milton achieves the extraordinary freedom from monotony, and the force of character, which distinguish his verse. And it has been recognised, with increasing decision, that he does not employ these means in a fashion merely con- tinuous or strung together, that his verse construction is really periodic or paragraphic—the sections corresponding in division of sense and substance, as it were, to long but unequal stanzas or strophes of verses identical at first sight, but individually variable.

If the reader will compare the sketches of the progress of English prosody given at intervals in this *History;* if he will remember that Milton was a careful scholar and a fluent writer of Latin verse; and if he will pay particular attention to the Rous ode in Latin, and to *Samson* in English—he will not have much difficulty in appreciating the position of the poet in regard to quality of versification. So far as Milton's historical position is concerned, he is almost the central figure in the whole history of our verse. Brought into definite form as that verse had been, after two centuries of experiment, by Chaucer; restored and reformed, after nearly two more of disarray, by Spenser; enormously varied and advanced by Shakespeare and the later Elizabethans—Milton found it liable to fresh disorders. He did not so much directly attack these as elaborate, for non-dramatic poetry, a medium practically involving all the order and all the freedom possible in English verse—yet without rime. And, in *Samson*, he returned to rime itself in choruses, though not universally or regularly, but, rather, with an extension of the occasional use which he had tried in *Lycidas*.

In the larger sense of style, Milton holds so great a place that we may almost let the arrangement of this chapter pass here into a conclusion-summary. He is, admittedly, in the least disputed sense of that much debated term, "the grand style," the grandest-styled of English poets. He never, indeed, attains to the absolute zenith of expression—as does Shakespeare often and, perhaps, Dante sometimes. He is, unlike them, strangely unmodern; he has, indeed, it has been quite correctly said, little even of the renascence about him, except those tricks and fashions of form which have been noticed. Biblical, classical and medieval influences almost alone work on him—especially the former two. Under their joint pressure, he has elaborated a manner so all-pervading, that, if it were not also great, it might, or must, be called a mannerism. But it is always a mannerism of grandeur and never —this is another of the points in which Milton is unique—one of grandiosity. It does break down sometimes, though rarely, when he attempts humour; when he lets himself prose, and so forth; but, even then, it does not become grandiose, still less bombastic: it is merely flat and dull or, sometimes, grotesque. Almost everywhere, the magnificent state and ceremony covers and carries off the occasion, the subject, resistlessly.

This manner has some modes and phases which are worth particularising, especially in the attempt to complete the presentation in little of the work and figure of so great a poet. One of the most remarkable of these is the famous "Miltonic vague"—the preference of vast but rather indeterminate pictures, tinted with a sort of dim gorgeousness or luridity, as the case may be—to sharper outlines and more definite colours. Another—as it may seem in a different sphere of thought—is the peculiar moral atmosphere of a kind of magnanimous *intransigeance* which pervades the whole. The common saying that "Satan is the hero of *Paradise Lost*" is merely a way of expressing this wider truth to the vulgar mind. It is not at all probable that Milton meant anything of the kind; according to "the rules," a hero ought to be victorious, and Satan's victory is exceedingly Pyrrhic; according to "the rules," he ought to be good, if not faultless, and certainly Milton did not think Satan good. But he has made Satan the most interesting person, and his unflinching nonconformity the most interesting thing, in the poem. In *Paradise Regained*, he enjoys a double presentation of this kind—the persistence of Satan, unconquered by past or future certainty of defeat, and the resistance of Christ, to which Milton's semi-Arian views must, as has been said, have given a peculiar interest. As regards *Agonistes*, the other common saying, that "Samson is Milton," contains the general truth again. Samson is incarnate resistance; he has resisted grace and the Philistines alike, in the past; his repentance and atonement consist in resisting his father, the chorus, Harapha, the officer, the lords, Dalila, everybody; and his final simulated compliance is only to obtain the means of making this resistance triumph. Even some forty years earlier, the centre of *Comus* is the invincible resolution of the Lady; and the real inspiration of *Lycidas*, apart from the poetry, is the defiant denunciation— utterly different from the parallel and, no doubt, suggesting passage in Dante—of St. Peter. Now this pervading irreconcilableness, wherein Milton and Dante, to some extent, come together again, can only be made poetical by a style of severe splendour; and it meets this eminently in both, but more exclusively and restrictively in Milton.

It is almost a necessary consequence of this peculiar kind of magnificence that Milton has always been more admired and written about than loved and read, except in his earlier and smaller poems. Some have been bold enough to say that even *Il Penseroso* is generally known only in a few passages of its brightest purple; and the extraordinary beauty of the latter part of *Comus* has not prevented persons who united cultivation with frankness from pronouncing it heavy. That this is unfortunate need hardly be said. To begin with, it is a loss, to him who does not read it, of some of the greatest poetry in the world—of poetry which scarcely ever declines below a level that most poets scarcely ever reach. But the loss is greater than this. Careless folk are sometimes found who decry the historic estimate altogether, and who maintain that a minor poet of the twentieth century is better worth reading than a minor poet of the thirteenth, though the later, for the most part, is simply a hand at the machine which the earlier had helped to construct. But Milton is not a minor poet, and his influence is omnipresent in almost all later English poetry, and in not a little of later prose English literature. At first, at second, at third, hand, he has permeated almost all his successors. Without Milton, you cannot understand, in the real sense of understanding, writers so different as Landor and Tennyson, as Thomson and Wordsworth. He might walk through English letters and, like the unwelcome apparition in one of Dickens's shorter stories, ejaculate "Mine!" as he laid his hand on rhythm after rhythm, phrase after phrase, design after design, in poetical arrangement. Although there was some plagiarism, even from his early poems, by men like Baron and Benlowes, he was not much followed immediately; but, as usual, the long germinating seed took the deeper and wider hold, and bore the most abun-dant and perennial crops. In particular, he, with Shakespeare, maintained the citadel of true English prosody through all the deviations and shortcomings of the eighteenth century.

With whatever allowance, in however grudging a manner, the greatness of these two was always allowed, and could be taken as pattern when the time came.

But this reflected and incidental glory, of course, is not the whole, or, with most people, the main, glory of Milton. His praises have been the theme of many excellent discourses; and it is quite superfluous, especially in such a place as this, to be rhetorical in regard to him. But the indication—if only the reindication—of the special quality and quiddity of writers great and small cannot be superfluous in a history of literature.

Although Dryden was merely repeating the common criticism on Homer and Vergil in ascribing "loftiness of mind" to the first and "majesty" to the second, and although his claim for a combination of the two in Milton is a sufficiently obvious figure of rhetoric, yet there was more of his own great critical genius in the hyperbole. One would, perhaps, rather choose "variety" and "nature" for Homer, "grace" and "perfection of art" for Vergil. But "loftiness of mind" and "majesty" (of expression, which, no doubt, was understood) remain true and keep their combination in regard to Milton. Great variety he has not; in his longer and later poems certainly not; while the contrast of later and earlier only supplies it to a limited extent. Although he is never unnatural, nature is never the first thing that suggests itself in him; and, though he is never (except in the rare instances often referred to) ungraceful, yet grace is too delicate a thing to be attributed to his work, at least after *Comus*. But in loftiness—sublimity— of thought and majesty of expression, both sustained at almost superhuman pitch, he has no superior, and no rival except Dante. That, despite this, he has had few admirers out of England and those few (like Scherer for instance) for more or less special reasons, is not surprising. For, in order to appreciate Milton, it is necessary to know the English language not merely, as has sometimes been said, with more than usual acquired scholarship, but thoroughly, and with a native intimacy. His subjects may attract or repel; his temper may be repellent and can hardly be very attractive, though it may have its admirers. But the magnificence of his poetical command of the language in which he writes has only to be perceived in order to carry all before it.

APPENDIX TO CHAPTER V

A CONSPECTUS OF MILTON'S PROSE WORKS, WITH A NOTE ON THE TEXT OF THE POEMS

It has been thought that, considering the number of these prose works, and the fact that there are very few modern editions of them, something more than merely bibliographical notice and the critical remarks in the text should be supplied.

1641. Of Reformation touching Church-Discipline in England. (English.)

Generally against Episcopacy: monarchy not attacked, although some stress is laid on the liberty of the subject. No small part occupied by instances of bishops being troublesome to rulers.

Of Prelatical Episcopacy. (English.)

Against the patristic arguments for it; "James Archbishop of Armagh" (Ussher) being expressly cited in the title, but not definitely named or very specially attacked in the text.

Animadversions upon the Remonstrant's defence against Smectymnuus. (English.)

Milton's temper here "gets ruffled by fighting," and the tract (in form of dialogue between the Remonstrant [Bishop Hall] and an Answerer) is, on the Answerer's side, entirely written in a savage and jeering tone. Not completely intelligible without the previous documents in the Smectymnuus controversy.

The Reason of Church-Government urg'd against Prelaty. (English.)

The argument against Episcopacy continued, chiefly on Biblical grounds. Tone more personal; "bishop Andrews" and "the primate of Armagh" named and both of them roughly handled; Milton's peculiar form of dialectic sarcasm here appearing, with invective against some of his poetic contemporaries and exaltation of his own studies and purposes.

1642. An Apology against a Pamphlet call'd a Modest Confutation of the Animadversions of the Remonstrant against Smectymnuus. (English.)

Begins with something in the more good-natured sense of its title, but quickly turns to an attack on Hall more violent than the former, diversified by fierce vindications of Milton himself, and bitter criticisms of the bishop's earlier literary work.

(Of Education, 1644, and Areopagitica, same year, are generally accessible, and are discussed in the text. They are in a more dignified tone of controversy, and are mentioned here in anticipation of their strict chronological order.)

1643–4. The Doctrine and Discipline of Divorce. (English.)

The first of the Divorce Tracts. Deals with the subject from various points of view, and is written with evidently restrained passion, but without avowing a personal interest.

1644. The Judgement of Martin Bucer concerning Divorce. (English.)

A sort of appendix to Doctrine and Discipline. Milton here sometimes translates bodily, and sometimes summarises his author, of whose agreement with his own views he represents himself as having been ignorant when he wrote the larger tract.

1644–5. Tetrachordon. (English.)

This, more widely known from the sonnet upon it than in itself, is the third divorce pamphlet and deals (whence its name) with four passages or batches of passages from Genesis, Deuteronomy, the Gospel of St. Matthew and the First Epistle to the Corinthians.

1645. Colasterion. (English.)

The fourth and last piece on divorce, replying, touchily and with much abuse, to a critic of Doctrine and Discipline.

1649. The Tenure of Kings and Magistrates. (English.)

Milton's first defence (though begun before the event) of the execution of Charles I. Being addressed to those members of the parliamentary and presbyterian party who had stopped short of regicide, it is, with a few outbreaks, for the most part written civilly and in a tone of sober argument.

Observations upon the Articles of Peace with the Irish Rebels. (English.)

The articles themselves and some documents appurtenant are first printed. Milton's comment is not long; and, like The Tenure, seems to have been written with some self-restraint, which, however, breaks down with relatively greater frequency than in the earlier piece.

Eikonoklastes. (English.)

In this reply to Eikon Basilike (the effect of which was greatly disturbing the regicides) a very few lines at the beginning seem to promise a continuance of the comparative moderation of the two previous pamphlets. But this is soon dropped, and every opportunity is taken of invective and innuendo furnished by a continuous analysis of Eikon, from the king's reading of Shakespeare and Sidney, through his political conduct, to his affection for his wife, and the ill-hap of his grandmother; from his "writing Oglio for Olla" to his repentance for the death of Strafford. Except in the preface, this line of bit-by-bit comment with hostile discussion is preserved throughout: there is no summary or peroration. As to Eikon Basilike, see *post*, Chap. VI.

(It is supposed that, during 1651, Milton may have written some articles for the Mercurius Politicus which he apparently censured; but they have never been authoritatively identified. See *post*, Chap. xv.)

1651. Pro Populo Anglicano Defensio. (Latin.) On this and the next three or four items, see text.

1654. Defensio Secunda. (Latin.) Followed by Pro se Defensio, 1655, and a Supplementum.

1658–9. A Treatise on Civil Power in Ecclesiastical Causes. (English.)

1659. Considerations touching the likeliest means to remove hirelings out of the Church. (English.)

A Letter to a Friend concerning the Ruptures of the Commonwealth. (English.)

1660. The Ready and Easy Way to Establish a Free Commonwealth. (English.)

Preceded by a letter on the same subject to Monck, and in the later printed form acknowledging that "since the writing . . . the face of things hath had some change." Argument against monarchy, with a good deal about the Areopagus and the Ephors.

1660. Brief Notes upon a late Sermon . . . by Matthew Griffith. (English.)

Opens with a reference to the last-named piece, and comments on the text in the style (a little softened) of the Answer to the Remonstrant and the Eikonoklastes.

1670. Written at uncertain dates.

The History of Britain. History of Moscovia. Both English; see text.

1673. Of True Religion, etc. against the growth of Popery. (English.)

Very brief and rather ambiguous in its attitude to "toleration." "Popery . . . is not to be tolerated in public or private." But, later, it seems that Papists may write "at least in Latin."

1674. Letters Patents of the Election of this present King of Poland, John the third. (Translated from Latin.)

1649-59. Letters of State. (Latin.) Published 1694.

1655. A Manifesto of the Lord Protector. (Latin.)

1625-66. Familiar Epistles (published 1674), including Milton's college Prolusiones. (Latin.)

(Posthumous.) De Doctrina Christiana. (Latin.)

Further light was thrown on the curious history of this after Sumner's publication of it (see *post* and *ante*) by Smith's Letters of Pepys, David Skinner, the depositary who handed over the MS. to Williamson, having been one of the diarist's numerous clients.

Besides these, Milton made collections, utilised by Phillips, for a Latin dictionary. He also issued the following compilations:

1669. Accedence commenc't Grammar (English, but on Latin, not English, grammar).

1672. Artis Logicæ Plenior Institutio. (Latin, and based on Ramus.)

With regard to the text of the poems, it may be useful to enumerate the sources. The whole (except the four sonnets to Fairfax, Cromwell, Vane and Cyriack Skinner (2), which were kept back for political reasons) was printed in Milton's lifetime; but the vast majority of the verses did not appear till after his blindness and, therefore, cannot possibly have been corrected by his own hand. For, however carefully he may have had read to him his dictated matter, the fair copies of it and the proofs, is it reasonably possible that every word can have been spelt to him at length and his alterations (if any) automatically and infallibly recorded? The importance, therefore, which was attached to the censor's copy (see *ante*) of Paradise Lost, Bk. 1, recently sold by descendants of Tonson, could be hardly more than an importance of curiosity.

On the other hand, the Cambridge MS., already referred to, is of the highest possible interest: for, with very few exceptions (and those almost entirely subsequent to the blindness), it is in Milton's own hand. There are also large corrections in that hand: so that, altogether, it is invaluable—not least so in regard to questions of versification and spelling. It gives us the whole of Arcades, Comus and Lycidas; all the sonnets except four (the "O Nightingale," "On the late

Massacher in Piemont," "When I consider" and the one to Lawrence), one or two minor things and the valuable notes of early planned or suggested subjects, to which reference has been made above. This is, practically, the only document of the kind that we have for the text of a very great English poet before the eighteenth century; and it can hardly be prized too highly.

Perhaps it should be added that, in some editions, translations, not Milton's own, of scraps of Latin verse in the pamphlets have been included without warning.

CHAPTER VI

Caroline Divines

IN the earlier years of Charles I, when, according to the view of intelligent contemporaries, there was the rare and happy union of *imperium* and *libertas* and few perceived the approach of the troubles which should lead to civil war, the English interest in preaching was, perhaps, at its greatest. The stormiest controversies of the reformation seemed, for a time, to have spent themselves. The church of England was in settled possession, with a king who was her devoted son. The wide interests of the Elizabethan age, which inspired theologians as well as men of affairs, had tuned the pulpits to themes of universal concern. As men thought and wrote, so men preached, of matters beyond the ken of the cloister; and the massive dignity of their fathers' prose was reflected from the lips and the pens of those who were set to give God's message to men. Nothing is more remarkable in an age of fading literary excellence than the way in which the thoughts and methods of the great poets and prose writers of the preceding generation were taken up and handled by the clergy of the national church. The earlier age of the Caroline divines was especially an age of great preachers.

For the most part, this development was confined to the church of England. Roman Catholics, obscure when they were not persecuted, did not seriously affect the national literature. Their training as theologians was exclusive and foreign. They did not write English very easily; and what they wrote had not a large audience. Roman Catholic writers, where they had influence at all, influenced English authors directly, as the Spanish school influenced Crashaw and Vaughan. In every sense, their English writings were exotic.

But, apart though this influence stands, it has not a little interest and charm, as may be seen in *Sancta Sophia, or Holy Wisdom . . . extracted out of more than forty Treatises written by the Venerable Father Augustin Baker* by Father Cressy, first published in 1657. Augustin Baker was a Welshman, who was taught at Christ's hospital and at Broadgates hall in Oxford and who, after a few years in practice as a country lawyer, became a Roman Catholic and, at the age of thirty-one, a Benedictine. In England and while he was at Cambridge, he wrote a number of ascetic treatises which, after his death, the more famous Father Cressy (an Englishman, and, at one time, chaplain to Falkland) collected and "extracted" into a devotional treatise of much beauty, to which he gave the name *Sancta Sophia*, a study of contemplation and prayer. The style is involved, and yet it is not cumbrous. There is a certain exactness, as it were of legalism, which affects the language with an obvious restraint. But, on the other hand, there are felicities of thought, and, more rarely, of expression, which give the book a definite place in the literature of devotion. Yet it is only necessary to compare it with the *Meditations* of Traherne to see how much the wider outlook of the English churchman has affected the literary expression given to thoughts that were common to meditative souls. The matter of *Sancta Sophia* is an instruction in the method of meditation, or the prayer of contemplation, owing a good deal to foreign mystics, whether orthodox like Saint Teresa or quietist, and, by a systematic rule, proceeding at last

unto the top of the mountain, where God is seen: a mountain, to us that stand below, environed with clouds and darkness, but to them who have their dwelling there it is peace and serenity and light. It is an intellectual heaven, where there is no sun nor moon, but God and the Lamb are the light of it.

The nearest parallel, in the English literature of the time, to the *Sancta Sophia* of Baker is the *Centuries of Meditations* of Thomas Traherne;[1] yet Traherne, above all things, is an Anglican. His residence at the university in times of puritan dominance did not give him any tincture of Calvinism. He

[1] See *ante*, pp. 48–51.

set himself to supply a private friend (as it appears) with thoughts for divine contemplation, in his *Centuries of Meditations*, a book which had the strange fortune to remain in manuscript for nearly two hundred and fifty years. What strikes the reader most, after the spiritual intensity of this remarkable volume, is the wide scope of the writer's survey. All heaven and earth he takes for the province of the pious soul, and the breadth of his conception of true religion is reflected in the richness of his style. From a book long undiscovered and still little known, it may be well to quote a passage which illustrates the freedom of the Anglican school to which Traherne belonged no less than the characteristic manner of his own English writing.

You never [he says] enjoy the world aright. . . . Till you can sing and rejoice and delight in God, as misers do in gold, and kings in sceptres, you never enjoy the world. Till your spirit filleth the whole world, and the stars are your jewels: till you are as familiar with the ways of God in all ages as with your walk and table: till you are intimately acquainted with that shady nothing out of which the world was made: till you love men so as to desire their happiness with a thirst equal to the zeal of your own: till you delight in God for being good to all: you never enjoy the world. Till you more feel it than your private estate, and are more present in the hemisphere, considering the glories and the beauties there, than in your own house: till you remember how lately you were made, and how wonderful it was when you came into it: and more rejoice in the palace of your glory, than if it had been made but to-day morning.

Fancy and insight are the masters of Traherne's imagination. From a well-stored mind, and an experience of men and things beyond that of his cloistered contemporaries, and equally remote from the jarring contentions of school and camp, from controversies about predestination or militia, he looks upon the hidden things of the soul, and, in them, he sees the image of the glory and love of God. The style is that of a poet who is also a master of prose; and there is no monotony in the richness of meditation after meditation on the eternal theme of the goodness and the splendour of God. Traherne is markedly the product of his age, in its ardour of expansion. He rivals Jeremy Taylor in richness of imagery, but has not Taylor's learning. He even suggests the style of the poet of two centuries later who brought into his prose the ardour of his poetry, Algernon Charles Swinburne.

Baker and Traherne may be compared, but, perhaps, as obviously contrasted. Another contrast is equally significant of the interests of the age of Charles I. If Roman Catholics lived and wrote apart from the general life of the nation, no one could say that this was true of the greater part of that large and ill-defined class to which the name of puritan was given. The secrecy of Martin Marprelate was a thing of the past, and, with it, for the most part, its scurrility and vulgarity. But there were puritans and puritans. The puritan literature of the earlier years of Charles I ranged, even in its theological aspect, from the solemn and pedantic extravagance of Prynne (notably in *Histriomastix*, 1632)[1] through ponderous verbiage with an occasional touch of humour, like *The Dipper Dipt, or the Anabaptist Duck't and Plung'd over Head and Ears in a Disputation by Daniel Featley, D.D.* (1645), to the rough force of Burton and Bastwick, and the mere ribaldry of the verses and fly-sheets against prelacy such as *Rot amongst the Bishops* and *Rome for Canterbury or a true relation of the Birth and Life of William Laud* (1641). And, when this is said, there is still omitted the solemn dignity of sermons like those of Stephen Marshall (printed in *A Brief Vindication of Mr. Stephen Marshal* by Giles Firmin, 1681) and the impressive mass of the whole literature produced by Richard Baxter.

To epitomise Baxter would be impossible—it was attempted for one of his works by Edmund Calamy: almost equally impossible is it to characterise in brief an author so stupendously prolific. *Reliquiae Baxterianae* is a storehouse of information for the religious and social history of the time, and it bears throughout the impress of the writer's energetic, restless and masterful mind. He describes the puritanism of his youth, exemplified in his own father, as not nonconformist but set in contrast to the loose living and laxity of the village where, on Sundays,

the reader read the Common Prayer briefly, and the rest of the day,

[1] See *ante*, Vol. VI, Chap. XIV.

even till dark night almost, except eating-time, was spent in dancing under a May-pole and a great tree, not far from my father's door, where all the town met together;

and his father, who "never scrupled the Common Prayer," was yet called puritan because he read the Scripture when the rest were dancing, and quoted it, too, to the reproof of the drunkards and profane. The clergy seemed to him lax, and, when one parish priest, being old, said the prayers by heart and got two working men to read the lessons, this employment of the laity was resented by the scrupulous young man, himself the son of a freeholder. He grew up with little education save what his own perseverance won, but with knowledge of life in the country and at court, eventually becoming a schoolmaster. He was ordained by bishop Thornborough of Worcester in 1638. Gradually, he adopted views of semi-conformity; there were things the church allowed which he could not approve. When he came to minister at Bridgnorth, he would not make the sign of the cross in baptism or wear a surplice. Thence, he went to Kidderminster, and, when the war broke out, he held, at different times, different posts of chaplain in the parliamentary forces. He came to deplore the growth of sectarianism; he worked as a pastor again at Kidderminster; he passed much time in country retirement, writing the book which made him famous. At the restoration, he was first offered a bishopric and, twenty years later, he was put in prison;[1] and he lived to see the revolution settlement. This varied life coloured the writing of one whose senses were peculiarly acute and whose sympathies were wider than his intellectual outlook. "I was but a pen," he said of himself, "and what praise is due to a pen?" He felt, indeed, of himself, what Shakespeare's editors thought was characteristic of their hero's work. Most probably, in all his voluminous writings, he never blotted a line. His style was himself. He wrote simply and naturally, with a choice of good phrases, sound words, straightforward constructions, as a man speaks who is well educated but not a pedant. It is this which makes *The Saints' Everlasting Rest* (1649/50) an English classic.

---

[1] He was in prison for a short time, illegally, in 1665, and, again, for a year and a half in 1685.

That book, which we all call immortal, though it is gradually sinking into the limbo whither much of seventeenth century prose, for all save scholars, has gone before, is, in many respects, "modern" in tone; and yet it is not so modern as Jeremy Taylor, because it has, or seems to have, much less art, as it certainly has much less glow. It is serious and direct; it is eloquent, after a simple, godly and appealing sort. Yet, after all, it is the matter not the manner which gives the book its place in English literature. There is no special thing in which you can say that Baxter influenced other writers; there is no individual influence on himself which you can trace from writers who preceded him. He would not have written as he did if Hooker had not written before him; but, then, that is true of the whole succession of post-Elizabethan prose.

Baxter's fame rests on other and better work than that of the pulpit; but it must not be thought that the influence of the preacher had ceased. It had its fluctuations, but it was still important so long as Charles I was on the throne. While sermons still stood midway between the learned world and the mob, and it was hoped that what suited the one would attract, instruct, or even amaze, the other into goodness and obedience to the ordered system of the national church, the pulpit in St. Paul's churchyard managed to hold something of its old position. "In an age when men read few books and had no newspapers, the sermon at Paul's cross or the Spital was the most exciting event of the week."[1] Times were changing: books were multiplied, there was a large manufacture of pamphlets to catch the popular ear and newspapers were just beginning, with a supply of suitable, selected or invented facts; but the sermon, spoken not read, died hard, and there was always an audience till men began to turn their ploughshares into swords. At Paul's cross, Laud preached on the anniversary of Charles's coronation; in 1640, Hammond delivered the striking discourse which he called *The Poor Man's Tithing;* in 1641, Frank preached a famous sermon on obedience. This last marked the beginning of the end. When bishops had suffered "the tumults about their houses and the riots upon their persons" and the "whole clergy" met with "daily insolences in your streets," the open pulpit had ceased to influence, it rather accepted the violence which it should have set itself to redress, and free speech was replaced by what the Londoners loved to hear. Paul's cross ceased to give Englishmen literature when they wanted only polemics. In May, 1643, the cross was torn down by the mob. A notable sermon by Steward, who was nominated dean in 1641, was among the last that was preached there. It was a denunciation of that Christianity which was of the lip not of the life, which kept plantations for criminals and did nothing to spread the gospel beyond the seas; when usury flourished (familiar lament) in spite of the banishment of Jews, when men might say "those words of Aeschines, εἰς παραδοξίαν ἔφυμεν, we are born the Paradox and Riddle of our times, a Reformed Church without a Reformation." Over against preachers such as these should be placed notable puritans such as Stephen Marshall, whose noble funeral eulogy of Pym is worthy to be placed high in the prose of his age.

Not all the preachers were theologians or men of letters; but few Caroline theologians were not famous preachers, and many men of letters were found among the ministers and preachers of the church. To these we may now pass. Henry Hammond, who has been called "the father of English Biblical criticism," is now chiefly remembered by Keble's beautiful eulogy; but, in his own time, no man had a more beneficent influence on the religious literature of the age. His own works were voluminous: his *Paraphrase and Annotations on the New Testament* (1653) was an achievement in English theological scholarship; his *Practical Catechism* (1644) occupies a position to some extent between the *Devotions* of Cosin and of Lewes Baily (*The Practice of Piety*, dedicated to Charles I when prince of Wales), and *The Whole Duty of Man*, with the origin of which he was undoubtedly acquainted. But the most valuable of all his work, as literature, are his sermons, models of the best Caroline prose in its simplicity, restraint, clarity, distinction. In his absence of conceits, he shows himself typically a Caroline rather than an Elizabethan. In his avoidance of anything approaching rhetorical adornment, he forms a marked contrast to the school in which we may place the gloomy splendour of Donne and the oriental exuberance of Jeremy Taylor. To write of charity, patience, toleration, befits him better than any other man of his age; and, when theologians and statesmen were wrangling over the limits of the church and the rights or wrongs of the individual in religion, his was almost the first, and certainly the clearest, voice to be lifted up in assertion of toleration as a plain Christian duty and in denunciation of the persecuting spirit as an enemy to religion and truth.

Parallel to Hammond's influence is that of another eminent theologian who was never a party man. James Ussher stands somewhat apart in principles from the dominant school of his time. He was an Irishman, a distinguished son of the great Irish university. In his own family, he had closer acquaintance with Roman Catholicism than had his English contemporaries, and the Calvinism of Dublin was much more definitely puritan than that of Oxford or Cambridge. His experience, as learner, as divinity professor, as bishop, was almost wholly Irish. Yet he, too, fell under the influence of Laud, was his constant correspondent for twelve years, was active in winning for him the chancellorship of Trinity college, Dublin, and shared his aims of anti-Roman defence and traditional reverence for Catholic antiquity. It was he who most boldly advised Charles not to consent to Strafford's execution and reproached him for yielding. Yet Cromwell ordered him a public funeral. "Learned to a miracle," as Selden calls him, Ussher, perhaps, was the last of the Calvinists in high place. His influence was very great, and it was all exercised in favour of peace and charity. Of his sermons, it was as true as of his personal influence that "he had a way of gaining people's hearts and touching their consciences that look'd like somewhat of the Apostolical age reviv'd." He was a voluminous writer, learned and exact; in manner an Elizabethan, who did not mark any important step in English letters. His contributions were to learning rather than to literature. Men used his information and incorporated it in their own works, but they did not copy his style; and it is significant, perhaps, that, while his contributions to historical study, in regard to subjects so different as the Ignatian letters and the early history of Ireland, have never lost their value, the only book of his which can reasonably be described as popular was *A Body of*

Divinitie (1645), which was little else but a commonplace
book that by no means always represented his own opinions.
The prominent place which Ussher's name occupies in contemporary accounts of the literature of the seventeenth
century is a proof, if one were needed, how much more influential, at the period of crisis which led to the civil war, were
personal than literary influences. Learning pursued its way
and scholars paid attention to it and, after their manner,
unduly exalted its achievements. Men who had won the
public ear kept it even when they had ceased very definitely
to teach their age. The "gentle soul" of Ussher made men
love him and attach more importance to his writings than they
deserved: such may well be the view of posterity, and it would
not be wholly unfair.

Robert Sanderson, who lived to become a bishop at the
restoration, and is embalmed in the exquisite prose of Izaak
Walton, was another of the Elizabethans who made the church
of England notable for its preaching power. The famous saying of Charles I is, perhaps, his chief title to distinction:
"I carry my ears to hear other preachers, but I carry my
conscience to hear Dr. Sanderson;" and, with it, Walton's
inimitable description of the talk "in a corner under a pent
house" till the rain forced them "into a cleanly house," where
they spoke "to my great comfort and advantage." Both show
him a man of wisdom and piety, "his learning methodical
and exact, his wisdom useful, his integrity visible." The
sermons are plain sober things, with "no improper rhetoric,"
indeed, as Walton notes, nor much of the fire which belongs
to the earlier masters of his school: didactic, mildly argumen-
tative, modestly learned, whether *ad aulam* (preached at
court), or *ad clerum*, or *ad populum*. The last-named were
preached some thirty years before the others, and they show
how consistent were his position and method. He wrote clearly
and without affectation; but he does not rank high among the
prose writers of his time. He was at his best in the revision of
The Book of Common Prayer, where the General Thanksgiving
(perhaps erroneously) had been ascribed to him, and for which
he certainly wrote the admirable preface which begins "It hath
been the wisdom of the Church." It is significant, perhaps,
that he wrote as easily and simply in Latin as in English.

Next to Sanderson may very fitly be named "his dear old friend Dr. Sheldon," one of those capable and strenuous men of business who, from time to time, have seemed marked out early in life—as Clarendon tells us was said of him—for the primacy of all England. No man was more bitterly criticised during the later years of his life than he, for he was a masterful exponent of the Clarendon policy. His literary remains, which are almost exclusively letters, still rest, for the most part in manuscript, in the Bodleian library; they are thoroughly in keeping, as regards manner and style, with the acute sobriety of his character, and a most valuable volume might be compiled from them. His only printed work is a sermon preached before Charles II just after the restoration, markedly in the style of Laud.

It is more than literature that links the names of Laud, Sanderson and Sheldon. The latter, who, early in life, had opposed the great archbishop in some of his university reforms and had been prominent, for example, in resisting the appointment of Jeremy Taylor to an Oxford fellowship, lived not only to carry on with a certain rigid determination the policy of the earlier primate but to assist in the preservation and publication of the memorials of his life. The association had been earlier, and in friendliness: for both Laud and Sheldon were concerned in the conversion from Roman Catholicism of the most conspicuous controversialist of the age of Charles I. This was William Chillingworth, who was an Oxford citizen, Laud's godson, a scholar of Trinity, a logician and disputant, a friend of the brilliant company which gathered at Great Tew. In an immortal passage, Clarendon has described the wits and theologians who were intimate with the fascinating Lucius Cary, Viscount Falkland. In his Oxfordshire house, he loved to consort with scholars of Oxford, he who had been the disciple of the last poets of the Elizabethan age, had himself written pretty verses and, perhaps, more than dabbled in acute theological difficulties. His mother Elizabeth (Tanfield) became a Roman Catholic, and it was in her house that Lucius met Chillingworth, when he, too, in search of an infallible guide, had abandoned his protestantism. Their talk, there is evidence to show, was often of Socinus and his rationalistic treatment of theology, and theological interests became more and more supreme in Falkland's mind. "His whole conversation," says Clarendon, "was one continued *convivium philosophicum* or *convivium theologicum*"; and the literary result was his *Discourse of Infallibility*, published after the restoration, in 1660. The literary coterie at Great Tew did not entirely abandon poetry: there was also, indeed, as of old in London, the "session of the Poets." But the main interests were theological. Lettice, lord Falkland's wife, was a typical product of the religious revival associated with Charles I's days. Her *Life* by her chaplain Duncon, one of the most interesting biographies of the time, shows her exact and scrupulous in all the devotional rules of the church; yet, in her religious, almost ascetic, household, the widest speculation was allowed her thoughtful and impressionable husband. There were Morley and Hammond; the former afterwards a notable bishop, the latter a preacher and devotional writer of singular charm and sweetness; Earle, author of *Microcosmographie*, who said that he "got more useful learning by his conversation at Tew than he had at Oxford"; Sheldon, Hales and Chillingworth. It is not unnatural to suppose that the foundations of *The Religion of Protestants* were laid at Great Tew: Falkland's book shows indebtedness to the same thoughts of rational disbelief in papal infallibility.

The Religion of Protestants a safe way to Salvation; or an Answer to a book Entituled Mercy and Truth or Charity Main.tained by Catholiques; which pretends to prove the contrary (1637) was the summing up of a long controversy which was begun as early as 1630 by a Jesuit named Edward Knott. It is hampered by a minute and complicated method, now of defence now of attack; but, out of pages of singularly complicated and involved discussion, there emerges a most clear and dogmatic assertion. Chillingworth's religion is to be found only in the Bible, insomuch that he will have no anathemas that he cannot find there; and his

desire is to go the right way to eternal happiness; but whether this way lie on the right hand, or on the left, or straightforward; whether it be by following a living guide, or by seeking my direction in a book, or by hearkening to the secret whisper of some private spirit, to me is indifferent.

A "safe way to Salvation" was to be found in free enquiry. The literary merit of Chillingworth, popular though his work became, is not conspicuous: his style is that of the sledge-hammer, dealing repeated blows. The arrangement of the book depends upon that which it is its aim to attack; we have to wait some time before the author emerges from the clouds that beset him; but, when his own thought comes directly before the reader it is conspicuously clear, and it is expressed very directly, in simple and forcible English, with a limited vocabulary but with trenchant emphasis. He is logical and he is tolerant, and there is in him, at his best, a remarkable breadth of charity. He cries for liberty, liberty which the times denied him and the search for which the puritan persecutor of his deathbed regarded as blasphemous: yet he is content to abide within the English fold and to ratify its apostolic claim. And all this comes out in clear-cut sentences, which men did not readily forget.

The difference between a Papist and a Protestant is this, that the one judges his guide to be infallible, the other his way to be manifest.

Another of those who frequented the "academy" of Falkland at Great Tew was the quiet but attractive John Hales, whose friends, after his death, caught the literary world's ear with their name for him of "the ever-memorable." A scholar, a recluse, a hesitating thinker and reluctant writer, he was yet a man whose words and character influenced all who knew him, and Laud left him, once Greek professor at Oxford, undisturbed at Eton, where he was happily at home: "a master of Polite, Various, and Universal Learning." And, to this, he added the rare perfection of character which made bishop Pearson say that it was "near as easy a task for every one to become so knowing, as so obliging" as he. His friend "that Reverend and Worthy Person, Mr. Farindon" tells us that, in his youth, he was a Calvinist till, at the synod of Dort, he said, "There, I bid John Calvin Good night." His breadth, as contemporaries record it, anticipates Thomas Arnold, for he would bring all Englishmen together by a common liturgy from which "all doctrinal points on which men differed in their opinions" were to be omitted. Yet Laud cherished and promoted him.

The *Golden Remains* of Hales (in the second edition, "with Additions from the Authour's own copy," 1673) contains many pleas for religious peace and arguments of the "great and irremediable inconvenience this free and uncontroulable venturing upon Theological Disputes hath brought upon us." But he was a positive teacher as well as one who dissuaded from extremes. His sermons, which, with a number of lively letters to Dudley Carleton, ambassador at the Hague, and a few fragmentary thoughts somewhat after Pascal's manner, constitute the precious volume, have a fine clarity and directness. The learning which men admired in him is almost laid aside or comes in only where it fitly illustrates the religious thought, unlike most of the sermons of his contemporaries. He speaks very plainly, at Eton, of the responsibility of riches, or, at the Hague, of the crime of duelling; he tells men how to know and love and worship God, as one whose simple object it was to find it out. His writing is straightforward and effective, as the writing of men is apt to be who, like himself, will not "pen anything till they needs must." But, behind it there lies, easy to be perceived, a depth of philosophic interest. Hales looked much further behind life than men like Sheldon, further, perhaps, than the piercing eye of Chillingworth; he had a basis of philosophy like Herbert or Traherne; he saw differences between earth and heaven, it may be, where they saw only correspondences; yet, while, like the former, he was the friend of courtiers and men of wit, he was, like the latter, a lover of solitude in the soul. He saw life whole and was original as a thinker in theology and philosophy: so he could not be a Calvinist. He was transparently sincere, and he came to have that sort of influence on the men who were making English literature as well as English politics which has often been exercised from the cloister, the college, or the country parsonage. The man who made the funeral oration of Sir Thomas Bodley, studied Shakespeare and belonged to Suckling's "session of the Poets," was a theologian who taught the next age in many subtle ways. He taught it breadth of view, and a passion for unity; he taught it to be critical and yet religious; and he taught it to pursue its speculations in the study and the church rather than in the market and the House of Commons.

But the name of Hales is not the only one to remind us that, while fightings without and fears within vexed men's souls and gave a new vehemence to their theological discussions, there were still those who possessed their souls in peace. The ordered system of the English church, when the fiercest storm of revolution and reformation had passed by, was at work in town and country, and in many a quiet village religious men were living peaceably in their habitations. The school of poetry, typically Anglican in its piety as well as in its humanity, was close-linked to the prose writers of the age. Crashaw, in 1635, printed a copy of verses as preface to Shelford's *Five Pious and Learned Discourses*—a book which Ussher thought popish; and Quarles was Ussher's secretary, "a very good man," as Aubrey calls him, and one whose meditative prose has been forgotten in the fame of his poetry. George Herbert, of course, was conspicuous in both. But, before we speak of him, we may briefly describe the literary work of the typical English household pledged to religion, the home of the Ferrars at Little Gidding.

Nicholas Ferrar was a man of affairs, like not a few of his time and temper, before he entered holy orders. He was a member of parliament, and active in the business of the Virginia company, a man who had travelled and mixed with his fellow-men. In "his travels over the western parts of Christendom," says Barnabas Oley, in his *Life of George Herbert*, men noted "his exquisite carriage, his rare parts and abilities of understanding and languages, his morals more perfect than the best," and sought to win him to the church of Rome; but he was fixed in attachment to his own church, and the collection of devotional books which he gathered abroad, and the devotional system which he witnessed in Italy, "rather inflamed him with a holy zeal to revenge their charity by transplanting their waste and misplaced zeal to adorn our Protestant religion." It was in the year of Charles I's accession that he retired to the secluded hamlet of Little Gidding; in the next year, he was ordained deacon by Laud, who, throughout his life, was in touch with the best devotion as well as the best theology of the day. For twenty-one years,

his "protestant nunnery," composed of the family of his
brother and his brother-in-law, carried on its life there, respected by all, visited with affectionate regard by Charles I,
and, as bishop, by the somewhat shifty Williams. Nicholas
Ferrar died in 1637, but the house itself survived for nine
years more till house and church were "ransacked" by parliamentary troops in 1646. "In this general devastation,"
says Pechard, "perished those works of Mr. Nicholas Ferrar
which merited a better fate."

The literary remains of Little Gidding are partly biographical—touching little histories of lives of exquisite charm—
together with the "Story Books" which still exist in five
manuscript volumes, chiefly written by Nicholas Ferrar himself and all bound by Mary Collet. The tales, which were
a collection of "divine interludes, dialogues and discourses
in the Platonic way," were the records of each day's literary
recreation, a mingling of piety with literature very well
suited to the lives of persons who had lived with great men and
great books before they came to give themselves wholly to
the life of contemplation and prayer. Of these volumes, only
about one and a half have, so far, been published. They are
quaint minglings of the romances of the age, just a touch
of Sir Philip Sidney, or a link here and there with Lyly, or
anticipation of Bunyan, with the sober ordered devotion
which traces all daily actions to their source and judges all
men and things by the standard of the Gospel. They do not
fear to deal with difficult matters, such as "the conversion
of a famous Courtesan," but it is in a spirit as placid as severe;
and the style partakes of the same simplicity, quietness and
restraint. With none of the vivacity of Bunyan, they have
yet a certain sting, which reminds the reader of William Law,
when they speak of fashionable follies and frivolities. They
are worth more attentive study than they have yet received,
because they show that the Elizabethan romance writers had
their successors, and they illustrate the manner in which
every branch of literature was being made subservient, as
the civil war approached, to the dominating interest of
religion.

Such lives as those of the Ferrars were imitated in many
parts of England; and an illustration of how closely the literary

and religious interests of Anglican England were knit together is afforded by the history of Lettice (Morison), lady Falkland, wife of the famous leader of the theological coterie of Great Tew.   After the fashion of Little Gidding, she planned

places for the education of Young Gentlewomen and for the retirement of Widows, . . . hoping thereby that learning and religion might flourish more in her own Sex than heretofore, having such opportunities to serve the Lord without distractions.

Her biography is a characteristic record of Anglican devotion, but, from the point of view of the historian of literature, it is chiefly noticeable for two things: the absence of rhetoric or ornament, with the precision of detail in which the tale is told, photographic in the exactness with which the daily life of a great lady of the time is realised; and the influence of Spanish and French mysticism both on the biographer and on the lady whose sayings he records.   Nicholas Ferrar had translated *A Hundred and Ten Divine Considerations* of Juan de Valdés, and it seems probable that Duncon himself was acquainted with the work in its Italian form.

The mysticism of these people was mixed with metaphysics: their letters are often almost as much philosophical as religious; and Traherne, their compeer, revels in speculations on the borderland of philosophy.   It is different with the other influence which profoundly affected them—that of George Herbert.

Herbert, courtier, public orator at Cambridge, country parson, was one of the happiest embodiments of the title "a scholar and a gentleman," but, before all things, he was a "priest to the temple."   His theory and practice are alike embalmed in an immortal book.

A Priest to the Temple, most familiarly known as "George Herbert's *Country Parson*," seems to have been finished in 1632, but did not appear in print for twenty years, when Barnabas Oley edited it with a "friendly prosopopoea" to John Echard, answering his "grounds and occasions of the contempt of the clergy."   Certainly, no one could contemn George Herbert's priest, for he is as good a man as Chaucer's clerk of Oxenford.   The sketch of him may take its place, it has been pointed out, among other character-sketches of the time, such as bishop Earle's. But it is conspicuous among them all for the minuteness of its observation, the exactness of its language and the fervent piety that animates the picture. Of its usefulness for its own time, Izaak Walton has said the last word, that it is "a book so full of plain, prudent and useful rules that that country parson that can spare 12d. and yet wants it, is scarce excusable." But, of the subtle beauty of its style, it is not easy to speak thus briefly. It abounds in happy phrases—such as that of "crumbling a text into small parts"—and touches of insight in words that exactly fit the thought. It is balanced in its parts, so that the effect of its sweet reasonableness is continuous and cumulative. It is not without verbal reminiscences of the writer's poetry; yet the prose is good prose, not poetry spoilt. And, indeed, its literary excellence is more consistently excellent than that of the writer's verse, because it has in it no straining for effect or quaintness, but proceeds naturally as though it flowed from ready lips and a full heart. If the poetry which Herbert sent, on his deathbed, by John Duncon to Nicholas Ferrar, was a picture, as he said, of his spiritual conflicts, the prose of *A Priest to the Temple* was an image of country tranquillity, bright and simple like the flowers of the field which he loved, and fragrant like the incense which he tells the parson to use on high festivals. The *Country Parson* marks an epoch in English literature. It shows character drawing at its perfection, and the character that is chosen is that of a profession which, transformed by the reformation, had stamped on itself a peculiar mark, of breadth and dutifulness and out-of-door piety, which, happily and for generations, embodied a spirit that was English as well as Christian in the lives of the English clergy. The publication of the book may well have had not a little effect in bringing about the restoration of the church with that of the king; for it showed men how liberal, how tolerant and candid, how kindly and rational, could that church be which the triumph of the sects had temporarily superseded. Not many books, indeed, have made so deep or abiding an impression. It has endowed the memory of its author with a peculiar claim to the affection of Englishmen. And it sums up the influence which men like Ferrar and Duncon and Traherne, like Hammond and Sanderson, were quietly exercising, amid days of disturbance, in the byways of English life.

This influence, it will already have been observed, is connected at point after point with the name of the dominating personality in the English church during the reign of Charles I, the determined and masterful archbishop of Canterbury, William Laud. Laud was the disciple of Andrewes, whom he regarded as his master in theology and the "light of the Christian world." He preached Donne's funeral sermon. He ordained Nicholas Ferrar. He was the considerate patron of Sanderson, Hales and Chillingworth. Thus, he linked the men of the new age to the times of the great Elizabeth. For he himself belonged undoubtedly to the system, theological and political, of the last of the Tudors. Brought up when England was stirred by the victory over the Armada, trained at Oxford by those who rejected another foreign influence, the dominant Calvinism, he gave his whole loyalty to the English church and king as national institutions yet related to a wider religious and political world.

His first literary work was as an anti-Roman controversialist. In 1622, he engaged in one of the common theological duels of the day, defending the cause of the English church. The book recording it came out first in 1624, was reissued more fully in 1639 and appeared in two more editions before the end of the seventeenth century. It became the standard defence of Anglicanism against Rome, and, as such, was recommended by Charles I to his children; and it laid down the lines on which controversy of this nature has proceeded practically down to the present day. The church, whether at Rome or in London, is the same church—"one in substance but not one in condition of state and purity." Rome has no ground of infallibility or universality: the eastern church as well as the reformation is a standing refutation of such an assertion. Laud declares England's adherence to the creeds and the fundamental unaltered doctrines of the church. His position with regard to the Bible is the typical Anglican one, acceptance, submission, not idolatry; and "the key that lets men into the Scriptures, even to this knowledge of them that are the Word of God, is the tradition of the church." Protestants have "not left the church of Rome in her essence but in her

errors"; and, to set matters right, the appeal must be to a true
general council, or, till that may be had, to the Bible.   Meanwhile, the church of England stands for liberty, enforces not
its articles as necessary to salvation, and is secure in the
confidence that

to believe the Scripture and the Creeds, to believe these in the sense
of the ancient primitive Church, to receive the four great General
Councils, to believe all points of doctrine generally received as
fundamental in the Church of Christ, is a faith in which to live and
die cannot but give salvation.

Laud, as a controversialist, is the true successor of Andrewes, and his whole attitude, as well as his particular
quotations, shows him to be a disciple of Hooker.   As a controversialist, he is, to some extent, in contrast to Richard
Mountague, a man of his own age and school, who is happily
described by Fuller in the words "very sharp the nib of his
pen, and much gall mingled in his ink, against such as opposed him."   Mountague, who afterwards, by Laud's influence,
became a bishop, was famed for his tart tracts *A New Gag for
an old Goose who would needs undertake to stop all Protestants'
mouths even with 276 places out of their own English Bible;
Appello Caesarem: a Just Appeal from two Unjust Informers;*
and a treatise on the invocation of saints with the title *Immediate Address unto God alone.*   In each of these he anticipated
a good deal that modern writers have advanced as new; his
general position is that of Laud and Andrewes, asserting the
"catholicity" of the English church; and his manner is biting
and epigrammatic, as he stands "in the gap against Puritanism
and Popery, the Scylla and Charybdis of ancient Piety."
But the importance of Mountague in English history is
theological and, perhaps even more, political, rather than
literary.   He is in style and language a man of his age, and
his age has better men in both.   He was not an influence on
others.   He stood rather at the wing of the anti-Roman army
of writers, and the permanent impression was made by men
who, if not more learned—for Mountague was well read and
won the admiration of the pedant king James—were more
sober and, therefore, more effective.   The other wing of the
army is well represented by Joseph Hall, bishop, satirist, poet,

preacher, as well as controversialist. In 1640, he issued, with
Laud's approbation and assistance, his *Episcopacy by Divine
Right Asserted*, which is anti-presbyterian. He declares the
supreme authority of bishops to be from Christ and "both
universal and unalterable." His meditations or "contemplations" are of more permanent value: they have been reprinted
again and again, and have passed into the stock material of
Anglican devotions, marked, as they are, by that quiet reticence and sobriety, relieved by quaint humorous touches, which,
since the time of Sir Thomas More, at least, seem to us, in
such matters, to be typically English.

In all this we are still close to the name of Laud, and,
because all the English theological literature of his day is
more or less connected with him, we may pause to consider
his sermons as typical of those of the reign of Charles I.

The sermons that are preserved are but seven, and they
were all preached on special occasions. Thus, they may not
be typical of the preacher's ordinary manner, for he preached
often and *ad populum:* here, we find him at court, where a
certain stiffness and freedom in quotation from fathers and
classics were expected. They were recognised at the time to
be "in the Bishop of Winchester's manner," but they have
not Andrewes's spiritual beauty. The text is most carefully
analysed, dissected, "crumbled": it is often made to bear more
than it can hold. The thesis is put clearly, and often repeated
for emphasis. The illustrations are from medieval writers
as well as the early fathers: moderns, outside England, are
little used, except Calvin—whom everybody knew and expected to hear referred to. But, most characteristic of the
writer and, to some extent, of the school to which he belonged,
are two outstanding features in every sermon. Laud continually refers to the psalms or lessons of the day; he was so
familiar with the church's daily services that he naturally
took them as providing each day with its lesson from God,
and that lesson should be the first he would employ for application or illustration. This was personal to the man: it
occurs again and again in his diary and tinges his prayers.
A second feature is historical allusion. Laud was more
historical, perhaps, than strictly theological in his outlook.
English society came before him as an ordered system which

had its roots in the past, its analogies with foreign developments, its debts to dead heroes and saints, its best hopes in imitations of the good things of byegone ages.   This thought is shown abundantly in historical reference, be it to Julius Caesar, Frederic *stupor mundi*, or Saladin, and even the quotations of which all the writers of the age were fond have, in his case, it seems, a special direction: they emphasise precedent as a part of the divine ordering of the world.

Such is what one finds expressed very clearly, very pointedly, very emphatically, in the writings of Charles I's chief religious adviser.   Two of those who may be regarded as Laud's disciples reflect his thoughts and his manner—William Juxon and William Sancroft.   The former published but one or two sermons, of no particular merit save that of consistent Anglicanism.   The latter did not issue his attack on Calvinism till just before the restoration (1658), and belongs, from a literary point of view, entirely to the later Caroline age; yet he must be just mentioned here because all that he wrote shows Laud's influence, and it was he chiefly who sought to preserve the archbishop's memory by the faithful publication of his literary remains—the little *Diary* and the long, weary, but indomitable, record of his *Troubles and Tryal*.

Besides these, there were, of course, many minor Laudians —some, in their writings, like Roger Mainwaring, of political rather than literary fame; others, such as William Strode, with a nice taste in poetry which showed itself happily in their sermons; others, again, like Richard Steward, one of the many notable fellows of All Souls who bore their part in the Laudian movement and stood for the king, with the church party, throughout the war and in exile.   He held office after office, and, at last, the deanery of Westminster—where, however, he never secured possession.   He was prominent among those who destroyed the influence of Calvin at Oxford and handed on the influence of Laud to the next generation.   He has already been named among the notable preachers.   Others who left few remains must not be forgotten.   The circle of the primate's friends and disciples was a wide one.

At the fringe of the literary and ecclesiastical party which looked to Laud as teacher and patron were wits like Abraham Wright, whose *Five Sermons* (1656) most cleverly took off

the different styles of his age, and showed the difference between "ship board breeding and the Universities"; and Giles
Widdowes, author of *The Lawless Kneeless Schismatical Puritan*
(a blow for lawyer Prynne), but as Anthony à Wood tells
us,

a harmless and honest man, a noted disputant, well read in the
schoolmen, and as conformable to and zealous in the established
discipline of the Church of England as any person of his time, yet
of so odd and strange parts that few or none could be compared
to him.

With not a few affinities in character to men such as these,
but strikingly unlike them in nature of his literary work,
there stands a writer whose powers have not even yet been
fully appreciated. John Gauden is one of the most remarkable figures in the literary history of his time. A singularly
adroit ecclesiastic, who was of the parliament's party and
yet not wholly repugnant to Laud, he was as well abused
as any clergyman of his day—which is saying a great deal—
but no man had a better skill in retort. His little known
*Anti-Baal-Berith or The Binding of the Covenant and all
Covenanters to their good behaviour* (1661) is as clever and
amusing a piece of controversial writing as the seventeenth century produced. Its sledge-hammer blows recall Martin Marprelate, and yet it never descends to mere
scurrility. One feels that Gauden knew extraordinarily well
how far he might go and carry people with him. And this is
true, in as striking a way, of his *Sermon preached in St. Paul's
Church London before the Right Honourable the Lord Mayor,
Lord General, Aldermen etc. on February* 28, 1659 (1660), the
day when there was public thanksgiving for the return of the
Rump. It is a most verbose and skilful—the verbosity itself is
skill—expression of what everybody at the moment was feeling,
and what the great persons of his audience particularly wished
to hear, as to the way of "healing the hurts of the kingdom."
Not a word that men could have him by the heels for is there in
it: no indiscreet references to the late king, or the late protector,
or the young man Charles Stewart; but just those hints which
go far enough to lead the hearers a little further, because they
show which way popular feeling is turning. No man ever

expressed with more fidelity the thoughts of his generation than John Gauden.

It is almost impossible to resist his claim to the authorship of the most important book of the day, *Eikon Basilike*, a "portraiture of his Sacred Majesty in his Sufferings." Internal and external evidence have been weighed again and again, as often as in the instance of the Casket letters, and it is difficult, indeed, to put aside the cumulative force of the facts. The long literary controversy which the claim occasioned has lasted to the present day. Briefly summarised, it turns upon the second-hand evidence of those who are said to have seen parts of the book in the handwriting of Charles I, and the counter-assertion of Gauden that he was himself the author, and upon the remarkable and detailed resemblance to his own writings. There is certainly no conclusive evidence that it was the work of the king. On the other hand, it is undoubtedly a masterpiece of expression of his principles, his personal feelings, his prejudices, his piety, his prerogative as it appeared to him at his moments of greatest sincerity and exaltation. Idealised, it undoubtedly is. Charles, perhaps, had never so deep a feeling of what kingship might mean to its worshippers. But a man who loved Shakespeare as Charles did may well have been inspired by his sufferings to write above the level of his constant thoughts. And it is at least possible that *Eikon* may be even more of a mosaic than it seems. The author knew what Charles had said on public occasions, and used it; he knew what the king felt on public questions; he knew what such a man, the disciple of Laud, the devout attendant at Anglican worship, would feel at a time of personal distress and imprisonment. The result is an incomparable picture of a stedfast prince, who acknowledges his weakness yet asserts the purity of his motives, the truth of his political and religious principles, the supremacy of his conscience. Such a dramatic presentment would not be above the ability of Gauden: and it is quite possible that he had before him, when he wrote, actual meditations, prayers and memoranda of the king, which perished when they had been copied and had found their place in the masterly mosaic.

Few books have had greater influence in English history. Forty-seven editions of it were produced with surprising rapidity: those who tried to answer it—Milton among them—

failed utterly to obliterate the impression it had created. The dull attempts at dignity and splendour which tried to relieve the exasperating vigilance and laborious monotony of the protectorate government and court were entirely powerless in face of this appealing pathos. The Stewart romance, which was to colour English history for another century, had its strongest impetus from this wonderful little book. The merit of the style is its simplicity and directness. It speaks straight to the heart. *Eikon Basilike* is, indeed, among the masterpieces of the age which produced the religion and the literature of Nicholas Ferrar and of George Herbert.

If *Eikon Basilike* is one of the most important books in English history, no one can rank its author among the immortals. But the last of the Caroline divines whom we shall name has a claim to that title. Jeremy Taylor may be regarded as the finished product of the school of Laud. It was Laud who procured him his fellowship at All Souls, and to whom his famous sermon on the Gunpowder plot was dedicated; and Laud's influence, at once in its attachment to ancient standards, in its antagonism to the theology of Rome and in its breadth of toleration, is evident in all his writings. His was a full life: he went through much affliction, and he had many consolations; he was an ardent scholar, a popular preacher, a bishop, a man of affairs; and all these experiences are reflected in books which are the most famous of all the work of the Caroline divines. No one of all that distinguished body, whose position in that age was summed up in the oft-quoted phrase *clerus Anglicanus stupor mundi*, was more eminent in his own day, and no one, except George Herbert, has so certainly won permanent place in the literature of England. He wrote voluminously; and few men who have written so much have left more books that still retain their value: the sermons, ingenious, fertile, convincing; *Ductor Dubitantium*, still the only English treatise of any importance on its subject;[1] the charm of *The Marriage Ring;* the piety of *The Golden Grove;* the sagacious, corrective, kindling instruction of *Holy Living* and *Holy Dying* and *The Worthy Communicant*—these are the abiding possession of the English people. Jeremy Taylor's controversial work has passed out of consideration with the greater part of all writing of the same

[1] See, *post*, Chap. XII.

kind that was contemporary with it: perhaps no English controversialist in theology save Hooker has secured a permanent place in English literature. Taylor's theology is of his age: his learning would not preserve his books from oblivion. But he remains a vital force in English letters, because of the wonderful combination of fine qualities which he possesses. Coleridge placed him among the four masters of early seventeenth century literature, with Shakespeare, Bacon and Milton; and later judgment shows no sign of reversing the verdict. But his character, as a writer, is very specially his own. First and obviously, by profession he was an Anglican priest. He had the ecclesiastical temper and the spiritual insight which befit his profession; and, in his firm adherence to the fundamentals of the Christian faith, combined with a wide tolerance in interpretation, a desire to admit and not to exclude, like Hales and Chillingworth and Laud, he was a typical Anglican of Charles I's day. Tradition, authority, faith, liberality, were harmonious, not contending, in his mind. Secondly, he was not less certainly a man of letters. His style is intensely artificial, not in the sense of insincerity, but in the sense of laborious achievement which has become facility and freedom. It is intensely individual. There are in it points of comparison with Sir Thomas Browne, with Donne, with Traherne, even with Burton; but the curiously mingled simplicity and gorgeousness are all his own. No one can, like Taylor, pile up splendour of description, exotic richness of phraseology, colour, tones instinct with music, and then turn in an instant to a sober, solemn, stately simplicity, direct and appealing like the call of a herald. Again, in his use of the ancient classics, if he is a man of his time, he works with a distinction of his own. . Now, he translates literally, incorporating the result in his own text; now, he quotes, now, paraphases; but he always handles his author as though he were familiar with him and loved him. Whether it be the *Greek Anthology*, or Petronius, or a Christian Father, he regards the book with a delicate appreciation which comes of pure passion for literature in itself. His taste is all-embracing, and he has an extraordinary aptitude for applying it to the matter, however far away, which, for the moment, is occupying his mind. Thus, you may often call his references, or his analogies, far fetched:

but, when you look more closely into the texture of his argument, you will see how fitly as well as how adroitly he has woven them in. This breadth of sympathy made Mason call him "the Shakespeare of English prose." The description is an extremely happy one. He is rhetorical like a dramatist. He abounds in arresting phrases, in haunting verbal felicities. He can be magnificent, and he can be most deeply pathetic. And, perhaps above all, his language is astoundingly popular and modern. To compare his prose with Milton's is to find one's self in a world of freedom as contrasted with the four walls of the scholar's study.

You cannot read Jeremy Taylor without feeling that, in spite of his preciosity, he is, in intention, before all things intensely practical; to this aim even his delight in expression and allusion yields again and again. You come continually on passages, for example, like that in which, after a list of diseases and a mention of Maecenas, he writes thus:

It was a cruel mercy in Tamerlane, who commanded all the leprous persons to be put to death, as we knock some beasts quickly on their head, to put them quickly out of pain, and lest they should live miserably: the poor men would rather have endured another leprosy, and have more willingly taken two diseases than one death. Therefore Caesar wondered that the old crazed soldier begged leave he might kill himself, and asked him, "dost thou think then to be more alive than now thou art?" We do not die suddenly, but we descend to death by steps and slow passages; and therefore men, so long as they are sick, are unwilling to proceed and go forward in the finishing that sad employment. Between a disease and death there are many degrees, and all those are like the reserves of evil things, the declining of every one of which is justly reckoned among those good things, which alleviate the sickness and make it tolerable. Never account that sickness intolerable, in which thou hadst rather remain than die: and yet if thou hadst rather die than suffer it, the worst of it that can be said is this, that this sickness is worse than death; that is, it is worse than that which is the best of all evils, and the end of all troubles; and then you have said no great harm against it.[1]

Taylor, it is true, had a variety of style. It is possible to trace "periods" in his literary manner, as it is to distinguish

[1] *Holy Dying*, chap. III.

the tone in which he dealt with different topics. He was a
controversialist and historian in *The Sacred order and offices of
Episcopacy* (1642); an advocate of toleration in *The Liberty
of Prophesying* (1647); purely a spiritual teacher in *The Great
Exemplar* (a life of Christ, 1649), *Holy Living* (1650), *Holy Dying* (1651) and *The Worthy Communicant* (1660); an opponent
of Rome in many treatises, a defender of Anglicanism in
others; but, in all, he was a man of wide outlook, of temperate
mind and of warm heart. Why Taylor has always been popular, has been, indeed, the Bunyan of the English church, is that
he obviously felt all he said, and was stirred by the very passion
which he sought to infuse into others. His work is not regular,
his style is hardly chastened; yet his feeling is restrained within
limits which not a few writers of his time transgressed to their
peril.   He is intense in feeling, up to the very verge of legitimate expression; he hardly ever oversteps it.   His style is the
servant, not the master, of the conviction or the passion which
breathes in every page that he writes.

When we survey the period of English prose of which
Jeremy Taylor is the brightest ornament, we are struck by the
fact that the divines of Charles I's day were conspicuously
English.   Spanish influence had passed by; French had hardly
yet come, as it came thirty years later; Latin and Greek were
still potent, but chiefly because they had taught men to write
English.   English they were, and, though some of those of
whom we have spoken had died before "the troubles," and the
voices of almost all were temporarily silenced during the years
after Charles's death, their influence was powerful in the next
generation—a generation enthusiastic for both church and
king.

CHAPTER VII

John Bunyan. Andrew Marvell

THE great civil war of the seventeenth century, while revolutionising English constitutional government, effected, also, an important break in the historical continuity of English literature. The years between 1640 and 1660, being years of prolonged and intense conflict, constitute, in the main, a distinct and well defined interval between the writers of the days of Elizabeth and James and those of the restoration. Above all other periods in our history, it was the age of the pamphleteer, of the writer who is concerned rather with the urgent needs of the hour than with the purpose of creating or developing the higher forms of literature. His aim was to reach the public mind directly and at once, and so shape the national policy at critical moments in the nation's life. What literature there might be of more permanent sort was the intellectual product of a generation which had either disappeared or was fast disappearing. Even Milton, recognised, as he is, as the great poet of the restoration, may, more properly, be said to belong to an earlier time. For the educative forces which shaped him, and the creative impulse which finally determined his path to fame, had exercised their influence upon him before ever the war began. All that is most characteristic of his genius belongs to the time when books were written to be read by scholars, and when classical learning gave form and pressure to English style. Very much the same thing may be said of Andrew Marvell. For, while his literary reputation rests mainly, if not exclusively, on poems not published till 1681, or three years after his death, they were actually composed, with few exceptions, during the early years of his manhood. They were the product of a time when

Donne's poetry, with its elaborate conceits and recondite analogies, was the fashion of the hour, and Donne himself the accepted poet of the younger men of the time, the leader by whose style and manner they were consciously, or unconsciously, influenced.

Taking into account, then, the effect of this hiatus in the literary continuity of the seventeenth century, it is not surprising that, in the succeeding period, we come upon writers who belong to no special class or school, and whose literary genealogy cannot be traced. Three names suggest themselves as furnishing illustrations of the kind: John Bunyan, who, with his vivid descriptions of character, his quaint turns of thought and his racy English style, stands alone; Daniel Defoe, with his unrivalled power of clothing with an air of reality the creations of his imagination; and Jonathan Swift, whose style defies description or classification, and, as he puts the case himself, "whose English was his own." John Bunyan, in creative genius the most gifted of the three, was, in educational advantages, the least favoured. Born in 1628, in the Bedfordshire village of Elstow, the son of an artisan, a brasier by trade, he was put to school, he tells us, to learn both to read and write "according to the rate of other poor men's children"; but, to his shame, he says, he has "to confess he soon lost that little he learnt, even almost utterly." Probably, if he had been bent on continuing the modest acquirements of the village school, he would have had small opportunity, for work at his father's forge began early, and literature was as scanty as leisure. Most likely, he was describing the kind of book within his own reach in those days when, in after years, he represents one of his characters as saying, "Give me a ballad, a newsbook, George on horseback, or Bevis of Southampton; give me some book that teaches curious arts, that tells old fables." And, even if books of a higher class of literature had been within his reach, opportunity for study scarcely could have been; for, during the civil war, the army regulation age was from sixteen to sixty, and in the very month in which Bunyan completed his sixteenth year he was drafted into service as a soldier in the parliamentary army. As we now know from the recently discovered muster-rolls of the garrison, he was on military duty at Newport Pagnell from November, 1644, to

June, 1647. He was here under the command of Sir Samuel
Luke, parliamentary scout master general, the puritan knight
whom Butler, in his well known satire, lampooned as Sir
Hudibras. And it is curious to notice, by the way, that
Bunyan, the writer of puritan books, and Butler, the merciless
satirist of puritan types, were both of them, at one and the
same time, in the service of the same worthy of Cople Woodend
—the one as a soldier in the garrison and the other as tutor or
secretary in his household.

On his release from military service in 1647, Bunyan returned to his native village, and married a year or two later.
It is in connection with this event in his life that he first refers
to any influence which books may have had over him. His
wife, he tells us,

had for her part *The Plain Man's Pathway to Heaven* and
The Practice of Piety which her father had left her when he died.
In these two books I should sometimes read with her, wherein I also
found some things that were somewhat pleasing to me.

A year or two later, he came under a more potent influence. One
day he happened to fall into the company of a poor man who

did talk pleasantly of the Scriptures. Wherefore, falling into some
love and liking to what he said, I betook me to my Bible and began
to take great pleasure in reading; but especially with the historical
part thereof. For as for Paul's Epistles, and such like Scriptures,
I could not away with them.

As yet, he had not entered upon that deep religious experience,
those intense struggles of soul, which he has vividly depicted
in his *Grace Abounding;* but, when that time came to him, he
turned again to his Bible with more living purpose—the book
to which, more than any other, his literary style was indebted
for its English clearness and force. "I began," he says, "to
look into it with new eyes and read as I never did before. I
was never out of the Bible either by reading or meditation."
So far as his native genius was shaped and directed by external
influence, it is here we come upon that influence.

"Bunyan's English," writes J. R. Green, "is the simplest and
homeliest English that has ever been used by any great English

writer, but it is the English of the Bible.　He had lived in the Bible till its words became his own."

Such was the main, and, so far as we know, the only influence of a literary sort under which Bunyan ever came, until he appeared before the world as an author.　This was in 1656, when he was twenty-eight years of age, and then only in response to what he felt to be the call of duty.　This first venture was brought about in a somewhat unexpected way. When his intense and memorable conflict of soul had passed into a more peaceful phase, he joined, in 1653, the fellowship of a Christian church recently formed in Bedford outside the national system.　A year or two later, these people prevailed upon him to exercise his gifts among them, and, in this way, he came gradually into active service as a preacher in Bedford and the villages round.　This brought him into collision with some of the followers of George Fox, founder of the Society of Friends, then a very aggressive body.　Like Fox himself, his followers went into places of worship and, in the presence of the congregation, assailed the preacher.　This they did with Bunyan, at one of his services.　He was not sufficiently mystical in his teaching for them.　They laid more stress upon the inward light and less upon historic fact and external revelation. They would have a Christ within, a resurrection within, a light within.　He, also, was desirous of these, but he would not let go the historic Christ, the historic facts of the Christian faith, or the Scriptures of revelation by which to guide and test the inward light.　A Quaker sister, he says, "did bid me in the audience of many 'to throw away the Scriptures.'　To which I answered, 'No, for then the devil would be too hard for me.'"

We are not here concerned with this controversy except in so far as to note the fact that, as its immediate result, it was responsible for the launching of Bunyan upon a career of authorship.　For the purpose of advancing what he held to be more scriptural teaching on the subject in dispute, he published, in 1656, a duodecimo volume of 270 pages, entitled *Some Gospel Truths Opened*.　This book, written rapidly and in a heat, was published at Newport Pagnell, and was immediately replied to by Edward Burrough, an eminent Quaker.

To this reply, Bunyan gave instant rejoinder in a further volume of 280 pages, his second book following his first, as he tells us, at only a few weeks' interval. These first literary ventures are not specially characteristic of Bunyan's genius; but they display the same ease of style, the same directness and naturalness of speech, which he maintained to the end, and are certainly remarkable as the productions of a working artisan of scantiest education, who had not long left the distractions of a soldier's life behind him.

Having thus ventured forth upon authorship in the interests of theological controversy, in 1658 Bunyan appeared again with a published treatise on the parable of the rich man and Lazarus, in which we have foretokens of his matured style in such characteristic touches as this: "The careless man lies like the smith's dog at the foot of the anvil though the fire-sparks fly in his face;" and this, "Some men despise the Lazaruses of our Lord Jesus Christ because they are not gentlemen, because they cannot with Pontius Pilate speak Hebrew, Greek and Latin." A further work of no special note, issued by him in 1659, brings us to 1660, when he entered upon the second and most important part of his life and literary history.

The restoration of monarchy to the state and of episcopacy to the church vitally affected the social and religious condition of nonconformists, and Bunyan was almost the first man among them to feel the change. In the November following the king's return in May, he was committed to Bedford gaol for preaching at a farmhouse in the south of the county, and, as he was convicted under the unrepealed Conventicle act of 1593, which required public confession and promise of submission before release could follow the term of imprisonment, he remained a prisoner for twelve years, that is, till the king's declaration of indulgence in 1672. So far as his literary history is concerned, these twelve years fall into two equal parts of six years each, during the first of which he published no fewer than nine of his books. The last of these, *Grace Abounding to the Chief of Sinners*, which appeared in 1666, is the first of the four outstanding creations of his genius. It is really his own autobiography, an intense record, written after he had "tarried long at Sinai to see the fire and the cloud and the darkness," and it has been recognised as one of the great books of the world on religious experience, and not unworthy to take its place by the side of the *Confessions* of Augustine. Another book which preceded this by a year, entitled *The Holy City, or the New Jerusalem*, is of interest to us as being a kind of foregleam of that celestial city to which, in after days, he conducted the pilgrims of his dream. At one time, there were no fewer than sixty other nonconformists in prison with him under the new Conventicle act of 1664, and they were accustomed to hold religious services among themselves in the common room of the county gaol. As he tells us in his preface to the book in question, it was his turn one Sunday morning to speak to the rest; but he felt so empty and spiritless that he thought he would not be "able to speak among them so much as five words of truth with light and evidence." However, as he turned over the pages of his Bible, in the book of *Revelation*, his eye lit upon the glowing picture of the city of God coming down out of heaven, her light like unto a stone most precious as it were a jasper stone clear as crystal. Musing upon this glowing vision, seen by that other prisoner in Patmos, Bunyan says, "Methought I perceived something of that jasper in whose light this holy city is said to come or descend;" and the Lord helped him to set this great hope before his brethren: "we did all eat and were well-refreshed." But the matter did not end there. When the sermon was over, the vision splendid rose before his mind again:

the more I cast mine eye upon it the more I saw lie in it. Wherefore setting myself to a more narrow search, through frequent prayer to God, what first with doing and then with undoing, and after that with doing again, I thus did finish it.

It has been truly said that, while Bunyan possessed in a remarkable degree the gift of expressing himself in written words, he had no appreciation of literature as such. In the preface of the book before us, he explains his mental attitude. He thinks his learned reader may blame him because he has "not beautified his matter with acuteness of language," and has not, "either in the line or in the margent, given a cloud of sentences from the learned fathers." As for the language of the learned, the sentences and words which others use, he does not give them because he has them not, nor has he read them: "had it not been for the Bible, I had not only not thus done it, but not at all." That is reason enough, but there is another behind it. Even if he had had the learning of the learned Fathers,

"I durst not make use of ought thereof," he says, "and that for fear lest that grace and these gifts that the Lord hath given me, should be attributed to their wits rather than the light of the Word and Spirit of God."

This way of regarding the literary gift as heaven-descended, therefore to be reverently used and not perverted to unworthy ends, was Milton's as well as Bunyan's. When he put in print a public pledge to execute his design of a great poem, Milton, at the same time, said that he conceived of it

as being a work not to be raised from the heat of youth or the vapours of wine, nor to be obtained by the invocation of Dame Memory and her Siren daughters, but by devout prayer to the Eternal Spirit who can enrich with all utterance and Knowledge, and sends out his Seraphim with all the hallowed fire of his altar to touch and purify the lips of whom he pleases.

This may not be the common way, but it was the puritan way of regarding the endowments of man's richer nature as gifts of the Spirit of God, as signs of his wider operation on the imagination and heart of the world. In the preface to his *Grace Abounding*, a book which, in some passages, seems as if it had been written with a pen of fire, Bunyan touches again upon the question of the relation of conscience to literature:

"I could," he says, "have stepped into a style much higher than this in which I have here discoursed, and could have adorned all things more than here I have seemed to do; but I dare not. God did not play in convincing of me . . . wherefore I may not play in my relating of these experiences, but be plain and simple, and lay down the thing as it was. He that liketh it let him receive it; and he that does not, let him produce a better."

While during the first six years of his prison life, as we have said, no fewer than nine books came from Bunyan's pen, for the next five years, so far as we know, that pen was laid aside. It was not till 1671 that he broke this long silence and published a book which he entitled *A Confession of my Faith, and a*

Reason of my Practice. This work, while giving a reasoned statement of his religious opinions, was, at the same time, a kind of *apologia pro vita sua*, a vindication of his conduct in resolutely standing by his convictions for a long time, while so weighty an argument as over eleven years' imprisonment was continually urging him to pause and consider again and again the grounds and foundation of those principles for which he thus had suffered. He maintains that he is a peaceable and obedient subject, and he appeals to his enemies themselves to judge whether there is anything in the opinions set forth savouring either of heresy or of rebellion rendering him deserving of almost twelve years' imprisonment. Still, he will suffer rather than yield. He goes on to say:

> If nothing will do, unless I make of my conscience a continual butchery and slaughter-shop, unless putting out my own eyes I commit me to the blind to lead me, I have determined, the Almighty God being my help and shield, yet to suffer, if frail life might continue so long, even till the moss shall grow on mine eye-brows rather than thus to violate my faith and principles.

Deliverance came at length. Seeing that "no fruit came of these forceful courses," in 1672 the king, apart from parliament, issued a declaration of indulgence, under power of which licences to preach were granted to nonconformist ministers, and to Bunyan among the rest. He was at once elected pastor of the church in Bedford of which, since 1653, he had been a private member; and he held that position, with freedom from state interference, for the next three years. At the end of that time, trouble broke forth again. The declaration of indulgence, being an unusual, and, to many in the nation, an unwelcome exercise of the royal prerogative, was withdrawn, and, as a consequence, nonconformists' licences were recalled. Bunyan, therefore, being once more exposed to all the penalties of the Conventicle act, was arrested and sent to prison for six months, this time to the small town gaol on Bedford bridge. It was during this second and shorter imprisonment that he wrote the first part of *The Pilgrim's Progress from this World to that which is to come.*

This allegory appeared in the early part of 1678, but received characteristic additions in a later edition of the same year, and, again, in the third edition, which appeared in 1679. In the first edition, there was no account of Christian breaking his mind to his wife and children, no Worldly Wiseman, no confession by Christian to Goodwill at the Wicket-gate, of his own turning aside. Christian's discourse at the palace, the name of which was Beautiful, was added afterwards, as were the accounts of Mr. By-Ends, his conversation and his rich relations, of Lot's wife as a pillar of salt and of Diffidence the wife of giant Despair. The description of the reception of the pilgrims on the further shore of the river was heightened, also, by the coming of the King's trumpeters to salute them with ten thousand welcomes, with shouting and sound of trumpet. On the other hand, some characteristic marginalia, such as "O brave Talkative!" "Christian snibbeth his fellow," "Hopeful swaggers," disappeared after the first edition.

The question of the originality of *The Pilgrim's Progress*, as to how far its author was indebted to previous allegorists, has been raised again and again. Comparisons have been instituted between this book and de Guileville's *Pilgrimage of the Sowle*, in which we have the vision of a city in the heavens acting as an incentive to a pilgrimage on earth, and in the course of which we come upon a wicket-gate and a reception in the house of Grâce Dieu, recalling that of Christian in the house called Beautiful. That there are ideas in common is obvious enough; but the probable explanation is that they had one common source. The looking for a city with eternal foundations was a New Testament idea as accessible to Bunyan as to the monk of Chaliz; while the house of Grâce Dieu and the Palace Beautiful, like the house of Mercy in *The Faerie Queene*, may well have been suggested by the old houses of entertainment prepared for pilgrims or travellers on their way. Spenser sets forth in allegory the dangers, the conflicts and the final victory of the Red Cross knight of holiness; but, apart from the question of the probability or otherwise of Bunyan's having access to *The Faerie Queene*, it may be noted that there is one important contrast between this allegory and his own. Spenser dealt mainly with abstract virtues and qualities, his book is an epic of the struggles and triumph of truth; whereas Bunyan, like Chaucer, drew personal portraits and gave concrete presentations of vices and virtues.

It would not be difficult to show that Spenser was weakest precisely where Bunyan was strongest.

Besides the two books referred to, others have been mentioned in which we have the regular introduction of the dream and the allegory, such as *The Palice of Honour* by Gawin Douglas, *The Goldyn Targe* by William Dunbar, *The Bowge of Courte* by John Skelton and *The Passetyme of Pleasure* by Stephen Hawes. But, before asking whether Bunyan could have been influenced by these or similar works, we must remember that he was in prison when the idea of the pilgrim journey first laid hold of him and would not let him go. And, even if he had thought of it beforehand, the literature of the subject which he might have studied by way of preparation for his theme was not easily accessible in those days to peasants and working artisans. But, apart from these considerations, we have Bunyan's own express declarations on the subject. The originality of the work was questioned in his own day: "Some say *The Pilgrim's Progress* is not mine;" but he will have none of this: "Manner and matter, too, was all mine own nor was it unto any mortal known till I had done it. The whole and every whit is mine." When the vision descended on him it surprised no one more than himself. He tells us that he was writing another book about the way and race of saints in his own day, when he

> Fell suddenly into an Allegory
> About their Journey, and the way to Glory.

Vivid fancies came so thick and fast upon him, that he resolved to put them down;

> This done, I twenty more had in my Crown,
> And they again began to multiply,
> Like sparks that from the coals of fire do fly.

It has been said that *The Pilgrim's Progress* was the last English book written without thought of the reviewer; its author goes further, and tells us it was written without thought even of a possible reader:

> I did not think
> To shew to all the World my Pen and Ink
> . . . nor did I undertake

> Thereby to please my Neighbour; no not I;
> I did it mine own self to gratifie.

This is the author's own account of the growth of his great masterpiece, and it goes far to account for its possession of that charm which lays hold of the hearts of men, they know not how.

But, while the book thus sprang into being, effortless and fair like a flower, it is not wanting in proportion or dramatic unity. The opening sentence lays hold of the reader, and, thenceforward, there is no unmown grass of weariness to wade through, no wilderness of tedium in which to wander. There are episodes by the way, but they never draw us so far aside that we forget the main story—on the contrary, they contribute to its effect. The book is remarkable, too, for the reality of its impersonations, for the rapidity and power with which its characters are drawn. They are no mere shadowy abstractions moving about in a mystical region far away from us, but real men and women living in our own every-day world. By a few strokes only, sometimes by the mere giving of a name, an abstraction rises up before us, clothed in flesh and blood. A contemporary tells us that Bunyan was "accomplished with an excellent discerning of persons," and it is this keen power of insight that gives permanent value to his work. He had the discriminating eye and, also, the broad sympathy and keen sense of humour which accompany that gift. Further, while he gives us quaint turns of thought, pithy expressions such as still linger on many a countryside, and revelations of character, which we recognise at once, the world of outside nature, with its manifold phases, comes in to complete the whole. We have the hill with its toilsome ascent, the mountain with its far-off vision of the city, the fearsome glen with its shadowy shapes. Then, at other times, we walk in "the King's gardens, into which the children of the land of Beulah go to gather nosegays for the pilgrims, bringing them with much affection." Our senses, too, are regaled with the fragrance of spikenard and saffron, calamus and cinnamon, with trees of "frankincense, myrrh, together with aloes with all chief spices." And, through the interlacings of green leaves, we hear, besides, the melodious notes of the country birds and the sweet sound of distant bells.

As to Bunyan's subsequent influence on English life and literature, it is to be remembered that, above everything else, his desire was to be a religious teacher, that it would have been against his conscience to aim at mere literary distinction and success. It would have gratified him beyond expression could he have known that *The Pilgrim's Progress* is one of the few books which act as a religious bond for the whole of English Christendom. As a creator of fictitious personalities, he has charmed the world, weaving them into a story of universal interest and lasting vitality. The most perfect and complex of fairy tales, as Hallam called the book, it has not only won the hearts of children at an age when its spiritual meaning is little perceived, but it has also been the interpreter of life to men perplexed with life's problems. "This is the great merit of the book," said Dr. Johnson, "that the most cultivated man cannot find anything to praise more highly, and the child knows nothing more amusing;" and even Swift could testify that he had been better entertained and more improved by a few pages of this allegory than by more pretentious books of another kind. Still, the literary class, as a whole, did not at the time, or long after, give the book appreciative welcome. Cowper was afraid to introduce Bunyan's name into his poetry lest he should provoke a sneer. Addison, in disparaging fashion, said that he never knew an author that had not his admirers, for Bunyan pleased as many readers as Dryden or Tillotson; and Mrs. Montague, following in his wake, called Bunyan and Quarles "those classics of the artificers in leather," laughing at them as forming the particular entertainment of her neighbours, the Kentish squires. On the other hand, Mrs. Piozzi asks, "Who shall say that Lillo, Bunyan and Antonio Correggio were not naturally equal to Jonson, Michael Angelo and the Archbishop of Cambrai?" And Horace Walpole evidently thought he was paying Edmund Spenser a compliment when he spoke of him as "John Bunyan in rhyme."

While the learned class differed widely in judgment, the general world of readers never wavered in their favourable estimate of the book. Between 1678, when it first appeared, and 1778, thirty-three editions of part I and fifty-nine editions of parts I and II together were issued, and then publishers left off counting. It is computed that one hundred thousand copies were sold in Bunyan's own lifetime. Nor was its literary influence confined to his own country. Three years after its publication, it was reprinted by the puritan colony in America, there receiving, as Bunyan himself tells us, "much loving countenance." And there it has continued ever since, in untold number of editions; and, with Shakespeare, it forms part of the literary bond which unites the two English-speaking peoples on each side of the Atlantic.

Bunyan's allegory was translated into Dutch and French in 1682. The first edition in German appeared in 1694, many successive editions following in its wake. F. H. Ranke tells us that, as a young man at Nürnberg, he met with a copy of an edition of 1703, translated from the Dutch, which made such an impression upon him that he formed classes of young men for the study of the book; and Gustav Kettner suggests that, in two of Schiller's poems, *Der Pilgrim* and *Die Sehnsucht*, Bunyan's influence is distinctly traceable. Jung-Stilling also records with what pleasure he read the book; Wieland, too, after telling an English traveller at Weimar how *The Pilgrim's Progress* had delighted him, went on to say, "In that book I learned to read English; English literature had great influence upon me, your puritan writings particularly."

Other translations of Bunyan's dream have gone on multiplying down to the present time. There are now versions of *The Pilgrim's Progress* in no fewer than one hundred and eight different languages and dialects, so that it is no mere poetical figure to say, as has been said, that it follows the Bible from land to land as the singing of birds follows the dawn.

Between 1656, when he gave his first book to the world, and 1688, when, a few weeks before his death, he saw his last book partly through the press, Bunyan sent forth, altogether, no fewer than sixty different publications as the product of his pen. While all these may be truly said to bear more or less the stamp and impress of his genius, there are four outstanding books which, by common consent, are recognised as surpassing all the rest in impressiveness and creative power—*Grace Abounding*, *The Pilgrim's Progress*, *The Holy War* and *The Life and Death of Mr. Badman*. It is generally agreed that, in point of personal interest and popular power, *The Holy War* contrasts unfavourably with the story of Christian and Christiana. Still, in the later book, also, there are fine passages and lofty conceptions, though it moves in a more abstract region than its predecessor. It is interesting, also, as throwing light upon Bunyan's own military experiences. The martial deeds of the various captains engaged in the siege of Mansoul are, doubtless, reminiscences of days in Newport garrison when he came in contact with the preaching and praying majors and captains of the parliamentary army. Apart from these things, however, Macaulay's verdict, as we all know, was that, if *The Pilgrim's Progress* had not been written, *The Holy War* would have been our greatest English allegory.

The remaining work—*The Life and Death of Mr. Badman* —though disfigured by grotesque stories and somewhat coarse passages, yet bears the characteristic marks of Bunyan's genius and is, admittedly, a work of power. He himself intended this book to be the companion picture to that of his dream; as the one set forth the progress of a Christian from this world to glory, the other was to present the life and death of the ungodly, their travel through this world to perdition. It is constructed on a different plan, the former being in continuous narrative, and this in dialogue form, disfigured by didactic discourses on the various vices of a bad man's life. It is a picture of low English life as Bunyan saw it with his own eyes in a commonplace country town in the degraded days of a licentious king, and, as such, it has its historical value. Froude has given a forcibly expressed estimate of the work. To him it is a remarkable story:

The drawing is so good, the details so minute, the conception so unexaggerated that we are disposed to believe that we must have a real history before us. But such supposition is only a compliment to the skill of the composer. Throughout we are on solid earth, amidst real experiences. Bunyan conceals nothing, assumes nothing, and exaggerates nothing. There the figure stands: a picture of a man in the rank of English life with which Bunyan was most familiar, travelling along the primrose path to the everlasting bonfire, as the way to Emmanuel's Land was through the Slough of Despond and the Valley of the Shadow of Death.

In passing from John Bunyan to Andrew Marvell we are conscious of making a great transition. There is a sense in

which they have both been classed as puritans—Bunyan as the
great puritan allegorist and Marvell as the one puritan of his
age besides Milton who acquired distinction in poetry. They
may even, through literary association, have been personally
known to each other, for Nathanael Ponder, the first publisher
of *The Pilgrim's Progress*, was also, about the same time, publisher of the second part of Marvell's *Rehearsal Transprosed*.
But, if we class both as puritans, we must do so with a difference; for, when Marvell was born, in 1621, his father was parson
of the parish of Winestead in Holderness, and all his life, as
his son tells us, he was "a conformist to the rules and ceremonies
of the Church of England, though, I confess, none of the most
over-running and eager in them." Moreover, this somewhat
measured description of the ecclesiastical standing-place of
the elder Andrew may very well be applied, also, to that of the
younger. It is true that he was for three years tutor in the
family of lord Fairfax, the parliamentary general, that he was
Milton's assistant as Latin secretary to Cromwell and that he
was in close personal association with many parliamentarians;
but it is also true that he numbered among his friends prince
Rupert and Richard Lovelace. And, while he wrote an *Ode
upon Cromwell's Return from Ireland*, it must be remembered
that in the same ode occur the memorable stanzas descriptive
of Charles I's kingly bearing on the scaffold, recording how

> He nothing common did, or mean,
> Upon that memorable scene,
> But with his keener eye
> The axe's edge did try.
>
> Nor called the gods with vulgar spite
> To vindicate his helpless right;
> But bowed his comely head
> Down, as upon a bed.

Then, too, it may be further said that, though in strenuous and
earnest language he resisted the attempts of Parker, afterwards
bishop of Oxford, to stir up persecution against nonconformists,
he himself expressly declares that he was not in the nonconformist ranks, that he merely wrote, to use his own words,
"what I think befits all men in humanity, Christianity, and
prudence towards dissenters."

Marvell, born 31 March, 1621, was educated at the Hull grammar school, of which his father became master in 1624, and, at the age of twelve, by the aid of an exhibition attached to the school, entered Cambridge, where he matriculated as a sizar of Trinity college, 14 December, 1633. On 13 April, 1638, he was admitted a scholar of his college and took his B.A. degree the same year.

His contributions to literature may be classified as consisting mainly of his *Poems*, which, for the most part, belong to the years 1650–2; the *Satires*, which he wrote on public men and public affairs in the reign of Charles II; the *News-letters*, which he regularly addressed to his constituents in Hull after his election as M.P. for the borough in 1659, and which extend from 1660 to the time of his death in 1678; and his *Controversial Essays* on ecclesiastical questions, written at intervals between 1672 and 1677.

It is upon his poems that Marvell's literary reputation mainly rests; yet, curiously enough, these were scarcely known at all to his own contemporaries. Some of them were circulated in MS. after the manner of the time, and were probably read by Milton and other personal friends; but, with few exceptions, they were not given to the world in printed form till three years after his death, when the small folio of 1681 appeared. Three or four fugitive pieces were printed earlier. Two poems, one in Greek and the other in Latin, addressed to the king, appeared as early as 1637 in *Musa Cantabrigiensis;* an occasional poem was printed in *Lachrymae Musarum* in 1649; one was prefixed to Lovelace's *Poems* the same year; and one to a new edition of Milton's *Paradise Lost* in 1671.

Marvell, like his friend Milton and other educated Englishmen, set forth on the accustomed course of European travel when he was twenty-one. From 1642 to 1646, he was abroad in Holland, France, Italy and Spain; but, beyond the fact that he was in Rome in 1645, we know nothing of his movements during these four years, save that Milton testifies that he spent them "to very good purpose and the gaining of those four languages." From 1646, he passes out of sight till we find him again at Nun Appleton house in Yorkshire, the seat of lord Fairfax, where, from 1650 to 1652, he acted as tutor to Fairfax's daughter Mary, a girl of twelve. Nun Appleton house, where Marvell thus came to reside for a while, is situated in the Ainsty of York, in a pleasant tract of country watered by the Ouse, the Wharfe and the Nidd. It was, indeed, an ideal place for a poet, for there nature seemed to conspire with genius to bring to perfection the flowering time of the poet's life; and it was here, under lord Fairfax's roof, that, so far as literature was concerned, Marvell did his best and most enduring work. Judging by the dates concerned, we may conclude that the first product of his pen, at this time, was the *Horatian Ode upon Cromwell's Return from Ireland;* and the title itself suggests one powerful influence which had much to do with the development of Marvell's poetic gift. Though classed among the poets of the reign of Charles II., it is generally recognised now that he really belongs to the earlier time, that his true place is with Herrick, Lovelace and Wither, rather than with Waller, Sedley, Dorset or Rochester. And, while he came under the influence of Donne, an influence paramount during the years of his Cambridge life, he, like Milton, was earliest shaped by his classical training, especially by his study of Horace, his chosen companion and friend. Of his first really great work, the *Horatian Ode,* it has been said that, better than anything else in the language, it gives an idea of a grand Horatian measure, moving, as it does, from end to end, with the solemn beat of its singular metre, strophe and antistrophe with the epode following. All its stanzas combine force with grace and originality with charm, leading Palgrave to say of it that it is "beyond doubt one of the finest in the language, and more in Milton's style than has been reached by any other poet."

Then, too, at a time when poets were not conspicuous for their love of nature herself, except so far as she could furnish similes and illustrations for poetic use, Marvell was an anticipator of Wordsworth in his sheer enjoyment of open air and country life for enjoyment's sake. In this, also, the influence of the Roman poet may, possibly, be seen. We have foregleams of some of Marvell's most beautiful poems in the second of Horace's *Epodes,* where he tells us how delightful it is to be among the sheep, the bees, the vines and fruit trees of his farm among the Sabine hills, and where he confides to us how willingly he would leave the luxuries of the city for the peaceful surroundings and charm of country life. In like manner,

Marvell encamps his mind among trees and gardens where the world toucheth him not, and exclaims, in joyous freedom of soul,

> Bind me, ye woodbines in your twines,
> Curle me about, ye gadding vines.

In his delight in gardens, fields and woods, he is the poet of the open air and the country-side. In his poem entitled *The Garden*, it has been well said that "he throws himself into the very soul of the garden with the imaginative intensity of Shelley in *The West Wind*." Here he has found Fair Quiet and Innocence her "sister dear." No city life for him.

> Society is all but rude
> To this delicious solitude.

Wondrous is the life to be lived here, where

> Ripe apples drop about my head;
> The luscious clusters of the vine,
> Upon my mouth do crush their wine;
> The nectaren and curious peach
> Into my hands themselves do reach;

and where, when he tries to pass, he is ensnared with flowers.

The Garden is composed in the short lines of the octosyllabic couplet. It is free, however, from the diffuseness which the facility of this form of composition too easily favours, possibly from the fact that it is an English version of lines first composed in Latin by Marvell himself: the classical mould exercising restraint upon mere unchartered freedom. Yet there is in it, in spite of this restraint, the poet's genuine love of gardens and woods, of birds and flowers.

Yet he is no merely sensuous epicure, even in his delight in nature. His poem entitled *The Coronet* shows he is not insensible how, in human life, the real ever falls short of the ideal; and, in his *Dialogue between the Soul and the Body*, he makes us realise the meaning of the struggle evermore going on between the lower passions and the higher nature of man. In the similar *Dialogue between the Resolved Soul and Created Pleasure*, also, the chorus comes in with the lofty strain proclaiming that

> Earth cannot show so brave a sight,
> As when a single soul does fence
> The batteries of alluring Sense.

In another poem, also, there is a beautiful simile, where "the orient dew, shed from the bosom of the Morn into the blowing roses," is by the warm sun exhaled back to the skies and so becomes the symbol of a soul,

> that drop, that ray,
> Of the clear fountain of eternal day,

in its upward ascent to its eternal source. In other poems, besides, we find not only grace and sweetness but, also, that high and excellent seriousness which Aristotle asserts to be one of the grand virtues of poetry, the high seriousness which comes of absolute sincerity. There is one other poem which, composed some five years after the Nun Appleton period, and combining delicacy and depth of feeling with charm of melody, should not escape notice. It is entitled *Bermudas*, and is descriptive of the experiences of friends of his who, in the days of Laud, were exiled to these islands for conscience' sake. Though banished, they were not desolate, for, as in their boat and by these shores they

> rowed along,
> The list'ning winds receiv'd their song.

It was a song of praise to Him who had led them "through the wat'ry maze, and, safe from the storms and prelat's rage," had brought them to a land of eternal spring, a land where, for them, the very rocks

> did frame
> A temple, where to sound His name.
> .   .   .   .

> Thus sung they, in the English boat,
> An holy and a cheerful note;
> And all the way, to guide their chime,
> With falling oars they kept the time.

While Marvell's poems were published in collected form in 1681, his *Satires* on the court and the court party, for obvious reasons, remained unpublished till the revolution of 1688 had become an accomplished fact. First circulated in MS. or, in some cases, printed clandestinely, in 1689 they appeared in collected form under the title *Poems on Affairs of State*, and throw curious light on the history of the reigns of Charles II and James II, the politics, manners and scandals of the time. As an example, take the one described as *An Historical Poem*. When Clarendon saw with a smile the wild rejoicings that greeted the return of king Charles on his progress from Dover to London, he could not but wonder, he said, where those people dwelt who had done all the mischief, and kept the king so many years from enjoying the comfort and support of such excellent subjects. In the satire referred to, Marvell expresses his own feelings in humorous fashion also, as he describes the king as:

> Of a tall stature and of sable hue,
> Much like the son of Kish, that lofty Jew,
> Twelve years complete he suffered in exile,
> And kept his father's asses all the while.

While these *Satires* came from Marvell's pen long after the poems of the Nun Appleton period, they were in fact, a return, to his earliest form, for, when in Rome, in 1645, he wrote the lampoon on Richard Flecknoe, an Irish priest, which is remembered now only as having suggested the satire by Dryden in 1682 on the laureate Shadwell. In Paris, also, somewhat later, Marvell wrote a satire in Latin on a French abbé, whom he pronounced a charlatan for undertaking to delineate character and prognosticate fortune from the sight of a man's handwriting. In turning to this form of literature he was but following in the wake of others whose work has been discussed in a previous chapter of the present work.[1]

When we consider the main body of Marvell's *Satires*, extending from about 1667 to the end of his life, we come to the conclusion that it was as a patriot that he became a satirist. Embittered by the degradation of his country in the disgraceful days when Dutch ships of war were actually sailing up the Medway, and feeling the hopelessness of anything like reform while corruption, open and shameless, reigned in the court and

[1] See *ante*, Vol. IV, Chap. XVI.

in public departments, in trenchant fashion he assailed the abuses against which he and the nobler spirits in the nation were contending. His longest rimed satire of 1667, dealing with the Dutch wars, is called *Last Instructions to a Painter*, a title derived from Waller's panegyric poem, and is believed to have been first published anonymously as a broadsheet in the August of that year. The painter, whom he is supposed to be instructing, is to picture the state as being without a fleet, and as being led by men whom neither wit nor courage did exalt; he is to lay bare the dissoluteness of the court, and the dishonesty of state officials who follow their leader, for he commands that pays; he is to show how, while "the Dutch their equipage renew," the English navy yards lie idle, the

<blockquote>
orders run,
To lay the ships up, cease the keels begun;
</blockquote>

meantime, store and wages find their way to the pockets of men who are the obsequious lackeys of the court—"the ships are unrigged, the forts unmanned, the money spent." These keen home-thrusts were keenly felt by some of those whom they most concerned. Pepys, himself a government official, felt compelled to own their truth. In his *Diary*, under date 16 September, he writes—"Here I met with a fourth Advice to a Painter upon the coming in of the Dutch and the End of the War, that made my heart ake to read, it being too sharp and so true." There were other satires of the same trenchant sort, and it has been said that Marvell's merciless dissection of the blunders and intrigues of the time led to the fall of Lord Clarendon, with all the consequences which that memorable event entailed.

Marvell's prose works consist of a long series of *News-letters*, which he wrote daily to his constituents on the doings in parliament, and also of certain controversial works to which he felt impelled by his love of fair play. The letters were discovered in the archives of the town of Hull by Edward Thompson and published by him in 1776. They are continuous from 1660 to 1678, with the exception of a break of two years when he was abroad in 1661, and another hiatus in 1671, and they throw valuable historical light upon the proceedings in parliament at a time when parliamentary reports had not yet begun. His chief prose work, of another character, was his *Rehearsal Transprosed*. The title of the book was suggested by a passage in the Duke of Buckingham's farce called *The Rehearsal*, which was the talk of the town. It occurs in one of the scenes where Bayes (meaning Dryden) speaks of what he calls his rule of transversion, by which he says he takes a book, and, if it be prose, he puts it into verse, and, if verse, he turns it into prose. To which Jonson replies that a process of putting verse into prose should be called transprosing. Marvell caught up this word, using it as part of the title of his book, in which he held up to ridicule the writings of Samuel Parker, one of the worst specimens of the ecclesiastics of Charles II's reign. Bishop Burnet tells us that Parker, in reply to several virulent books,

was attacked by the liveliest droll of the age, who wrote in a burlesque strain read with pleasure from the king down to the tradesman. He not only humbled Parker but the whole party. The author of the *Rehearsal Transprosed* had all the men of wit, (or, as the French phrase it,) all the *laughers*, on his side.

Yet, with all the grace and humour that light up his pages, there was in Andrew Marvell a deep vein of serious earnestness; and in his writings we find, not only wit and banter, but, also, passages of powerful advocacy of great truths and of defence of public rights wantonly violated. In other words, there was the puritan strain in him, a spirit which resented and resisted unrighteousness and wrong.

When we consider the number of editions of Marvell's *Poems* issued between 1681 and 1776, it cannot be said that his works lacked appreciation when they first appeared, and yet, in the last quarter of the eighteenth century, they seem to have passed out of sight, to be rediscovered in the century following. In a sonnet of 1802, Wordsworth spoke of Marvell as one of the great men there have been among us—

> hands that penned
> And tongues that uttered wisdom—better none;

ranked him with those "who called Milton friend," who "knew how genuine glory was put on," and who taught us

what strength was, that would not bend
But in magnanimous meekness.

Six years later, Charles Lamb, with his usual fine taste, appreciated what he called the "witty delicacy" of Marvell's poems, and others who have come after have endorsed this judgment, so that it may be said that, after two centuries and a half, this seventeenth century writer has come to his own, and "is winning as high a place as poet as he occupied as a patriot."

CHAPTER VIII

Historical and Political Writings

I

STATE PAPERS AND LETTERS

IN the period of English history covered by this volume, the system of government under which the nation still has its being was, in a great measure, determined, while the religious movement which dominated the great conflict of the age deeply influenced, for centuries to come, the principles followed by Englishmen in their social relations and in the conduct of their lives. In such times, when the minds of men are constantly strung up to action, and when history, as the phrase runs, is being made every day, there cannot but be a great storage, accompanied by an inevitable waste, of historical materials. Now, materials of history, as such, cannot claim to form part of historical literature, although some of them— many speeches and letters, for instance—may often possess artistic qualities entitling them to be included in it. Again, much that is ostensibly meant to find a place among historical works is often designed by the writer with a political intent; while, in some exceptional instances, political writings, by virtue of their dignity and fulness, come to rank as historical classics. In an age when the two branches of composition were not only inextricably interwoven, but, more or less consciously, confounded, with each other; in which biographies and personal memoirs were frequently written for public or party ends; while private letters were habitually written for wide circles of readers; while speeches were, at times, drawn up as summaries of long and complicated public transactions—an exact classi- fication of historical and political writings under accepted heads becomes extremely difficult. Yet, obvious distinctions being kept generally in view, it may prove possible both to illustrate the remarkable accumulation in this period of materials for historical and political research and study, and to show to what degree the national literature was directly enriched by contemporary efforts in the corresponding fields of literary production. It is not, however, purposed in any part of this or the following chapter to attempt more than a selection, for mention or for comment, of writings marked out as possessed of typical or individual interest.

The first great collection of English state papers is that of John Rushworth, who was appointed clerk-assistant to the House of Commons in April, 1640, and secretary to the council of war in 1645. Whatever may have been their political bias, his labours, if only because of their priority to all others in the same field in England, would deserve the lasting gratitude of all students of English history. But his *Collections of Private Passages of State, Weighty Matters in Law, and Remarkable Proceedings in Five Parliaments*, of which the first volume, extending from 1618 to 1629, was published in the year before the restoration, were no mere tentative beginning. The author's design was both comprehensive and deeply thought out. Being desirous of furnishing a faithful account of the contention between the advocates of prerogative and those of liberty which "gave the Alarm to a Civil War," and for which he was in possession of an unusual abundance of materials,[1] he resolved to devote his attention mainly, though not exclusively, to the domestic struggle, and, since, with regard to this, he found forgery and fiction rampant in the unbridled pamphlet literature of the age, to make the documents on which his narrative was based the substantial part of his work. Thus, in this and the following seven volumes of this edition (of which the last, not published till 1680, ends with the trial of Strafford), he set the first example of pragmatic history to be found in our literature, and reviewed, under the searchlight of first-hand evidence, a period whose records ran the risk of being permanently distorted by a partisanship that cleft the very depths of the national life.[2]

[1] See *post*, Chap. xv, as to Rushworth's newspaper called *The London Post*.

[2] How erroneous it would be to suppose Rushworth's *Collections* to be a dry

The most important body of authentic materials for the history of both the domestic and the foreign policy of Oliver Cromwell, is the *Collection of the State Papers of secretary John Thurloe* (1616–68), which extends from the year 1649 to the restoration, with the addition of some papers belonging to the last eleven years of Charles I. Against Thurloe, an "antidote," if it is to be so called, was posthumously supplied in the important collection known as the *Clarendon State Papers* preserved in the Bodleian and calendared in three volumes. The first of these volumes, which reaches to the year 1649, deals, to a great extent, with documents collected for the use of Clarendon when he was writing the earlier books of his *History of the Rebellion*, together with his own letters and the correspondence of his secretary Edgeman. The second volume is concerned with copies of Charles II's disguised correspondence with members of the royal family and royalists in England, and a series of news-letters addressed to Edgeman by Richard Watson, an ejected fellow of Caius college, and a similar series sent from London to Sir Edward Nicholas at the Hague. The third contains a list of the state papers of the years 1655 to 1657—records of plots and negotiations for the restoration of the king, of which only a small proportion had been previously printed.

If it is not always easy to discriminate between the public and private letters of sovereigns, or of their ministers and agents at home and abroad, and other important functionaries of state, this difficulty often becomes an impossibility in the period now under review. So long as the personal authority of the sovereign was the very essence of the existing system of government, the sense of that authority dominated all his communications, whether with members of the royal family or with others; while a more or less direct personal relation to the sovereign seemed to pervade despatches, reports and letters of all kinds on business of state. This feature finds abundant illustrations in the letters, noted below, of ambassadors of the

---

series of business documents, is shown, *e.g.*, by the extremely interesting narrative by archbishop Abbot of his own sequestration (1627) reported in vol. 1 of the *Stuart Tracts* (1903) from *The English Garner*, which includes not only a clear, and, in the circumstances, fair, account of the system of Laud but, also, a curious sketch of the rise of Buckingham.

type of Sir Henry Wotton; and, no doubt, some of the mental characteristics of James I led his diplomatists to adapt their communications to the idiosyncrasy of the recipient. The king's curiosity was endless, and his sagacity fell little short of his curiosity; he loved a good story and was quick in understanding the point of a joke.[1] But it should also be remembered that the early Stewart age had inherited from the Elizabethan a prose diction intent upon the display of two qualities not always mutually reconcileable—amplitude and point; so that few men and women, least of all those whose epistles were likely to pass through a succession of hands, sat down to write a letter without the desire of leaving it, when done, a finished production in the way of style.

The letters of queen Henrietta Maria, including her correspondence with the king, have been collated by Mrs. Everett Green from both the English and the French archives. Though, in the case of the daughter of Henri IV, everything turned to failure as, with him, most things ended in success, and, though, with the best of intentions, her efforts largely contributed to aggravate the misfortunes of her consort, she was a true daughter of the one, as she was, in another sense, the true wife of the other, king. Her letters have a style of their own, which, in the earlier among them, is accentuated by her pretty broken English. As the toils close round the king and she is perpetually urging him to burst through them, the letters to her "dear heart" gain in intensity what they lose in charm. The correspondence, which ought to have come to a close with her joyful message to her son on his restoration—"if you are torn to pieces in England with 'kindness,' I have my share of it also in France"—drags to a weary end, full of the miseries of money troubles and veiled personal mysteries which seem still not to have been quite set at rest.

A few words may seem in place here on the letters, and the speeches, of Oliver Cromwell, which are alike familiar to modern readers in Carlyle's subjective presentment. As Mrs. Lomas, the latest editor of these remains, puts the matter, Cromwell was an accurate writer; and this makes it both possible and desirable to restore the actual text of his letters. But the case is quite different with the speeches; here, we have

[1] See bibliography as to *The Prince's Cabala.*

only what Cromwell is reported to have said, sometimes taken down in shorthand only, and often under disadvantages of time and place.

On the other hand, the frankness with which his thoughts are laid bare as his sense of responsibility to the Divine source of authority causes him to ignore all other considerations prevails more and more completely as the speeches progress; while such is not the case with the letters. On the contrary, some of the early letters, from the point of view of sincerity, are more "convincing" than a diplomatic communication to Mazarin or a mandate to Cambridge university. Yet, as a whole, Cromwell's letters, which, when necessity obliged, were matter-of-fact and businesslike, are full of those touches of intimacy and those suggestions of individual conviction which give to a letter its true charm and its real force. Cromwell, if one may so put it, was a born letter-writer. Fairfax seems to have left to him the task of drawing up despatches to Speaker Lenthall describing victorious actions; and Carlyle and Gardiner agree that it was Cromwell himself who composed the fateful manifesto of the army to the city of London. Few more powerfully written state papers exist than the declaration of the lord lieutenant of Ireland (in reply to the Roman Catholic council of Kilkenny, 1650), though its account of earlier Irish history may be regarded as more than doubtful.[1] Nothing, in its way, could be more dignified than his message accepting the Oxford vice-chancellorship,[2] or, again, more broad-minded than his advice to his son Richard to recreate himself with "Sir Walter Raughley's History."[3] Among Cromwell's speeches, it is a difficult task to select the most noteworthy. But it may not be amiss to direct attention to two of them, as typical of his treatment of some of the problems with which, in the course of his career, he found himself face to face. In the great speech to the Barebones parliament,[4] he raises a whole edifice of theory as to the eloquence of words and that of deeds; and the speech challenging the confidence of his own first parliament is an unmistakably able pronouncement, especially in reference to his own position.[5] Probably the most trustworthy text of any of his speeches is that of the speech against

[1] Vol. ii, pp. 5 ff. (Mrs. Lomas's edition).   [2] Vol. ii, p. 180.
[3] Vol. ii, p. 54.   [4] Vol. ii, pp. 272 ff.   [5] Vol. ii, pp. 339 ff.

the Levellers, revised by himself as delivered in January, 1655.[1]

The value of ambassadorial despatches as materials of history was recognised at an early date. According to Bacon,[2] they are *ad historiam pretiosissima supellex;* and, in Sir George Carew's introduction to his *Relation of the State of France*, addressed to James I on Carew's return from his embassy to Henri IV,[3] the original letters and papers of leading actors in the management of affairs are described as "the only true and unerring sources of history." But, though Sarpi (father Paul), the illustrious historian of the council of Trent (1619), by his use of materials of this nature, had already set an example which, before long, was to be followed by English historical writers, it had not occurred to the statesmen and diplomatists of the reigns of Elizabeth and James I to publish, or allow to be published, their "works" of this description; and, had it occurred to them, they would probably soon have been made to change their minds.

It may be disputed whether the golden age of English diplomacy should be placed in the years in which the great queen was warily staving off, though she knew it to be inevitable, the critical struggle with Spain, or in the reign of her successor, confident, almost to the last, of his ability to gain by negotiation the European authority which he was unprepared to assert by the alternative method of blood and iron. But it is certain that few publications of diplomatic history have exercised a greater effect than one which was given to the world in 1654, when a new epoch was opening in English foreign policy and the protector's military state, after asserting itself as the dominant great power of Europe, seemed about to become the head of a protestant alliance holding the balance in both hemispheres.[4] It was at this time that there appeared in print a posthumous publication by Sir Dudley Digges, late master of the rolls (1583–1639),[5] entitled *The Compleat Ambassador: or Two Treaties of the Intended Marriage of Qu. Elizabeth of Glorious Memory.* In this work, the history of the

---

[1] Vol. ii, p. 405. [2] *De Augmentis* (1623). [3] Printed in Birch's *Negotiations*.
[4] Cf. Stählin, K., *Sir Francis Walsingham und seine Zeit* (Heidelberg, 1908), vol. i, *ad fin.*
[5] As to his and his son's pamphlets, see bibliography.

negotiations as to the Anjou and Alençon matches carried on during Walsingham's embassy (1570–3, dates covering that of the massacre of St. Bartholomew) became public property in the shape of the despatches of Walsingham, and the replies of Burghley, Leicester and Sir Thomas Smith.   No similar revelation had hitherto taken place in England, where, notwithstanding the assiduous exertions of James I's diplomatists, very little attention had been paid to their activity by outsiders.   But the publisher, encouraged by the success of *Cabala*,[1] a curious medley of letters and papers of the reigns of James and Charles I which appeared in 1654, anticipated a great success for his experiment, and was not deceived.   The time was propitious for a study of the diplomatic processes of the most aggressively protestant of queen Elizabeth's ambassadors, whose policy of securing the alliance of France against Spain was just about to experience a revival.   Thus, the book, having rapidly gone into a second edition, was, in due course, translated into French, and came to be repeatedly cited in Wicquefort's celebrated manual, *L'Ambassadeur et ses Fonctions*.

Sir Henry Wotton, of whose writings some general account has been given in a previous volume,[2] was one of the most accomplished, as he was one of the most voluminous, letter-writers of his age.   Many of his letters are printed in the successive editions of *Reliquiae Wottonianae;* but a very large number have been added by the zeal of his most recent biographer.[3] In the case of a considerable portion of these letters, it is useless to seek to distinguish between what is of the nature of private or of public information.   Intended primarily for the eye of his royal master, Wotton's semi-official letters blend the report of high affairs of state and the offer of grave political advice with table-talk.   Of this he was a master; he practised it to perfection with the members of his embassy at Venice, and he seasoned it with a great deal of wit.   The genial humour of his later years, when, in his Eton provostship, he had found such mental repose as is possible to an active spirit, was, necessarily, of slower growth.

[1] To be distinguished, of course, from *The Prince's Cabala*.
[2] See Vol. IV, pp. 188, 189, *ibid*. bibliography, pp. 551, 552.
[3] *The Life and Letters of Sir Henry Wotton* (1907) by Logan Pearsall Smith.

While, as a diplomatist, Wotton exercised, at least at Venice, a stronger influence than quite suited his master's policy, his literary ambition, except in a poetic gem by which it would have surprised him to find himself most widely remembered, never carried him far in the direction of achievement. His authorship of *The State of Christendom*, a survey of the political world in 1594, still remains doubtful, and, as a historian, he never accomplished more than the *Characters* of Essex and Buckingham, with *Some Observations by way of Parallel;* a short *Life and Death* of the former favourite; a Latin *Panegyrick of King Charles*, written at Eton not long before his death, and, among a few other fragments or incidental pieces, a page of an intended *History of Venice*, which no man could have seemed either by experience or by insight more competent to write. The history of England from Henry VIII, which it was the wish of Charles I that Wotton should execute, he never seems to have taken in hand. In the world of letters, he was a man of projects, as in that of politics he was a man of designs — and it is this perennial freshness of mind which, added to the nobility of his aims and the grace of his style, makes him a delightful letter-writer.

A species of correspondents which is more fully discussed elsewhere in this volume,[1] cannot be altogether passed by in the present connection. "Intelligencers," as they were called, played a part of some importance in the earlier Stewart period. They were professed writers of news employed by ambassadors residing abroad, or by persons of consequence at home, to furnish them with a continuous budget of news concerning events in England and in other countries. Obviously, the value of these communications was enhanced, if private letters could be added from persons connected with the court and likely to be *au courant* of its secrets or, at all events, of its gossip, or from others filling important positions abroad. It is of such "intelligence" as this that is composed the collection transcribed by T. Birch from various sources and published from his MSS. in the British Museum under the title *The Court and Times of James I*. The most prolific "intelligencer" in this collection is John Chamberlain, who is responsible for not less than 116 in the first, and 122 in the second, volume. Most of

[1] See chapter on The Beginnings of English Journalism, *post*.

his letters are addressed to Carleton, to whom, when in Paris, all but one letter of another series are likewise addressed. Chamberlain's letters, or many of them, possess some of the qualities of later journalism, without some of its defects. Their news includes gossip of all sorts, but they are straightforward in statement, while their simplicity of style must have refreshed diplomatists, who had "oratory" enough to compose on their own account. It must not be forgotten that these were private letters intended for private recipients, and that the freedom of comment which makes them pleasant reading would not have been possible under any other circumstances.[1]

Letters in which public and private ingredients intermix were familiar already to the Elizabethans, as they must be to every age in which a sense of form has come to affect all varieties of written, and not a few of spoken, composition. Bacon, as is known, was a great letter-writer and owed something of the strength which he shows even in this relatively loose branch of writing to the example of his mother.[2] This lady identified herself to an extraordinary degree with the interests of her sons, though her puritanism was of a hard flawlessness to which neither of them could attain. Bacon himself was in so many respects greater than his age that the chief significance of his own priceless letters lies in their biographical value. But the light which they throw on affairs of state in which he was an actor, or of which he was an interested spectator, or (as in the early Essex episode[3]) something of both, is of the utmost importance for the historical student; and the fact that, in not a few of these letters, Bacon appears as a keen politician nurtured in the Elizabethan traditions of a patriotic hatred of Spain, is only part of their general evidence showing the many-sidedness of his nature, by no means alien from the sympathies and antipathies common to those around him. A special literary interest attaches to the interesting letters to Sir Toby Matthew on *Instauratio Magna*, and to the *Letter to the King*

---

[1] Francis Osborne, the author of *Advice to a Son* and other easy-going manuals of knowledge and conduct, declares, in the first-named work, that "it is an Office unbecoming a Gentleman to be an Intelligencer, which in real Truth is no better than a Spie."

[2] See her letters in Spedding's *Letters and Life*, vol. I, pp. 110 ff.

[3] *Ibid.*, vol. II.

upon the sending unto him of a beginning of a History of His Majesties Time.[1]

In the reign of Charles I, few historical students will fail to turn to the letters of the great statesman by whom the king's councils were guided in the most critical period of his rule. *The Earl of Strafford's Letters and Despatches*, extending over the years 1611 to 1640, show forth a man who, though overwhelmed by the "violent hate" of a people refusing to be coerced into good government, thoroughly knew his own mind and could forgive his sovereign for not knowing his own.[2]

As we pass into the period of the civil war, our attention is claimed, after the letters of Oliver Cromwell already noticed, by *The Fairfax Correspondence*, and the *Memorials of the Civil War* which forms the conclusion of the series. Unfortunately, these volumes, which relate the history of a family genuinely English in its temperament and bearing, and include correspondence with many personages prominent in the struggle, are written in the confusing form, popularised by Carlyle, of running narrative interspersed with original letters. The same form is more successfully adopted in one of the most attractive records of family history belonging to the period from the outbreak of the civil war to the revolution of 1688 (and beyond); but, in this instance, the design is carried out with so much of both objectivity and freshness as to leave little room for cavil.

The *Letters and Papers of the Verney Family* down to the end of the year 1639 were first printed in 1833. They are documents of a family history which goes back to the reign of king John, covers the wars of the Roses and the Tudor reigns, and relates the story of the journey into Spain of Charles prince of Wales, on whom Edward Verney attended. But the collection ends with the Scottish expedition of king Charles, when his standard-bearer, Sir Edmund Verney, was again in his train, in 1639. Here, the tale was taken up by pious hands and carried on through three series of *Memoirs of the Verney Family* during the civil war, during the commonwealth and from the restoration to the year 1696. The story, like the stately and hospitable English house which forms its centre, is full of portraits; but, in their book, the tact of the editresses has allowed these to

---

[1] Spedding's *Letters and Life*, vol. iv.
[2] First published in 1739. See bibliography.

be mainly self-painted. The Verneys, before and during the seventeenth century, were, in the words of the elder lady Verney,

an ordinary gentleman's family of the higher class, mixing a good deal in the politics of their times, with considerable country and local influence; Members of Parliament, sheriffs, magistrates, soldiers—never place-men—marrying in their own degree, with no splendid talents or positions to boast of, no crimes, either noble or ignoble, to make them notorious, and, for that very reason, good average specimens of hundreds of men or women of their age.

They were, at the same time, a family that cherished, in prosperity and in adversity alike, the principles of conduct in both public and private life to the observation of which the greatness and the freedom of England are deeply indebted; and, in their case, the principles in question were practised not less constantly by the women than by the men. Sir Edmund Verney, *ultimus Angliae Bannerettus*, who, with many misgivings as to the policy of Charles I, had loyally adhered to his cause, fell at Edgehill, his right hand, with the royal standard in its grasp, being severed from his arm; the responsibilities of the headship of the family descended to his son Ralph and remained with him for nearly half a century. While Sir Edmund was described as "one of the strictness of a Puritan, of the charity of a papist, of the civility of an Englishman," Sir Ralph is an admirable example of the best class of country gentleman of his or any day, gentle and courteous, the mainstay of his brothers and sisters and kinsmen and kinswomen of every degree, a thorough man of business, sober in his religious views, and, in his political, loyal to his convictions, but with a self-reliant loyalty unintelligible either to courts or to mobs. Though he had taken the side of the parliament during the civil war, he went into exile rather than accept the covenant, and remained there for several years—even after the sequestration of his estates had been removed, thanks to the self-sacrificing exertions of his wife Mary, the heroine *par excellence* of the Verney records—"Mischief," as Sir Ralph fondly called her and, in person, another Henrietta Maria,[1] though not in the

---

[1] There is a *prima facie* resemblance between the portraits of the two ladies, both of whom were small in stature.

benefits which her services brought to her husband. After
its chief had quitted house and country, the remainder of the
family seemed to fall to pieces—the brave Sir Edmund Verney
the younger, slain at Drogheda; Tom, the black sheep of the
family, a most "unfortunate traveller" by land and sea, and
the rest of them. But Sir Ralph survived his beloved wife for
nearly half a century, and, in the days of Charles II and James
II, again sat in parliament, and was again found on the side
of civil and religious liberty. The history of the times, public
as well as private, is spread out before us in this family correspondence, as it had been in no previous collection since the
Paston letters. It may, perhaps, be added that the influence
of literature or learning upon the Verney family is not per-
ceptibly important, though some of them had been partly
educated at Oxford. The education of ladies in the seventeenth century was, undoubtedly, inferior to that of some of
their Elizabethan predecessors;[1] their penmanship is execrable,
and their spelling purely phonetic.

The *Correspondence of the Family of Hatton* (1601-1704),
though it cannot compare in breadth of interest to the Verney
papers, is one of the most amusing of the collections dating from
this period; though what has been published only forms part of
a larger family correspondence,[2] and mainly dates from post-
restoration times. Lord chancellor Sir Christopher Hatton,
of Elizabethan fame, left a son and namesake who, after the
restoration, became governor of Jersey, and was succeeded in
this office by his son, afterwards first viscount Hatton, to whom
most of the letters now printed were addressed. Nothing can
be more characteristic of the "frank age" from which they
date than these outspoken family communings, of which the
spelling, by no means the least of their charms, has, happily,
not been modernised by their editor.

For final mention among the letter-writers of this period it
has been thought well to reserve one who may, perhaps, be

---

[1] This does not specially apply to Anne and Mary Fitton, passages from whose
letters have been published under the title *Gossip from a Muniment Room* (by
lady Newdigate-Newdegate, 1897), and carry us back to the years 1574-1618.
Mary played only too conspicuous a part at queen Elizabeth's court. Anne may
be regarded as one of the worthies of Warwickshire. Their letters contain more
of the prose than of the poetry of women's experience.

[2] The MS. *Finch-Hatton Correspondence* in the British Museum.

considered as the most widely representative of them all, inasmuch as, while himself not unaccustomed to the lower walks of diplomacy, it is rather as an "intelligencer" of long standing, and as a more or less private letter-writer, that he established his claim to the place which he holds in the history of English literature. At the same time, his general literary activity was such that it would be neither just nor convenient were not some general account of his literary labours to be attempted in this place.

Although James Howell earned his appointment by Charles II as historiographer royal of England by a long succession of publications to be classed as historical, his enduring title to literary fame rests on his *Familiar Letters* (*Epistolae Ho-Elianae*), which can only in part be described as historical writing. They occupy a place of their own in the literature of essays and table-talk clothed in the mainly fictitious form of personal letters. Before he began his literary career, James Howell had led an active life, which had extended over some forty-five years since, to use his own phraseology, he "came tumbling into the world a grave Cadet, a true Cosmopolite; not born to Land, Lease, House or Office." He had seen many cities and the dwellers therein beyond the limits of England and his native Wales; he had been engaged in commercial dealings in Venice and in diplomatic negotiations in Spain, besides being temporarily employed in foreign service in Denmark and in France; he had held an administrative post in York, and had thus come to sit for a time in parliament; and he had been sent on a confidential mission by Strafford from Dublin to Edinburgh and London. In 1642, before he had actually begun to perform the duties of clerk of the privy council, into which office he had been sworn, he was imprisoned in the Fleet—because of his loyalty or because of his debts, or for both reasons. During the eight or nine years of his imprisonment, he lived the laborious life of a man supporting himself by his pen, and produced a large proportion of his numerous writings. In these, he at first kept up a display of antagonism to presbyterianism, becoming, as a matter of course, involved in controversy with Prynne; but this attitude he modified, and, in 1651, he was released on bail. During the protectorate, he sought to secure the good-will of Cromwell, advocating a compromise between him and the royal pretender. The restoration, naturally, he welcomed; but he obtained nothing from the crown beyond a small gift of money (£200) and the office aforesaid. Some ironical consolations addressed to him by disappointed cavaliers led to a controversy between him and Sir Roger L'Estrange, who had not much trouble in pointing out certain inconsistencies in Howell's political profession. He died in 1666.[1]

Such a life might well provide abundant materials for the volume of *Letters* which Howell published from his prison in 1645, and which was succeeded by a second volume in 1647, and a new edition of both, with a third volume, in 1650. A fourth was added in a collected edition which appeared in 1655. The reader will not be long in discerning the fictitious character of many of these letters. Even so outspoken a writer as he was would hardly have cared actually to send to Buckingham, when at the height of his power, the "few advertisements" of the letter of advice (dated 13 February, 1626/7), "which I would not dare to present, had I not hopes that the Goodness which is concomitant with your Greatness would make them venial," or have troubled Charles I, not long after Marston moor, with variations on the consolatory fact that, in the past, other kings had found themselves in an even worse plight. There is further internal evidence to support the same conclusion, besides the occasional great length of these letters, their *sans gêne*, remarkable even in an age not habituated to reticence, their excess of anecdotes (though often good in themselves, and always well told) and of verse, with which an experienced man of the world would scarcely have tired most of his correspondents. Moreover, as a matter of fact, the few letters from Howell actually preserved by those to whom they were sent are in a shorter and more businesslike form.

Of the letters as we have them, some are lucid, as well as readable, summaries of the political condition and historical development of particular countries or communities—Venice, the united provinces of the Netherlands, the Hanseatic league and Spain (which he studied with particular curiosity); statements as to the distribution of different religions on the earth, of the Jews in Europe, and the like; accounts of the inquisition, and of

---

[1] He was buried in the Temple church, where his monument is preserved, though not on its original site.

particular episodes of recent or contemporary history. Others
are practically nothing else than short essays—"middles," as
journalists would call them—on social or literary topics of
divers kinds, especially problems of language—for Howell was
a scholar by training as well as by instinct, and, in 1623, after
some of his travels were over, was elected a fellow of his college
(Jesus) at Oxford. His scientific interests appear to have been
few, though he could speculate on the changes in the human
body, and, in moral science, on the mysterious ways of Providence in its dealing with man,[1] and on demonology, for he was
no exception to his generation in his belief in witchcraft.
Occasionally, he turns to more material topics—the potations
of the chief nations of the globe (from "whisky" to "cauphe")
and the virtues of tobacco, which even king James acknowledged in circumstances of stress.[2]

All these matters, and a great many others, Howell discusses
in "these rambling Letters," "which indeed," he writes,[3] "are
naught else than a Legend of the cumbersome Life and various
Fortunes of a Cadet;" and he deprecates the assurances of his
correspondent that

> some of them are freighted with many excellent and quiet passages
> delivered in a masculine and solid style, adorn'd with much eloquence
> and stuck with the choicest flowers pick'd from the Muses garden.

But the praise was not, in all respects, undeserved. Howell
combined instruction and entertainment with admirable effect,
and possessed what was still the rare gift of imparting information that was not only to a large extent new, but, also, true so
far as its purveyor could ascertain its truth. Accuracy of
detail, in the matter of dates and places, was not his forte;[4]
on the other hand, neither was a tendency to exaggeration, or a
habit of garbling his facts so as to suit his point of view,
among his foibles. And, above all, he said what he had to say
clearly, often with not a little force, and with a humour usually
apposite and sound. His anti-puritanism (as the later conduct

---

[1] Letter 4 in book IV (Jacobs's ed.), there can be little doubt, is the original of
Parnell's famous tale of the hermit.

[2] When he found himself in a pigsty.

[3] From the Fleet, 5 May, book II, letter 61.

[4] "Syracuse, now Messina" (book I, sect. I, letter 27), is, perhaps, a rather
out-of-the-way instance of looseness.

of his life shows) was not very violent, and sometimes takes a rather ingenious turn;[1] his personal piety was quite unaffected, though his way of placing on record his religious habits may savour rather too much of what he calls "striking a talley in the Exchequer of Heaven."[2] And if, on this and other occasions, he may seem to talk overmuch about himself "what subject," as Thackeray asks in a passage where James Howell is honoured by being coupled with Montaigne,[3] "does a man know better?" Thus, his letters as a whole, and especially the earlier (for the later are not altogether exempt from the decline noticeable in most continuations) do not fall far short of his own description of "Familiar Letters" as

the Keys of the Mind; they open all the Boxes of one's Breast, all the cells of the Brain, and truly set forth the inward Man; nor can the Pencil so lively represent the Face as the Pen can do the Fancy.[4]

James Howell's literary activity was very far from being exhausted by his letters; during the years from 1642 to 1651, his pen was never at rest, and the habit, once acquired, was never relinquished. But, in one way or another, most of his lesser productions seem more or less supplementary to the work on which his literary reputation rests. An apparent exception is *Dendrologia, Dodona's Grove, or the Vocall Forest* (1640), the earliest of his publications, which may be described as an allegorical gallery of characters conveying, under the thin veil of the names of trees or of designations derived from them, the political sympathies or antipathies of the writer.[5] An allegory of this sort admitted of easy multiplication, and Howell appended to it a series of skeleton pleas, similar in design, for

---

[1] See the clever comparison (it hardly deserves a higher kind of commendation) between the advantages of prayer and those of praise (book II, letter 67).

[2] Book I, sect. IV, letter 32.

[3] *Roundabout Papers : On Two Children in Black.*

[4] Book II, letter 70.

[5] "Cedar" is the emperor; "Oke, Vine, Beech" are the kings of England, France, Sweden and Poland; "Elder" is duke Maximilian I of Bavaria ("so-called both from his age and the ill favour he hath amongst us"); "Elmes," the nobility; "Ampeluna," France; "Adriana," Venice; "Alchorana," Turkey; "Druina," England; "Boetia," the university of Oxford, etc. That the opinions suggested by the allegory are not altogether conventional is shown by the character of "Elaiana" (Spain, the land of oil), which displays discriminating insight.

the monarchical form of government.[1] A second appendix, *England's Teares for the present Warres*, is a rhetorical lament by London's mother, England.[2]

In a different vein—one of rough satirical humour—are two curious pieces of Howell's later years, which, as it were, travesty the sober summaries exemplified in his letters — *A Brief Character of the Low Countries under the States* (1660) and *A Perfect Description of the Country of Scotland* (1659). The satire against the Dutch[3] is at least accompanied by a recognition of some of their merits; but the anti-Scottish tract descends into invective so bitter and so coarse that its date alone can excuse it;[4] the unerring instinct of Wilkes, more than a century later, selected it for reproduction, with a sly preamble, in No. 31 of *The North Briton* (August, 1762).

In his capacity as a traveller, Howell, though familiar only with western, and parts of southern and central, Europe, promulgated *Instructions for Forreine Travell* (1642, republished 1650, with a new appendix "for Travelling into Turkey and the Levant parts," which, unlike Fynes Moryson and Coryate, he had himself never visited[5]).   The little book is a very divert-

[1] The Great Conjunction or Parliament of Stars; Ornilogia (*sic*), or The Great Consult of Birds; Anthologia, or Parliament of Flowers; The Assembly of Architects (on the value of such a pillar as an ancient court of justice); The Insurrection of the Winds (against rebellion).

[2] It ends with the expression of a desire that, if England "and her Monarch miscarry, her Epitaph may be written by her dearly beloved Childe, James Howell."

[3] "There are spiders as bigge as Shrimps, and I think as many"—"You may sooner convert a Jew, than make an ordinary Dutch-man yeild to Arguments that Crosse him."

[4] If the Almighty came down from heaven in the last day with His Angels in their whitest garments, the Scots "would run away, crying, The Children of the Chappel are come again to torment us, let us flie from the abomination of these boys."

[5] Of Coryate and his *Crudities* (1610), as well as of other English travellers, something has been said *ante*, Vol. IV, pp. 104 ff. Midway between Coryate's over-advertised, but, as a matter of fact, unjustly decried, book and James Howell's *Instructions*, there appeared so much as up to a recent date was allowed to become publicly known of Fynes Moryson's *Travels*. The first three parts of his *Itinerary* were published in 1617; but part IV, with an *imprimatur* dated 1626, remained, unprinted, at Corpus Christi college, Oxford, till the more important portions of it were published, thanks to the energy of Charles Hughes, in 1903. The whole work was originally written in Latin, in which form it is preserved among the Harleian MSS. in the British Museum. The English version is also by Fynes Moryson. On the whole, he was an impartial, as well as a candid, observer,

ing, but, at the same time, very rational anticipation of the
introductions to guidebooks of later days, containing, as it
does, much valuable historical, political and (allowing for the
philological shortcomings of the age) linguistic observation
interspersed with interesting observations on men and
manners.

It could, however, hardly be that he should not be most at
home in London, where, by his own choice, or lodged by the
parliament, he spent a large portion of his life; and his *Lon-
dinopolis; An Historical Discourse or Perlustration of the City
of London* (1657), a careful guidebook of London, with a survey
of its several wards, and special mention of its lawcourts, is
among the last literary fruits of his life, bearing the characteristic motto *Senesco, non segnesco.* It makes no pretence of
being wholly original; and, indeed, the author confesses that, in
this instance, he has followed the examples of "the Lord
Bacon's Henry the Seventh, and my Lord Herbert's Henry the
eighth," of which the noble authors,

> though the composition, and digesting be theirs, whereby they
> determined their Books, yet, under favour, touching the main in-
> gredients . . . took them from others, who had written the life of
> these Kings before.

Yet the work is far from deficient in vigour, and includes a
"Parallel with other great Cities," showing in which of twenty
several points they are respectively inferior to London.

---

whose eyes were open to national vices, such as Italian immorality and German
intemperance. Though by no means infallible in his statements of fact, he is not
habitually inaccurate. He writes in good Elizabethan prose, but without any
effort at displaying his scholarship after the fashion of James Howell.

CHAPTER IX

Historical and Political Writings

II

HISTORIES AND MEMOIRS

IN the present chapter, which has to deal with a number of more or less conscious endeavours to put the results of historical study or of personal experience into a literary shape, it seems well to begin with a notice of some of the works produced in the period under discussion which aimed at being "perfect history" or history proper. Whether the master-piece of the historical works of the age, Clarendon's *Rebellion*, viewed in connection with his autobiography—from which (as will be seen) there is no possibility of detaching it—be regarded as history proper, or as partaking of the character of memoirs, it must mark the height of our survey of the histories of the age, and will, at the same time, serve as a transition from these to the accumulation of memoirs, diaries, contemporary biographies and autobiographies, and personal narratives of various sorts from which some selection will be attempted. What has to be said of political literature, for the most part, will be added as occasion may arise, for it would not be feasible to spread the net widely over the sea of unnumbered pamphlets of an age in which every subject in church and state was regarded as contentious, and few were left undiscussed in "fundamental" argument and with a vast expenditure of printer's ink.

The days of the later Tudor annalists and chroniclers, thoroughly national in their spirit and sympathies, had not passed away when upon some few far-seeing minds had dawned the conception of historical writing which, while still furnishing a full account of the events of the past should, at the same time, interest the political thinker and satisfy the demands of literary art.

Bacon's *Historie of the Reigne of King Henry the Seventh* (1622), which may practically be regarded as the earliest of English historical monographs, was actually composed in 1621, probably after Bacon, on his release from the Tower, had returned to Gorhambury. In the circumstances, as Spedding points out,[1] the book could not be written otherwise than at second-hand; for, during all but the last six weeks of the four or five months within which the task was executed, the author was excluded from London and from the house of Sir Robert Cotton, who supplied him with some of his material. It is, consequently, in the main, founded on Bernard André and Polydore Vergil, with Fabyan and the later chroniclers, and a few additions by Stow, and, more especially, by Speed, some of whose mistakes were copied by Bacon. Yet this *Life* was by no means a piece of mere compilation, either in design or execution. The conception of the character of Henry VII dates from an early period of Bacon's career, as is proved by a fragment of a history of the Tudor reigns from Henry VIII to Elizabeth, discovered by Spedding;[2] which also seems to refute Mackintosh's idea that the *Historie of the Reigne of King Henry the Seventh* was written, not only (as, in a sense, it certainly was) to justify James I, but, also, to flatter him by representing Henry VII as a model king and the prototype of the reigning monarch. For the rest, if features are observable in Bacon's king Henry which seem to support Mackintosh's view (thus, Henry was "careful to obtain good intelligence from abroad"), there are others in which the resemblance is most imperfect ("for his pleasures, there is no news of them"; "he was governed by none")—though it might be possible to see in this very unlikeness the most subtle flattery. There is certainly no flattery to be found in some touches of unmistakable irony—in the reference to Henry's great attention to religious foundations as he became old, or in the turn given to the application of the phrase "his Salomon of England (for Salomon also was too heavy upon his people in exactions)." On the whole,

[1] Bacon's *Literary and Professional Works*, vol. 1 (VI), pp. 23 ff.
[2] See *ibid.*, pp. 17–22.

Henry VII, in the mirror of Bacon's narrative, appears, not as a man of genius, but as a wise and singularly ready politician, and as one of whom it might be said that "what he minded he compassed." It need hardly be added that the spirit of the book is thoroughly monarchical; the writer's contempt for "the rude people," always intent upon being deceived, is especially noticeable in the narrative of the attempts of Lambert Simnel and Perkin Warbeck. The style of this work possesses a kind of charm absent from few of Bacon's writings, which always have the fascination belonging to deep waters, and the concluding sentence of the work is exceedingly graceful. The author's fondness for Latin forms ("militar," "indubiate," and so forth) is very obvious; the Latin translation of his book seems to have been made either by himself or under his own eye.

Lord Herbert of Cherbury's *Life and Reign of King Henry the Eighth, together with which is briefly represented A general History of the Times*, marks a very conscious advance in historical composition. There is here, coupled with a dignified ease of style characteristic of most of the author's writings, and of his *Autobiography* in particular, an evident wish to make as full use as possible of the original documents at the historian's disposal. No doubt, the work was also written with a personal purpose, and of this it is impossible to lose sight in estimating the literary effect produced; indeed, it is to be discovered in most of Herbert's historical writings. They were composed at a later period of his life than the *Autobiography*, which only reaches the year 1624, and the merits of which are surprisingly exiguous for an author commanding a wide experience of the world and possessed of original intellectual power.[1] Yet the characteristic qualities of the book, both for better and for worse, have been much exaggerated. Horace Walpole (who first printed the MS. at Strawberry Hill in 1764) must have been beyond the mark in describing it as "the most curious and entertaining" produced by his press;[2] and, if, as he states, he and lady Waldegrave could not "get on" with it "for laughing and screaming,"[3] their sense of the ridiculous must have been

---

[1] An estimate of lord Herbert of Cherbury's position among modern speculative thinkers has been given in Vol. IV, pp. 335–338.

[2] *Letters*, ed. Cunningham, vol. IV, p. 156.

[3] *Ibid.*, p. 252.

excessively acute, though, to be sure, on one occasion, at least, the autobiographer all but falls into the Falstaffian vein.[1]

Beyond all doubt, Edward Herbert was inordinately vain of his powers as a duellist—whether on foot or on horseback—which, in his opinion, evidently entitled him to say to all comers (including ministers, governors, and ambassadors) "*Je suis Herbert*," as one of his French rivals declared "*Je suis Balagny*"; and in his relations with women he certainly had the advantage of sublime self-confidence. But duelling was the most fashionable vice of the time;[2] added to which he took his vows as knight of the Bath most seriously. Though vainglorious and quarrelsome, he was free from revengefulness and any sort of meanness; and, though something of a lady-killer,[3] he was not wanton. Notwithstanding his remarks on education, and his contributions both to natural science and household medicine, it cannot be said that, except as a picture of manners, his *Autobiography* has much serious interest before the period of his embassy to France (1619–24); and, even then, though his narrative of the Spanish and French marriage negotiations is worth reading, as well as his characterisation of Louis XIII, de Luynes, and Gondomar, he seems to reserve the substance of his political experiences for treatment in another form.

The *Autobiography*, of which the style is measured but agreeable, though the record of some of the writer's youthful exploits in camp and court, at times, has an almost pedantic solemnity, breaks off with Herbert's recall from Paris. The remainder of his life was given up to a series of endeavours to re-enter the active service of the crown by conciliating the royal goodwill, and to literary labours which, in part, are to be reckoned among these efforts. Among them was the defence of Buckingham, drawn up in reply to violent attacks upon the memory of the favourite after his assassination, and dedicated to Charles I. Sir Henry Wotton expressed his admiration of

---

[1] See *Autobiography*, ed. Lee, S., p. 185, for Herbert's night escapade, when he was about to start on his embassy in 1619.

[2] See the appendix on "Duelling in France and England in the early years of the Seventeenth Century" in Lee's edition.

[3] He believed himself to have endangered the peace of mind of no less august and devout a personage than Anne of Denmark.

it while it was in the making; but it brought no recompense to its author.

Among these efforts, also, was his *Life of Henry the Eighth*, on which he seems to have been at work as early as 1632, and on which he was still engaged seven years later. The use of original documents by which it is distinguished has been already noted. It was not completed till 1645, when he was also bringing to an end his chief philosophic labours. The rest of Herbert's life was occupied by a painful and unedifying struggle for his estates.

Many indications of the growing interest in historical writing in the reign of James I and in the earlier years of that of Charles I must be passed by. Edmund Bolton, who, under the pseudonym of "Philanactophil," dedicated to Buckingham a translation of Florus's epitome of Roman history, in order to demonstrate the superiority of histories to "epitomes," took occasion, from the publication of an epistle by Sir Henry Savile lamenting the existing state of English historical literature, to advocate, in a tract called *Hypercritica*, the production of a complete *Corpus Rerum Anglicarum*—"a felicity wanting to our Nation, now when even the name thereof is as it were at an end." And we know how Milton contemplated on his own account a history of Britain from the origins, of which he only executed a fragment.[1] On the other hand, Thomas May, secretary of the Long Parliament, obeyed its authoritative behest by publishing, in 1647, the history of the great assembly which had begun its labours seven years earlier, together with "a short and necessary view of some precedent years." May, who was a writer of considerable versatility,[2] had produced, besides a translation in rimed couplets of Lucan's stirring epic on the second civil war of Rome, two moderately inspiring English poems on the reigns of Edward III and Henry II, in

[1] See, as to Milton's *History of England*, and his *History of Moscovia*, *ante*, Chap. v. Milton's *Reflections on the Civil War in England*, etc., which inveighs against the decay of religion during the civil wars and the period of uncertainty which ensued, is rptd. in Maseres's *Select Tracts*, etc., part II. For a review of Milton's historical work, see Firth, C. H., *Milton as a Historian*, Publications of the British Academy, 1909 (x).

[2] See, as to his tragedies and comedies, of which the earliest is dated 1622, *ante*, Vol. VI, p. 264. He also wrote a Latin play, *Julius Caesar*, which remained in manuscript.

which "Philip and all her beauteous train" and Fair Rosamond
do not fail to appear; but his *History of the Parliament of
England*, which began 3 November, 1640, in conformity with the
claim advanced, in the title as well as in the motto of the book,
that its distinctive quality was veracity, exhibits both straight-
forwardness of manner and dignity of tone. A succinct introduction dwells specially on the relations with Rome, with whom
James I is described as having "temporised," but holds the
balance fairly between the personal virtues of Charles I and
his errors as a ruler. Strafford's trial and death, we are told,
did at last as much harm to the kingdom as had resulted from
his action while he was in power. The work, in which some
important speeches and documents are inserted *verbatim*, ends
with November, 1643.

By way of contrast with the official historian of the Long
Parliament may be mentioned a faithful, though by no means
uncomplaining, follower of Charles I and Charles II, to whom,
indeed, he successively acted as a kind of historiographer in the
campaigns of 1644, 1645 and 1650. Sir Edward Walker, garter
king-at-arms, held the posts of secretary at war and secretary
extraordinary to the privy council both before and during the
siege of Oxford, and was allowed to assist Charles I in the ill-
fated negotiations at Newport; he afterwards accompanied
Charles II to Scotland in 1650 and formed part of his court
in exile till the restoration. Thereafter, he held sway at
the Heralds' college for the rest of his days. He had
many grievances to urge, and many controversies to conduct; so that there was much to include in the *Historical
Discourses upon several Occasions*, published posthumously
in 1705.

A word should, perhaps, be added as to *Secret Observations
on the Life and Death of Charles King of England*, by William
Lilly, "student of Astrology," which forms part II of a larger
tract entitled *Monarchy, or no Monarchy in England* (1651).
In part I, various prophecies are in good faith treated as ful-
filled—especially Ambrose Merlin's famous prophecy of the
white king, dating nine hundred years back. Part II is a historical account of the life of Charles I from his childhood to his
death, which is fair to certain sides of his character, though the
animus of the whole is anti-episcopalian and anti-royalist.

As a matter of course, no important occasion is allowed to go by without a horoscope.

One historian of note remains to be mentioned, before we pass from England to Scotland and Ireland. Peter Heylyn loved learning from his youth; but his belief in the value of discipline can hardly have exceeded his craving for publicity. He began his career as a historical writer in 1621 with the publication of his *Geography*, a subject on which, as connected with history, he had lectured at Oxford in his eighteenth year, and which, with the aid of some experience of travel, he afterwards developed into that of his *Cosmography*. He had been king's chaplain for many years, as well as a prebendary of Westminster, when his personal troubles began with the downfall of Laud, whose ecclesiastical policy he had supported; and he was brought up before the Commons as having helped to get up the case against the author of *Histriomastix*. After the civil war broke out, he was commissioned to keep a record of public occurrences in *Mercurius Aulicus;* but he speedily lost his benefice (Alresford) with his house and library; nor was it till 1656 that he could again venture to come to the front. In 1659, he published his *Examen Criticum*, the first part of which adversely criticised Fuller's *Church History*, but the pair managed to make friends. His next controversy was with Baxter.

When the restoration came, Heylyn returned into residence at Westminster, and the brief remainder of his life was spent in tranquillity. His pen continued active to the end. In 1661, he brought out his chief work, *Ecclesia Restaurata, or The History of the Reformation*, which passed through several editions. This book, which carries on the history of the church of England from the accession of Edward VI to the Elizabethan settlement (1566), is notable as an attempt to view the changes effected by the reformation with as much of impartiality as was to be expected from a prelatist opposed to reunion with Rome. Among Heylyn's writings published posthumously are *Cyprianus Anglicus, or The History of the Life and Death of Archbishop Laud* (1668), defending him against Prynne's elaborate invective, and described by Creighton as "the chief authority for Laud's personal character and private life"; and *Aerius Redivivus, or The History of Presbyterianism* (1670), which traces back to Calvin the origin of puritanism, here described

as the source of England's internal troubles. This remarkable
man was no bigot, and was capable of looking on things as a
historian rather than as a professional apologist; but controversy was irresistible to him, and apt to expand and multiply
in his hands like a river plant in its favourite waters.

Of the two kingdoms whose destinies were interwoven with
those of England, the one was not brought into personal union
with her till near the beginning of the period treated in this
chapter; whereas the other, for centuries, had been riveted to the
side of her dominant partner by conquest and reconquest, and
was perpetually striving to burst her bonds asunder. Though
Scottish history had to tell of a long series of conflicts with the
neighbouring kingdom, and of periods of subjection as well as
of revolt and war, yet it ran its own course in both church and
state, and the ecclesiastical history of Scotland in particular,
the interest in which outweighed that of all other kinds of
history north of the Tweed, covers a field of its own. The
earliest record of the Scottish reformed church is *The Booke of
the Universal Kirk of Scotland*, of which a most important portion was consumed at the fire of the two houses of parliament
in 1834. But what remains is an invaluable document for much
of the national history, and, so far as the history of the church
is concerned, testifies at once to the conservative spirit of the
Scottish reformers and to their firm adherence to the presbyterian form of church government set up by them from the first.
One prelatical and one anti-prelatical history of importance
belonging to this period deal with the material at the command
of the writers. Of archbishop Spottiswoode's *History of the
Church of Scotland*, beginning A.D. 203, and continued to the
reign of king James IV, the first edition was printed in 1665;
but the book had advanced gradually in its author's hands, and
the earliest MS. of it extends only to the year 1602. The work
was written in tranquil times by a calm-minded man, who was
singularly free from a spirit of ecclesiastical bitterness. On the
other hand, David Calderwood's *Historie of the Kirk of Scotland, beginning at Patrik Hamilton and ending at the death of
James the Sixt*, is the work of an indefatigable adversary of prelacy, whose opinions, on this head, caused his expulsion from
presbytery and assembly in 1608, and, nine years later, though
expressed with moderation, led James to denounce him to his

face as "a very knave." After undergoing both imprisonment and exile, he returned to Scotland in 1625,[1] and, in 1641, was allowed to sit in the general assembly, though without the rights of a member. Two years before his death, he was granted a handsome pension in order to complete his *History*, which is a methodised and corrected revision in three volumes of the larger work—the latter being regarded by him rather as a common-place book of facts and documents than as a finished history. Yet, to students, the complete work is the most valuable, as containing the actual language of Knox and the other reformers, which, in the revised edition, Calderwood more or less assimilated to his own.

In the works dealing with Irish history from the Elizabethan age to the time of the Cromwellian settlement, it is, of course, difficult to separate the historical and political elements from each other; or, rather, the former are dominated by the latter. Of these works, the most celebrated has been reserved for a notice in this place. Spenser's *Veue of the Present State of Ireland* possesses a great biographical interest; while it supplements, or illustrates one of the books of *The Faerie Queene*—the Vth, containing the legend of Artegall, or Justice—which seeks to immortalise the poet's patron as the incarnation of the policy advocated by the poet himself as the only cure for "Ierne's ills."[2]

In 1598 broke out the rebellion which, by October in that year, had placed all Munster in the hands of the insurgents, and which put an end to Spenser's sojourn in Ireland. It had amounted altogether to fourteen years, more or less, and had for ever associated the land of his adoption with his epical masterpiece as well as with one of the noblest of English lyrics (*Epithalamion*). That the rebellion, which cruelly blighted Spenser's personal prospects, left him, in dean Church's words, "a ruined and broken-hearted man," is, in all probability, an exaggerated statement;[3] but there can be no question that *A*

---

[1] Calderwood's *Recantation* (1623) is a forgery.

[2] See the striking argument that there is an extraordinarily close parallel between the *Veue* and the two cantos of *Mutabilitie*, the chief burden of the former being the need for consistency in the policy to be pursued by the crown in Ireland, in C. Litton Falkiner's interesting essay, "Spenser in Ireland," in *Essays relating to Ireland* (1909), pp. 26, 27.

[3] *Spenser*, English Men of Letters (1879), p. 177.

Veue of the Present State of Ireland was composed under the influence of profoundly moved personal feeling. It was certainly composed in 1596, during the visit of Spenser (Irenaeus) to England, which lasted from 1595 till (probably) 1597.

Spenser's historico-political essay opens with a lengthy review of the evils existing in the state of Ireland, which are described as being of three kinds—"the first in the Lawes, the second in Customes and the third in Religion." Parts of this demonstration, hackneyed though it may have seemed even to the public to which it was addressed, were very forcibly put—especially the clear illustrations as to the evil effect of laws bad in themselves, and the bold assertion that "the most of the Irish are soe farre from understanding of the popish religion as they are of the protestants profession." There are, too, some pregnant passages, such as the opening sentences of Irenaeus, suggesting, as a possible explanation of the apparent hopelessness of the condition of Ireland, that, peradventure, God "reserveth her in this unquiett state still for some secrett scourdge, which shall by her come to England;" and the proposal, which strikes at the root of the barbarism overshadowing "Ierne," that a schoolmaster shall be maintained in every parish of the land. Though some of the historical and philological information may be questionable, the essay furnishes constant proof, not only of a careful study of the people itself, but, also, of a genuine interest in the associations which have always meant so much for its life—conveyed in ballads and legends and folklore of all sorts. The description of the influence of the bards, or Irish chroniclers, as radically tainted by inveracity, is curious; and there is a double edge in the denunciation of the folly of the Irish in deriving their origin from the Spaniards—"of all nations under heaven (I suppose) the most mingled, most uncertayne, and most bastardly." The Anglo-Irish—*ipsis Hibernis Hiberniores*—the dialogue declares to be "more malicious to the English than the very Irish themselves."

As to the moral of the whole treatise—the supposed necessity of a firm and vigorous policy of repression, and of doing away with native customs of all sorts and the establishment of a strong rule, represented by numerous garrisons throughout the country—nothing further need be said here. Lord Grey de

Wilton, as whose private secretary Spenser came to Ireland in 1580, tried this system for two years, and was recalled; and it has been tried since, for longer periods, with no more success. It has been, rather cynically, said[1] that the readers of Spenser's *Veue* and other writings of his expressing similar sentiments should "forget that he was a poet and remember that he was trying to improve forfeited lands." But there is nothing more unsatisfactory to the highest conception of a great writer than this sort of analytical separation of functions. The style of the essay is businesslike, and the dialogue form is used with ease; though there is far too much talk about the method of conducting the discussion—always a tedious ingredient in any kind of discourse.[2]

The important historical narrative *Pacata Hibernia*, originally published in 1633, was almost entirely composed by some one who stood very near to the person of Sir George Carew (afterwards lord Carew of Clopton and earl of Totnes), president of Munster during the three years (1600–3) through which the book traces the history of that province, ending with the suppression of the insurrection there. Possibly, the author was lieutenant Thomas Stafford, who served under Carew, but whose name is mentioned only a single time in the entire narrative. The book, which, in the words of its editor, Standish O'Grady, "deals with the stormy conclusion of a stormy century, the lurid sunset of one of the wildest epochs in Irish history," shows how complete, in the days of Mountjoy's viceroyalty,[3] was the absence of anything like patriotism or public spirit from all but a very few of the Irish lords and that of all sense of honourable dealing from English officials.

Carew, who seems to have taken a warm interest in Irish history, translated, from the French, with illustrative notes, Morice Regan's *History of Ireland*, as well as the story of Richard II's last visit to Ireland by a French gentleman in his suite. These were included in part I of *Hibernica* (1770), which contains various documents of interest, including the project for

[1] Bagwell, R., *Ireland under the Tudors*, vol. III (1890), p. 458.

[2] Spenser also wrote in dialogue form a *Discourse of Civill Life, containing the Ethike Part of Morall Philosophie* (not published till 1606).

[3] For an account of Mountjoy's rule, by a friendly hand, see Fynes Moryson's *Itinerary*, part II, ptd. 1735 as his *History of Ireland from 1599 to 1603*.

the division and plantation of Ulster. The policy advocated by Spenser was carried out by Sir John Davies, who, in succession, was solicitor- and attorney-general for Ireland during the years 1603–11, became speaker of the (Irish) House of Commons in 1613, and was appointed chief-justice of Ireland just before his death. His rare administrative ability was exercised in the great historical operation of the plantation of Ulster, as well as in the organisation of local government, especially in that province, and in the reform of the parliamentary system, which he established on the lines followed by it for nearly two centuries. His *Discovrie of the True Causes why Ireland was not entirely subdued . . . until the beginning of his Majesty's happie Raigne* (1612, rptd. 1613) marks out the lines on which the system of government consistently pursued by him was conducted; the parliament over whose House of Commons he presided was, consequently, the first in which a majority entirely controlled by the English council was confronted by a nationalist opposition.[1] The historical interest of his book is, therefore, exceptionally great.

The last works on Irish history which call for mention here deal with a later period. Richard Bellings's contemporary *History of the Irish Confederation* (to which he was secretary) *and the War in Ireland*, 1641–3 (edited by J. T. Gilbert) is accompanied by many documents, and necessarily takes a view of Irish affairs directly opposed to that of a better known work, intended as a vindication of the government of the duke of Ormonde and his royal master before the outbreak of the Irish troubles under Charles I. The authorship of the *History of the Irish Rebellion and Civil Wars in Ireland, with the true State and Condition of that Kingdom before the Year* 1640, has been disputed; but there seems to be no doubt that it was the work of Clarendon, with whose name it was brought out in 1721, and in whose *History*, as afterwards published, it was incorporated, as a seventh volume, under the title *A Short View of the State and Condition of the Kingdom of Ireland, from* 1640 *to this time*. Clarendon's authorship of the work was attested by his successor in the earldom, and the internal evidence would almost have sufficed to settle the question. For the narrative is composed in his most forensic style, and throughout displays

---

[1] See Falkiner, C. Litton, *u.s.* pp. 54, 55.

his indiscreet pertinacity as well as his lucidity in argument. He is said to have written it at Cologne, and to have had the assistance of Ormonde in defending his conduct. The special object of the work is to refute the Roman Catholic point of view, while an appendix[1] shows how the "Rebels of England" retaliated upon "the Papists that rebelled in Ireland."

Thus, through an *apologia* composed by the great statesman and historical writer for a chapter of the royal government in which he had no share,[2] we are brought to consider, however briefly, his contributions—half history, half memoir—to the records of a period of the national history in which he played a part of high significance. In any survey such as the present no other name can vie with that of Edward Hyde, first earl of Clarendon—a great writer, whose literary powers laid the foundation of his political greatness and, without any disparagement of his lifelong services to crown and country, remain his foremost title to enduring fame. He abhorred the unconstitutional designation of prime minister, though, during the septennate of his ascendency after the restoration, he came almost as near to realising a complete conception of that office as any English statesman before or since; but he would not have disdained the palm of which no rival can deprive him, adjudged to him by the unwavering consent of posterity as one of the great masters of English prose.

Few readers of Clarendon's *Life* are likely to have forgotten a passage, towards the close of what remains of the autobiographical narrative proper, which may serve as a text for the few comments it is possible to add on the present occasion. "He was wont to say," he writes of himself, with that impersonality of form which covers an exorbitancy of self-consciousness:

that of the infinite blessings which God had vouchsafed to confer upon him almost from his cradle . . . he esteemed himself so happy in none as in his three acquiescences, which he called "his three vacations and retreats he had in his life enjoyed from business of

---

[1] *A Collection of some of the Massacres and Murthers committed on the Irish in Ireland, since the 23rd of August*, 1641.

[2] His long vindication of his relation to Irish affairs after the restoration, including the results of Charles II's gift to him from Irish sources, in vol. II of the *Life*, belong, of course, to another period.

trouble and vexation, and in every one of which God had given him
grace and opportunity to make full reflections upon his actions, and
his observations on what he had done himself, and what he had seen
others do and suffer; to repair the breaches of his own mind, and to
justify himself with new resolutions against future encounters. . . .
The first of these recesses or acquiescences was, his remaining and
residing at Jersey, when the prince of Wales, his new majesty, first
went into France."

These years, from 1646 to 1648, between the so-called first and
second civil wars, were a dark period in the fortunes of the
royalist cause, with which Hyde had identified himself since, as
a young man without any special advantages of birth or wealth,
he had raised himself, by his own abilities and capacity for
forming friendships with his superiors, to a good position at
the bar; had, by his powers as a speaker, caught the ear of the
House of Commons,[1] and had placed his skilful pen at the
service of the king with great effect in the critical months
preceding the outbreak of the civil war.   And the darkness was
intensified by dissensions between the royal councillors, headed
by Hyde, and his constant adversary the queen, who insisted
on the prince of Wales coming to France instead of holding
out so long as possible in England or near its coasts, while, at
the same time, eager that he should purchase the goodwill of
the Scots by throwing over the episcopal church of England.
It was under the pressure of all this trouble that Hyde sat down
on 18 March, 1646, in his exile in one of the Scilly isles, to write
his *History of the Rebellion* and carried on his task during a
period of two years in Jersey.   "By the spring of 1648," says
Firth, "he had brought the story down to the opening of the
campaign of 1644, and had written seven books of the work,
and a few sections of the eighth."

Hyde's purpose was to recount, not for publication, but for
the use of future statesmen, and after a fashion which would
be appreciated by them, the origin of the great struggle whose

---

[1] Burnet and Pepys both attest Clarendon's gifts as a speaker.   The speeches
which remain from his later days, though delivered on important occasions and
under the responsibility of high office, are easy and often almost chatty in tone,
while seasoned with quotations and anecdote.   Occasional passages rise to eloquence; but, altogether, the style of these speeches suggests what may have been
an excellent "House of Commons manner" and is altogether lighter than Clarendon's usual style of writing.

present issue seemed to have overwhelmed both crown and church; to tell of all the errors that had been committed from the point of view of constitutional principle, as well as of the great sacrifices that had been made, in order that they might be remembered, and not remembered in vain, by later and more fortunate generations. Though, in this first version of the earlier part of the great work, there is very little personal mention of the writer, his whole heart and mind were with the country from which he had been driven because of his loyalty to her ancient institutions in church and state. In this loyalty, he had been born and bred as the descendant of an old Cheshire family, as a student of the university where his name was afterwards to be gratefully cherished, as an inns of court man and lawyer, and as a constitutionalist member of parliament, who had separated from the popular party so soon as it had begun to tamper with the interests of the episcopacy, and whose advice to king Charles I, since he had been taken into the royal confidence, had consistently been that in any steps the sovereign might take, or in any concessions he might make, he should remain within the limits of the law and the constitution.

Hyde's second "recess or acquiescence" was during the two years which, with lord Cottington, he spent in Spain as the ambassador of the titular king Charles II. Dark as had been the days of his Jersey exile, at this later stage all hope for the recovery of the royal cause had been extinguished, except such as could be extracted from an alternative policy of abject submission on the part of Charles (whom Hyde had joined in Paris six months before the axe fell at Whitehall) or intrigue with Irish rebels or a foreign power not to be trusted much further than they. Hyde, who inclined to the latter line of policy, set his hand to assist in weaving a web of diplomacy which he could not but know to be futile. Of the fourteen years of exile during which he was the chief adviser of the younger Charles, this period of waiting upon Providence at Madrid was probably that in which public trouble, private sorrow and the sickness of hope deferred weighed most heavily upon his trained self-control and extraordinary elasticity of mind; it was during his embassy in Spain that he took comfort from the *Psalms of David*, and produced the bulk of those *Contemplations and Reflections* upon them which fill half the folio volume of his *Miscellaneous Works*.

But he could not, in these years of a depression which hardly ever lifted, though it failed to affect a fidelity which never swerved,[1] resume the self-imposed task undertaken by him long since; and, even when they came to an end, it seemed as if, during the remainder of his days, his hand would be on the helm of state, and he would be able to enforce in practice the lessons which he had sought to place on record in the first large instalment of his *History*. But this was not to be.

"And the third was his last recess, by the disgrace he underwent, and by the act of banishment. In which three acquiescences," the passage cited concludes, "he had learned more, knew himself and other men much better, and served God and his country with more devotion, and he hoped more effectually, than in all his life." There was no conscious hypocrisy in Clarendon, but the forms which his self-confidence assumed were Protean in their variety.

This third retreat upon himself, to which his comment upon all three must, of course, be intended to apply with special force, was by far the longest in duration, and one from which there was to be no return to action or power. The abrupt and sultan-like taking from Clarendon of the great seal, held by him for seven laborious years since the king's return, to the accomplishment of which no other of his subjects can have contributed so much thought and labour, and the subsequent flight from England of the disowned minister, followed by his impeachment and banishment, put an end to his public life. To the last, however—and this should not be overlooked by readers of the works which were the chief occupation of the remaining seven years of his life—he was scheming and hoping for his return, or, at least, when even hope began to grow faint, anxious to spend his last days in the country of his birth and state. It was all in vain: neither king nor country had any wish to see him again.

As a matter of course, the topic of his downfall and its causes dominated the thoughts of his later years; in his *Life*, he demonstrated the injustice of his doom in a series of answers to the articles of impeachment drawn up against him, extending over some seventy or eighty pages; while, in the preface to the first edition of his *History*, he discusses the subject on broader lines.

[1] The active services of Clarendon to the royal court cannot be described here.

He here comes to the conclusion that the chief authors of his catastrophe were papists and women; and, so far as the immediate agencies of his overthrow were concerned, he was probably not far mistaken. In truth, however, Clarendon, who, in his youth, had justly gloried in his capacity for making friends, found very few to uphold him in the days of his downfall. He was confronted by antagonistic interests with which he scorned to hold parley—the catholics, whose advance he strove to stem, and the protestant nonconformists, of whom he openly avowed his detestation.[1] He was incapable either of the duplicity of gaining the gratitude of the hungry rank and file of the royalists by seeking, or seeming to seek, to advance their personal claims, or of the meanness which is ready to cringe to mistresses and favourites, and affects to be hail-fellow with the revel rout of frivolity and pleasure. Thus, Clarendon paid the penalty of an isolation due, at the same time, to his qualities and their defects. He says of himself, on one occasion, that (like Laud) he was "too proud of a good conscience." Possibly so; but it is certain that, in his days of power, Clarendon, even with the aid of the church which he upheld with unselfish consistency, failed to create a party that would have rallied round him in his season of adversity, and might have saved his name from being added to the list of victims of a fickleness not confined to democracies.

No sooner had Clarendon, after chicaneries and discomforts, settled down at Montpellier and indited his replies to the articles exhibited against him,[2] than he began, as, with his essentially literary temperament, he could not have failed to do, to write his reminiscences. The portion of *The History of the Rebellion* which he had composed twenty years earlier he had left behind him in England with the rest of his manuscripts. Moreover, his present design differed from that which had occupied him during his two years of continuous labour in Jersey; what he had at heart now was the vindication of his own career in the eyes of his children—a memoir of his own life,

---

[1] See for instance, his remark, *Life*, vol. II, p. 121, on the unhappy policy of making concessions to "that classis of men." Charles II, it may be added, broke his promise to the protestant dissenters chiefly because of Clarendon's advice.

[2] The *Vindication*, which is also included in the *Life*, forms part of the *Miscellaneous Works*, and is dated Montpellier, 24 July, 1668.

introducing, of course, some of the great events or transactions
with which he was in contact, rather than a history of the great
struggle and its ultimate issue, in which he, too, played his part.
Thus, during two or three years, working, we may rest assured,
con amore, but without haste or even allowing the whole of his
literary energies to be absorbed by his task,[1] he composed so
much of his *Life* as preceded the date of the restoration.   (This
amounted to more than half of the first of the three printed
volumes.) In this part of the autobiography, the literary powers
of the author are displayed at their height, while the freedom
with which, in the absence of a great pressure of materials, he
could allow himself to write, gives a flow to his composition
which is not characteristic of the completed *Rebellion*.   This
earlier part of the *Life* contains some of the most admirable
among the many admirable characters drawn by Clarendon—
a gallery which, in their different ways, neither Thucydides nor
Macaulay has surpassed—including the exquisite miniature of
Sydney Godolphin the elder, the delightful portraits of Hales,
Earle and Chillingworth, the discriminating sketch of Colepeper
and, above all, the famous character of Falkland.   Here and
there occur some of those indications of an intuitive perception
of the weak sides of human nature which, in Clarendon, are at

---

[1] It is impossible to date most of Clarendon's miscellaneous writings, of which
a list will be found in the bibliography.   The *Contemplations and Reflections upon
the Psalms of David*, already mentioned as, to a large extent, composed at an earlier
date, were concluded at Montpellier on 27 February, 1670, and the dedication "to
my children" is dated in the following year; the concluding personal note, which
has both dignity and pathos, still breathes the hope that the writer may be restored to the favour of the king.   Among *Essays Divine and Moral*, that *Of
Human Nature* is dated Montpellier, 1668; that *Of Liberty* is an attack on Hobbes;
that *Of Repentance* has a very practical bearing on the question of the restoration
of property taken away in the rebellion.   The others, for the most part, are moral
rather than polemical, and very readable.   The essay on the old debating problem
of the comparative advantages of *An Active and Contemplative Life*, argues very
strongly against monastic vows; and the essay *Against multiplying Controversies*,
etc., may be described as, in purport, an elaborate defence of the laws for the
maintenance of the church of England and for keeping the Roman Catholics in
order.   Finally, there are two well sustained dialogues *On the Reverence due to
Old Age* and *On Education*, conducted by a group of representatives of the previous
generation, among whom, however, are to be found advocates of conservative
reform.   The dialogue *On Education* has a few good points and a few which are
not quite out of date; but it is not, on the whole, a very luminous contribution to
the discussion of a theme which some of Clarendon's contemporaries had treated
with far greater power and profundity.

all times compatible with a very imperfect openness to his own failings—the recognition of the sharpness which marred the dignity of Laud, and the insight into the true nature of the relations between Charles I and his consort, and, again, of those between the king and his "servants." In Clarendon's account of his own early days, his narrative, like the memoirs of so many successful lawyers, furnishes us, unintentionally, with instruction as to the art of "getting on"; as he progresses, he falls into a way of attributing prejudice against, or dislike of, himself to small and more or less accidental causes (see his account of his early quarrel with Cromwell), and begins his long list of *nolo's* with a statement as to his resolution not to be named secretary of state.

In 1671, Clarendon's son Lawrence (afterwards earl of Rochester) visited him in his exile, bringing with him the unfinished MS. of the *Rebellion*, mainly written in Jersey. It was now that Clarendon made up his mind to a process of contamination for which, considering the scale on which it was conducted and the rare importance of the writings to which it was applied, a parallel cannot easily be found in literary history.[1] Taking the MS. *History*, so far as it went, as the framework of his book, he inserted into it a great number of passages from the portion of the *Life* which he had recently written; and then added, as books X – XVI of the work, the whole of the latter part of the *Life*, from the restoration to his days of exile. By way of a link between the earlier and later parts of the work, he wrote book VIII and part of book IX, as more or less new matter, and then, after putting the whole into a shape which, so far as possible, concealed the operations by which it was joined together, he left the whole *History of the Restoration* in the condition in which, after his death, it was given to the world (in 1702).

Inasmuch as the original *History* and the first part of the *Life*, as has been seen, were written with different ends in view, the result of the dovetailing process could not but be what Firth, perhaps rather sternly, calls patchwork. It is, however, equally clear that, in the whole work, we shall find some of the qualities which belong to a reasoned history, and some of those

---

[1] The process summarised by Firth in his lecture on Clarendon is detailed by him in three articles contributed to *The English Historical Review*, 1904.

that belong to a personal memoir, fresh from the hands of an actor in the scenes and events narrated by him. Among the former is the faculty of taking and conveying a comprehensive view of an entire situation or conjuncture in the affairs of the nation, or of the court, or of a party or influential section of the community. The picture of happy England (before the outbreak of the great civil war) is, indeed, more or less conventional, and will be found in the *Life* as well as in the *History*. But how excellent, in the *History*, is the connected and succinct narrative of the Spanish journey of the prince of Wales and Buckingham, and of the triumph of the latter over the better judgment of his master king James; how persuasive, without any attempt at a whole-hearted defence, is the pleading for the action of king Charles I in the critical matter of Strafford's catastrophe; how ingenious is the sketch of the attitude of the foreign powers after the death of Charles I himself; how masterly, too, in the later portion of the *Life*, is the description of the jealousies and other foibles of the royalist party in the period preceding the restoration!

Of some of the characters in the early portion of the *Life*, mention has already been made; others, in the *History*, are Buckingham, Coventry, Weston, Arundel and Pembroke; Hampden (very skilfully drawn), archbishop Williams (very bitter), the two Vanes (a touch of high comedy in the midst of tragic action); and, at a much later stage of the *History*, the cruelly antithetical labelling of Lauderdale, and the vignettes in acid of Bradshaw and Harrison. Excellent, too, in the *Life*, is the note that St. Albans (Jermyn) "had that kindness for himself that he thought everybody did believe him," and the sly remark that the duke of Albemarle (Monck) "knew that his wife was no wiser than she was born to be." There are many touches of this kind in Clarendon, which, to the observant reader, are hardly less attractive than are the elaborate portraits in which he delighted.

The final character of Charles I (in vol. VI of the *History*) is very tender, and at the same time, probably, not far from being just. On the other hand (in vol. I of the *Life* and elsewhere), the weaknesses of Charles II are suggested with considerable tact and (in a remarkable passage of vol. III) the transmitted failings of the Stewart family—their tendency

to follow the advice of inferior men, and their inability to refuse
favours to those who asked them—are pointed out with admirable insight.   Clarendon is least tolerable when he appears
as an apologist for himself—a task which he seems incapable of
performing without an excess of protests and an inordinate
flow of unction.   His defence of his conduct in the matter of
his daughter Anne's marriage is detestable in tone; the history
of his actual downfall he could not be expected to relate without
taxing the patience of his readers.

Clarendon's style, like every style that attracts or interests,
is the man; and it would not be what it is without the constant
desire to please which had animated him as a member of parliament and a courtier, or without the consciousness of his own
dignity and rectitude which made him stand erect through misfortune and obloquy.   He sometimes comes near true wit, and
occasionally has a picturesque turn; but he very rarely rises
into actual eloquence.   For this, he lacked the power of imagination in which he showed himself wanting in more ways than
one—more especially in his incapacity of recognising the virtue
or the greatness of an adversary or of appreciating the stand-
point of a political party or a religious denomination other than
his own.   Even in the characters of his dramatic dialogues
(which, in detail, are happy enough), he could not travel beyond the range of those who had been born about his own
time, and who, more or less, thought as he thought.   But the
style proper to nearly everything written by him, from his
History to his occasional tracts, is never out of keeping with
itself, always deliberate without being dull, and dignified without being (except on fit occasions) solemn, and, more frequently
than it is the custom to assume, breaking into a ripple of pleas-
antry which prevents it from growing tedious.   Few memoir
writers have succeeded in so steadily sustaining the attention
of their readers as has Clarendon; few historians have been
less pretentious or mannered than he.   His style is not a literary
style in the sense in which this, in different ways, can be pre-
dicated of the style of Gibbon or of that of Macaulay; if it has
a model, this has still to be sought, as with all the prose of the
age, in Latin literature rather than our own.   In his dialogue
On Education, he argues in favour of the conversational (not
the vulgar colloquial) practice of Latin in schools, whether by

means of discourse or the acting of plays and the like; and how such a training can inform the style of a writer is shown by Clarendon's own prose, which Latin influence helped to mould, without proclaiming its presence as in the case of the magnificent but exotic Latinisms of Milton. It has been pointed out that, in Clarendon's later writing, the influence of his lone residence in France and familiarity with the French tongue is very distinctly perceptible; and this may help to account for the fact that the *Life*, as well as some of the detached *Essays*, is particularly readable. In any case, Clarendon was original enough, in essentials, to form his own style; and the first great historical writer in our literature is, at the same time, a great writer of English prose.

The memoir literature proper of the earlier Stewart period is far too extensive to admit of more than a cursory survey, though one or two works may be singled out as having, by their literary qualities, secured to themselves a wider remembrance. The list may be headed by a well known short production, of which the most interesting portion carries us back into Elizabethan days. The *Memoirs of Robert Carey*, earl of Monmouth, written by himself, have always enjoyed a certain popularity, if only because of the account they furnish of queen Elizabeth's last moments and of her successor's reception of the great news of her death; the writer having been an eye-witness in both cases. He survived into a third reign; but the entire record, though brightly written, would not fill a hundred folio pages. *Fragmata Regalia, or Observations on the late Queen Elizabeth, her Times and Favourites*, by Sir Robert Naunton, are still more compendious, and were, accordingly, reprinted with Carey's *Memoirs* and other works in succession. There is considerable force, and not a little malice, in some of the short characters making up the collection of secretary Naunton, of whom Bacon said that he "forgot nothing."

From the reign of Elizabeth, though from its very last year, dates, also, the *Diary of John Manningham*, barrister-at-law of the Inner Temple. Among the eminently miscellaneous entries in this there chances to be one which has a special interest for students of Shakespeare. Whether in this connection or generally, the opening sentence of this celebrated repository

of anecdotes and witty sayings, as well as of extracts from
sermons,[1] sufficiently illustrates the miscellaneous nature of the
writer's interests, and his unwillingness to narrow their range.

In the reign of Charles I, the stream of memoir literature
flows copiously. Precedence may be allowed to two autobiographical works by men of high intellectual eminence, of which
that of lord Herbert of Cherbury has already received notice.[2]
The other, likewise, is a book *sui generis*, but of a strange
fantastic character, such as cannot be said to belong to lord
Herbert's monument of his own excellences. The *Private
Memoirs of Sir Kenelm Digby, Gentleman of the Privy Chamber
to King Charles the First*, are a narrative of Digby's wooing, and
finally wedding, a celebrated beauty, the names of persons and
places being veiled under more or less fictitious disguises.
This, together with the long sentimental dialogues, gives an
appearance of unreality to the book (which the author calls
"Loose Fantasies," and which he states himself to have written
in order to preserve his virtue by evoking the remembrance of
his heroine, when beset by the favours of certain ladies in the
"island of Milo").

The result is a production as unreadable to modern generations as a Scudéry romance, which, indeed, in form it very much
resembles. To the curiosity of contemporaries, however, these
Memoirs, though they can have circulated in manuscript only,
must have commended themselves in more ways than one.
Sir Kenelm Digby had in him something of the genius of
Ralegh and something of the impudence of Dr. Dee (Digby's
celebrated "sympathy powders" make the comparison permissible); but he was also a fine gentleman, an able diplomatist[3] and, on occasion, a successful naval commander.[4]
In person he was of "gigantic" proportions, but, according to
Clarendon, "marvellously graceful"; and, in accordance with
the fashion of the times, he was an eager duellist. He was
vainglorious in other respects also, and persuaded himself that
Mary de' Medici was in love with him. Digby was master of
six languages and well seen in divinity—in 1636 he returned to

---

[1] "A puritan is a curious corrector of things indifferent."
[2] *Ante*, pp. 232, 233.
[3] He was in Spain during the stay of Charles and Buckingham in 1623.
[4] See his *Journal of a Voyage into the Mediterranean*.

the church of Rome of which he had originally been a member; and he seems to have possessed genuine scientific insight as well as philosophising acumen.   (He sat on the council of the Royal Society when it was first incorporated.)   His political instability was more signal than that of his religious opinions; and, indeed, his attitude towards causes and persons was a strange mixture of knight-errantry and criticism, the passion of action running through all.   In his *Memoirs*, he is Theagenes and Venetia Stanley is Stelliana.   Mardontius, her other lover, is now held to be Sir Edward Sackville.   The narrative is embedded in a great deal of moralising and speculative writing, which, here and there, assumes a tone of impassioned ardour.   The manuscript is stated to contain several sensuous passages, which have been excised from the published edition but which should not be left out of account in estimating Digby's strange idiosyncrasy.

We re-enter a homelier sphere in mentioning among records covering the earlier, as well as the later, years of Charles I's fateful reign, the *Historical Notices* of Nehemiah Wallington of St. Leonard's, Eastcheap, London, which, indeed, go back as far as 1623, and occasionally refer to much earlier dates.   This worthy annalist, a London shopkeeper without family connections of a higher social order, was, at the same time, bookish in his tastes and a great reader of tracts, which he constantly quotes.   His chronicle is of a miscellaneous sort, noting all kinds of unusual sights and occurrences, and remarkable judgments of God, as, for instance, upon those that break the Sabbath day.   Public events he notes in the same strain; on the meeting of the Long Parliament, he recognises the flow of God's mercies in the judgments done upon Strafford and Laud; the troubles in Ireland are brought home to him by the sufferings there of his wife's brother Zechariah; and the memoranda end with the execution of the king, on which he comments: "Whatever may be unjust with men, God is righteous and just in whatever he doth."

Of more importance, though in some respects not very different in spirit, is the *Autobiography and Correspondence of Sir Simonds d' Ewes, Bart.*[1]   After serving as high sheriff of

---

[1] The family letters subjoined to the *Autobiography* in some instances touch on public affairs during the period 1600–49.

Suffolk in 1640, he in 1642 entered parliament as member for
Sudbury. He took the covenant. The *Autobiography*, which
becomes a record of affairs abroad (the great German war in
particular) as well as at home, shows forth a man who is not
a violent partisan. He judges the character of James I fairly,
without ignoring his "vices and deviations," and, in the following reign, wished for mutual concession and reconciliation between king and parliament, but was equally opposed to Rome
and to the Anglicanism of Laud. He had in him something of
the genuine spirit of puritanism, and disliked his own university,
Cambridge, not only because of the licence of life, but, also,
because of the "hatred of all piety and virtue under false and
adulterate nicknames," which he found obtaining there. There
are touches of other kinds which go some way towards recon-
ciling us to the pedantry of a man who, though no great orator, [1]
was probably an excellent specimen of the average member of
parliament in his day. For the rest, the *Autobiography* ends
in 1636, some years before he took his seat, with the pathetic
mention of the death of the writer's "sweet and only" surviving
son, "whose delicate favour and bright grey eyes were deeply
imprinted in our hearts."

In contrast to the *Autobiography* of Sir Simonds d'Ewes may
be mentioned that of Sir Henry Slingsby of Scriven, who, after
being created a Nova Scotia baronet in 1638, sat for Knares-
borough in both the Short and Long Parliaments, and in 1641
was one of the fifty-nine members who voted against the bill
for the attainder of Strafford. In 1642, he appears to have
ceased to attend; but his *Diary*, which begins in 1638, continues
to 1649, the death of Charles I being the last public event noted
in it. [2] Slingsby's estates, though sequestered, were bought in
for him by friendly trustees; but he had to live in privacy, and
having been involved in a plot for a northern rising, underwent
imprisonment at Hull. He was afterwards entrapped into
mixing himself up with Ormonde's design, and, after being
tried in London, was beheaded on Tower hill, June, 1658. His
Diary is interesting as exhibiting the life of a country gentle-

---

[1] He mentions with pride the compliments paid to him on one of his speeches
by the earl of Holland (vol. II, p. 289).

[2] "He end'd his good life upon the 20th of January, 1648-9, I hear: *heu me, quid
heu me? humana perpessi sumus.*"

man, as well as on account of its political memoranda. He
writes with businesslike directness but not without feeling, and
can rise to saying of life here and hereafter: "Every man loves
his Inn rather than his home."

A special interest belongs to the *Diary* of John Rous, in-
cumbent, from 1625 to 1643, of Santon Downham, Suffolk.
John Rous, educated at Emmanuel college, Cambridge, was,
for the last third of his life, minister of a village or hamlet
adjoining the parish of which his father was rector. Thus,
nothing could have been more humdrum than the course of
his life; but his *Diary*, which seems to have been intended
entirely for private use, probably gained, rather than lost, from
the conditions of his existence. For, while paying much attention to political and religious controversy, he was a lover of
literature; and thus he was led to preserve, from no party
point of view, an amount of contemporary satirical verse
which, considering the limits of his *Diary*, is curiously large,[1]
besides occasional political and other documents. At the same
time, he was a thinking man, and one who expressed his
opinions, temperate as they were, with distinctness; so that,
notwithstanding his moderation, it is clear that he believed
time to be on the side of the parliament rather than on that of
the king. What remains of his *Diary* has, accordingly, a
flavour and value of its own, while forming a sort of repertory
of contemporary satirical literature.

Leaving aside, as referred to elsewhere in this volume,[2] the
personal records of archbishop Laud, and merely mentioning,
together with the vindictive *Memoirs* of Denzil, lord Holles,
the modest account of his own services written by Fairfax,[3]
we are constrained to pause on the *Memoirs* of Edmund Ludlow, which, though those of a contemporary, are not always
those of an eye-witness; thus, he was in Ireland during the
period after Worcester, in which, in his opinion, Cromwell's
designs first clearly manifested themselves. Of these designs,
and of everything which made for the superiority of the military over the civil power, and of the monarchical over the de-
mocratic principle, he was a consistent adversary; and the

---

[1] "I hate these following, railing rimes
    Yet kepe them for president [precedent] of the times" (p. 109).
[2] See *ante*, Chap. VI.   [3] See bibliography.

simple strength of his convictions invests his narrative with a
moral interest which neither the dogmatism of some of his
later utterances nor his occasional lack of intellectual sincerity
can, in the long run, obscure.   His censures on Charles I and
on Oliver Cromwell necessarily gave rise to a great deal of controversy, including a *Just Defence of the Royal Martyr King
Charles I from the many false and malicious aspersions in Ludlow's Memoirs*, etc. (1699), and a *Vindication of Oliver Cromwell from the accusations of Lieutenant General Ludlow* (1698).
The latter of these tracts was honoured by a brief "moral"
from the pen of Carlyle, who could not, perhaps, be expected to
recognise the fact that it is on the completeness with which
they are assimilated by "partly wooden men" that the enduring
influence of great currents of opinion "partly" depends.   Ludlow's *Memoirs* form one of the historical documents of English
republicanism.

From a literary point of view, however, no biographical
work of the time equals in interest the life of yet another parliamentary officer, written, in this instance, by his wife.   *The
Memoirs of the Life of Colonel Hutchinson, Governor of Nottingham Castle and Town, etc., etc.   Written by his Widow Lucy,
daughter of Sir Allen Apsley, Governor of the Town, etc.*, are
inseparable from *The Life of Mrs. Lucy Hutchinson, written
by herself*, albeit the latter is only a fragment.   It extends in
fact over only a few pages; but it is an excellent piece of writing, descriptive of the authoress's birth and parentage, and
giving a curious picture of an overtrained but self-controlled
girl who, when about seven years of age, "had at one time eight
tutors in several qualities, languages, music, dancing, writing
and needlework, but her genius was quite averse from all her
book."   The picture of her mother has much charm, and proves
what a woman's kindness can do in any surroundings—for the
wife of the governor was "a mother to all the prisoners that
came into the Tower."   The character of her husband which is
subjoined, and which she drew up for her children, opens with
a nobly worded reference to his dying command to her "not to
grieve at the common rate of desolate women," and purports to
be "a naked, undressed narrative, speaking the simple truth
of him."   But it appears that Mrs. Hutchinson was so dissatisfied with what she had written that she made another

essay, which, however, her husband's descendant Julius Hutchinson suppressed in favour of what he thought the less laboured and more characteristic effort of the two. It certainly brings out with much force colonel Hutchinson's deep religiosity, his perfect veracity, his piety in his affections—which seemed his most distinctive qualities to his sorrowing widow, who says of herself that "all that she is now at best is his pale shadow."

The biography proper of colonel Hutchinson is a work composed with great care and elaboration. We see him at "Peter House," where "he was constant at their chapel," and "began to take notice of their stretching superstition to idolatry." We follow him to Lincoln's inn and witness his courtship, in which he gained the hand of a woman, at first sight terribly superior to himself, "after about fourteen months' various exercise of his mind, in the pursuit of his love." Then we have an account of the condition of the kingdom before the outbreak of the civil war—not very original, or more fair in one way than Clarendon's is in another, but of great interest as a direct apology for the puritans. They were not, as they were believed to be, "an illiterate, morose, melancholy, discontented, crazed sort of men." On the other hand, the moral purity of the king's court is acknowledged. At the end of this disquisition, the writer refers her readers to May's *History*, on which, indeed, it is largely based. The account of the civil conflict in Notts (one of the counties whence the godly had to emigrate, and where the castle and adjoining town alone remained in the hands of the parliament) is full of interest. Hutchinson was long in expectation of a siege, first by Newcastle and then by prince Rupert; but he held his own both against these dangers and against the perpetual worrying of the parliamentary committee, till times changed after Marston moor. Yet his worst troubles began after he had come up to London, as a member of parliament; and his wife's story now has to accompany him through a tortuous course, which, after bringing him into relations of deep mutual distrust with Cromwell, finally exposed him, as one of the "regicides," to the vengeance of the restoration. Although, with the skilful aid of his wife's exertions, he escaped with his life and with most of his estate, he became suspect in connection with the so-called Yorkshire plot, and was finally brought home from prison to his grave. His "murderers,' writes his uncompromising biographer, had confined him in Sandown castle, where "the place had killed him."

The character of Colonel Hutchinson, as drawn by his widow, need not be accepted exactly as presented by her. It was some time after the outbreak of the civil war that, as he phrases it, he found "a clear call from the Lord" to take up arms on the side of his choice; and, again, he retained his seat in the House of Commons even after proceedings to which his wife states him to have objected. According to the same authority, he was a regicide on compulsion; and this, perhaps, made it easier for her, at the restoration, to plead in his name a "signal" and not inopportune "repentance." She may have gone rather far in asserting that "there was nothing he durst not do but sin against God"; in return, her high spirit and enthusiasm, together with her learning and ability, more than justify her husband's dying commendation of her "above the pitch of ordinary women," while her heroic devotion to him, during a long succession of perils and trials, entitles her to a place near that of Alcestis among the "good women" of all time. The form of her book is worthy of its spirit, and contributes to illustrate the supreme force which belonged to religious conceptions and associations as determining conduct in the age of which she was a representative. The dignity of her style does not interfere with its candour; on the other hand, the general sobriety of her narrative is not out of harmony with occasional passages of deep personal feeling and, now and then, of emotion almost passionate in its directness.

The only royalist commander who played an important part in the civil war and of whom a contemporary biography remains to us was not less fortunate than colonel Hutchinson in the fact that this record is from the hand of his wife. *The Life of William Cavendish, duke of Newcastle*, too, may be regarded as one of the lesser classics of English biographical literature, and contains, like its counterpart, a supplementary *True Relation of the Birth, Breeding and Life* of his faithful companion in adversity as well as in prosperity. It is true that many different estimates have been formed by different critics of the literary claims of Margaret, duchess of Newcastle, who, as became a loyal wife, has left behind her a biography of her husband which may be described as ample, but only a brief re

lation of what was personal to herself.   Among her contemporaries, at a season when the university of Cambridge was
prostrating itself *in corpore* before both their graces, Pepys
confided to his cipher that the writer of this biography was
"a mad, conceited, ridiculous woman," and the duke "an ass
to suffer her to write what she writes to him and of him"—
for her literary monument to her husband, singularly enough,
was erected during his lifetime.   On the other hand, Charles
Lamb said of the book that "no casket is rich enough, no casing
sufficiently durable, to honour and keep such a jewel," and indulged in other paradoxes of praise with regard to the letters[1]
of "that princely woman, the thrice noble Margaret Newcastle."
Her "output," if such a phrase be permissible, amounts to thirteen volumes in print besides a great deal more in manuscript
and what is accessible to posterity in prose or verse, and in
most known species of either—dramatic, narrative, didactic
and, above all, aphoristic—reveals, with much queer philosophy and other eccentric cleverness, not a little genuine
mother-wit and occasional felicity of gnomic phrase.   She
cherished a scorn, which she did not care to conceal, for any
fetters upon the most active part of her nature, her mind;
and, though she had what might be called "anti-suffragist"
leanings, she confessed that in all things, from essays in
natural philosophy and plays in which she ignored Aristotle
to mere "accoutrements of habits," originality was her *foible* as
well as her *forte*.   Thus, while she illustrates the force of natural talent, however thinly beaten out, and the irresistible impulse of the pen,[2] she proves even more signally the value of
that orderly training which she never underwent and openly
contemned.

   But it is only the biography of her husband and the devotion which it displays that have secured her the niche which
she occupies among the unforgotten writers of her age.   The
first duke of Newcastle, who played a prominent part in the
great civil war, who bore himself gallantly till his withdrawal
to the continent after Marston moor and who sacrificed a vast
fortune for the king's cause, was a most honourable and ac-

[1] No doubt *The ccxi Sociable Letters* (1664).
[2] "That little wit I have, it delights me to scribble it out and to disperse it
about," *Autobiography*, p. 307.

complished,[1] but far from extraordinary, man; in fact, he was manifestly born to be master of the horse, though Monck deprived him of that phase of greatness.   In his life, as in that of his wife, there was much moral dignity, and in her personality, as it stands forth from her brief autobiography, there was something which, if less than heroic, is more than merely attractive. The fortunate conformity of tastes and dispositions between the pair, enabled them to weather bravely the protracted storm and, in the end, cheered the rural solitude to which they were relegated by a callous sovereign.   The duchess, to alter slightly her own words, "had been bred to elevated thoughts, not to a dejected spirit; her life was ruled with honesty, attended by modesty, and directed by truth."   These qualities give a charm to her portraiture of herself and her husband from which all her vanities and oddities of thought and style glance off harmlessly; and if literature, arduously as she pursued it, was to her only a noble diversion, it was, nevertheless, an organic part of a noble life.

Turning from military men to statesmen, we find an important contribution to history in Bulstrode Whitelocke's *Memorials of the English Affairs* from the accession of Charles I to the restoration, first published in 1682, with a somewhat pretentious preface (by the earl of Anglesea).   Though in these *Memorials* the writer does not make any apparent attempt to disguise his opinions, he betrays no intention of colouring his statement of facts either to suit those opinions or to gratify any demand for literary display.   By the Whig writers of the earlier part of the eighteenth century he was contrasted to his advantage with Clarendon;[2] but, in point of fact, there is no basis of comparison between them; for the substance of Whitelocke's *Memorials* was not put together till after the restoration, and their form admitted of their being extracted at second-hand from the most ordinary sources.   At the same time, they are, to make debates more easily understood, interspersed with some more or less verbatim reports of speeches delivered by the writer, as well as with detailed accounts of transactions in which he was personally engaged

---

[1] Though hardly, as his wife calls him (*Life*, ed. Firth, p. 201), "the best lyric and dramatic poet of his age."

[1] See Oldmixon, *Clarendon and Whitelocke compared* (1729).

(such as the Oxford peace negotiations in 1644), together with other fragments of his various autobiographical productions. Thus, the spirit has not entirely gone out of the compilation, and these *Memorials* retain a value not only for lawyers and students of constitutional history, though their importance as an actual narrative of facts has probably, from more points of view than one, been greatly overrated. Whitelocke occasionally deviates into subjects of less severity—such as his long account of the Inns of court masque in October, 1633,[1] ending with the telling phrase: "These dreams passed and these pomps vanished." The *Memorials*, of course, increase in interest as the times become more and more critical; the account of the king's trial is full of sympathy, which may or may not have been *ex post facto*. Indeed, in general, Whitelocke showed throughout the civil troubles, the moderation which accorded with his training and his disposition; and this quality which, at the restoration, preserved to him the bulk of his fortune, is impressed upon the character and style of his *Memorials* at large.

Equally well known is Whitelocke's *Journal of his Swedish Embassy in the years 1653 and 1654*. Here, the narrative is Carried on throughout in the third person but is interspersed with a number of conversations with Oxenstjerna and others, given in direct dialogue form. The *Journal* is extremely interesting and entertaining, and offers a picture at first-hand of that most extraordinary woman, queen Christina. She received Whitelocke very politely and, according to English custom, was his valentine on 14 February, when he presented her with a very large looking-glass. Their conversation was at times varied by the offering of copies of Latin verse, which on one occasion the ambassador translated into indifferent English. In the course of his embassy, the queen's design of giving up her crown was communicated to Whitelocke, who witnessed the ceremony of her resignation and the coronation of her successor (30 May, 1654) and departed "rejoicing" on the following day. For his experiences had not been altogether agreeable, and, at night time, there had been occasional disturbances outside his house, and shouts of "Come out, ye English dogs, ye king-killers, rogues."

[1] Vol. 1, pp. 53–62.

Whitelocke, who had tried to anticipate Monck's fateful march to London by inducing Lambert to attack him, did not attend the Long Parliament on its reassembling, but, after sending the great seal to the Speaker, withdrew into the country, where he survived for many years. His *Notes upon the King's Writt* for choosing members of parliament (1662), which occupied him for some three or four years, and in which Scriptural arguments hold a prominent place, form a most elaborate comment on the system of English constitutional government. To an earlier date belongs his share in the conference held by him and other heads of the law with the protector and a committee of parliament (April, 1657), which ended with Cromwell's declining the title of king. The report of this was published in 1660 under the title *Monarchy Asserted to be the best, most Ancient and legall form of Government.* Whitelocke left behind him manuscripts, still unprinted and preserved in the British Museum, which are autobiographical in their contents and addressed to his children.[1]

In the period under notice, the number was necessarily large of narratives dealing with campaigns or other episodes of military and naval life. Several of these are noted elsewhere;[2] but one of them may, in conclusion, find mention here, both because it typifies at once the military and the religious spirit of the age, and because the remembrance of it is evoked in one of the most famous of English books.[3]

Colonel Robert Munro's—*Robertus robore Munro*—narrative of his *Expedition with the worthy Scots Regiment called M'Keyes Regiment levied in August*, 1626, was published four years after his death, in 1637, with a dedication to Charles Lewis elector Palatine, "as it was through the line of his mother that Munro's comrades went out to war." The regiment served under Christian IV of Denmark in the Lower Saxon war, and then under Gustavus Adolphus, and, after

---

[1] See bibliography.   [2] See *ibid*.

[3] In *Waverley*, vol. II., chap. XXXVI, where the baron of Bradwardine excuses the devastation of the house of his ancestors by the reflection that "doubtless officers cannot always keep the soldier's hand from depredation and spuilzie; and Gustavus Adolphus himself, as ye may read in Colonel Munro his Expedition with the worthy Scotch regiment called Mackay's regiment, did often permit it." "Tavie" (Gustavus) is, or was recently, still a familiar name in Sutherlandshire.

his death, under Oxenstjerna and his generals. After the unfortunate battle of Nördlingen the regiment, as the title-page proceeds to say, was reduced to a single company. Colonel Munro, like the great king whom he served, was as pious as he was brave; and the appendixes to his celebrated book comprise together with an "Abridgment of Exercises, and divers practical observations, for the younger Officer his Consideration," "the Souldiers meditations going on service." The narrative itself is characteristically divided into sections called "Duties discharged (for instance, 'The twenty-fourth Duty discharged of our March to Mentz, etc.') and Observations thereon"—the soldier's life being thus treated as a sort of pilgrim's progress.

CHAPTER X

Antiquaries

SIR THOMAS BROWNE. THOMAS FULLER. IZAAK WALTON.
SIR THOMAS URQUHART

THE three writers to whom it is proposed to devote the bulk
of the present chapter, more particularly Sir Thomas
Browne and Fuller, agree in being men who, while
showing a lively interest in the present, devoted especial attention to the past; they agree still more—and here without any
qualification—in being, though in ways distinctly different,
exponents of that extraordinary gift of prose-writing which
distinguished the mid-seventeenth century in English literature.
The fourth, Sir Thomas Urquhart, had great schemes for the
improvement, as he thought it, of the future; but he, also,
"catched the opportunity to write of old things"; and, with a
special Scottish *differentia*, represented the learned and intensely anti-"modern" quaintness of the time in thought and
style.

The first and greatest of them—who has been held by certain good wits to have hardly a superior in one kind of English prose, and whose matter, as is not always the case, fully
matches his manner—was of a good Cheshire family; but his
father had gone into trade as a mercer, and Thomas Browne
was born in London on 19 October, 1605, in the parish of St.
Michael-le-Quern, Cheapside. His mother was Anne Garra-
way, of a Sussex family. There were three other children,
but the father died early, and the mother married again, her
second husband being Sir Thomas Dutton, apparently the
opponent and slayer of Sir Hatton Cheke in a fierce, and rather
famous, duel on Calais sands. It is said that the youthful

Thomas was defrauded by his guardian; but his stepfather seems to have been guiltless in the matter, and there are not at any time in Browne's life any signs of straitened means, though, towards the close, he complains, like other rich fellows enough, of losses. He was admitted to a scholarship at Winchester on 20 August, 1616; and, in 1623, being then eighteen, went, not to New college, but to Broadgates hall, Oxford, which, during his own residence, was erected into Pembroke college. Here, he graduated B.A. on 30 June, 1626, and M.A. on 11 June, 1629. Somewhere about this time, he seems to have accompanied his stepfather to Ireland, where Dutton held a post as inspector of fortresses.

The future author of *Religio Medici* began his professional studies at Oxford, and is said to have actually practised in the county; but this must have been later. Then, and for long afterwards, it was customary to supplement home training in physic by visits to famous foreign schools; and to the two most famous of these, Montpellier and Padua, Browne proceeded— as well as later to the younger school of Leyden, where he took his first doctor's degree. He was abroad three years in all, spending, probably, a year at each place; and he returned home in 1633. After an unknown interval—which may have been occupied by the Oxfordshire practice above referred to— he established himself in a dale south-east of Halifax in York-shire, in a house, no longer in existence, named Upper Shebden hall. Here he is supposed to have written or finished *Religio Medici;* but the circumstances of his books will be dealt with later. On 10 July, 1637, he took his M.D. degree at Oxford; and, in the same year (apparently at the suggestion of some old Oxford friends), he moved to Norwich, where he passed the rest of his life. Two years earlier, while at Halifax, he had become a member of the college of physicians; and, four years later, in 1641, he married Dorothy Mileham, daughter of a Norfolk gentleman, with whom he lived for more than forty years and who survived him. Of their numerous children— ten, or eleven, or, according to the best authorities, twelve— only one son, Edward Browne, himself a man of distinction, and three daughters, survived their father. Few details of his life are known, though we have a relatively large number of letters from and to him; but the chief biographical points may be conveniently separated from the story of his books. The civil war broke out shortly after his marriage; Browne was a royalist, and a sincere one, refusing subscriptions for parliamentary purposes at the beginning, and rejoicing heartily in the restoration at the end. But a man of his temperament could hardly have been a violent partisan, or an extravagant self-sacrificer; and it was, perhaps, lucky for him that the district in which he lived was so generally disaffected as to make overt royalist enterprise almost impossible; while his personal popularity, and the respect in which he was held, prevented any persecution of him for mere opinion. For the better part of twenty years he seems to have practised, read, collected and written in the most even tenor of life; and during this time all his principal finished work was executed. From the restoration to his death, we hear a little more of him. His younger son Tom, after some business experience in France, entered the royal navy, and distinguished himself in the Dutch war: what became of him later we do not know. In 1664, came the famous trial at Bury St. Edmunds in which, before Sir Matthew Hale, Browne incurred the indignation of certain persons by giving—not on his own motion but when directly appealed to by the judge—testimony as to his belief in the reality of witchcraft, an expression of belief in which ninety-nine out of every hundred of his best educated contemporaries in England would probably have agreed with him. At the end of that year, he was made honorary fellow of the college of physicians, receiving his diploma next year; and, in the year after, 1666, he made a present of fossil bones to the Royal Society, of which, however (contrary to what used to be stated), he was never a fellow. On 28 September, 1671, Charles II, visiting Norwich, knighted him. Eleven years later, on his birthday, 19 October, 1682, he died and was buried in the church of St. Peter Mancroft, Norwich.

Browne had thus enjoyed nearly half a century of quiet professional life, and five and forty years of it in the same place. He was well off; he had plenty of books and collections round him; and he was in correspondence with many learned men of tastes similar to his own—Evelyn being the chief of them so far as England was concerned, though even Iceland was reached by his curiosity. He had read very widely; to speak disrespectfully of Browne's learning would be more than a little rash, and might provoke doubts as to the coextensiveness of the speaker's own erudition. Above all, he had an intense idiosyncrasy of mental attitude, and a literary gift hardly surpassed in its own special way. It was impossible that such a combination of gift and circumstance should not find its expression.

The first instance of that expression, and, in some eyes, the most considerable, *Religio Medici*, appeared in a fashion which could not but provoke comment, but which, perhaps, has actually provoked it to an unnecessary extent. That Browne may have conceived the idea, or parts of the idea, of the book during his foreign tour is highly probable; but there is not any reason to doubt the tradition—supported by or founded upon, a positive chronological reference of his own, which throws it back seven years from 1642—that it was written during his residence at Halifax, in or about 1635. Like much of the literature of the age—a fact which Dr. Johnson somewhat sceptically ignored—it was copied in manuscript again and again. There still exist some half dozen of such copies; and one of these, getting into the hands of a printer, Crooke, was published in the year above mentioned, 1642. A copy having fallen in the way of the earl of Dorset was by him recommended to Sir Kenelm Digby; and that remarkable Amadis-Paracelsus made it the subject of *Observations*, written in the space of considerably less than twenty-four hours, which came to Browne's knowledge and extracted an elaborately courteous reply from him, part explanation, part disavowal—at least of the thing having been authorised. He then took it into his own hands and, in 1643, issued "a true and full coppy of that which was most imperfectly and surreptitiously printed before."

If Johnson was unduly suspicious of this transaction, Browne's excellent editor, Simon Wilkin—it is rare luck for any man to have two such editors as Wilkin and Greenhill—has been justly thought to have been unnecessarily indignant at the suspicion. Very likely Browne did not instigate the publication; it is equally likely that he was not wholly sorry for it. The book, not unassisted by the discussion with Digby, became popular; and, being translated (again, it would seem, without Browne's direct privity) into Latin by John Merryweather in 1644, it achieved a continental reputation extremely uncommon in those days in the case of the work of an English author. Guy Patin's notice, with the curious but not inappropriate description of Browne as *un mélancolique agréable en ses pensées* is one of the commonplaces of the subject. The book's combination of theology and physics exactly suited the bent of the time, and, though its great literary excellence could only be perceived by readers of the original, and those not the first-comers, the peculiarity of the mental attitude was of wider appeal. In both respects, some special notice must be taken of it.

The original cause of the book, at least the ostensible cause, is, of course, clear enough: a defence of himself, if not, also, of his brethren, from the ancient imputation of irreligion which Chaucer has epigrammatised. But those circumstances of the time which already have been glanced at complicated the conditions. On the one hand, there was the still raging battle of sects and churches—as obstinate and as confused as the famous conflict in Spenser, where the knights are constantly changing their allies and their enemies; on the other, there was the steady rise of what was not yet called materialism or anti-supernaturalism. Browne took in all these things and, of course, was (as he could not but have anticipated) claimed as a partisan, or denounced as an enemy, by the most opposite parties. Nor has there ever yet been reached any distinct or complete agreement as to his position, of which we shall ourselves, perhaps, be able to take a clearer view when we consider his *Vulgar Errors*. In reading *Religio*, a man need not have been—need not even be—an absolute fool if he is somewhat irresolute between Browne's apparently inconsistent declarations, or, rather, between his positive declarations on the one hand, and the qualifications—still more the atmosphere and background of thought—by which they are accompanied, surrounded and thrown into relief. He proclaims, almost ostentatiously, belief in some literal interpretations of the Bible, and in some general acceptances of the supernatural which, even at his time, were not uncommonly questioned by the knowing. Yet, in some cases, even of these, he hints "new and not authentic interpretations" (such as those to which, he says, a Jesuit once objected), and his whole attitude and atmosphere are those, rather, of a man arguing for his own right to believe if he lists, than of an Athanasian positiveness. Against such a man, it is sure to be a case of *Hinc movet Euphrates, illinc Germania bellum.* Eastern dogmatism will doubt the logician and western scepticism will contemn the believer.

The success, however, of the expression of this attitude can hardly be hidden from anyone who has the slightest appreciation of the beauties of English prose, unless that appreciation be as one-sided as it is slight. Coleridge who was nevertheless a warm, and might have been expected to be a thoroughgoing, admirer of Browne, does, indeed, accuse him of being a corrupter of the language. But the passage in which the accusation occurs is a mass of anachronisms; it was evidently written in one of the well known Coleridgean fits of "fun," as Lamb called them, that is to say, of one-sided crotchet; and the corruption alleged is that of a purely fanciful standard of Elizabethan English which appears to have been blended for himself by the critic out of two such isolated, anything but contemporary, and singularly different, exemplars as Latimer and Hooker.

As a matter of fact, Browne does not corrupt, but develops, the principal tendencies of his predecessors—rhythmical elaboration, highly coloured language and conceit. His special characteristic in the lower aspects of style may, indeed, be called a corruption, if anyone chooses, and an audacious, but often real, improvement, at the pleasure of anyone else. In that lower aspect, it is the adoption, or, if need be, the manufacture, of Latin or, sometimes, Greek compounds with English terminations, in fuller indulgence than any other known case supplies, except that of his contemporary, namesake and fellow in knighthood Sir Thomas Urquhart. These manufactured words appear to annoy some people very much; but there are few of them which, with a moment's thought, will give much trouble to any decently educated person, while, for others (as Sir Thomas might even have said, though he rarely reached the quip modest), he did not write.

There is, however, a further peculiarity, the approval or disapproval of which may, once more, be a matter of taste, but which does make a somewhat heavy demand, not merely on the erudition, but on the strength and quickness of intellect, of the reader. Browne is not quite content with using an uncommonly Latinised vocabulary. He must, in many cases, employ that vocabulary itself with a peculiar sort of *catachresis;* so that its plain and straightforward meaning, even if known, will not fully illuminate the passage. A phrase of his own, contrasting "to construe" with "to understand," is often very applicable to himself; and a man might not merely be able to construe but, to some extent, to understand, the meaning of every word in such a sentence as "commutatively iniquous in the valuation of transgressions" without apprehending the true drift of the whole phrase.

In *Religio Medici*, however, he had not arrived at this pitch; while, if he had, likewise, not attained the utter magnificence of combined rhythmical cadence and imaginative illustration which distinguishes *Urn Burial* and *The Garden of Cyrus*, there were good foretastes of it. How much importance he himself attached to the book is not very clear. His later references to it are rather slighting, and yet not quite in the way either of mock humility, or of that mannerly deprecation which was not the worst point of old-fashioned courtesy. He may have been annoyed by the comments and controversies upon it; or he may have repented of a certain youthful egotism which certainly does characterise it, and of such unguarded confessions to the vulgar as that of his dislike (very rare and suspicious then, very intelligible and common now) of the word "protestant," of his fits of Origenism and of belief in prayers for the dead and so forth. At any rate, his next and largest work (1646) is of a much less esoteric character. Its Greek and English titles *Pseudodoxia Epidemica* and (for short) *Vulgar Errors* are not, as has been sometimes erroneously thought, translations of each other. "Pseudodoxy" is opposed, in the abstract, to "orthodoxy"; but the treatise, after a few chapters on the general subject, divagates, with most obvious gusto, into an enormous collection of particular examples which Browne subjects to treatment with the mild but potent acid of his peculiar scepticism.

Perhaps, though it is less attractive to purely modern tastes of the most diverse kinds than the smaller works, an appreciation of *Pseudodoxia* is the real touchstone of appreciation of Browne generally. It is not unnatural that, to the mere man of science or the mere modernist of any kind, it should seem a

scrap-heap of out-of-date observations, and its criticism hardly
more valuable than its credulity.   But it is surprising that even
Walter Pater should have complained of Browne's having
"no true sense of natural law," as Bacon had, of his having
achieved "no real logic of fallacies."   If recrimination were
argument, or if argument of any kind on the subject were in
place here, one might retort that Bacon's true sense of natural
law did not prevent him from being as much of an anti-
Copernican as Browne was, and that an elaborate exposure of
fallacies, nearly always on strict logical principles, is no bad
preparation for that "real logic" of them which can probably
only be achieved when the last human being has achieved his
last example of fallacy itself.

· The fact is that Browne's obvious and, indeed, almost
ostentatious desultoriness, and the subtle "two-sidedness"
of his scepticism, have led too many modern critics into the
opposite and complementary error to that of some of his contemporaries.   These latter were suspicious of him, or indignant
with him, because he doubted or denied some things; the former
are contemptuously, or, at least, compassionately, surprised,
because he admits or, at least, does not question other things.
But it may be very seriously questioned whether his attitude,
when the conditions of his time and his opportunities are duly
weighed, does not become a far more reasonable one than that of
either set of censors.   Browne had mastered the fact—which
the Alexander Rosses[1] and even the Kenelm Digbys had not
mastered—that, where a fact or an opinion previously adopted
by a sufficiently *communis sensus* is open to trial by experiment,
and experiment does not prove or justify it, you should give it
up.   But he had also mastered the fact—which some, at least,
of his modern critics have not mastered—that, where such

[1] Butler's famous couplet about the "sage philosopher, that had read Alexander
Ross over," and, perhaps, some remarks in editions and notices of Browne, have
occasioned a sort of general idea of Ross as a pattern *Dunce* or *Obscurus Vir*.   He
was, however, nothing of the kind; but an original, who, with great learning
and not small acuteness, put both at the service of a crotchety conservatism,
seeking only, as he says himself, for causes "which may stand with the grounds
of Divinity and Philosophy."   John Robinson, of Norwich, "fellow citizen and
colleague," as he proudly calls himself, of Browne, to whom he is very polite,
was a much duller man.   His *Endoxa* are chiefly minute technical demurrers.
His notion of wit may be gathered from his remark on sugar: *Saccharum, quod
per jocum ego soleo sal charum dicere.*

a fact or an opinion is not open to experiment, or where experiment has, as yet, been insufficiently applied, you are at liberty not to give it up, and to doubt the wisdom of those who do.

There is no space here to follow out this consideration; and, if there were, it might be improper to do so. It is enough to say that from *Religio Medici* to *Christian Morals*, though the dissolvent principle may appear uppermost in the one, and the conservative principle in the other, this double scepticism is the hinge and centre of Browne's thought; that, naturally enough, it is as disagreeable or unintelligible to those who hold certain kinds of modern view, as it was to others of an opposite temper in his own times; and that, perhaps, there is room for not entirely unintelligent or uninstructed folk who choose to do so to hold it, with the adjustments with which Browne would certainly have held it to-day. And it may further be deemed to have some real connection with the astonishing *chiaroscuro*, the mixture of shaded sunlight and half illuminated gloom which makes the charm of his style and habit of expression; while its connection with the singular charity and equity of his temper and judgment is quite unmistakable.

For the admitted desultoriness, no apology seems to be required, because the objection, and the want of objection, to it are equally matters of individual taste. And a tolerably brisk student, undertaking the task as a matter of postgraduate study, could classify Browne's materials prettily in any one of half a dozen different ways, and make it almost a pattern monograph. But Browne did not choose to adopt this method. He simply took—sometimes in more or less apparent or real connection, sometimes at haphazard—examples of pseudo-orthodoxy (as he might, perhaps, have even better entitled the treatise) and submitted them to the microscope or *aqua fortis* of his method—applying now experiment, as in the case of the kingfisher and its supposed virtue as a vane; now investigation of historical or other proof or disproof; now considerations of probability, analogy, decency and the like. His command of these different lines of evidence is remarkable: he scarcely ever confuses them, or the degree of certainty which they may be supposed to import; but the immense range of his subject — natural and other history of almost every conceivable kind except pure literature, upon which, strangely

enough,[1] he never touches—and the open flouting of any attempt at consecutiveness, may afford some excuse for the failure, in some cases, of critics to recognise this.

On the other hand, in no book has he been so parsimonious
of that nectar of his style which modern readers have been
wont to take as the solace of his supposed sins of desultoriness,
credulity and unscientific conduct generally; and in none is
that humour, which some have strangely ignored or refused to
recognise, subtler and less obtrusive, though it is tolerably pervading.   "It is delivered with *aiunt* and *ferunt* by many," he
says of the story of pope Joan.   Oppian, he informs us,

abating the annual mutation of sexes in the hyaena, the single sex
of the rhinoceros, the antipathy between two drums, of a lamb and
a wolf's skin, the informity of cubs, the venation of Centaures, the
copulation of the murena and the viper, with some few others, he
may be read with great delight and profit.

The quintessential dryness of that "with some few others" between the list of abatements and the commendation can only escape a palate predestined not to taste it.   And it is equally
difficult to understand the missing of the humour in the famous
prefatory declaration—that, "if elegancy still proceedeth . . . we
shall, within few years, be fain to learn Latin to understand English"—by a man who, before he had finished, was to observe how
something "handsomely sets forth the efficacy of assuefaction."

For twelve years—years of the utmost trouble and turmoil
to England but, apparently, unhistorical with him—Browne
published nothing; but, in 1658, when his political redemption
was drawing nigh, he was moved to two wonderful deliverances
which may have occupied him for a longer or shorter time, but
which certainly contain the quintessence both of his thought
and of his expression. *Hydriotaphia or Urn Burial* was
directly inspired by the discovery of certain sepulchral vessels
in Norfolk; no equally definite origin is assigned for its singular
companion *The Garden of Cyrus*—a discussion of the ubiquity
and virtues of the quincuncial arrangement (: · :).   Both, however, are, in effect—though the first not quite so much as the

---

[1] Yet his purely literary knowledge was certainly not small; and he is, perhaps, the only great Englishman of letters of his day, except Milton, who shows
familiarity with Dante.

second—occasions, if not occasions merely, for the outpouring
of their author's remarkable learning, of his strange quietist
reflection on the mysteries of the universe, of his profound
though unobtrusive melancholy, of the intensely poetical feeling which denied itself poetical expression[1] and, above all,
of his unique and splendid style.   They were the last things
that he himself published—uniting them, a year after their first
appearance, to *Pseudodoxia* in its third edition, and *Religio*
in its fifth authorised form.   The folio of 1659 may, in a sense,
be called his *Works*, so far as he published these himself, *A
Letter to a Friend*, *Christian Morals* and the various *Miscellanies* being, in some cases quite obviously, in almost all
probably, destitute of final revision, though all but a quarter of
a century passed between 1658 and his death.

These posthumously published works contain, as will be
pointed out presently, better things than some critics have
found in them.   But their author, whatever pains he had taken
with them, could hardly have made any—even the fragment
on *Dreams*—into a thing more magnificent than *Urn Burial*.
Its companion, like the posthumous pieces, has sometimes been
rather harshly judged.   Everybody of competence admits the
splendour of the peroration "But the quincunx of heaven runs
low," with its sign-manual or hallmark of Brownism in the
observation "To keep our eyes open longer were but to act our
Antipodes."[2]   But the whole of the fifth or last chapter leads
us to this in a fashion which has not universally been perceived
or acknowledged, and chapter 1, despite its touch of the whimsical, is no ordinary prelude.   Even the three central chapters,
for all their bewildering hunt of the quincunx through arts and
sciences, buildings and beds, botany and zoology, are not long
enough to be tedious, and, despite the prevailing motive, are
too various to incur the charge of monotony.   But a certain
allowance must always be made in the praise of *The Garden*

[1] Browne has left little verse, and that little of less merit.   The best, as well
as the best known, is the evening hymn in *Religio Medici*, II, § xii, which recalls
to all readers bishop Ken's later one, and may recall to a few the similar composition of Flatman, which came, perhaps, between the two.   All three, it is worth
observing, were Wykehamists, and, as such, accustomed to Latin hymns.

[2] There are few better examples than this of the truth of Sir Henry Craik's
observation, that the object of seventeenth century "wit" was "not to excite
laughter but to compel attention."

of Cyrus: in that of *Urn Burial* there is none necessary or even permissible. That Browne thought his urns older than they really were is perfectly immaterial, even if true; and no faults of a more serious nature occur. On the other hand, the author, on the very first page, has struck, and has maintained with wonderful fugue-variations to the close, a note at once directly appealing to ordinary humanity, and susceptible of being played upon with the strangest and remotest harmonies. This is not merely derived from the contrast of death and life— it is the result of a sort of double or triple consideration of the shortness of individual life, the length of time as contrasted with this and the shortness, again, of time, as a whole, contrasted with eternity. Now, one of these sides of the thought is uppermost; now, another; now, two, or all three, are kept in evidence together, with the most rapid shifting, while the changes illumine or are illumined by the phantasmagoria of Browne's imaginative learning. The purely historical part is much shorter than the corresponding portion of *The Garden of Cyrus;* and it seems relatively shorter still because of the more human interest of the subject, and the comparative, if not entire, absence of merely trivial scientific detail. But the really important point is the constant illumination just referred to— the almost continuous series of imaginative *explosions* where the subject catches fire from the author's spirit or *vice versa*. The greatest triumph of this pyrotechnical[1] explosion is, of course, the famous "Now since these dead bones" at the beginning of the fifth and (for in both these tractates Browne kept to his sacred number five) last chapter, where the display continues unbroken to the very conclusion, the longest piece, perhaps, of absolutely sublime rhetoric to be found in the prose literature of the world. But the tone has been only a little lower throughout the treatise; the very first lines "When the funeral pyre was out and the last valediction over" set a rhythm which is never too metrical and yet always cadenced beyond ordinary prose; and the imagination of the reader is constantly invited to incandescence corresponding to that of the writer, in such phrases, prodigally scattered over every

---

[1] There is no reason why any connotation of artificiality or triviality should be attached to this word. Summer lightning and the Aurora Borealis are only pyrotechnics on the great scale, and the effect of these against a dark sky is exactly that of Browne's rhetoric on a smaller.

page, and in almost every paragraph, as "What virtue yet sleeps in this *terra damnata* and aged cinders" and "his soul was viewing the large stations of the dead," which occur within a dozen lines of each other.

There are few provocatives to a similar enthusiasm in the posthumous miscellanies, with the exception above noted; and it would be unreasonable to complain of their absence, seeing that these miscellanies are somewhat unceremoniously "gnawed," if not "knaved," out of the author's unguarded "remains" in commonplace-books, scientific memoranda and the like. But the two major *posthuma* are in a different position. They have a curious interconnection—for certain passages occur in both, and it is impossible to say whether, if Browne had ever finally decided on publishing either, he might not have issued the two as one. Actually, *A Letter to a Friend* begins by a description— curiously blended between medical *sangfroid* and human sympathy—of (apparently) a case of rapid consumption; which description passes into remarks on the dying man's thoughts and so forth, while these, in their turn, fray out into general moral reflections and precepts; the whole being almost more deeply suffused than any other piece with Browne's intense, though quiet, melancholy.

Of such reflections and precepts, *Christian Morals* is entirely composed; and these ingredients, no doubt, have accounted for a recent tendency to depreciate them, the later nineteenth and earlier twentieth centuries being, as is well known, in no need of religious and ethical instruction. But readers who are not merely of, or for, their own age, may, perhaps, still find profit and pleasure in the treatise. Its most remarkable characteristic, from the strictly literary point of view, is an exaggeration of Browne's habit of Latinising ("Upon a *curricle* in this world depends a long course in the next"; "Trust not too much unto suggestions from the *reminiscential* amulets"), while there is a certain deficiency of his finer cadences and more harmonious rhetoric. Yet, these last traits appear not unfrequently in such splendid phrases as "Acquaint thyself with the Choragium of the Stars," "Behold thyself by inward opticks and the Crystalline of thy Soul." And, if a more ungenerous interpretation may assign both exaggeration and deficiency to failing powers, it is no irrational charity to prefer

the hypothesis of a simple want of revision and "making up."
At any rate, the tractate is no unworthy evensong to a day's
work of hardly surpassed quality.

A few words may, perhaps, be added about his letters. It
should surely not surprise anyone, though it has actually
seemed to surprise some of the very elect, that the style of these
is in the greatest apparent contrast to that of the printed works.
About Browne, there was no pose whatever. When he
appeared in public, he showed respect to himself, and to the
public at the same time, by assuming the garments of ceremony.
He did not "talk book" to his children and his friends. His
letters to his son Tom, of whose actual end, as has been said,
we do not know anything, though it was certainly premature,
are delightfully easy, full of matter, not in any way derogating
from the fatherly character, but, while maintaining this, still
the letters of friend to friend. To Edward, they are the
same, with an additional touch of the colleague—the fellow-
experimenter and student. With his learned acquaintances he
is a little more formal, though not much, and, naturally,
less playful. But, throughout, he shows how entirely equal he
was to either function of prose composition; and that, if he had
lived in the next generation and had been disposed rather to
adopt the "middle," than the sublime, style of that composition,
he could have been little less skilful at it than Addison or Steele.
It is fortunate that he did not so live for, as it is, we have both
them and him. But the correspondence is a special warning
not to limit our classifications too rashly; and, especially, not
to think that a great bender of the bow must always bend it.

Thomas Fuller, a curious contemporary, complement and
contrast to Browne, was born three years later, in 1608, at the
village of Aldwinkle, afterwards the birthplace of Dryden, but
in its other parish, St. Peter's, of which his father, also a Thomas,
was rector. The mother was Judith Davenant, sister of a
divine, who, becoming president of Queen's college, Cambridge,
and bishop of Salisbury, exercised important influence over his
nephew's career. But, when Fuller, after attendance at a
local school, went to Queen's on 29 June, 1621, at the age of
thirteen, his uncle had already been promoted to Salisbury;
and, though the nephew went through the regular course,

becoming B.A. in 1624/5 and M.A. in 1628, he was, despite Davenant's recommendations, disappointed of a fellowship there, as well as later at Sidney Sussex, which college he had also entered. He took orders, however, and obtained the curacy of St. Bene't's, where he buried Hobson, Milton's carrier. His first publication consisted of some inferior verse entitled *Davids Heinous Sin*, 1631 : in the same year, his uncle gave him the prebend of Netherbury in the diocese of Salisbury, following it, two years later, with the living of Broadwindsor in that of Bristol. Between the two appointments, in 1632, Fuller's father died; but he was already provided for, and had begun the process of making friends with persons of quality which afterwards stood him in good stead. In 1635, he took the degree of B.D., and, before 1638, he married. Up to this time, he seems to have been—as, indeed, would have been usual enough—chiefly or frequently absent from his prebend and his rectory, for he speaks of himself, later, as being "seventeen years [apparently 1621–38] resident in Cambridge." But Fuller's language is so much subdued to special antithetic and other quips that it does not do to take it too literally. Indeed, the context stating that his seventeen weeks in Oxford cost him more than these seventeen years at the other university shows, almost certainly, that he is speaking figuratively —of his prosperity during the one period, and of the loss of his benefices during, or about, the other.

However this may be, the quiet part of his life was over, or nearly so, by 1638. In 1640, the year after he had published his first important book, *The Holy War*, he became a member of convocation and, though already taking the moderate line for which he was afterwards famous, he signed the much contested canons of that year; and, if the House of Commons could have had its way, would have been fined £200. In 1641, a son was born to him, but his wife died; and in this year he published *The Holy and Profane State*. When the struggle actually broke out, he further illustrated that rather willowy policy of his by voluntarily abandoning—though, of course, not formally resigning—his preferments in the west; he went, at first, not to the royalist camp but to London, where, for some time, he was preacher at the Savoy. However, he could not stay there, and retired to Oxford (Lincoln college) and then to Hopton's army, where he became chaplain, and, fixing himself for a time in Exeter, was also titular of the same office to the baby princess Henrietta—the ill-fated "Madame" of the next generation. *Good Thoughts in Bad Times* was published here (1645). When Exeter had to surrender, he went once more to London; and the protection of divers powerful friends who were members of the other party, or had made their peace with it, not only saved him from molestation, but enabled him, with certain breaks and difficulties, to continue his ministration. In 1651, he married Mary Roper, daughter of viscount Baltinglas. He wrote, as well as preached, busily during this time; but was rather harassed by members of his own party, such as South and Heylyn, who disliked his moderation, objected to his fantastic style and made some fun of him personally. He seems, however, to have been reconciled to Heylyn, if not to the far greater and more formidable South.

The restoration (which he had advocated by a pamphlet for "a free parliament") seemed likely to do him much good. He proceeded D.D. by king's letters; he recovered his prebend and his rectory, in which latter, however, he characteristically left the intruder as curate; and he was made chaplain extraordinary to the king. But he caught a fever, died of it at his lodgings in Covent Garden on 15 August, 1661, and was buried at Cranford. His great collection *The Worthies of England* was posthumously published.

Nothing that has been said about Fuller's moderation must be construed into a charge against him of truckling or time-serving. It is true that, if not exactly (what some have called him) a puritan, he was probably more definitely anti-Roman than was usual on the cavalier side. But he not only saw active service in the non-combatant way at Basing, at Oxford with Hopton and at Exeter; his London residence in 1643 gave opportunity for hardly less active exercise in the royalist cause, for several of his sermons at the Savoy were strong, and, in the circumstances, not very safe, advocacies of that cause, and of the indissolubly allied cause of prelacy. He publicly and, for him, pretty sharply rebuked Milton's anonymous tractate *Of Reformation . . . in England;* was in his turn sharply taken to task by a Yorkshire puritan divine, John Saltmarsh; and was actually stopped (*i. e.* arrested) for a time by the Commons' orders, when proceeding to Oxford with a safe conduct from the Lords. And his later *Appeal of Injured Innocence*, when Heylyn had attacked his *Church History*, though much too long and hampered by its scholastic arrangement of regularly scheduled objection and reply, is an effective vindication of his general position.[1] As a man, he seems to have been perfectly honest and sincere; a better Christian than most men on either side; not quite destitute, perhaps, of a certain innocent vanity and busybodiness; but without a drop of bad blood in his composition. It is, however, as a man of letters that we are here principally concerned with him.

His verse is quite negligible and, fortunately, there is little of it; of the very large and never yet collectively edited body of his prose, certain features are pretty generally known. They have been characterised concisely (but with something of that want of accuracy and adequacy combined which conciseness often carries with it) in Coleridge's famous dictum that "wit was the stuff and substance of Fuller's intellect." Hair-splitting criticism may ask whether wit is not rather a form, a habit, a bent of the intellect, than, in any case, its stuff and substance. But, undoubtedly, in the wide and contemporary, as well as in the more modern and narrow sense, "wit" is the most prominent characteristic of Fuller's writing. Although it was apparently the subject of an acrid rebuke from South as a feature of our author's sermons, it cannot, since the collected presentation of these by Bailey and Axon, be said to be specially prevalent there. Indeed, he seems to have been conscious of his foible and to have tried to avoid giving way to it in the pulpit. But, in all his other work, from *The Holy War* (1639) to the posthumous *Worthies of England*, even in definitely "divine" examples like *Good Thoughts in Bad Times* and its sequels, he either does not make any attempt at resistance or fails entirely to resist. St. Monica's maid is "her partner in potting"; in the case of another (crippled) saint "God, who denied her legs, gave her wings." These

---

[1] It is, perhaps, not quite so effective as an actual defence of the book; he was, as will be pointed out again, an early user of "the document" in history, but his wandering life and his habit of subordinating everything to sallies of wit made him rather an inaccurate one. Still, the concluding letter to Heylyn (which was taken in a manner highly creditable to its recipient) is a model of courtesy, dignity and good feeling.

things please some of us well enough; but, in times when there is a straightlaced notion of dignity and decency, or when (neither of these being specially attended to) the sense of humour is sterilised and specialised, they have been, and are, looked on with little favour.

It is said, though statements of the kind are very difficult to check or control, that *The Holy and Profane State* has been Fuller's most popular work. If it be so, popular taste has not gone far wrong in this instance. The book does not, indeed, give so much room as others for the exhibition of one very creditable quality which was by no means common in Fuller's time—attention to documents and appreciation of their comparative value. Part of the cause of Heylyn's attack on *The Church History* (1655) is supposed to be Fuller's observation that "no *Historian* hath avouched" a certain anecdote of Henry VI, though both Brian Twyne and Heylyn himself had given it. Fuller was by no means incapable of mischief; but it is more than probable that, by "historian," he meant contemporary historian, and, of course, Twyne and Heylyn did not stand in that relation to the times of Henry VI. The fact, of course, is that, to the present day, both in history and literature, it is the most difficult thing in the world to get people to attend to this simple distinction of evidence. Fuller, with slips and errors, no doubt, did try to attend to it, especially in his *Church History* and the *Worthies*, but, everywhere, more or less. It is, however, not a popular attempt; and, though he did not fail to make it to some extent in *The Holy and Profane State* itself, as well as in *The Holy War* earlier and in the biographies he contributed to *Abel Redivivus*, these three works gave scope for a far more popular talent, and one in which he was to take and give one of his own "Pisgah Sights" of a yet unexploited and almost unexplored province of English literature. In all,[1] but in *The Holy and Profane State* especially, the narrative faculty is specially in evidence. This curious book is a sort of blend of the abstract "character" popular at the time, and of examples which are practically short stories with real heroes and heroines, Monica or Joan of Naples, Andronicus Comnenus or Drake. *Andronicus* was actually published

---

[1] Heylyn makes this (and the introduction of verse) a general objection to the *Church History*—"rather like a Church romance," quoth he, disdainfully.

separately; and one can see that Fuller's fingers unwittingly
itched (as Gibbon's did afterwards) to make the not yet born
historical novel out of it.   Even in the enormous miscellanies
or *collectanea* of the *Church History*, of its part conclusion part
sequel *The History of the University of Cambridge* and of *The
Worthies of England* the narrative impetus is no more to be
checked than witticisms or antiquarian details.   Lists of
sheriffs, of heads of colleges, of country gentlemen at the last
visitation, alternate with stories about some of them (or
about somebody or something else) and with dry observations, as to wax, "being yellow by nature [it] is by art made
white, red and green—which I take to be the dearest colours
especially when appendant on parchment."

Undoubtedly, however, it is the witticisms themselves
which, for the most part, delight or disgust readers of Fuller,
and, though they take the benefit of the above quoted dictum
as to the purpose of "wit" at this time being not merely
comical, they require more "benefit of clergy" in this kind
than those of most other writers.   He has been called epigrammatic, even "the father of English epigram"; but this does
not seem very appropriate either to the Greek or to the modern
sense of the term.   The famous idea of "images of God cut by
him in ebony not ivory" is not an epigram, but it is very much
of an emblem; and, perhaps because of the immense abundance
of emblem literature in those days, Fuller's conceits were constantly emblematic.   "The soldier at the same time shoot[ing]
out his prayer to God and his pistol at his enemy"; the question
"Who hath sailed about the world of his own heart, sounded
each creek, surveyed each corner, but that there still remains
much *terra incognita* to himself?" both appeal vividly to the
mind's eye.   Indeed, the conceit almost necessarily, even in
similes of the most solemn cast, leads to witticism intended or
unintentional; for each is intimately concerned with the discovery, elaborate or spontaneous, of similarity or dissimilarity.
Even the serious Browne, in his most serious work, has become almost Fullerian in his remark on the deluge that "fishes
could not wholly have escaped, except the salt ocean were
handsomely contempered by a mixture of the fresh element."
But Fuller himself positively aims at these things; or, at
least, certainly in his less professional work, and sometimes

elsewhere, never spares a jest when it presents itself to him.

It is almost unavoidable that such a style should incline less to the continuous harmonic cadence than to shorter moulds and measures. Fuller is by no means jerky, and he would not have been of his time if he had never used long sentences. But he does not incline to them; and his paragraphs are apt to be even shorter proportionally than their constituents. He has all the love of his day for an aphoristic and apophthegmatic delivery; though an occasional cause of lengthening in his sentences is his habit of shading or tailing off a serious statement of fact or axiom of opinion into a jest.

Fuller invites selection and has had his share of it. Hardly any book of his has so formal a plan or such consecutiveness of argument that piecemeal citation injures it; and it may well seem that the process of "creaming" can be justly and safely applied to a writer who is both desultory and jocular. But it may be doubted whether such selections give the reader a fair idea of his author, even if that reader be well disposed towards both the mid-seventeenth century and its characteristic quaintness. For, we must once more remember that the conceits and the quips were by no means intended merely to amuse; they were meant, partly, to act as sugarplums for the serious passages, and, partly, to drive these passages closer home by humorous application or illustration. To expect all or many readers to read all Fuller's books would be unreasonable; but nobody should think that he understands Fuller until he has read at least one of them as a book.

Except in regard to *Reliquiae Wottonianae*, and, perhaps, even to this in most points beyond its title, the work of Izaak Walton, by which he is almost universally known, may not seem to "intrude him upon antiquaries" as Browne has it; but he was no mean example of the temperament, then common, which creates the antiquarian tendency. Born in East Gate street, Stafford, on 9 August, 1593, he represented, through his father James, a family of yeomen; but he was early sent to London to be apprenticed to Thomas Grinsell and became a freeman of the Ironmongers' company on 12 November, 1618, having previously settled down in the neighbourhood of Fleet street and Chancery lane. His residence near St. Dunstan's brought him into contact with Donne. Jonson, Drayton, bishops Hall and King, Sir Henry Wotton and others were, also, his friends; and, by 1619, his connection with literature is, to some extent, shown by the dedication to him of the poems of a certain "S. B." For a long time, we hear nothing of him; but, in 1640, he published his life of Donne, and, four years later, left London, though he was back at the time of Laud's execution. In 1650, he is found living at Clerkenwell, and, next year, published *Reliquiae*. In an unobtrusive way, he seems to have been a trusted member of the royalist party; and he had Charles II's "lesser George" confided to his care after Worcester. In 1653, *The Compleat Angler* (not yet complete) appeared; five years later, he wrote his name on Casaubon's tablet in Westminster abbey; and, in 1662, took up his abode, after the hospitable fashion of great households in those days, with his friend bishop Morley of Winchester. His other *Lives* followed at intervals. In 1683, he published Chalkhill's *Thealma and Clearchus*,[1] and he died at the house of his son-in-law Hawkins (a Winchester prebendary who had married his daughter Anne) on 15 December, 1683. He had been twice married: first, in 1626, to Rachel Floud (a collateral descendant of archbishop Cranmer), who died in 1640; then, in 1646, to Anne Ken, half and elder sister to the future bishop who wrote Walton's epitaph. His second wife died twenty years before him.

Walton's long life was thus divided into two periods; and it was only in the later of these that he had full leisure. But this was a leisure of forty unbroken years; and it is not likely that the work of the earlier time was very severe or strenuous. That his tastes, his avocations, his associations were thoroughly literary, there is no doubt; but they do not seem to have prompted him to any extensive or frequent literary exercise. The world-famous *Compleat Angler* and the widely known *Lives* go together in one moderate-sized volume (even with Cotton's part of the firstnamed). There is no valid reason whatever for crediting him with the authorship of *Thealma and Clearchus*. And the minor works and *anecdota*, which the diligence of

[1] See *ante*, Chap. IV.

R. H. Shepherd collected some thirty years ago, are of little importance and less bulk.

It has generally been conceded that the absence of quantity is more than made up by the presence of quality, but the quality of that quality itself has been made the subject of dispute, sometimes unnecessarily (and, in reference to Walton, most inappropriately) ill-tempered. In *The Compleat Angler*, it has been pronounced by some to be the result of consummate literary art; while, to others, it seems to be—there almost exclusively, and, in the *Lives*, to no small extent—purely natural and unpremeditated, the spontaneous utterance of a "happy old man" (as Flatman, with complete felicity, if not complete originality, called him), who has lived with men of letters, and is familiar with letters themselves, but who no more thinks of picking words and turning phrases than a nurse does in telling tales to a child. But this dispute could hardly be settled without settling what "literary art" is, and that would be a long process. Nor is the settlement of the actual quarrel a matter of absorbing interest. The fact remains that the singular and golden simplicity of Walton's style—in *The Compleat Angler* more especially but, except when the occasion seems to insist on more ceremony, also in the *Lives*—is matter of common ground and of no dispute whatever. Walton was a man of no inconsiderable reading; and he could not have been a man of his time if he had been shy of showing it, however completely his character might lack pretension. But not Bunyan himself can use a plainer and purer vernacular than Walton when he chooses, as he generally does choose. On the much rarer occasions when he "talks book" a little (as in the passage about the "silver stream gliding towards the tempestuous sea," which preludes the scene with Maudlin and "Come live with me and be my love"), he may, possibly, be aiming higher, but he goes much wider of his mark.

If this naturalness of style be duly considered, it will, perhaps, be found to diminish, if not to remove altogether, any surprise that might otherwise be felt at the production of so little work in so long a life; at the remarkable excellence of the product; and at its curious variety. Personal interest, and nothing else, appears to have been the sole starting influence, so far as matter goes, in every case, even in that of the life of

Hooker;[1] and personal quality, and nothing else, to have been the fashioner of the style. Anything—country, scenery, old-fashioned manners, piety, the strange complexity of Donne, the simplicity (patient in life, massive and independent in letters) of Hooker, the various characteristics of Wotton and Herbert and Sanderson, the pastoral-romantic fairy-land of Chalkhill—all these things, in one way or another, were brought directly home to him, and he made them at home without parade, and, with perfect homeliness and ease, as Philemon and Baucis did the gods who visited them, to speak in the manner of his own time.

The result was what ease generally brings with it—charm. There have been, from his own time downwards, fishermen who were contemptuous of his fishing; and recent biographers have been contemptuous of anyone who should be content with the facts of his biographies. The competent *orbis terrarum* of readers has always been careless of either contempt. In his case, as in almost all, the charm is not really to be analysed, or, rather, it is possible to distinguish the parts, but necessary to recognise that the whole is much greater than these parts put together. The angling directions might fail to interest, and the angling erudition succeed in boring; as to the subjects of the *Lives*, though they were all remarkable men in their different ways, only Donne can be said to have an intense interest of personality. The source of attraction is Walton, not the "chub or chavender," or the Hertfordshire meadows and streams, or Maudlin and "red cow," or the decent joviality of my brother Peter, or Hooker's misfortunes in marriage, or Sir Henry Wotton's scholarly urbanity, but these things, as Walton shows them to us, with art so unpremeditated, that, as has been said, some would deny it to be art at all, yet with the effect of consummate *mimesis* of presentation of nature with something of the individual presenter added. But it will hardly be denied that his grace is positively enhanced by the characteristic which he shares with the other subjects of this chapter—the quaint, and, in him, almost unexpected seasoning of learning. He has it, no doubt, least of the four; and what he has he neither obtrudes and caricatures like

---

[1] Walton quotes from Hooker the words "as discernible as a natural from an artificial beauty." They were not without application in his own case.

Urquhart, nor makes his main canvas like Browne, nor associates pell-mell with play of conceit and purpose of instruction, as does Fuller. With him, it is a sort of silver or gold lacing to the sober grey garment of his thought and diction, though it should always be remembered that grey is capable of almost more fascinating shades than any other colour, and sets off the most delicate textures admirably.

To dwell at any length on the fashion in which this sober grace is brought out in *The Compleat Angler* would be superfluous; but a word or two may be permitted. No book so well deserves as a motto that stanza of *The Palace of Art* which describes the "English home," "a haunt of ancient Peace," with "dewy pastures, dewy trees." There is no dulness and no stagnation; the characters walk briskly, talk vigorously and argumentatively, fish, eat, drink like men of this world, and like cheerful and active men of a world that is going pretty well after all. But there is also no worry; nothing ugly, vulgar or jarring. It is the landscape and the company of *The Faerie Queene* passed through a slight sieve of realism, and crimeless; only, in the distance, perhaps, an erring gentleman, who reprehensively derives his jests from Scripture or from want of decency. A land of Beulah in short—with a somewhat less disquieting atmosphere of lack of permanence, which the land of Beulah itself must have carried with it.

The birth-year of Thomas, afterwards Sir Thomas, Urquhart, or Urchard[1]—the best Scottish representative of the peculiar seventeenth century character which was exhibited in different ways in England by Burton earlier, and by Browne and Fuller in his own time—used to be assigned to the same date as Browne's, 1605. But this date has now, on good evidence, been shifted six years later, to 1611. His father, another Sir Thomas, represented the Urquharts of Cromarty, a family whose pedigree has been verified to the year 1300, while it may reasonably be extended to Adam, though the acceptance of the particulars (supplied, with characteristic pedantry and humour mingled, by the subject of this notice) may be facultative. The younger Thomas's mother was Christian Livingstone of the

---

[1] He sometimes, if not always, signed himself so; using. as well, the initials "C. P.," *i. e.* "Christianus Presbyteromastix."

noble family of that name. His father succeeded to considerable estates; but was either a determined spendthrift or a very
bad manager; and, in his later years (1637 to his death in 1641),
appears to have been subjected to rather peremptory treatment
including personal restraint, by his eldest son and other members of a self-constituted family council. It is certain that, all
his life, our Sir Thomas himself was the victim of creditors;
though, perhaps—when one considers his foreign travels, and
the fact that, at Worcester, he lost four trunks of fine clothes
besides three of MSS.—not entirely without his own contribution to the difficulties. He entered King's college, Aberdeen
in 1622, and must have studied there vigorously; while, after
completing his course, he travelled much abroad, learnt more,
acquired accomplishments of various kinds and, according to
his own account, displayed martial and patriotic prowess resembling that of the Admirable Crichton (whose chief celebra-
tor he himself was), and of "Squire Meldrum" still earlier. He
emerges into public life at the time of the at first successful but
soon suppressed royalist rising in the north of Scotland which
is known as the Trot of Turriff (1639).

After the failure of this, he went to England, was knighted by
Charles I at Whitehall in 1641, but took no part in the civil war
proper, making another excursion to the continent in 1642–5.
In the last named year, he returned and settled at Cromarty.
Three years later, he was made "officer of horse and foot" and,
after the king's execution in 1649, shared in the abortive rising
at Inverness, was declared a traitor, but, in 1650, was dismissed
by the General Assembly after examination. He joined
Charles II in the expedition to England, fought at Worcester,
lost the seven trunks above mentioned, was taken and thrown
into the Tower, but leniently treated, transferred to Windsor
and, finally, liberated by Cromwell. Then he returned to Scotland and, in 1653, published his great translation of the earlier
part of *Rabelais*. From this time, we know nothing whatever
about him. That he died abroad of rapture or laughter on
hearing of the restoration is a legend. But, in August, 1660,
his brother Alexander laid claim to the hereditary office of sheriff
of Cromarty, which practically implies Sir Thomas's death.

For people who like a clear and consistent character, classi-
fiable under ordinary conventions, Urquhart must be a hope-

less puzzle; indeed, most of his critics have got out of their
difficulties by the easy suggestion-door of "a little mad," which
may be allowed, but is insufficient. From his portraits—one
exhibiting a gentleman in cavalier dress, spruce, mustachioed,
beribboned to the very "nines" of the irresistible vernacular,
and suggesting, in one of his own admirable phrases, "one of
the quaintest Romancealists" of the time; the other, the same
gentleman enthroned and crowned by muses and other mythological personages—the enquirer turns to the works they adorn,
where the coxcomb, though he remains, shows quite a different
kind of coxcombry, and blends it with a pedantry which
is gigantesque and almost incredible. His *Epigrams* (1642)
are not specially remarkable for this, being mostly sensible
enough commonplaces expressed in hopelessly prosaic verse.
But, in the series of elaborately Greek-named treatises which
followed, the characteristics are quite different. Mathema-
ticians do not seem quite agreed as to *Trissotetras* (1645), but
at least some competent authorities are said to have allowed
it possible merit, if only it had been written in a saner lingo.
As it is, it informs us that "The axioms of plane triangles are
four viz. Rulerst, Eproso, Grediftal and Bagrediffiu," while
Rulerst branches into Gradesso and Eradetul, and is under the
directory of Uphechet. This mania for jargonic nomenclature
pursues Urquhart throughout, and seems sometimes to have
been the very mainspring or exciting cause of his lucubrations.
The indulgence of it must have counted for something in his
famous and (even in his own time) much ridiculed genealogy
of the Urquharts (*Pantochronocanon*, 1652) from Adam, with
invented names for all the fathers and mothers from Seth's
wife downwards, whom history does not mention or whom he
cannot borrow from it. It dictated more than the titles of
Logopandecteision (1653), a scheme for a universal language,
and *Ekskubalauron* (1652), a treatise of his own rescued from
the gutter after the dispersal of his property at Worcester.
When it descends from proper names, it dictates, in its severer
moods, remarks about "disergetic loxogonosphericals"; in its
lighter, intimations that he will "proceed to the catheteuretic
operation" of something, and sneers at "the ministerian philo-
plutaries" who deprived a friend of his of a living for what
Urquhart thought insufficient cause.

Yet he is not mad all round the compass. The best known passage of his work outside *Rabelais*, the account of the Admirable Crichton, though it may somewhat embroider the plain canvas of truth, is vigorously and effectively written. Intensely patriotic as he is—a very "bur-thistle" in his aggressive proclamation of Scottish merits and virtues—he, in the mid-seventeenth century and in mid-war-time between England and Scotland, argues stoutly and sensibly for a union parliament, representing both divisions of the island. When his coxcomb-familiar is not playing tricks with him on the one side, or his pedant-familiar on the other, or both together—sometimes, in flashes, even when they are doing their worst—he shows himself not merely, what he always is, a scholar and a gentleman, but a man of most excellent differences, acute, fanciful, stocked with pregnant ideas and possessed of a very noteworthy faculty of expression for them, whenever the fiend of jargon does not simply possess and speak through him.

It may be questioned, however, whether his most glaring faults and foibles did not stand him in almost as good stead as his gifts and graces, when he took it into his head to give an English version of *Gargantua* and *Pantagruel*. It is true that they led him to exaggerate the peculiarities of his original; and that this exaggeration has undoubtedly passed into the usual English estimate of Rabelais himself. But only a man who had practised jargon, largely combined with learning, for years could, even by exaggerating it, have excogitated a lingo capable of reproducing the wonderful genius-*galimatias* of Master Francis. Urquhart could coin words as easily as he could write, blenched at no extravagance, would have scorned to rationalise any apparent nonsense, sympathised thoroughly with, and could understand, his author's undoubted learning, and had quite enough shrewdness, good feeling and even exaltation of thought and sentiment to interpret these qualities when they met him in that author.

The result, as is pretty generally granted, is an almost ideal translation, perhaps enlarging slightly, as has been said, the moles and warts of his subject—the gibberish, the "broad" language, the torrents of grotesque synonyms (in this last respect, Sir Thomas was especially lavish) but reproducing the general effect amazingly. Very often, scholars in originals

are the harshest critics of translations. It may be said with
confidence that those who have known their Rabelais best in
his own shape and language have been the heartiest admirers
of his English presenter. Motteux, Urquhart's successor, did
his work very well, but something has departed in it; and Sir
Thomas remains the last and greatest of the great translators
of the larger Elizabethan period.

These four royalist writers—Urquhart, to some extent, but
by no means wholly, being what Browne calls a "monstrous
draught and caricatured representation" of what Browne
himself presents magnificently, Fuller ingeniously and Walton
in the simplest and least pretentious fashion—agree in something more than in their royalism and in that determined
attention to the past which undoubtedly they all display.
They represent their own age, not merely in the learning which
attracted and rewarded that attention, and in which the
earlier seventeenth century probably surpassed every other
period, not merely in the obstinate quaintness which was also
characteristic of it, but in a peculiar command of prose style
which is likely to remain inimitable and unique. To set this
down to something like an accident of time, the dying down or
approaching extinction of the more "insolent and passionate"
spirit of poetry and its temporary taking refuge in prose, is
not irrational and is probably correct, but it is not quite
sufficient. More went to the making of the group—and especially of Browne—than this; even if we leave to the idiosyncrasy
of the individuals its first and incalculable value. Perhaps not
a little should be allowed for the existence of a body of readers,
not very large, perhaps, but not inconsiderable, interested in
learning and thought and not yet accustomed to "light" reading of the more modern type. Something more may be set
down to the absence of the restrictions of conventional grammar, conventional vocabulary, conventional propriety of various kinds. The revolt of the plain style, the demand for "a
naked natural way of speaking" and the like may have been
justified even by Browne and Fuller to a certain extent and
more than amply by Urquhart in his serious work. Even
Walton, though he speaks "naturally" enough, might be
thought by a man like Sprat not to speak sufficiently nakedly—

to dress his thought with too many tags of learning and flights of fancy. But, if there was any sin, there was mighty and manifold solace. Without the liberty of syntax, to some extent; without the unrestrained abundance and variegated colour of vocabulary to a much greater; without the endless decoration of learning, and arabesque of imagination and conceit, the quaint flashing wit of Fuller would find itself miserably hampered and (which is of far greater importance) the magnificence of Browne could not exist. The wit may tease some and the magnificence appear too solemn and cumbrous, too much a matter of apparatus and circumstantial peroration to others. If so, these authors are not for those readers. But, fortunately, there are others for whom they are, and who should be able to perceive that without what, from some points of view, may seem their defects, their qualities could hardly exist. Walton's simplicity would not be what it is without the contrast of its mannerism; and, though a little of the original writing of Urquhart may go a very long way, and to read too much, even of Fuller consecutively, is not well, the parenthetic and metaphysical wit of Broadwindsor can be returned to again and again with satisfaction, and a moderate dose even of *Logopandecteision* and *Ekskubalauron* has no unwelcome gust. On the other hand, the charm of Walton is unfailing and unfading; and the *Rabelais* of Sir Thomas of Cromarty has not merely a borrowed, but an earned and contributory, place in the utterances of the comic spirit of the world. While, as for those of the graver genius, the work of Sir Thomas of Norwich, its scepticism tempered by imagination and its style incrusted with the rarest gems of phrase and rhythm, stands practically alone, even in its own time—some things in Donne excepted—and without anything similar or second at any other.

CHAPTER XI
Jacobean and Caroline Criticism

T HE great names of Jonson and Bacon meet us at the threshold of the seventeenth century, and the names of Milton and Hobbes are soon added to theirs; but disappointment awaits the scholar who expects to find their achievement in poetry and philosophy matched by a similar achievement in the field of criticism. It is doubtful whether any of these four justified one of the most significant of the critic's functions by interpreting a poet to his contemporaries, or by making an unknown name a real possession of English literature: not a single author was better understood because of any light shed by them. The utterances of Jonson concerning Shakespeare impressed themselves upon his countrymen, and, in a sense, increased Shakespeare's vogue and prestige; but, for the most part, they understated rather than illuminated the contemporary taste which they confirmed. Yet, it would be untrue to say that these critics did not accomplish anything, for they changed the attitude of men toward literature and the criticism of literature; and, by modifying the literary outlook of Englishmen, they so transformed the spirit of criticism that the transition from the age of Sidney to the age of Dryden seems not only intelligible but inevitable.

At the outset, we are met by Bacon, and it is no less true of him than of the others that his services to contemporary thought are not the measure of his services to criticism. But he, too, helped to transform the theory of literature, or, at least, to bring order out of the chaos of theory; and he created a new conception of literary history, which served as a touchstone to scholars from the moment he enunciated it, though its real

significance was not apprehended for many generations to
come.   It was he who first defined the relation of poetry to the
imagination, and attempted a classification of the arts and
sciences based on the divisions of the mind, according to which
poetry bears the same relation to the imaginative faculty that
history and philosophy bear, respectively, to memory and reason.   The Spaniard Huarte, in his *Examen de Ingenios*, had
already classified sciences and arts in a similar way, and Bacon
adopted this foreign system.   But, in elaborating it, he gave
it a significance for criticism as well as for philosophy; and his
classification became a more or less permanent possession of
English thought and taste.   Within the scope of the imagination, he included allegorical poetry; and, to his rationalising
mind, this seemed the highest expression of poetic genius.   He
finds no difficulty in justifying this inclusion, though his conception of the imagination as a transformation of the realities
of life into forms more sympathetic to the human mind, as
external nature idealised, forces him to separate the lyric from
truly imaginative poetry and to place it with rhetoric and
philosophy.

All this may seem to have little to do with the actual progress of criticism; but it must be remembered that the critics of
the preceding age had not thus definitely connected literature
with the mental faculty that creates it, and that Bacon, in doing
this, is a herald of the attitude of Hobbes and his successors.
It is by his conception of literary history, however, that he has
made his most important contribution.   Just as literature was
regarded as a product of the imagination, and not merely as
something interesting in itself and by itself separate from the
mind of man, so, here, he conceives of it as having certain external relations with the age in which it is produced, not a thing
in vacuo but something expressive of the *Zeitgeist*, of which
he was the first to have a fairly adequate conception.   Yet,
with all these ideas about the place of poetry in the scheme of
the sciences and the meaning and function of literary history,
Bacon has given us very few concrete judgments in respect to
literature that are of any considerable value.   His method of
interpreting poetry is either through allegory, as in *The Wisdom
of the Ancients* and elsewhere, where poetic truth becomes
merely a symbol of moral truth, or through history, where a

record of external changes in style and in manner passes for
criticism, without for a moment grappling with the secret of
an author's power or charm. His influence, both by his specific
achievements and by his general theory, was in the direction
of rationalism and science; yet he was an Elizabethan, and
touched by the romantic longings of his time. His statement
that art becomes more delightful when "strangeness is added
to beauty" foreshadows Pater's definition of romanticism, and
his assertion that art works "by felicity not by rule" places
him in opposition to the whole tendency of criticism in the
century that was to follow.

It was his contemporary Jonson, in fact, who first made
this conception of "rule" native to English thought. In the
prologue of *Volpone*, he boasts that he has followed all the
laws of refined comedy,

> As best Criticks have designed;
> The lawes of time, place, persons he observeth,
> From no needfull rule he swerveth;

and it was his critical function throughout his life to make
Englishmen realise that literary creation is not determined by
individual whim, but by an external and ideal order given by
literary tradition, and not to be swerved from without the
sacrifice of art. This was the chief influence which he exerted
on his younger contemporaries; and, in *Jonsonus Virbius*, the
monument of verse reared to his memory, John Cleiveland
could say that it was Jonson

> Who first reform'd our Stage with justest Lawes,
> And was the first best Judge in your own Cause;
> Who, when his Actors trembled for Applause,
> Could with a noble Confidence preferre
> His own, by right, to a whole Theater,
> From Principles which he knew could not erre.

"Laws" and "principles which could not err" first entered
English criticism through the agency of Jonson. It is true that
Sidney, in his *Defence of Poesie*, had espoused the three unities,
on the authority both of Aristotle and of "common reason,"

and it was from Sidney that Jonson may have derived his
original impetus toward the acceptance of the classical tradition.   Sidney's conception of the high dignity of poetry, of
dramatic form and of humours in comedy are all to be found in
the early writings of Jonson; and, though this early glow of
Elizabethan fervour cooled with age, in the prefaces, prologues
and epilogues of his plays, in epigrams and poems, he continued
to expound the message of order in literature, of classical form,
of the tempered spirit as opposed to boisterous energy and
emphasis.   He took counsel with the Latin rhetoricians, with
Cicero, Quintilian, Seneca, Pliny, Petronius and, later, with the
humanists of the continent, Erasmus, Daniel Heinsius, Justus
Lipsius and Julius Caesar Scaliger.   The star of scholarship in
criticism was passing northward from Italy to Holland; and
the deliberate and moderate classicism of the Dutch Latinists,
their reasonableness and common sense, made a deep appeal to
Jonson.   Though his own classicism became more and more
rigid, he never failed to echo their assertion of the "liberty of
poets" and their conception of the classics as "guides, not
commanders."

The chief result of these studies, and the chief monument of
Jonson as a critic, is to be found in his *Timber or Discoveries*,
published, posthumously, in 1641.   It is a commonplace
book, certainly not intended for publication in its present form,
and, possibly, never intended for publication at all.   Certainly,
not one of the utterances which it contains in respect to poetry
and poetic criticism is the result of Jonson's own thought.   Recent scholarship has been able to trace nearly every one of its
famous passages to some contemporary or classical origin, and
it is fair to assume that the slight remnant is equally unoriginal. [1]

If it were our purpose to judge Jonson as a literary artist,
this would be of slight consequence, for the artist may consider
the world as all before him where to choose, and may demand
that we consider not whence he has borrowed his materials but
what he has done with them.   The critic's case is different.
We have a right to expect of him that he shall have reflected
on literature; that, out of the ideas of others, he shall mould
ideas which shall seem as if they were his own.   Jonson has
translated his originals *verbatim*, and has not added a single

[1] See *ante*, Vols. IV., pp. 398, 594, and VI., pp. 9, 10.

idea that was not already full-grown in them. If we were merely studying the taste of the dramatist Jonson, all this would have high interest for us; but it would be idle to dispute that Jonson the critic suffers from the discovery. The "constant good sense, occasional felicity of expression, conscientious and logical intensity of application or devotion to every point of the subject handled or attempted," which Swinburne found in the critical portions of *Discoveries*, are virtues that must be credited to Jonson's originals rather than to Jonson himself.

Yet, though Dryden's statement that "there are few serious thoughts which are new" in Jonson has proved truer with time, this did not affect the influence of his selective translation on the age that was to follow; and Dryden himself could say that, in *Discoveries*, "we have as many and profitable rules for perfecting the stage as any wherewith the French can furnish us." As an influence, Jonson remains what he was; as an original critic, he indubitably loses in prestige. His influence was immediately exerted on the younger men about him; some of its results may be observed, for example, in the comments on poets and prosemen in Bolton's *Hypercritica;* and, even now the tremendous effects of this influence on restoration poetry and criticism are only partly comprehended. It was due to him that the pregnant utterances of post-classic rhetoricians and the lucid and rational classicism of Dutch scholars became part and parcel of English thought.

Despite changes of taste, a number of Elizabethan survivals may be found in the very heart of this period. The chapter on poetry in Peacham's *Compleat Gentleman* (1622) forms a kind of text-book borrowed from Puttenham and Scaliger. The chapter begins with a long and enthusiastic defence of poetry and a rhapsody on its history, quite in the Elizabethan manner, and this is followed by a brief survey of Latin and English poetry; but Peacham has nothing to say concerning the Latin poets that had not already been uttered by Scaliger, and nothing concerning the English poets that had not been said by Puttenham. In similar manner, Sir William Alexander, in his *Anacrisis* (1634?), reverts to the tradition of Sidney's *Defence of Poesie*, and summarises the taste begun with *Arcadia* and culminating, after his own day, in the heroic romances. Yet, even here, the new ideals of Caroline taste are beginning to

assert themselves.   Not only is modern poetry summed up in
the prose romances, not only are Tasso and Sidney, Vergil and
Lucan, his idols, but a comparison of poetry to a formal garden
stands side by side with an attack on Scaliger and a defence of
poetic freedom.   Balzac's letters and the writings of other men
of the new French school furnish us with the models of his style,
and we are here on the threshold of D'Avenant's preface to
Gondibert in manner and feeling.   A new and tentative classicism was struggling through the ordeal of *préciosité*.   To this
period, too, belongs Suckling's *Session of the Poets*, with its
casual and ironical judgments of some of his contemporaries;
and a few minor essays of like character illustrate similar
tendencies of the time.

   In the next decade or two, the results of contact with France
appear, also, in the new theory and practice of translation and
in the critical trend toward simplicity in style.   In France, a
number of brilliant translators were adapting the classics to the
taste of their countrymen.   Of these, Perrot d'Ablancourt was
the chief exemplar, and the prefaces of his numerous translations enunciate most clearly this new philosophy of paraphrase.
"I do not always limit myself to the words or even to the
thoughts of this author," he says, in his version of Lucian, "but,
mindful solely of his purpose, I accommodate it to the French
air and manner"; and, in his complete version of Tacitus, he
goes so far as to say that an injustice is done to a translation by
comparing it with its original.   When this theory reached England, it came into contact with the Jonsonian tradition of literal
translation, and, for some time, these two schools existed side
by side.   Cowley, in the preface to his *Pindaric Odes*, claims
for himself the credit of having introduced the new way into
England; his biographer Sprat assumes that Cowley was not
the first to recommend it, but insists that he was one of the
first to practise it.   The acknowledged herald of the new
method was Sir John Denham, in the well known verses prefixed to Fanshawe's version of *Il Pastor Fido* (1647):

> That servile path thou nobly dost decline
> Of tracing word by word and line by line . . .
> A new and nobler way thou dost pursue
> To make Translations and Translators too;

> They but preserve the Ashes, Thou the Flame,
> True to his sense but truer to his fame.

Nine years later, Denham restated the argument in the prose preface to his *Essay on Translation*, which had been begun much earlier and which is one of the first English attempts to put the theory of loose paraphrase into practice.

The critical trend toward simplicity, which, also, received an impetus from French influence, was especially directed to the elimination of the conceits of the metaphysical school and the current perversions of poetry and prose. That school had not had any adequate expression in English criticism, just as the Elizabethan drama was really without its true critical expounders and defenders; but Henry Reynolds's *Mythomystes* (1632) illustrates the perverse effect of the school in the realms of criticism. In this work, the friend of Drayton and translator of Tasso's *Aminta* has systematically applied Neoplatonism to the interpretation of poetry. Bacon had already indicated the road, but Reynolds follows it into a tropical forest of strange fancies. The cabalists and neoplatonists, Philo and Reuchlin, but especially Pico della Mirandola and Alessandro Farra, here find an English voice. *Mythomystes* has another historical interest in its relation to the controversy respecting ancients and moderns. It professes to contain a brief for the ancients; but it argues their claims on grounds utterly repugnant to neo-classicism, not their superior portrayal of the fundamentals of human nature but their defter manipulation of the cabalistic mysteries. For Bacon, allegorical interpretation seemed to furnish an opportunity for the scientific explanation of poetry; Reynolds's method implies the negation of science. It was against such perversities of taste as these that the new exponents of simplicity now directed sporadic attacks; but no systematic expression of this new movement is to be found at this period, and it did not gain real headway until the age of Dryden.

The critical position of Milton, who began to write about this time, has been defined by himself. In the treatise *Of Education* (1644), he commits himself unequivocally to the tradition of "that sublime art" which is taught "in Aristotle's *Poetics*, in Horace, and the Italian commentaries of Castelvetro,

Tasso, Mazzoni, and others"; and to the tradition of renascence criticism he remained faithful throughout his life.   In the preface to *Samson Agonistes* (1671), this attitude remains unmodified except by an occasional touch of puritan conscience; even the somewhat earlier attack on rime he inherited from Trissino and Tolomei.   In the judgment of literature, he has little to offer save a venomous onslaught on Hall's satires (referring, especially, to the cacophonous "pace of the verse" and to the "poorness and frigidity" of the imagery), and contemptuous allusions to Sidney's *Arcadia* and Shakespeare's *Richard III*.   But his conception of the imagination as that which alone makes literature vital, his veneration for the poet's consecrated office, his passionate defence of literary freedom, his ideas concerning the spiritual unity of poetry and religion, were heritages which he passed on to the critics of the following age; and, indirectly at least, he helped to fructify not only poetry but criticism as well, through the agency of such men as Edward Phillips, Dennis and the two Wartons.

Bacon, as we have seen, gave poetry a definite place in a scheme of the arts and sciences; he referred it to the imagination, and used this term to explain the idealising process by which poetry transforms the materials of life into forms of art. But he did not attempt to analyse this process, or to explain the sources and mutual relations of the various functions of the mind.   This is the peculiar work of Hobbes.   The critics of the sixteenth century had dealt with literature as an external phenomenon; they isolated the work of art from its position in space and time, and from its relation to the mind which created it.   This generalisation does not imply that the historical sense did not make itself felt in some literary controversies, or that such words as "wit," "fancy," "imagination" and the like do not occasionally and casually occur in criticism; the Spanish critic Rengifo, for example, asserts a vehement imagination, *furor poeticus* and *agudeza de ingenio* to be essentials of the poet.   But such words as these are casual and unreasoned; they are not analysed; they remain, one might say, abstract virtues of the poet, and are not brought into fundamental relation with the work of art itself.   The concrete work is tested *in vacuo*, and the critic is concerned with its unity, probability, regularity, harmony and the like.   The seventeenth century first attempted to deal accurately with the relation between the creative mind and the work of art; it began to analyse the content of such terms as "wit," "fancy" and "taste." Hobbes is here a pioneer; he left an impress on critical terminology, and his psychology became the groundwork of restoration criticism. The relation of Descartes to French classicism suggests the position of Hobbes in Stewart England.

Hobbes's theory of poetry is a logical result of his philosophy of mind. For him, a mechanical universe continues to make itself felt on the *tabula rasa* of the human mind; these impressions the mind retains, arranges and combines. "Time and Education" (as he puts it briefly, in popular fashion, in the letter to D'Avenant prefixed to *Gondibert*) "begets experience; Experience begets Memory; Memory begets Judgement and Fancy; Judgement begets the strength and structure, and Fancy begets the ornaments of a Poem." Here, "fancy" and "judgment," like Bacon's "imagination," are mental processes which re-arrange the materials of experience into forms of art; but, for Hobbes, the imaginative process is no longer sufficient or even vital; fancy furnishes the "ornaments" and judgment the "strength and structure" of poetry. His distinction between the two became a commonplace of criticism in the period of classicism: "wit," the current term for fancy, denotes quickness of mind in seeing the resemblances between disparate objects; judgment, or reason, finds differences in objects apparently similar. This distinction had been suggested by the Italians of the later renascence, and had been more clearly indicated, as a difference in human temperament, by Bacon; but, with Hobbes, who first gave it precision, it became part and parcel of English thought, and was adopted by Robert Boyle, Locke, Temple, Addison and others, until Harris pointed out that a distinction of this sort would place Euclid's *Geometry* among the supreme works of fancy. The French had realised the critical significance of the antithesis for some time, but they never formulated it so clearly as this. Throughout the second half of the century, in both countries, the terms "wit" and "judgment" were placed in a sort of conventional opposition, like the *doctrina* and *eloquentia* of the humanists, and the clash resounds through neo-classical criticism.

Hobbes's distinction of the poetic genres is the logical outcome of his philosophy.   He conceives of them as conditioned
by the divisions of the external world—heroic, comic and pastoral, corresponding to court, city and country—and man
simply arranges what nature gives in forms of his own speech,
narrative or dramatic.   The poetry of the court thus assumes
the form of epic or tragedy; the poetry of the city, satire or
comedy; the poetry of the country, bucolics or pastoral comedy.
Here, there is no place for lyrical forms; they are "but essayes
and parts of an entire poem."   Bacon had set the example for
this indifference, and, later, Temple followed in the path of
Hobbes.   Nor is there any place for didactic or descriptive
verse, for the subject of poetry is not natural science or moral
theory, but "the manners of men," presented in the guise of
lifelike fiction.   The exclusion of didactic verse is Aristotelian,
and had furnished the subject for infinite controversy in the
renascence; but the seventeenth century tended more and
more to follow Roman practice rather than Aristotelian precept
in this respect.   Yet Hobbes's "manners of men" fails to
suggest that the whole content of human life (in its inner as
well as its outer manifestations) is the theme of poetry, and is
Horatian rather than Aristotelian.

The theme of poetry, then, is the manners of men; its
method is that of verisimilitude, or resemblance to the actual
conditions of life; and Hobbes's scorn for ghosts and magic
is the natural outcome of this insistence on *vraisemblance*.
From acquaintance with the manners of men, rather than from
books, the poet is to obtain the elements of style, or "expression."   To know human nature well, to retain images of it in
the memory that are distinct and clear, are the sources of per-
spicuity and propriety of style, and of "decorum" in character-
drawing; to know much of it is the source of variety and novelty
of expression.   Hobbes's aesthetic is consistent and logical
throughout, the first of its kind in English literature.

When he wields this body of theory in the concrete field of
criticism, his discretion fails.   A quarter of a century inter-
vened between the publication of his letter to D'Avenant (1650)
and the preface to his translation of Homer (1675), but the
theory has not fundamentally changed.   Edward Phillips
preferred the latter because of the bias and friendly compli-

ment of the former, and, certainly, Hobbes's judgment of
Gondibert and of Howard's *British Princes* must be approached
with at least as much caution as the flattering dedications of
the period. In the later preface, he justifies his taste by the
preference of Homer to both Vergil and Lucan. He formulates
seven "virtues" of the epic—in diction, style, imagery, plot,
elevation of fancy (which, he says, is usually overestimated as a
virtue of poetry), the amplitude of the subject and the justice
and impartiality of the poet—and he then compares Homer
with Vergil and Lucan in respect to these essential qualities.
Dryden complains that Hobbes "begins the praise of Homer
where he should have ended it," meaning that Hobbes first
considers the choice of words and the harmony of numbers
instead of the design, the manners and the thoughts; and it is
true that he also fails to express several of the other main
tendencies of neo-classicism. Unlike his more orthodox contemporaries, he does not give to the logical structure of a poem
the same sort of exaggerated importance that the theorists of
art for art's sake have given to the externals of style; he cares
nothing for the rules which the French had inherited from the
Italians; he has serious doubts about a fixed standard of taste.
The method of comparison which he urges was to have an
important bearing on the progress of criticism. This was a
conventional exercise from the time of Scaliger to that of
Rapin, but Hobbes's way of basing his judgments on general
qualities of style and content is an advance on theirs. The
method was adopted by Rymer in his preface to Rapin (1674);
and it was from Hobbes, also, that Rymer acquired, especially
later, something of the same external and mechanical outlook
on life, the same political philosophy and spirit of conformity,
the same clangour of style, the same magisterial attitude, and
that intellectual arrogance which made Dryden compare the
sage of Malmesbury with Lucretius.

D'Avenant's long preface to *Gondibert* (1650) is a dilution
of the aesthetic theory of Hobbes, but Tasso's discourses on
the epic and Chapelain's preface to Marino's *Adone*, doubtless,
served as his models. Nothing could differ more widely than
the prose styles of the two men; the style of Hobbes foreshadows
Rymer, while Cowley and D'Avenant prepare the way for
Dryden and Temple. Of the four men who associated them-

selves with the composition of *Gondibert* in Paris, Hobbes was
sixty-two years of age, D'Avenant and Waller forty-four and
Cowley thirty-two; obviously, the eldest of these was less
likely than the others to succumb to the influences of French
taste.   The heroic poem (like the pastoral, an artificial product
of the later renascence) was in the air in Paris at that time.
Chapelain had been at work on *La Pucelle* for nearly fifteen
years, Lemoyne on his *Saint Louis* somewhat less; and D'Avenant's preface bears a remarkable resemblance to those which
were soon to precede these and many other French epics in the
dozen years that followed.   The spirit with which they worked
explains that of D'Avenant.   It explains his conception of epic
practice as a merely mechanical consequence of epic theory;
it explains how experience of human nature, which Hobbes
considered essential to the writing of great poetry, tends to
limit itself to "conversation"; it explains the talk about "nature," which was to be more and more fundamental for English
criticism, and the attack on "conceits," one of the first of its
kind in our language.   The *concetti* of the Italians had lost
ground in France for some time; D'Avenant was a pioneer in a
campaign that, thenceforth, was sustained without a break in
England.   In both countries, there had been a metaphysical
school of poetry; but only in Italy did the principles of the
school receive a critical formulation; and neither England nor
France had any contemporary equivalent for such important
works as Tesauro's *Cannocchiale Aristotelico* or Pellegrini's
Fonti dell' Ingegno.   D'Avenant himself shows his natural
leanings toward the older school in his conception of poetry as
a presentation of truth "through unfrequented and new ways,
and from the most remote Shades, by representing Nature,
though not in an affected, yet in an unusual dress."   This is
Bacon's "strangeness added to beauty," and is far from the
principle of Pope's "what oft was thought but ne'er so well
expressed."   The defence of the stanza form, the confused
conception of "wit," the insistence on religion as well as nature
and reason as the basis of poetry, all suggest D'Avenant's place
in this transitional period of English criticism.

Cowley, the junior of D'Avenant by a dozen years, occupies
a similar position.   The influence of his poetry on contemporary
taste was powerful; but taste does not become criticism until

it has received reasoned expression. His keenest intellectual powers expressed themselves, however, in his verse; in his prose, he aimed rather at charm and clarity, after the fashion of the new standards of France: here, his critical opinions are casual and fragmentary, and, unlike Milton's, they explain the externals rather than the essence of his own poetic practice. His chief critical utterances are contained in the 1656 edition of his poems, both in the general preface and in the notes to *Davideis*. This preface contains a passage acknowledging the triumph of the commonwealth which he omitted from later editions, and for which his first biographer apologises at some length. The spirit of the commonwealth exhibits itself in the insistence that poets should avoid obscenity and profaneness, and in the impassioned defence of Biblical material for modern poetry. In the decade which opens with D'Avenant's preface to *Gondibert* (in which the Christian epic had been defended), heroic poems, sacred and profane, were coming forth from French presses with the speed of the modern novel; Mambrun had published his treatise *De Poemate Epico;* and Desmarets de Saint-Sorlin inaugurated his long campaign in favour of the *merveilleux chrétien*. Cowley does not accept their moralistic theory; for him, as for Waller, "to communicate delight to others is the main end of Poesie," and a soul "filled with bright and delightful Idæas" the fountain of poetic creation. In charming prose, he has paraphrased Ovid's complaint that poetry will not bear fruit in a troubled mind or body, and he has extended the principle to the influence of climate and of a "warlike, various, and a tragical age," which is "best to write of, but worst to write in": this is the logical outcome of Hobbes's psychology. His later work connects itself largely with the foundation and progress of the Royal Society, and, through it, with the Baconian tradition; and he played so important a part (if we may believe Evelyn) in the attempt of the Society to organise a literary academy for the refinement of English, that, at his death, the whole scheme was dropped.

The influence of Hobbes's political philosophy on Restoration thought and conduct is well known; his outlook on life, and, more especially, the psychology by which it is explained, were scarcely less influential in the domain of letters. Tempered and refined by the social and literary influences

proceeding from France, they became, in the hands of younger
men (not least of all in Cowley's *Odes*), instruments of power.
No member of this group accepts an absolute standard of taste;
they do not yield a complete subservience to classical authority
or to the pseudo-classical rules; the rationalistic temper has
not, as yet, flooded criticism to the exclusion of all imaginative
elements.   They logically connect the critical activity of the
first and the second Caroline periods; and Dryden begins his
work at the point where D'Avenant and Cowley leave off.

It will be noticed that most of these critics concern themselves with literary principles, and only on occasion (and with
doubtful success) enter the field of critical judgment.   But,
even here, some progress may be observed.   In the "censure"
of authors, the Elizabethans had seldom gone beyond the
repetition of a few traditional phrases.   Impassioned on the
subject of poetry in general, its antiquity, its dignity, its
beauty, they became timid and reserved so soon as they faced
the concrete problem which every critic must face in the
individual poet or the individual poem.   Their method, for
the most part, was the method of the "roll-call," a catalogue
of poets, in which one name follows another, each with its tag
of critical comment.   These comments are limited by a narrow
range of critical terminology, a few words of praise or blame,
some commonplace, some more highly coloured, and the judgments that they express are those of a well established literary
tradition or of the common opinion of their time.   The first
extended critique in English seems to be that which Sidney, in
his *Defence of Poesie*, devotes to the tragedy of *Gorboduc;*
here, for the first time, critical principles are applied systematically to a work of English literature.   Yet, Sidney has little
to say of *Gorboduc* except that it has ignored the dramatic
unities; he has few terms with which to express its positive
qualities, its special beauties or defects, and no method of
summing up the general effect in the form of literary portraiture
or appreciation.   In the case of other works, he adheres to the
method of the roll-call.   "I account the *Mirrour of Magistrates*
meetely furnished of beautiful parts; and in the Earle of Surries
Liricks many things tasting of a noble birth, and worthy of a
noble minde."

This is the staple of his judgment of authors.   Nor do his

contemporaries and his successors stray beyond the range of
the roll-call. Of the seventy-four chapters of Puttenham's
Arte of English Poesie, which attempts to cover the whole field
of poetical criticism, a single chapter is devoted to a "censure"
of the English poets; and here we are told that "for dittie and
amourous ode I finde Sir Walter Rawleyghs vayne most loftie,
insolent, and passionate; Maister Edward Dyar, for elegy most
sweet, solempne, and of high conceit; Gascon, for a good
meeter and for a plentifull vayne," etc. This is a typical
example of roll-call criticism, the most primitive form of literary
characterisation; literary history, unguided by any organic
principle, is as yet unable to express itself save by adding
name to name and epithet to epithet. Harington, it is true,
argues against the charge that "Ariosto wanteth art," and re-
peats some of the commonplaces of Italian criticism; but, for
the rest, he is limited to disjointed and intemperate eulogy
the same incense that Sidney burnt at the altar of Vergil.
It is tradition and not criticism which speaks in both. As
they approach the poets of their own tongue, even more as
they approach their own time, they lose their certainty of
utterance; they have no terminology to give precision to their
vague impressions; they have no form or method which gives
unity or logic to their disjointed thoughts. It is at this point
that Jonson enters the field. It is not merely that he makes
Quintilian and Scaliger native to English criticism, by translating or paraphrasing their ideas in a language both sane and
robust; but, under their guidance, he attempts the literary
"portrait." Yet, note how cautiously he works this new vein.
The brief note on Shakespeare in *Discoveries* is made up of
classical echoes; and the masterly portrait of Bacon as an orator
follows, almost word for word, the elder Seneca's description of
Severus Cassius. Such a portrait was as yet impossible in
English, and, not unwisely, Jonson leans heavily on Roman
crutches. But it is in the famous lines to Shakespeare that he
is at his best, for the uplift of verse has helped him to sureness
and swiftness of speech. This is the first adequate tribute to
a great English poet; this, and the portrait of Bacon, are the
first of their kind in English.

The first training in adequate characterisation of the poets
seems, then, to have been given (however tentatively) by Jon-

son, and it was certainly among his own disciples that literary
portraiture first began to flourish.   Verse rather than prose was
the surer vehicle, and the chief training ground seems to have
been the commendatory verses prefixed to plays and poems.
Those, for example, that appeared in *Jonsonus Virbius* (1638),
or in the 1647 folio of Beaumont and Fletcher, contain some
of the most acute criticism of the first half of the seventeenth
century, amid much that is the merest distortion of ingenious
eulogy.   But what is new (and effective for criticism) in them
is the complete realisation of a great literary background.
Shakespeare, Fletcher, Jonson, Spenser, had imposed themselves on criticism; and criticism grew rich (as it always does)
by accepting and passing these great poets as current coin of
the realm.   There was a more or less serious attempt to understand them, to appraise them, to express their significance;
they jostled one another in every discussion; and it was the
most natural thing in the world to compare and contrast them.
It is this comparative criticism which is employed to good use
in these commendatory verses.   A few lines from Cartwright's
tribute to Fletcher will illustrate the acuteness of some of this
criticism:

> Jonson hath writ things lasting and divine,
> Yet his love-scenes, Fletcher, compar'd to thine,
> Are cold and frosty, and express love so,
> As heat with ice, or warm fires mix'd with snow . . .
> Shakespeare to thee was dull, whose best jest lies
> I' the ladies' questions and the fools' replies;
> Old-fashion'd wit, which walk'd from town to town
> In turn'd hose, which our fathers call'd the clown,
> Whose wit our nice times would obsceneness call,
> And which made bawdry pass for comical.

Yet, elsewhere, for the most part, critics continued to follow
the roll-call; and even Jonson, here bookish rather than
critical, uses it in a brief note on the chief writers of English
prose (embedded in the borrowed material of *Discoveries*) and
in other places.   His curt *dicta* in conversation with Drummond seem almost typical of the method of contemporary
criticism; and, despite all the changes of time, this method
retained its vogue up to the middle of the century.   Peacham,

Bolton, Drayton, Alexander, Reynolds, Suckling, all employ it, though some of them have amplified its narrow scope or transformed it even in using it. Bolton, in *Hypercritica* (1618?), gives a catalogue of his favourite poets in crabbed prose; Drayton, in the *Epistle to Henry Reynolds, of Poets and Poesy* (1627), strings together a necklace of famous names on a silken thread of verse. Drayton's comments are brief, but often singularly appropriate and just; some of them have remained memorable utterances of poetic criticism, as in the lines on the "fine madness" of Marlowe and the kinship of his genius with the "brave translunary things" of the first poets. But, after all, they retain the marks of the roll-call; singly, as it were, they are mere *obiter dicta*, like Jonson's conversations with Drummond, utterances oracular and compact; together, they have no other framework than that furnished by the familiar epistle in verse. Neither singly nor jointly do they give any consistent criticism of poets or poetry.

In Reynolds's *Mythomystes*, there is a serious attempt to arrive at some consistency in the criticism of poetry by means of a systematic interpretation of its content. But the allegorical method, complicated here by an admixture of Neoplatonism and cabalism, though it may offer opportunities for subtle interpretation of mythological or mystical poetry, fails to explain most of the moderns; and in his brief introductory survey of modern poetry, Reynolds does not divest himself of the cataloguing spirit of his predecessors.

Though efforts to enrich the content and amplify the scope of the roll-call failed, an attempt to bind its *disjecta membra* into some kind of unity may be said to have succeeded temporarily. As the Italians had bound their *novelle* together by an artificial framework, so critics adopted a device from classical mythology to perform a similar function. This new framework makes of the term roll-call no longer a metaphor but a poetic fact. In Suckling's *Session of the Poets* (1637?), the poets of the time are represented as claimants for the laureateship at the court of Apollo; each argues his claims, and hears them discussed by his fellows; until, finally, Apollo decides in favour of a rich alderman whose money makes up for his lack of skill. The discussion is rather personal than literary, the talk of a coterie of artists

and wits, and is interesting as indicating the flavour of literary
discussion during the first Caroline period, much as the conversations of Jonson and Drummond shed light on Jacobean
taste.   Yet, even here, not much has been added since Jonson's day, for lady Would-be, in the third act of *Volpone*,
anticipates, by more than thirty years, the very note of Suckling's criticism, in such lines as these:

> Hee [Guarini] has so moderne and facile a veine,
> Fitting the time, and catching the court-eare;
> Your Petrarch is more passionate, yet hee
> In dayes of sonnetting trusted 'hem [*i. e.* plagiarists] with much;
> Dante is hard, and few can understand him;
> But for a desperate wit, there 's Aretine!
> Only his pictures are a little obscene.

The Italian poet Caporali, taking a hint from Lucian, had
first systematically used mythological allegory for the purpose of literary criticism or satire; and, in Spain, Cervantes
had followed his example in the *Voyage to Parnassus*.   But it
was the Italian proseman Boccalini who, in his *Ragguagli
di Parnaso*, gave European prestige to this form; his work
was translated and imitated in all the languages of Europe;
and, in England, besides Suckling, Sheppard's *Socratic Session, or the Arraignment and Conviction of Julius Scaliger*
(1651) and Wither's (?) *Great Assises holden in Parnassus*
(1645) illustrate the character of its influence.   This framework transfigures the dead bones of the old roll-call, and, in
Suckling and others, gives wit and fancy an opportunity to
enliven the casual utterances of criticism.

As we follow the course of the seventeenth century, we
note that the tags which follow the names of the roll-call
develop in amplitude.   They still remain more or less conventional, but they have been extended from a brief clause
or a succession of adjectives to sentences and paragraphs.
Thus, D'Avenant, in a page or two, traces the growth of epic
poetry from Homer to Spenser, devoting to each poet a paragraph of his own; and though, for example, that on Spenser
merely objects to the "obsolete language," "the unlucky
choice of the stanza" and the allegory, critical utterance
has become more facile and self-expressive, has, in fact,

developed a manner of its own. But it was not until the age of Dryden that the roll-call disappears entirely, and is displaced by the critical study of a poet and his work. The critique of *The Silent Woman*, the literary portraits of Jonson, Shakespeare and Fletcher, in *An Essay of Dramatic Poesy* (1668), mark a new stage in the growth of English criticism. The commendatory verses of many poets, the new aesthetic of Hobbes, the prose style of Cowley and D'Avenant, and many tentatives in the art of character-writing have made such things possible; but it is the *discours* and *examens* of Corneille (1660) that furnished Dryden with his true models. With Dryden, then, the intensive study of works of literature begins, and displaces the mere tags and epithets of the older criticism. But literary history was not born in England for another quarter of a century; and, in Rymer's *View of Tragedy* (1693), despite an exaggerated animus against Elizabethan tragedy, real learning was placed at the service of criticism, and the first connected account of the rise of modern literatures attempted.

The critical literature of the first half of the century is interesting, therefore, for its direction, rather than for any accomplishment of its own. It revolutionised aesthetic principles, but accomplished little or nothing in the field of concrete criticism. It did not adequately explain or appraise the works of the great poets and playwrights of the Elizabethan age. Englishmen were slowly beginning to realise the greatness of their literary past, but criticism did little to direct or encourage this new taste. The playwrights themselves scattered comments on their own art throughout their plays, and the modern scholar may arrange these isolated utterances at his pleasure into a unified code; yet, no critic of this age brought order and meaning out of the chaos of hints and hopes, and the romantic drama remained without its thoroughgoing exponents or analysts. New ideas in respect to poetry were, indeed, being developed. But, though Jonson elaborated a classical point of view and Hobbes a new aesthetic, these ideas were not consistently or intelligently applied to the literary heritage of the English people. Not until after the restoration was the clash of romantic and classical achievement truly apprehended, and its meaning analysed and explained.

CHAPTER XII

Hobbes and Contemporary Philosophy

THE philosophical writings which belong to the period following Bacon's death show but slight traces of Bacon's influence. His genius was recognised, and he was quoted, now and again, on special points; but his leading doctrines were generally ignored. No new logic appeared on the lines described in his *Novum Organum*. The writers of logical treatises followed the traditional scholastic method, or adopted the modifications of it introduced by Ramus. Even Milton's logic, which is founded on that of Ramus, pays no attention to the Baconian revolution. It is worthy of note that, in the middle of the sixteenth century, a beginning had been made at writing works on logic in English. In 1552, Thomas Wilson published *The Rule of Reason, conteining the arte of logique*. The innovation was not without danger at the time, if it be true that his publication on this subject in a vulgar tongue led to the author's imprisonment by the inquisition at Rome. His example was followed, in safer circumstances, by Ralph Lever, who, in his *Arte of Reason rightly termed Witcraft, teaching a perfect way to argue and dispute* (1573), not only wrote in English, but used words of English derivation in place of the traditional terminology—*foreset* and *backset* for "subject" and "predicate," *inholder* and *inbeer* for "substance" and "accident," *saywhat* for "definition" and so on. This attempt was never taken seriously; and a considerable time had to elapse before English became the usual language for books on logic. In the seventeenth century, as well as in the sixteenth, the demands of the universities made the use of Latin almost essential for the purpose. The work of Richard Crakanthorp,

Logicae libri quinque de Praedicabilibus (1622), was one of the best known of these text-books. The question of method which had ruled the thought of Bacon, was less prominent in the English philosophy of the following period and did not lead to any new work of importance.

Religion is as powerful a stimulus to philosophical thought as science is, and it is apt to lead more directly to the study of ultimate problems. It was the chief interest in the speculative writings of Herbert of Cherbury, and the same interest is even more directly obvious in other writings. In 1599, Sir John Davies had published his philosophical poem *Nosce Teipsum*, in which a view of the nature of the soul and arguments for its immortality are "expounded in two elegies." Utilising Platonic, as well as Aristotelian, ideas, the author worked out a spiritual philosophy in which the soul is regarded as akin to the universal order,

> For Nature in man's heart her lawes doth pen;
> Prescribing *truth* to *wit*, and *good* to *will*,
> Which doe *accuse*, or else *excuse* all men,
> For every thought or practise, good or ill:

and, therefore, the soul can find no true satisfaction in earthly things:

> *Wit*, seeking *Truth*, from cause to cause ascends,
> And never rests till it the *first* attaine:
> *Will*, seeking *Good*, finds many middle ends,
> But never stayes, till it the *last* doe gaine.

The same influence led to work of a philosophical kind among theologians, usually conveyed in a scholastic manner. In his *Atheomastix* (1622), Martin Fotherby, bishop of Salisbury, relied chiefly on St. Thomas Aquinas in his demonstration of the being of God, and maintained that there is a "natural prenotion" that there is a God. The work of George Hakewill, archdeacon of Surrey, entitled *An Apologie or Declaration of the Power and Providence of God* (1627), touches on philosophy without being genuinely philosophical in character. Bacon is referred to for his "noble and worthy endeavour . . . so to mix and temper practice and speculation together, that they may march hand in hand"; but his new method is not spoken of, though both Ramus and Lully are referred to in the section on advances in logic. Nor does the discussion on truth contain any observations beyond the ordinary commonplaces: it does not show any knowledge of Herbert of Cherbury's enquiry, and can hardly have suggested ideas to lord Brooke. The real importance of the book lies in the fact that the author's eyes are turned to the future, not to the past. It is an elaborate argument against the view that the history of the world is a record of deterioration from an earlier golden age. As described on the title-page, it is "an examination and censure of the common error touching nature's perpetual and universal decay."

Much more important is the work of lord Brooke, in whom the puritan temper was combined with the mystic. Robert Greville, cousin and adopted son of Fulke Greville, first lord Brooke, was born in 1608, and entered parliament in 1628. In the civil war, he acted as a general of the parliamentary army, gained the victory of Kineton in 1642, took Stratford-on-Avon in February, 1643, and was killed at the attack on Lichfield a few weeks later. He was an ardent puritan, and, in 1641, wrote *A Discourse opening the nature of that Episcopacie which is exercised in England*, aimed at the political power of the bishops. In the same year was published his philosophical work *The Nature of Truth*. In this work, he refuses to distinguish between philosophy and theology. "What is true philosophy but divinity?" he asks, "and if it be not true, it is not philosophy." He appeals to reason and reflection alone for an answer to his question; but his method differs from that of Herbert of Cherbury in dealing with the same subject: it is less logical and thorough, and more mystical. He had "dived deep," his editor says, "into prophetic mysteries." He was also well read in speculative, especially Neoplatonic, writings. The revival of Platonism had already affected English literature; its influence may be seen in the works of Sir Thomas More, and in Davies's *Nosce Teipsum*, and it had coloured the Aristotelianism of Everard Digby; but Brooke was the first Englishman to present in an original treatise the fundamental ideas which, later in the same century, bore riper fruit in the works of the Cambridge Platonists. The two doctrines of the unity of reality and the emanation of all things from God rule his thought; and he thinks that difficulties about truth are solved when we see that the understanding, the soul, light and truth are all one: "all being is but one emanation from above, diversified only in our apprehension." Faith and reason differ in degree only, not in nature; knowledge and affection are but several shapes under which truth is present to our view: "what good we know, we are; our act of understanding being an act of union." The author goes on to explain that all the diversities of things —even space and time themselves—are without reality and are only appearances to our apprehension. The whole physical world, accordingly, is merely phenomenal; in it, there is no true being, nor are there any true causes, though it is allowable, "when you see some things precede others," to "call the one a cause the other an effect." In these expressions have been found anticipations of the idealism of Berkeley and of Hume's theory of causation. In presenting his doctrine, Brooke wrote like a seer, rather than as a logician who has tested its consistency and adequacy. But he had the seer's vision, and the vision gave him courage, "for if we knew this truth," he says,

that all things are one, how cheerfully, with what modest courage, should we undertake any action, reincounter any occurrence, knowing that that distinction of misery and happiness, which now so perplexeth us, has no being except in the brain.

Nathanael Culverwel, fellow of Emmanuel college, Cambridge (B.A. 1636), was thrown among the group of men who afterwards became famous as the Cambridge Platonists. Whichcote and Cudworth (both, originally, of Emmanuel), and Henry More of Christ's college, were his contemporaries. But he can hardly be counted as belonging to the group. He was not a Platonist. Unlike More, he would not come to terms with the doctrine of the pre-existence of souls, and he even rejected the theory of ideas. The mysticism of lord Brooke was, also, alien to him; he had no sympathy with the union of contradictories; and he quotes with approval the criticism of Brooke published, in 1643, by John Wallis, under the title *Truth tried*. Nor can Culverwel be described as a "latitude man." He remained constant to Calvinism, and, on the whole, to the puritan spirit. But he was far removed from the extremists of his party, of whom he writes that "if you do but offer to make a syllogism, they will straightway cry it down for carnal learning." The purpose of his book *Of the Light of Nature* (published, posthumously, in 1652) is to show the true relation between faith and reason: "to give faith her full scope and latitude, and to give reason also her just bounds and limits. This," he says, "is the first-born, but the other has the blessing." Two propositions sum up his doctrine:

(1) That all the moral law is founded in natural and common light, in the light of reason; and (2) That there is nothing in the mysteries of the gospel contrary to the light of reason.

The law of nature belongs to reason, not to sense, and is essential to a rational creature. The voice of reason promulgates the law; but its obligation and binding virtue rest

partly in the excellency and equity of the commands themselves; but they principally depend upon the sovereignty and authority of God himself, thus contriving and commanding the welfare of His creature, and advancing a rational nature to the just perfection of its being.

As Aquinas holds, the law of nature is a copy of the eternal law, and "this eternal law is not really distinguished from God himself." This view of the laws of nature is not altogether new, even in English. Hooker had already given classical expression to a doctrine essentially the same and drawn from similar sources. But no one had a clearer view than Culverwel of the essence of the doctrine. He never inclines to the theory that all knowledge arises out of sensation, and yet he never lapses into mysticism. His theory is a pure and elevated rationalism, though he holds that our reason needs illumination from the fuller light of faith. His style is worthy of the subject, if, perhaps, too full of learned references and, occasionally, oratorical; and it is hardly too much to say of the book that "it is almost a poem in its grandeur and harmony of conception, and the lyrical enthusiasm with which it chants the praise of reason."[1]

The doctrine of a law of nature was commonly relied upon by the more philosophical writers who dealt with the details of moral duty. Among the moralists of this class may be reckoned William Perkins, author of *Armilla aurea* (1590) (Englished as *A Golden Chaine*, 1600), and of *The Whole Treatise of the Cases of Conscience* (1608); William Ames, a Calvinistic theologian, who wrote *De Conscientia et ejus jure vel casibus* (1630); and Robert Sanderson, bishop of Lincoln, who wrote not only a Latin compendium of logic (Oxford, 1615), but many works besides, including *De juramenti promissorii obligatione* (1647), and *De obligatione conscientiae*. The former of these is said to have been translated into English by king Charles during his imprisonment. Joseph Hall, bishop of Norwich and satirist, was the author of *Characters of Vertues and Vices* (1608) and of *Decisions of diverse Practicall Cases of Conscience* (1649). But the greatest work of the kind in English, and, perhaps, the greatest treatise on casuistry ever written by a protestant theologian, is the *Ductor Dubitantium* of Jeremy Taylor (1660). Publishing shortly after the restoration, and dedicating his book to the king, the author rejoices that "now our duty stands on the sunny side." He professes to open out a way untrodden before. He will not collect individual cases of conscience, for they are infinite; but he seeks to provide a "general instrument of moral theology, by the rules and measures of which the guides of souls may determine the particulars that shall be brought before them." The work opens with a description of conscience as a reflection of the divine law— "the brightness and splendour of the eternal light, a spotless mirror of the divine majesty, and the image of the goodness of God." It proceeds to describe the characteristics of individual consciences when brought into contact with the problems of conduct; it passes on to an enquiry into the nature of law in general and of particular laws, divine and human; and it closes with a discussion of the nature and causes of good and evil. The whole forms a comprehensive treatise on

[1] Tulloch, J., *Rational Theology and Christian Philosophy in England in the Seventeenth Century*, vol. II., p. 411.

Christian ethics, based, undoubtedly, on traditional scholastic doctrines, but holding firmly to the inwardness of morality, and illustrated by an extraordinary wealth of concrete examples.

It is only to a small extent that the writings of John Selden, historian, jurist and political writer, fall within the scope of this chapter. His treatise *De Dis Syris* (1617), his *Historie of Tithes* (1618) and most of his other works lie beyond its range. But, in his treatment of the law of nature, he enters upon topics which are common to him and the philosophers. In his *Mare Clausum* (1635), he maintains two propositions against Grotius: first, that, by the law of nature, the sea is not common to all men, but is capable of private sovereignty or proprietorship, equally with the earth; and, secondly, that the king of Great Britain is sovereign of the surrounding seas, as an individual and perpetual appanage of the British empire. As was usual in his day and for long afterwards, he identified the law of nature with international law. This identification is seen in the title of his work *De jure naturali et gentium juxta disciplinam Hebraeorum* (1640). But here he has in view not the law or custom which regulates the relation of state to state, but the natural or moral law which is common to all men independently of positive enactment divine or human. With the wealth of learning in which he was without a rival in his day, he traces the opinions of the Jews on the subject of moral obligation, and, at the same time, brings out his own view of the law of nature. He holds, with most jurists, that law requires an authority to prescribe it, and that, therefore, reason cannot be the source of law. At the same time, he allows that God has imprinted certain moral rules in the minds of all men.

Speculation on these and kindred topics was soon to enter upon a new stage under the impulse derived from the original mind of Hobbes. Before his work is dealt with, two other writers may be mentioned. Sir Kenelm Digby, remarkable in many departments of life and letters, was, also, a philosopher, and wrote a treatise on the immortality of the soul (1644). In 1655, Thomas Stanley, well known as a classical scholar, published the first *History of Philosophy* written in the English language.

Thomas Hobbes was born at Westport, adjoining Malmesbury in Wiltshire, on 5 April, 1588. His father, the vicar of the parish, says Aubrey,

> was one of the ignorant Sir Johns of Queen Elizabeth's time, could only read the prayers of the church and the homilies, and valued not learning, as not knowing the sweetness of it.

His mother came of yeoman stock. Of her, we know nothing beyond the story of her dread of the Spanish Armada; the air was full of rumours of its approach; and her terror led to the premature birth of her second son. As he put it long afterwards, "she brought forth twins—myself and fear." The expression is significant, used, as it was, when he could look back on more than eighty years of life, begun amidst the terror of invasion and afterwards harassed by civil war and unstable government. To seek peace and follow it became, in his view, the fundamental law of nature; and the philosopher was himself (to use his own phrase) a "man of feminine courage." "The first of all that fled" at the threat of civil war, he was afterwards quick to return when the French government seemed likely to offer less protection than the commonwealth. But the importance of these events for his life and doctrine has sometimes been exaggerated. He had passed his fiftieth year before the threat of danger touched him, and, by that time, he had already completed a work which contains, in outline, the essential features of his philosophy. Throughout the long years of preparation which fitted him to take his place among the greatest of modern philosophers, Hobbes led a sheltered and leisured life, and it is not to be supposed that dreams of the Armada disturbed his quiet. His education was provided for by an uncle, a solid tradesman and alderman of Malmesbury. He was already a good Latin and Greek scholar when, not yet fifteen, he was sent to Magdalen hall, Oxford. The studies of the university were then at a low ebb; and no subsequent reforms affected his low opinion of them. Yet he seems to have learned the logic and physics of Aristotle, as they were then taught, though he preferred to "lie gaping on maps" at the stationers' shops. On leaving Oxford, in 1608, he became companion to the eldest son of lord Cavendish of Hardwick (afterwards created earl of Devonshire), and his connection with the Cavendish family lasted (although not without interruptions) till his death. Through this connection, he gained security and leisure for his own work, opportunities of travel and ready admission to the society of statesmen and scholars.

Three times in his life, Hobbes travelled on the continent with a pupil. His first journey was begun in 1610, and in it he visited France, Germany and Italy, learning the French and Italian languages, and gaining experience, but not yet conscious of his life's work. On his return (the date is uncertain), he settled down with his young lord at Hardwick and in London. His secretarial duties were light, and he set himself to become a scholar; with the society and books at his command, he did not "need the university" (he said); he read the historians and poets both Greek and Latin, and taught himself a clear and accurate Latin style. To these studies, his first published work bears witness—an English translation of Thucydides, sent to press in 1628, but completed some years earlier. To this period, also, belongs his acquaintance with Bacon, Herbert of Cherbury, Ben Jonson and other leading men of the time. Of his association with Bacon (probably sometime in the years between 1621 and 1626), we know little beyond what Aubrey tells us—that he translated some of Bacon's essays into Latin, that, on occasion, he would attend with ink and paper and set down Bacon's thoughts when he contemplated and dictated "in his delicious walks at Gorhambury" and that "his lordship would often say that he better liked Mr. Hobbes's taking his thoughts, than any of the others, because he understood what he wrote." There is no evidence, however, that their discourse turned on strictly philosophical questions; nor does it appear that philosophical interest had, as yet, become dominant in Hobbes's mind; certainly, he was never a pupil of Bacon; and it is an error to attempt, as has sometimes been done, to affiliate his philosophy to the Baconian. They agreed in their opposition to medievalism, and both attempted to elaborate a comprehensive scheme; the vague term "empirical" may, also, be applied to both; but Hobbes set small store by experiment,[1] and his system differed fundamentally

---

[1] *English Works*, ed. Molesworth, vol. IV., pp. 436–7; vol. VII., p. 117.

from Bacon's in method, temper and scope. One important point only was common to both—their acceptance of the mechanical theory; and, for this theory, there is ample evidence, external as well as internal, that Hobbes was directly indebted not to Bacon but to Galileo.

Hobbes's master and friend died in 1628, two years after the death of the first earl; his son and successor was a boy of eleven; his widow did not need the services of a secretary; and, for a time, there was no place in the household for Hobbes. In 1629, he left for the continent again with a new pupil, returning from this second journey in 1631 to take charge of the young earl's education. Little is known of his travels, but this period of his life is remarkable for two things—his introduction to the study of geometry, and his first effort towards a philosophy. As regards the former, there is no reason for doubting Aubrey's story, which throws light both on his early education and on the controversies of his later years.

He was forty years old before he looked on geometry, which happened accidentally; being in a gentleman's library in . . . Euclid's Elements lay open, and it was the 47 prop. lib. 1. So he reads the proposition, "By G—," says he, "this is impossible!" So he reads the demonstration of it, which referred him back to another, which also he read, et sic deinceps, that at last he was demonstratively convinced of that truth. This made him in love with geometry.

About this time also, or soon afterwards, his philosophical views began to take shape. Among his manuscripts, there is a *Short Tract on First Principles*,[1] which has been conjectured to belong to the year 1630 and cannot have been much later. It shows the author so much impressed by his reading of Euclid as to adopt the geometrical form (soon afterwards used by Descartes) for the expression of his argument. It shows, further, that he had already fixed on the conception of motion as fundamental for the explanation of things, but, also, that he had not yet relinquished the scholastic doctrine of species in explaining action and perception.

[1] Printed as an appendix to Hobbes's *Elements of Law*, edited by Tönnies, F., 1889.

When Hobbes made his third visit to the continent, which lasted from 1634 to 1637 and on which he was accompanied by the young earl of Devonshire, he is found taking his place among philosophers. At Paris, he was an intimate of Mersenne, who was the centre of a scientific circle that included Descartes and Gassendi; and, at Florence, he held discourse with Galileo. There is an earlier record, in January, 1633, of Hobbes searching the shops in London for a copy of Galileo's *Dialogue*, and searching vainly, as the small supply had been sold out. And now he seems to have arrived at the view that not only is motion the fundamental conception for explaining the physical world, but that man and society also can be explained on the same mechanical theory. After his return to England, he wrote, with a view to publication, a sketch of his new theory, to which he gave the title *Elements of Law natural and politic*. The physical doctrine of which he had taken firm hold lies at the basis of this work, but it deals in detail only with the mind of man and the principles of social order. The introduction to his *Thucydides* had already shown his interest in the latter subject, and the side of politics to which he leaned himself, by the emphasis he laid on the historian's preference for the monarchical form of government. In his dedication of *The Elements* (dated 9 May, 1640), Hobbes says that his object is to reduce the doctrine of justice and policy in general to "the rules and infallibility of reason" after the fashion of mathematics. This volume is the "little treatise in English" to which he afterwards referred as written in the days of the Short Parliament.

Of this treatise, though not printed, many gentlemen had copies, which occasioned much talk of the author: and had not his majesty dissolved the parliament, it had brought him into danger of his life.

The treatise was never published by Hobbes, nor did it appear as a connected whole until 1889, although, in 1650, probably with his consent, its first thirteen chapters were issued with the title *Human Nature*, and the remainder of the volume as a separate work *De Corpore Politico*. In November, 1640, when the Long parliament began to show its activity, Hobbes fled to France, where he remained for the next eleven years.

These years were fruitful in many ways. From the beginning, he was in constant intercourse with Mersenne and the brilliant group of men of science who frequented his monastery. Soon, too, he was followed to Paris by other English emigrants of the royalist party, among whom was the marquis of Newcastle, a member of the Cavendish family, to whom the unpublished *Elements of Law* had been dedicated. By his influence, Hobbes was appointed to teach mathematics to Charles, prince of Wales, who arrived in Paris in 1646. His position in the exiled court was ultimately rendered impossible by the suspicions of its clerical members; but Charles's friendship was of importance to him in later years, after the restoration of the monarchy. It was Newcastle's desire to hear both sides of a question that led, during his residence in France, to discussion, and, afterwards, to a somewhat acrimonious controversy on the problem of free-will, with John Bramhall, bishop of Derry. Of greater interest is another literary correspondence which followed close upon his arrival in Paris. Mersenne was then collecting the opinions of scholars on the forthcoming treatise by Descartes, *Meditationes de prima philosophia*, and, in January, 1641, Hobbes's objections were ready and forwarded to his great contemporary in Holland. These, with the replies of Descartes, afterwards appeared as the third set of *Objectiones* when the treatise was published. Further communications followed on the *Dioptrique* which had appeared along with the famous *Discours de la méthode* in 1637. Descartes did not discover the identity of his two critics; but he did not approve of either; and, indeed, as regards the subject-matter of *Meditationes*, the thinking of the two philosophers moved in such different worlds that mutual understanding was almost impossible. To Descartes, mind was the primal certainty and independent of material reality. Hobbes, on the other hand, had already fixed on motion as the fundamental fact, and his originality consisted in his attempt to use it for the explanation not of nature only but, also, of mind and society. Two or three years after his correspondence with Descartes, Hobbes contributed a summary of his views on physics and a *Tractatus Opticus* to works published by Mersenne.

At latest, by the beginning of his residence in Paris in 1640, Hobbes had matured the plan for his own philosophical work. It was to consist of three treatises, dealing, respectively, with matter or body, with human nature and with society. It was his intention, he says, to have dealt with these subjects in this order, but his country "was boiling hot with questions concerning the rights of dominion, and the obedience due from subjects, the true forerunners of an approaching war," and this cause, as he said, "ripened and plucked from me this third part" of the system—the book *De Cive*, published at Paris in 1642. Hobbes's first political publication was thus directly occasioned by the troubles of the time. Only a small edition seems to have been printed. Gassendi spoke of the difficulty of procuring a copy, and expressed his satisfaction when the author allowed a new and enlarged edition to be printed at the Elzevir press in Amsterdam in 1647. In this edition, the description of the book as the third part of a philosophical system was removed, at the publisher's request, from the title-page, and a new preface was added in which the author explained his plan. The book was a tract for the times as well as a philosophical treatise; but it was not till four years later, when stable government seemed to have been re-established by the commonwealth, that he had it published in London, in an English version from his own hand, as *Philosophical Rudiments concerning Government and Society*. The same year, 1651, saw the publication, also in London, of his greatest work, *Leviathan*, and his own return to England, which now promised a safer shelter to the philosopher than France, where he feared the clergy and was no longer in favour with the remnant of the exiled English court. In the case of *De Cive* and, still more, in that of *Leviathan*, the political situation led to greater fulness of detail and, also, to a more fervid manner of utterance than had been shown in his earliest treatise. In particular, the danger arising from the claim to independence or to direction on the part of the ecclesiastical power gave occasion for a much more comprehensive treatment of the subject of religion. As early as 1641, he had expressed the opinion that the dispute "between the spiritual and civil power has of late more than any other thing in the world, been the cause of civil wars in all places of Christendom," and had urged that "all church government depend on the state and authority of the kingdom, without which there can be no unity in the church." This was not palatable doctrine to any of the sects, and there was much more to cause them alarm in the theological discussions contained in his *Leviathan*. But, after the restoration, in a dedication to the king, he was able to claim that all had been "propounded with submission to those that have the power ecclesiastical," holding that he had not given any ground of offence "unless it be for making the authority of the church wholly upon the regal power; which I hope your majesty will think is neither atheism nor heresy."

The last twenty-eight years of Hobbes's long life were spent in England; and there he soon returned to the house of his old pupil the earl of Devonshire, who had preceded him in submitting to the commonwealth, and, like him, welcomed the king on his return. For a year or two after his home-coming, Hobbes resided in London, busied with the completion of his philosophical system, the long-delayed first part of which, *De Corpore*, appeared in 1655, and the second part, *De Homine*, in 1656. The latter work contains little or nothing of importance that Hobbes had not said already; but the former deals with the logical, mathematical and physical principles which were to serve as foundation for the imposing structure he had built. A new world had been revealed to him, many years ago, when, at the age of forty, he had first chanced upon Euclid's *Elements*. He had designed that his own philosophy should imitate the certainty of mathematics. In the dedication to his first treatise, he had called mathematics the one branch of learning that is "free from controversies and dispute." Yet, strangely enough, when we remember how provocative of controversy were all his leading views, it was disputes about the most certain of all subjects that filled and harassed the last five and twenty years of his life.

The author of *Leviathan* could hardly have expected to escape controversy, and he did not do anything to avoid it. The views of human nature set forth in the book became, for generations, the favourite battle-ground for contending philosophies; its political theory was not fitted to please either party; and on its religious doctrine, the clergy would have something to say when they came to their own again. His dispute with Bramhall on the question of free-will began in his Paris days and has been already recorded. But it was not allowed to be forgotten. In 1654, the tract *Of Liberty and Necessity*, which he had written eight years before in reply to the bishop's arguments, was published by some person unnamed, into whose hands it had fallen. Not suspecting Hobbes's innocence in the matter of the publication, Bramhall replied with some heat on the personal question and much fulness on the matter in hand in the following year; and this led to Hobbes's elaborate defence in *The Questions concerning Liberty, Necessity, and Chance*, published in 1656. By this time, however, the storm of controversy had already broken out in another quarter. Hobbes remembered Oxford as it was in his student days, and made little allowance for altered manners and the reform of studies. In the fourth part of *Leviathan*, which is devoted to "the kingdom of darkness," he had taken occasion to pronounce judgment on the universities; they are a bulwark of papal power; their philosophy is but "Aristotelity"; for them, "till very late times," geometry was but an "art diabolical." But Oxford had undergone a change since the days when Hobbes could afford to despise its learning. In particular, the Savilian professorships, founded in the interval, were held by two men of eminence, Seth Ward and John Wallis—the latter, a mathematician of the first rank. They were acknowledged masters of a science in which Hobbes seems to have been only a brilliant and capricious amateur—the greatest of circle-squarers. The dispute began, mildly enough, in a vindication of the university by Ward against another critic, Hobbes being dealt with in an appendix. This was in 1654; but, next year, Hobbes's own mathematical discoveries were published with much parade in *De Corpore*. The opportunity was then seized by Wallis, who, in a few months, was ready with a reply in which the pretended demonstrations were torn to shreds. From this time onwards, the war of pamphlets waged unremittingly. Hobbes maintained his opinions with a tenacity which would have been wholly admirable if they had been better grounded; and he was bold enough to carry the war into the enemy's camp, though with unfortunate results, and to engage other adversaries, such as Robert Boyle, with no better success. It is unnecessary to follow the controversy in detail,[1] but, incidentally, it produced one document of great personal interest—a defence of his own reputation in the form of a letter to Wallis, written in 1662.

In addition to these and connected controversies, more serious trouble threatened the philosopher's later years. After the restoration he was well received by the king, who took pleasure in his conversation. But he had an enemy in the clergy; his opinions were notorious; it was easy to connect them with the moral licence shown in high places; and, after the great Plague and the great Fire, at a time when recent disaster made men's consciences sensitive and their desires welcome a scape-goat, Hobbes was in no little danger. A bill aimed at blasphemous literature actually passed the Commons in January, 1667, and *Leviathan* was one of two books mentioned in it. The bill never got through both houses; but Hobbes was seriously frightened; he is said to have become more regular at church and communion; he studied the law of heresy, also, and wrote a short treatise on the subject, proving that there was no court by which he could be judged. But he was not permitted to excite the public conscience by further publications on matters of religion. A Latin translation of *Leviathan* (containing a new appendix bringing its theology into line with the Nicene creed) was issued at Amsterdam in 1668. Other works, however, dating from the same year, were kept back—the tract on *Heresy*, the answer to Bramhall's attack on *Leviathan* and *Behemoth: the History of the Causes of the Civil Wars of England*. About the same time was written his *Dialogue between a Philosopher and a Student of the Common Laws of England*. His *Historia Ecclesiastica*, in elegiac verse, dates

---

[1] A lucid and admirable sketch of its successive stages is given in Croom Robertson's monograph on Hobbes (1886). It should be added, however, that Tönnies (*Hobbes*, 1896, p. 65) is of opinion that Robertson has dealt too hardly with Hobbes in his account of the controversy.

from about his eightieth year. When he was eighty-four, he wrote his autobiography in Latin verse. Neither age nor controversy seemed to tire him. Although controversy had the last word—he published *Decameron Physiologicum* at the age of ninety—he turned in old age for solace and employment to the literature which had been his first inspiration. In 1673, he published a translation in rimed quatrains of four books of the *Odyssey;* and he had completed both *Iliad* and *Odyssey* when, in 1675, he left London for the last time. Thereafter, he lived with the Cavendish family at one of their seats in Derbyshire. He died at Hardwick on 4 December, 1679.

Hobbes is one of a succession of English writers who are as remarkable for their style as for the originality of their thought. Bacon, Hobbes, Berkeley and Hume—to mention only the greatest names—must be counted amongst the masters of language, wherever language is looked upon as conveying a meaning. And, in each case, the style has an individual quality which suits the thought and the time. Bacon's displays a wealth of imagery and allusion significant of the new worlds which man's mind was to enter into and to conquer; it has the glamour not of enchantment but of discovery; greater precision and restraint of imagery would not have befitted the pioneer of so vast an adventure. The musical eloquence of Berkeley is the utterance of a soul rapt in one clear vision and able to read the language of God in the form and events of the world. Hume writes with the unimpassioned lucidity of the observer, intent on technical perfection in the way of conveying his meaning, but with no illusions as to its importance. Hobbes differs from all three, and, in his own way, is supreme. There is no excess of imagery or allusion, though both are at hand when wanted. There is epigram; but epigram is not multiplied for its own sake. There is satire; but it is always kept in restraint. His work is never embellished with ornament: every ornament is structural and belongs to the building. There is never a word too many, and the right word is always chosen. His materials are of the simplest; and they have been formed into a living whole, guided by a great thought and fired by the passion for a great cause.

Aubrey tells us something of his method of work:

> He had read much, if one considers his long life, but his contemplation was much more than his reading. He was wont to say, that if he had read as much as other men, he should have continued still as ignorant as other men. The manner of writing [*Leviathan*] was thus. He walked much and contemplated, and he had in the head of his cane a pen and ink-horn, carried always a note-book in his pocket, and as soon as a thought darted, he presently entered it into his book, or otherwise might have lost it.

This careful forethought for idea and phrase was always controlled by the dominant purpose, which was to convince by demonstration. How the method worked may be seen from a characteristic passage. Speaking of undesigned trains of thought, he says

> And yet in this wild ranging of the mind, a man may oft-times perceive the way of it, and the dependance of one thought upon another. For in a discourse of our present civil war, what could seem more impertinent, than to ask (as one did) what was the value of a Roman penny? Yet the coherence to me was manifest enough. For the thought of the war introduced the thought of the delivering up the king to his enemies; the thought of that brought in the thought of the delivering up of Christ; and that again the thought of the 30 pence, which was the price of that treason; and thence easily followed that malicious question; and all this in a moment of time; for thought is quick.

Here, the illustration strikes home; the sarcasm hits the party he hated most; and the last four words clinch the whole and bring back the discourse to the matter in hand. Attention is arrested, not diverted, so that the single paragraph in which these sentences occur may be taken as having started the line of thought which issued in the theory of association, for a long time dominant in English psychology.

To understand the underlying ideas of Hobbes's philosophy, portions of his Latin work *De Corpore* must be kept in view; but his lasting fame as a writer rests upon three books: *Elements of Law, Philosophicall Rudiments concerning Government and Society* (the English version of *De Cive*) and *Leviathan*. The first of these books is a sketch, in clear outline and drawn with unfaltering hand, of the bold and original theory which he after-

wards worked out and applied, but never altered in substance.
It contains less illustration and less epigram than the later
works, but it yields to neither of them in lucidity or in confidence. The circumstances which led to its issue in two
fragments, arbitrarily sundered from one another, have hindered
the general recognition of its greatness. Nor did it appear at
all till *De Cive* was well known and *Leviathan* ready for press.
The latter works are less severe in style: they have a glow from
the "bright live coal" which (we are told) seemed to shine from
Hobbes's eye when he spoke. *De Cive* is restricted to the political theory; but his whole view of human life and the social
order is comprehended in *Leviathan*.

The title-page of this book depicts its purpose. The upper
half of the page has, in the foreground, a walled town with tall
church spires; behind, the country rises towards a hill out of
which emerges the figure of a man from the waist upwards; a
crown is on his head; his right hand wields a sword, his left
grasps a crosier; his coat of mail consists of a multitude of
human figures, with their faces turned to him, as in supplication.
On the lower half of the page, on either side the title, are represented a castle and a church, a coronet and a mitre, a cannon
and lightning, implements of war and weapons of argument,
a battle-field and a dispute in the schools. Over all runs the
legend *Non est potestas super terram quae comparetur ei*. This
is the design "of that great Leviathan, or rather (to speak more
reverently) of that mortal God," whose generation and power
Hobbes sets out to describe.

The figure of the leviathan dominates the whole book, and
Hobbes argues over and over again that there is no alternative
between absolute rule and social anarchy. Its lurid picture of
the state of nature, contrasted with the peace and order instituted by sovereign power, undoubtedly reflects the troubles
and emotions of the time; but it is no mere seventeenth century
version of *In darkest England and the way out*. Far less is
Hobbes's whole philosophy to be put down to the fear of civil
tumult and the desire to think out a theory of government
adequate to its restraint. *Leviathan* is a work of great and
enduring importance just because it is not a mere political
pamphlet. It owes life and colour to the time at which it was
written; but another force also contributed to its making—

a conception of larger scope, which gives it the unity of a philosophical masterpiece.

This underlying conception and all the author's most striking ideas are to be found in the treatise completed in 1640—when political troubles were obviously at hand, but, as yet, no personal danger threatened. In logic and lucidity, this earlier treatise is not surpassed by the later work, though it fails to give the same constant impression of reality. It is a text-book such as philosophers have sometimes written for statesmen, to instruct them in the principles of their craft; and it did not entirely escape the usual fate of such efforts. Before Hobbes set about writing it, the fundamental idea of a philosophy had taken root in his mind; and this idea he owed to the new mechanical theory, and, in particular, to Galileo's teaching. Motion, he came to think, was the one reality; all other things are but "fancies, the offspring of our brains." He did not now, or, indeed, afterwards, work out a mechanical theory of the physical universe, as Descartes, for instance, was doing. But he had a bolder—if an impossible—project. Descartes restricted mechanism to the extended world, maintained the independence of mental existence and held the latter to be of all things most certain. Hobbes did not thus limit the applications of his new idea. He thought he could pass from external motions to "the internal motions of men," and, thence, to sovereignty and justice. This is his own account, and it agrees with what we know otherwise. Neither the mechanical theory, nor the psychology, is an afterthought introduced to bolster up a foregone political conclusion. They have their roots too deep in Hobbes's mind. It is true, the desired transitions could not logically be made, and Hobbes found out the difficulty later. But, when civil disturbance forced his hand and led to the elaboration of his ethical and political doctrine, this doctrine was found to be in harmony with the idea from which his view of the universe started. The external and mechanical character of the political theory is an indication of its unreality, but it bears witness, also, to the unity of conception that dominates the whole philosophy.

All things, according to Hobbes, "have but one universal cause, which is motion." But, for him, as for other writers of his day, "motion" is not a merely abstract conception; it includes movement of masses or of particles. From geometry, which treats of abstract motion, he thus passes, without a break, to physics, and, thence, to moral philosophy; for the "motions of the mind" have physical causes. And, by this synthetical method, proceeding from principles, we "come to the causes and necessity of constituting commonwealths." This method he always kept in view, and it gives unity to his theory. But he never carried out the impossible task of applying it in detail. He admits that there is another and an easier way:

> For the causes of the motions of the mind are known, not only by ratiocination, but also by the experience of every man that takes the pains to observe those motions within himself.

If he "will but examine his own mind," he will find

> that the appetites of men and the passions of their minds are such that, unless they be restrained by some power, they will always be making war upon one another.

By adopting this method, Hobbes thinks he can appeal to each man's experience to confirm the truth of his doctrine.

Leviathan is divided into four parts, which treat, respectively, of Man, of a Commonwealth, of a Christian Commonwealth and of the Kingdom of Darkness. Man comes first, for he is both the matter and the artificer of the Leviathan; and, at the outset, he is considered alone, as an individual thing played upon by external bodies; "for there is no conception in a man's mind which hath not at first, totally or by parts, been begotten upon the organs of sense." Diverse external motions produce diverse motions in us; and, in reality, there is nothing else; "but their appearance to us is fancy," though this name is commonly restricted to "decaying sense." The thoughts thus raised succeed one another in an order sometimes controlled by a "passionate thought," sometimes not. By

> the most noble and profitable invention of speech, names have been given to thoughts, whereby society and science have been made possible, and also absurdity: for words are wise men's counters, they do but reckon by them; but they are the money of fools.

Reason is but reckoning; addition and subtraction are its processes, logic is "computation." So far, man is regarded as if
he were a thinking being only. But he is also active. The
internal motions set up by the action of objects upon the senses
become reactions upon the external world; and these reactions
are all of the nature of tendencies towards that which "helps
the vital motion," that is, ministers to the preservation of the
individual, or tendencies away from things of an opposite
nature. Thus, we have appetite or desire for certain things,
and these we are said to love, and we call them good. In a
similar way, we have aversion from certain other things, which
we hate and call evil. Pleasure is "the appearance or sense of
good"; displeasure, "the appearance or sense of evil." Starting from these definitions, Hobbes proceeds to describe the
whole emotional and active nature of man as a consistent
scheme of selfishness. The following characteristic summary
comes from *Elements of Law :*

The comparison of the life of man to a race, though it holdeth
not in every point, yet it holdeth so well for this our purpose, that
we may thereby both see and remember almost all the passions
before mentioned. But this race we must suppose to have no
other goal, nor other garland, but being foremost; and in it: To
endeavour, is appetite. To be remiss, is sensuality. To consider them behind, is glory. To consider them before, humility.
To lose ground with looking back, vain glory. To be holden,
hatred. To turn back, repentance. To be in breath, hope. To
be weary, despair. To endeavour to overtake the next, emulation.
To supplant or overthrow, envy. To resolve to break through a
stop foreseen, courage. To break through a sudden stop, anger.
To break through with ease, magnanimity. To lose ground by
little hindrances, pusillanimity. To fall on the sudden, is disposition to weep. To see another fall, disposition to laugh. To
see one out-gone whom we would not, is pity. To see one out-go
we would not, is indignation. To hold fast by another, is to love.
To carry him on that so holdeth, is charity. To hurt one's-self
for haste, is shame. Continually to be out-gone, is misery. Continually to out-go the next before, is felicity. And to forsake the
course, is to die.

Out of this contention of selfish units, Hobbes, in some way,
has to derive morality and the social order. Yet, in the state

of nature there are no rules for the race of life—not even the
rule of the strongest, for Hobbes thinks that there is little
difference between men's faculties, and, at any rate, "the weakest has strength enough to kill the strongest." Thus, for gain,
for safety and for reputation (which is a sign of power), each
man desires whatever may preserve or enrich his own life, and,
indeed, by nature, "every man has a right to everything, even
to one another's body." Thus, the natural state of man is a
state of war, in which "every man is enemy to every man."
In this condition, as he points out, there is no place for industry, or knowledge, or arts, or society, but only "continual
fear and danger of violent death; and the life of man solitary,
poor, nasty, brutish, and short." Nor, in this state, is there
any difference of right and wrong, mine and thine; "force
and fraud are in war the two cardinal virtues."

Hobbes betrays some hesitation in speaking of the historical
reality of this state of universal war. But the point, perhaps,
is not fundamental. What is essential is the view of human
nature as so constituted as to make every man his neighbour's
enemy. The view was not entirely new; he was not the first
satirist of the "golden age." His originality lies in the consistency of his picture of its anarchy, and in the amazing skill
with which he makes the very misery of this state lead on to
social order: the freedom of anarchy yields at once and forever
to the fetters of power. The transition is effected by the social
contract—an instrument familiar to medieval philosophers
and jurists. So long as the state of nature endures, life is
insecure and wretched. Man cannot improve this state, but
he can get out of it; therefore, the fundamental law of nature
is to seek peace and follow it; and, from this, emerges the
second law, that, for the sake of peace, a man should be willing
to lay down his right to all things, when other men are, also,
willing to do so. From these two are derived all the laws of
nature of the moralists. The laws of nature are immutable
and eternal, says Hobbes, and, in so saying, conforms to the
traditional view—but with one great difference. Hooker,
who followed the older theory, had said that the laws of nature
"bind men absolutely, even as they are men, although they
have never any settled fellowship, never any solemn agreement
amongst themselves." But Hobbes holds that their authority,

for any man, is not absolute; it is strictly conditional on other men being willing to obey them; and this requires an agreement of wills—a contract. Contracts, again, require a power to enforce them: "covenants of mutual trust where there is a fear of not performance on either part are invalid"; and the only way to obtain such a common power is for all men to give up their rights to one man, or one assembly of men, and to acknowledge his acts as their own "in those things which concern the common peace and safety." This man, or assembly, will thus bear the "person" of the whole multitude. They have contracted with one another to be his subjects. But the sovereign himself is under no contract: he has rights but no duties.

From this, it follows, logically, that sovereignty cannot be limited, divided, or forfeited. The conduct of the commonwealth in peace and war, and the rights of subjects against one another, are decided by the sovereign. He is sole legislator, supreme ruler and supreme judge. And this holds, whether the sovereignty lies in one man or in an assembly. Hobbes always maintained the superiority of monarchy to other forms of government; but he never thought that this superiority was capable of the demonstrative proof that he claimed for his general theory. There is a story that, before leaving Paris, Hobbes told Edward Hyde (afterwards earl of Clarendon) that he was publishing *Leviathan* because he "had a mind to go home." If he was serious in making the remark reported by Clarendon, he must have been referring to the "Review and Conclusion," with which the work closes, and in which he speaks of the time at which submission to a conqueror may lawfully be made. The book in no way modifies his earlier views on the merits of monarchy.

A man cannot serve two masters: "mixed government" is no government; nor can the spiritual power be independent of the temporal. The doctrines "that every private man is judge of good and evil actions," and "that whatsoever a man does against his conscience is a sin," are seditious and repugnant to civil society. By living in a commonwealth, a man takes the law for his conscience. These positions may seem to complete the political theory, and few readers now care to pursue the matter further. But Hobbes's commonwealth professes

to be a Christian commonwealth.   He must show the place
which religion occupies in it, and also expose the errors which
have led to nations being overshadowed by the spiritual power.
His theory is Erastianism pushed to its extremest limits.   The
inner life—the true home of religion for the religious man—
shrinks to a point; while its external expression in doctrine and
observance is described as part of the order that depends on
the will of the sovereign.   Hobbes can cite Scripture for his
purpose; he anticipates some of the results of modern Biblical
criticism; and he has theories about God, the Trinity, the atonement and the last judgment—all of them in harmony with his
general principles.   His doctrine of God is, in modern phrase,
agnostic.   The attributes we ascribe to Him only signify our
desire to honour Him: "we understand nothing of what he is,
but only that he is."   In this, Hobbes follows the doctrine of
negative attributes, worked out by some medieval theologians.
But his doctrine of the Trinity is, surely, original.   It is

in substance this: that God who is always one and the same was
the person represented by Moses, the person represented by his
Son incarnate, and the person represented by the apostles.

Again, the kingdom of God is a real kingdom, instituted by
covenant or contract: which contract was made by Moses,
broken by the election of Saul to the kingship, restored by
Christ and proclaimed by the apostles.   But the kingdom of
Christ "is not of this world"; it is of the world to come after
the general resurrection; "therefore neither can his ministers
(unless they be kings) require obedience in his name."
     There are two things specially opposed to this theory.   On
the one hand, there is the enthusiasm which results from the
claim either to personal illumination by the spirit of God or to
private interpretation of Scripture.   On the other hand, there
is the claim to dominion on the part of the organised spiritual
power.   Both claims were rampant in Hobbes's day, and he
seeks to undermine them both by criticism.   There is no argument, he says, by which a man can be convinced that God has
spoken immediately to some other man, "who (being a man)
may err, and (which is more) may lie."   And, as regards
Scripture, it is for sovereigns as the sole legislators to say which

books are canonical, and, therefore, to them, also, must belong
the authority for their interpretation. Of all the abuses that
constitute what Hobbes calls the Kingdom of Darkness, the
greatest arise from the erroneous tenet "that the present church
now militant on earth is the kingdom of God." Through this
error, not only the Roman, but, also, the presbyterian, clergy
have been the authors of darkness in religion, and encroached
upon the civil power. The Roman church alone has been
thorough in its work. The pope, in claiming dominion over
all Christendom, has forsaken the true kingdom of God, and
he has built up his power out of the ruins of heathen Rome.
For "the papacy is no other than the ghost of the deceased
Roman empire, sitting crowned upon the grave thereof."

Taken as a whole, Hobbes's *Leviathan* has two characteristics which stamp it with the mark of genius. In the first
place, it is a work of great imaginative power, which shows
how the whole fabric of human life and society is built up out
of simple elements. And, in the second place, it is distinguished
by a remarkable logical consecutiveness, so that there are very
few places in which any lack of coherence can be detected in the
thought. It is true that the social order, as Hobbes presents
it, produces an impression of artificiality; but this is hardly an
objection, for it was his deliberate aim to show the artifice by
which it had been constructed and the danger which lay in
any interference with the mechanism. It is true, also, that the
state of nature and the social contract are fictions passed off as
facts; but, even to this objection, an answer might be made
from within the bounds of his theory. It is in his premises,
not in his reasoning, that the error lies. If human nature were
as selfish and anarchical as he represents it, then morality and
the political order could arise and flourish only by its restraint,
and the alternative would be, as he describes it, between complete insecurity and absolute power. But, if his view of man
be mistaken, then the whole fabric of his thought crumbles.
When we recognise that the individual is neither real nor
intelligible apart from his social origin and traditions, and that
the social factor influences his thought and motives, the
opposition between self and others becomes less fundamental,
the abrupt alternatives of Hobbism lose their validity and it
is possible to regard morality and the state as expressing the

ideal and sphere of human activity, and not as simply the chains by which man's unruly passions are kept in check.

The most powerful criticism of Hobbes's political theory which appeared in his lifetime was contained in the *Oceana* of James Harrington, published in 1656; and the criticism gained in effectiveness from the author's own constructive doctrine. This he set forth under the thin disguise of a picture of an imaginary commonwealth. The device was familiar enough at the time. More and Bacon in England, and Campanella in Italy, had already followed the ancient model by describing an ideal state, which both More and Bacon placed in some unknown island of the west. The *Utopia* of Sir Thomas More was published in 1516 and Englished by Ralph Robynson in 1551. The work is a political romance. The spirit of the renascence was still fresh when the author wrote, and it made him imagine a new world to which the old order might conform, and, by conforming, escape the evils of its present condition. There is not any attempt at a philosophical analysis of the nature of the state, but only an account of a government and people devoted to the cause of social welfare. Supreme power is in the hands of a prince, but he and all other magistrates are elected by the people; and it is in its account of the life of the people that the interest of the work lies. They detest war "as a thing very beastly" and "count nothing so much against glory as glory gotten in war." Their life is one of peace and freedom, of justice and equality. There is not any oppression, industrial or religious; but work and enjoyment are shared alike by all:

In other places, they speak still of the commonwealth, but every man procureth his own private gain. Here where nothing is private, the common affairs be earnestly looked upon. . . . Nothing is distributed after a niggish sort, neither there is any poor man or beggar. And though no man have any thing, yet every man is rich.

Bacon's fable *New Atlantis* (1627) is only a fragment, and has little of the charm that distinguishes More's romance. Its interest lies in the description of Solomon's house, which may be taken as Bacon's ideal of the public endowment of science. We are told that "his lordship thought also in this present fable to have composed a frame of laws, or of the best state or mould of a commonwealth"; but, unfortunately, he preferred to work at his natural history, so that we learn nothing about the government of his ideal community, and little about the social characteristics of the people, though he descants on the dignity of their manners and on the magnificence of their costumes.

Harrington's *Oceana* is a work of a different kind. It has none of the imaginative quality of *Utopia* or even of *New Atlantis*. Much of it reads like a state paper or the schedules of a budget. The reference to present affairs is too thinly disguised for any artistic purpose. "Oceana" is, of course, England, and the lord Archon pervades the book as his prototype, Oliver, pervaded the English government. In all the councils of Oceana, he has always the last word, and his speeches are long, convincing and wearisome; he will even digress into sketching the history of the world. The author was probably ill-advised when he threw his work into the romantic form. He has a real insight into politics, and can see some things which were concealed from Hobbes's vision. He never loses sight of the important fact that government is only one factor in social life. The form of government will follow the distribution of property: "where there is inequality of estates there must be inequality of power; and where there is inequality of power there can be no commonwealth." The commonwealth should exhibit equality both in its foundation and in the superstructure. The former is to be secured by an agrarian law limiting the amount of property which can be held by one man, so that "no one man or number of men, within the compass of the few or aristocracy, can come to overpower the whole people by their possessions in land"; and Harrington explained the recent change in the government of the country by the gradual shifting of the balance of property from king and lords to the commons. Equality in the superstructure will be attained by means of a rotation or succession to the magistracy secured by "the suffrage of the people given by the ballot." In this way will be constituted the three orders: "the senate debating and proposing, the people resolving, and the magistracy executing." The need for distinguishing the orders is emphasised in Harrington's *Political Aphorisms*, where he says that "a popular assembly without a senate cannot be wise," and that a "senate without a popular assembly will not be honest." A commonwealth thus rightly instituted, so he thinks, can never swerve from its principles, and has in it no "principle of mortality." Yet the constitution which he proposed comes short of consistent democracy, and falls in with the spirit of the time. The function of the one great man is recognised: "a parliament of physicians would never have found out the circulation of the blood, nor would a parliament of poets have written Virgil's Aeneis." Thus, the great man is right to aim at the sovereignty when the times are out of joint, so that he may set them right and establish the reign of law; and the book ends with his proclamation as lord Archon for life. The nobility or gentry have, also, their place:

there is something first in the making of a commonwealth, then in the governing of it, and last of all in the leading of its armies, which . . . seems to be peculiar only to the genius of a gentleman.

Like Milton, Harrington argues for liberty of conscience in matters of religion—though he would disallow "popish, Jewish, or idolatrous" worship. Unlike Milton, however, he does not exclude the state from the sphere of religion:

a commonwealth is nothing else but the national conscience. And if the conviction of a man's private conscience produces his private religion, the conviction of the national conscience must produce a national religion.

Sir Robert Filmer was also among the critics of Hobbes's politics, though he owes his fame to the circumstance that he was himself criticised by Locke. He maintained the doctrine of absolute power as strongly as Hobbes did, and, like him, thought that limited monarchy meant anarchy; and he had written on these topics in king Charles's time. But he would not admit that this power could rest on contract, and, in his *Originall of Government* (1652), attacked Hobbes as well as Milton and Grotius. His own views are set forth in his *Patriarcha, or the Natural Power of Kings*, first published in 1680, twenty-seven years after his death. Filmer was by no means devoid of critical insight. He saw that the doctrine that all men are by nature free and equal is not true historically and, therefore, is no good ground for making popular consent the origin of government.

Late writers [he says] have taken up too much upon trust from the subtle schoolmen, who to be sure to thrust down the king below the pope, thought it the safest course to advance the people above the king.

He thinks that "a great family, as to the rights of sovereignty, is a little monarchy," and Hobbes had said the same; but Filmer traces all kingship to the subjection of children to their parents, which is both natural and a divine ordinance. There has never been a more absolute dominion than that which Adam had over the whole world. And kings are Adam's heirs. In developing this thesis, the author diverges into a reading of history more fantastic than anything suggested by Bellarmine or Hobbes, and delivers himself up an easy prey to Locke's criticism.

Edward Hyde, earl of Clarendon, is also to be counted among the critics of Hobbes's political theory. His *Brief Survey of the dangerous and pernicious Errors to Church and State in Mr. Hobbes's book* (1674) is a protest against the paradoxes of *Leviathan*, but is lacking in any element of constructive criticism.

John Bramhall, bishop of Derry, and, afterwards, archbishop of Armagh, was one of the most vigorous and persistent of Hobbes's critics. His first work was in defence of the royal power (1643). Afterwards he engaged in a discussion of the question of free-will with Hobbes when they were both in France. When the controversy was renewed and became public, he wrote *A Defence of the True Liberty of Human Actions from Antecedent and Extrinsicall Necessity* (1655). Hobbes replied, and Bramhall followed, in 1658, with *Castigations of Mr. Hobbes*, to which there was an appendix called "The Catching of Leviathan the Great Whale." In this appendix, more famous than the rest of the treatise, he attacked the whole religious and political theory of Hobbes, and gave rise to the complaint of the latter that the bishop

hath put together diverse sentences picked out of my *Leviathan*, which stand there plainly and firmly proved, and sets them down without their proofs, and without the order of their dependance one upon another; and calls them atheism, blasphemy, impiety, subversion of religion, and by other names of that kind.

Two younger polemical writers may be mentioned along with Bramhall. Thomas Tenison, a future archbishop of Canterbury, was one of the young churchmen militant who must needs try their arms "in thundering upon Hobbes's steel-cap." In *The Creed of Mr. Hobbes examined* (1670), he selected a number of Hobbes's confident assertions and set them together so as to show their mutual inconsistencies. In two dialogues, published in 1672 and 1673, John Eachard, afterwards master of St. Catharine's hall, Cambridge, adopted a similar method, and showed no little wit and learning in his criticism.

These writers are the most notable of a number of early critics of Hobbes who made no independent contributions of their own to philosophy. And their criticism dealt with results rather than with principles. A satisfactory criticism of Hobbes has to penetrate to the principles of the mechanical philosophy which he adopted, and to the view of human nature which he set forth in conformity with those principles. Criticism of this more fundamental kind was attempted by certain of the Cambridge Platonists,[1] especially by Cudworth and More; and they were fitted for the task by their sympathetic study of the spiritual philosophy of Plato in the ancient world and of Descartes in their own day—two thinkers for whom Hobbes had no appreciation.

Joseph Glanvill was intimately associated with some members of the Cambridge school—in particular, with Henry More—but he was himself educated at Oxford, and he was not a Platonist. He had, however, many points of sympathy with them. He was attracted by the new philosophy of Descartes—he calls it the "best philosophy"—whereas he had nothing but criticism for the Aristotelianism that still ruled the schools of Oxford. He was in sympathy, also, with the broad and reasonable tone that distinguished the theology of the Cambridge Platonists from the prevailing attitude of the

[1] A chapter on the Cambridge Platonists will appear in the next volume of this work.

puritan divines. Glanvill's mind was sensitive to all the influences of the time, the new science, the human culture, the contending doctrines in philosophy and theology. The result was a distrust of all dogmatic systems, combined with a certain openness of mind—a readiness to receive light from any quarter. His first and most famous book was *The Vanity of Dogmatizing* (1661), and a revised edition of the same was published in 1665 with the title *Scepsis scientifica: or Confest Ignorance the way to Science*. This was dedicated to the Royal Society, of which he had become a fellow in 1664. In philosophy, Glanvill professed himself a seeker. He discoursed on the defects in our knowledge even of the things nearest to us, such as the nature of the soul and the body: he held that reason is swayed by the emotions, so that "most of the contests of the litigious world pretending for truth are but the bandyings of one man's affections against another's." His chief censures were for the dogmas of the Aristotelians, and this involved him in controversy with "the learned Mr. Thomas White," a priest of Douay, collaborator with Sir Kenelm Digby, and a voluminous author, who answered *The Vanity of Dogmatizing* in a Latin treatise entitled *Sciri, sive sceptices et scepticorum a jure disputationis exclusio*. It is in his reply to this writer that Glanvill defines his scepticism as a "way of enquiry, which is not to continue still poring upon the writings and opinions of philosophers, but to seek truth in the great book of nature." The Royal Society, realising Bacon's prophetic scheme of Solomon's house, had adopted this method, and had done more for the improvement of useful knowledge "than all the philosophers of the notional way since Aristotle opened his shop in Greece." Glanvill himself ventured upon a "continuation of the New Atlantis" in his essay *Antifanatick Theologie, and Free Philosophy*. His openness of mind and his conviction that authority and sense are our only evidence on such matters led to his belief in supernatural appearances. He thought that "the testimony of all ages" established their reality. And he distrusted the dogmatism of what he called "modern Sadducism": to him, it was a "matter of astonishment that men, otherwise witty and ingenious, are fallen into the conceit that there 's no such thing as a witch or apparition."

Other writers of the period showed the influence of the new

ideas. From the scholastic point of view, Samuel Parker, bishop of Oxford, criticised both Hobbes and Descartes, a treatise on Cartesianism having been published in England in 1675 by Antoine Legrand, of Douay, a Franciscan friar and member of the English mission. In his *Court of the Gentiles* (1669–77), Theophilus Gale traced all ancient learning and philosophy to the Hebrew scriptures. John Pordage wrote a number of works, the mysticism of which was inspired by Jacob Boehme. The treatise *De legibus naturae*, published in 1672, by Richard Cumberland, afterwards bishop of Peterborough, is much more than a criticism of Hobbes. It is a restatement of the doctrine of the law of nature as furnishing the ground of the obligation of all the moral virtues. The work is heavy in style, and its philosophical analysis lacks thoroughness; but its insistence on the social nature of man, and its doctrine of the common good as the supreme law of morality, anticipate the direction taken by much of the ethical thought of the following century.

CHAPTER XIII

Scholars and Scholarship, 1600-60

THE starting-point of English scholarship and learning in the seventeenth century is not the humanism of the early renascence. The main current was diverted from its onward flow by the events of the reign of queen Mary and the political and ecclesiastical exigencies of queen Elizabeth's reign. From the moment of the return of the English exiles from Geneva, Frankfort and Strassburg, the conviction set in of the necessity of a discipline in life and learning founded on the Bible. This conviction permeated every activity of the nation, putting energetic representatives of learning and education in the very front of the propaganda, and reserving meditative scholars as the very bulwarks of defence. William Chillingworth's *Religion of Protestants* maintained that the Bible alone is the religion of protestants; and, in the thought of the age, the Bible, also, was the centre towards which all scholarship could gravitate most profitably and creditably, and by which it could most certainly gain acceptance and stability. The usefulness of learning became almost axiomatic, so long as "human" was kept subsidiary to "divine" learning. The older humanism which dominated Erasmus, Thomas More and Thomas Elyot was crushed. The day had passed for placing Aristotle, Plato, Seneca, side by side, in the joyful enthusiasm for new found comrades, with New Testament writers, or with St. Chrysostom and St. Jerome, fearlessly running the risk of unifying sacred and profane, in the common appeal to antiquity. The fires of Smithfield in Mary's reign and the penal inflictions of Elizabeth, together with the St. Bartholomew massacres in France, stirred, in the minds of both the opposing parties, the intuition that the struggle between Roman Catholics and

protestantism was a personal concern as well as a national issue
—and, if there was authority on the one side, there must be
authority on the other.   The issue, necessarily, was the church
versus the book.   If the contest was not to be by fire and sword
solely, the only alternative was that in the arena of scholarship.   The extreme puritan view of a discipline in religion,
based only on the Bible, was soon found to be ineffective against
opponents like the Jesuits, who commanded all the resources
of Bible erudition, as well as of scholarship in ecclesiastical
history, for disputational purposes.   The most redoubtable
protestant advocates were, of necessity, increasingly driven to
include in their scholarly studies the early Fathers as well as
the Bible, and to agree that the primitive church had at least
a high degree of authority.   But the main point in tracing the
course of this scholarship is to realise that the church, the early
Fathers, the Bible, constituted authorities to which appeal could
be made, and that both Catholics and their opponents had to
pursue, with an intensity of application unequalled before or
since, the history of antiquity in so far as it concerned these
issues.   Christianity, whether of the church or of the Bible,
was a historical religion—and to imply either aspect was to
bring the argument into the historical environments within
which these crucial sanctities had their origin, development
and continuity.

    The puritans, who staked their all intellectually on Bible-
centred knowledge, might have confined English scholarship
to the narrowest of limits.   England, as J. R. Green has said,
became "the people of one book, and that book the Bible."
But there were other influences at work, in this period, which
tended to enlarge the scope of intellectual interests.   The spirit
of national enterprise and sea exploit that characterised queen
Elizabeth's reign continued to mark the Stewart period, and
transferred itself into intellectual efforts in new directions
The companies of Merchant Adventurers made a discovery
of the east, as Columbus had discovered America.   Eastern
languages were learned and transmitted, and oriental MSS.
were triumphantly brought home to eager scholars.   Physical
adventure in east and west tended to provoke fearlessness of
enquiry into natural science.   The old sea groups of Hawkins,
Ralegh, Frobisher gave place to the *camaraderie* of intellectual

centres like the society of Antiquaries, gatherings of gentie-
men-investigators, such as Falkland's group at Great Tew,[1]
Hartlib's group in London and the groups at Oxford, Cambridge, London, which coalesced into the Royal Society.[2] All
these and other groups were fascinated by the expanding
spaciousness of physical research and the love of truth, and
ideals of independent enquiry stimulated them to complete the
knowledge of the *Orbis Visibilis* and *Orbis Intellectualis*, and
to supply "gaps" such as those indicated by Bacon.

Besides native sources of wider development than could be
gained from the Bible centre alone, the close connection of
English scholars with foreign scholars must be taken into account. England was drawn close to the continent after the
return of protestant exiles. Of the twenty-one bishops whom
queen Elizabeth appointed, thirteen had passed most of
queen Mary's reign in Germany or Switzerland, and the 650
letters on theological subjects published by the Parker society
show the close relationship between English protestants and
their fellow believers abroad. English bishops remembered
Geneva in the days of her tribulation, by the practical method
of sending remittances for the relief of distress when the duke
of Savoy was harassing that city. In 1583, by royal brief, a
collection for the Genevese was made in the churches of England, which brought in £5039. Calvin's *Institutes* was translated into English in 1559, by Thomas Norton, and ran through
many editions. Almost all the chief Elizabethan divines were
Zwinglian or Calvinist in doctrine, and were in communication
with foreign theologians and scholars. When the Spanish
armies of Alva were devastating the Low Countries, distressed
protestant Fleming refugees came to England in hundreds,[3]
while the earl of Leicester and Sir Philip Sidney took some
thousands of Englishmen to fight for the Dutch cause. Previously, Sir Walter Ralegh had fought for the Huguenots in
France. The duke of Buckingham's duplicity and feeble-
ness in attempting the relief of La Rochelle in Charles I's reign
caused boundless indignation in England. The sympathy of

---

[1] See *ante*, Chap. VI.   [2] See *post*, Vol. VIII.

[3] The frequent immigrations into England of Huguenots and other foreign
religious refugees form an important subject in English commercial history. See
Cunningham, W., *Alien Immigrants to England*, Chaps. IV and VI.

Cromwell and the English people with the protestants of Piedmont was sufficient, in 1655, to open the national exchequer for grants to schoolmasters, ministers, physicians, even to students in divinity and physic.

The continuity of these close relations, political and personal, with foreign protestants, is of capital importance in understanding the history of English scholarship. For, while England largely owed its concentrative group of Bible studies to Geneva, the greatest classical scholarship of the sixteenth century had been shown by French Huguenots, and the chief glories of scholarship in the seventeenth century were clustered together in Holland; and France and Holland, in each age, respectively, were the countries with which our divines and scholars were in closest touch. Thus, in the sixteenth century, French scholarship had been transfigured by the genius and research of Budaeus, Turnebus, Lambinus and the Stephenses, and the succession into the seventeenth century included Casaubon and Salmasius. In 1593, Joseph Scaliger went to Holland to the university of Leyden (founded 1575). Dutch scholarship was the ripest in Europe from 1600-60 and included G. J. Vossius, Isaac Vossius (his son), Claude Saumaise or Salmasius, P. Cluverius,[1] Daniel Heinsius, N. Heinsius (his son), Hugo Grotius, J. F. Gronovius. The interest of this list consists in the fact that all these distinguished scholars were in direct touch with English scholars. The older Vossius corresponded, for instance, with Thomas Farnaby; Isaac Vossius actually left Holland and lived in England, where he held a prebend at Windsor for sixteen years (1673-88). Salmasius had the famous controversy with Milton. From his contemporary, Daniel Heinsius, Ben Jonson borrowed freely in his *Timber*. Heinsius's son Nicholas travelled in England. Hugo Grotius wrote his famous *Mare liberum* (1609) to assert the international right of the seas, and John Selden in 1635 published his answer *Mare Clausum*, written about 1619. The brother-in-law of G. J. Vossius, Franciscus Junius, himself a man of no mean learning, left Holland to come to England as librarian to the earl of Arundel, and remained in this post for 30 years. He published his *De Pictura Veterum*, in

[1] P. Cluverius was one of the many "sojourners" with John Prideaux, rector of Exeter college, Oxford.

Latin, in 1637, and, in English, in 1638.   Junius was drawn
into the enthusiasm for British antiquities and produced an
edition of Caedmon, in 1655, and the Moeso-Gothic text of
Ulfilas in 1664–5; and he left in MS. an English etymology
which served the turn of Johnson's *Dictionary*.

The direct influence of these great French and Dutch
scholars was reinforced by the general state of culture prevalent among foreign protestants.   Travelling was a constituent
part of the education of the well-to-do.   The travelling of men
with messages of goodwill, or of advice to the various churches
abroad, brought about an appreciation of standards of knowledge and learning.   Correspondence between learned men and
religious leaders filled the place of modern reviews and newspapers.   Reports of new books and learned investigations
penetrated into remote corners and at a pace unexampled in
the previous history of the world.   Frankfort and Leipzig fairs
collected and circulated books broadcast.   Dutch presses
found a large English market.   England was thus within
reach of the best of foreign culture, because she was protestant after the Genevan type; and much of the most solid
foreign scholarship, in the seventeenth century, was directly
or indirectly under the spell of Calvin.   An interesting indication of the religious sympathies which united English and
foreign protestants is the growth of the custom of sending boys
and girls to French Huguenot academies and pastors, or English youths to the university of Leyden; on the other hand, an
English scholar such as Thomas Gataker could maintain for
some time a private seminary in his house at Rotherhithe, and
"many foreigners went and lodged with him, that they might
enjoy the benefit of his advice."   Casaubon, when in straitened
means in Paris, received lord Herbert of Cherbury as boarder
as he had received young Henry Wotton in his house at Geneva.
Before the Pilgrim fathers went to America, they had sojourned
in Dutch cities, established congregations there and appointed
ministers in Amsterdam and Leyden.   There was an English
congregation at Rotterdam, whose minister was William
Ames, who, for twelve years, had been professor in the university of Franeker in Friesland.   William Bedell, who was
chaplain to Wotton at Venice for about three years, penned his
sermons in Italian and Latin, wrote an English grammar so

that Italians might learn to read English sermons and translated father Paul's works into Latin for all protestant Europe to read. The great mathematician John Wallis wrote an English grammar (in Latin) for the use of foreigners. The great English disputant John Featley lived three years in France and "did great honour to his nation and protestantism by disputing successfully against the most learned papists." Matthew Slade, an Oxford graduate, became rector of the academy at Amsterdam and distinguished himself by entering the lists against the scholar Conrad Vorstius. David Primrose, a Scot, became minister of the Huguenot church at Rouen. The chaplaincies of the Merchant companies of England, especially the Levant company, at Aleppo, furnished important opportunities for the cultivation of oriental languages. The greatest of these chaplains was Edward Pococke. The name of Thomas Davies, resident at Aleppo, is memorable for his services in securing oriental MSS. for archbishop Ussher (1624-7).

Many were the distinguished foreigners who found a home in England. Antonio de Dominis, once Roman Catholic archbishop of Spalatro, was made dean of Windsor in 1617, and maintained the rights of national churches, but left England in 1622 and recanted. Saravia and Peter du Moulin, like Isaac Vossius, held English prebends. John Verneuil, of Bordeaux, was appointed second keeper of the Bodleian library in 1625. Matthias Pasor lectured on oriental languages at Exeter college, Oxford, 1625-9, whilst Christian Ravis of Berlin taught the same subjects in Gresham college, London, in 1642. John Milton, in 1649, was appointed secretary for foreign tongues, succeeding G. R. Weckherlin, a native of Stuttgart, fluent in German, French and English, and a writer of verses in each of those languages. The great Albericus Gentilis had lectured on law in Oxford. Isaac Casaubon took up his abode here from 1610 to 1614 and held a prebend at Canterbury with a pension of £300 a year.

The influence of Roman Catholic scholarship perhaps constituted the most potent stimulus to the prodigious efforts of protestant erudition in this period. In the latter half of the sixteenth century, Jesuits had regained France and southern Germany for Rome, and protestants were in peril of their lives.

Jesuits had taken the lead in polite letters and had trained themselves in classical style. Yet the whole course of their studies, "however deeply grounded in erudition or embellished by eloquence, had one perpetual aim—the propagation of the Catholic faith." Jesuit colleges were the admiration of every scholar. Three years' work was devoted to philosophy, and four years' drill was given in theology. Thus were trained the combatants who gained back France and part of Germany to Rome, and bid fair, at the beginning of the seventeenth century, to extirpate protestantism everywhere. Towering above the army of disputants thus produced, cardinal Bellarmine swept the field in controversial theology. In these controversies, England was not unrepresented, but English writers found it increasingly necessary to equip themselves further in specialistic learning and dialectical skill in order to meet their opponents. The war was carried on in England by William Whitaker, the great Calvinistic scholarly churchman of queen Elizabeth's reign, and, in the same reign, and in that of James I, by Matthew Sutcliffe, afterwards dean of Exeter; by John Rainolds, king James I, Lancelot Andrewes and Francis Mason. On the Catholic side, one of the most distinguished English disputants was William Rainolds, brother of John Rainolds.

Inconsiderable in point of learning as some of these theological disputations may be, the controversies largely determined the line of direction of scholarly effort. It is significant that, in 1610, James I incorporated a college to be called by his name at Chelsea. Matthew Sutcliffe gave considerable funds to the project, and was appointed provost. Its occupants were to be "men of war," reserved for polemical studies. Besides the study of divinity, two historians were to be maintained, "to record and publish to posterity all memorable passages in Church and Commonwealth." The college, ultimately, was seized by parliament during the interregnum. Samuel Hartlib, in 1655, in a letter to John Worthington, master of Jesus college, Cambridge, laments its confiscation. "Bishops and Deans are gone," he says. It would be a scandal, if "we betray or destroy an incomparable engine already prepared . . . for the defence of the Truth."

But a still higher stimulus to protestant learning was

provided in 1588–1609 when the greatest of Roman Catholic
researchers, cardinal Baronius, produced his twelve folios of
Annales Ecclesiastici.

"The whole case," says Mark Pattison, "of the Romanists
and especially the supremacy of the See of Rome was here set
out in the form of authentic annals. . . . The *Annales* transferred to the Catholic party the preponderance in the field of
learning which ever since Erasmus had been on the side of the
innovators."

It became the object of protestant learning to devote itself
to the effective criticism and refutation of the statements and
arguments of Baronius. No mere reliance on scriptural texts
could meet the emergency. Learning could only be fairly and
finally met by learning. Zealously English scholars strained
themselves to the utmost. John Rainolds, president of Corpus
Christi college, Oxford, attempted, from the puritanic side,
the task of refuting Baronius in 1602. All English efforts,
however, pale into insignificance beside the work of Isaac
Casaubon, *De rebus sacris et ecclesiasticis exercitationes XVI
ad Baronii annales* (1614).

Next to Joseph Scaliger in Leyden, who died in 1609, Isaac
Casaubon was regarded as the most learned scholar in Europe,
and his residence in London from 1610 to 1614 proved the
attractiveness to his scholarly mind of the theological attitude
of men like Lancelot Andrewes. Casaubon's residence in
England was an incalculable stimulus to the industry and research of the new "Anglican" school that was rising over the
heads of the puritan groups.

Whilst Casaubon was admired by the protestant world for
his classical and patriotic scholarship, there was not a little
misgiving that he lost his opportunity in his *Exercitationes* of
refuting the doctrinal theology of Baronius, and it was feared
that he had failed to return the undermining attacks of Jesuits
on protestant bulwarks. But Casaubon was not a gladiator
like Scioppius. He had gone through fiery torments of in-
decision in taking the one side rather than the other. In the
inner sanctity of his conscience, the cause of truth was en-
shrined. The older ideal of imitation, both in form and in

substance, of the great classical writers of antiquity had now passed. It was essential for those engaged in theological conflict on an intellectual plane *to know*. But knowledge, which goes to the root of matters, must use both a trained judgment and the results of independent enquiries into the ideas and thoughts as well as the surroundings of the ancient world, if it is to represent a solid basis for the thought of the present. To the keenest scholars of the seventeenth century, among whom Casaubon was conspicuously the first, the foundations of theological truth necessarily had to be sought in the earlier centuries of the Christian era. Casaubon had devoted his faculties, heightened and refined by almost incredible application, unparalleled even in that age of classical scholars, to critical work in respect of the writings of Strabo, Athenaeus, Persius and Polybius. On all these, he brought to bear a knowledge of classical antiquity which seemed at once universal in its comprehensiveness and selective in its adequacy for the point in hand, so much so that his commentary on Strabo has not been superseded.

Casaubon only lived to complete the first half of the first volume of his criticism of Baronius's mighty tomes. Much of the 800 folio pages is occupied with a re-tracing of Baronius's tracks, correcting and rebutting, point by point. Constructive work, indeed, there was, in the form of dissertations. But the essential significance of the history of seventeenth century scholarship is the object-lesson which its productions furnish, providing students in the Bible studies, in patristic learning and in church history with a standard of research, intellectual persistency, scholarly apparatus and equipment.

The dissatisfaction of English controversialists with Casaubon's method of critical correction rather than of concentration on doctrinal disputation was made manifest in the effort of Richard Mountague, who, in his *Analecta Exercitationum ecclesiasticarum*, 1622, "went over the same ground again, to show how Casaubon ought to have done it but could not." Mountague and the Greek professor of Cambridge, Andrew Downes, had been among the coadjutors of Sir Henry Savile in the production of the wonderful eight volume Eton edition of St. Chrysostom's works (1612). Savile had collected MSS. of Chrysostom, and, with Casaubon's aid, he had had the MSS.

in the Royal library of Paris collated, and had organised the
revision of the text by the most learned Greek scholars in
England, himself defraying the cost of production, computed
at £8000. No edition of a Greek author, in England or in
Europe, in the first part of the seventeenth century, could vie
with this work in the splendour of its production. Casaubon
and Savile, though not on good terms personally, were united
by the publication in England of two of the greatest works of
scholarship of the age, and in the inauguration on the highest
plane of that patristic study which constituted the chief
feature of English scholarship in the period 1600–60.

Throughout the period, works of learned men, whether
divines or laymen, abound in allusions disclosing a knowledge
of the Fathers, the councils and ecclesiastical history. Calamy,
a member of the Westminster assembly, is said to have read
through St. Augustine's works five times, and to have thoroughly
mastered the *Summa* of Aquinas. Thomas Holland, the
Oxford professor of divinity, was familiar with the Fathers
"as if he himself were a Father and in the schoolmen as if he
had been a seraphical doctor." Henry Jackson, a country
rector in Gloucestershire, collected several of the works of
Abelard from ancient MSS., and revised and collated them;
but, in 1642, his collection was scattered by parliamentary
soldiers. Archbishop Ussher, at 20 years of age, resolved to go
through all the Fathers by himself and "to trust no eyes but
his own." He took eighteen years over the task, "strictly
confining himself to read so much in a day and suffering no
occasion whatever" to divert him from it. Laymen as well as
divines were close students; physicians, lawyers, schoolmasters
knew the Fathers, at least for the purpose of embellishing their
writings. In the directions which James I issued to the
universities in 1616, students in divinity were

to be incited to bestow their times in the Fathers and Councils,
Schoolmen, Histories and Controversies, and not to insist so long
upon Compendiums and abbreviations as the grounds of their
study in Divinity.

Thus, the spread of patristic learning in England in the first
half of the seventeenth century is not to be judged merely by
the incidental scholarship shown by Anglican divines. It also

pervaded many puritan divines; it characterised many of the leading preachers, like Jeremy Taylor. Different as the subjects of these writings are, Robert Burton, in his *Anatomy of Melancholy*, Sir Thomas Browne, in his *Religio Medici*, William Prynne, in his *Histriomastix* (who quotes testimony from 71 Fathers and 55 synods) show that writers found in the Fathers a court of appeal with an authority generally recognised, and the literature of the period revels in multitudinous quotations patristic as well as classical.

The higher criticism which now is occupied with the Bible then lavished its learning on the Fathers. For, though John Daillé, the most learned French pastor in patristic knowledge, in his *Traicté de l'employ des saincts pères*, 1628, deprecated absolute reliance on this authority, the subject was acknowledged, by all interested in scholarship, to be of profound relative importance, and only to be transcended by a thorough knowledge of the Scriptures themselves, which, again, depended upon light thrown on them by patristic studies.

The seventeenth century entered into a noble heritage of accumulated knowledge of the classics. The sixteenth century had been a period of acquisition and ingathering of knowledge of classical authors; and grammars, rhetorics and logics, together with phrase-books, colloquies, vocabularies and dictionaries, collections of adages, apophthegms, epigrams, proverbs, emblems, synonyms, were rapidly produced. Not only were the whole of the available literary remains of Rome and Greece thus presented, but they were broken up into such a systematic analysis that every detail was at hand for the synthetic process of composition modelled on the style of Cicero or Demosthenes. With marvellous skill and prodigious research, analytical and inductive methods were applied more and more daringly to writing on topics concerning Roman and Greek antiquities, as well as on medieval and modern history and contemporary events and interests. As the fifteenth and sixteenth centuries had developed style and form in writing the classical languages, the seventeenth century entered into assured possession of literary instruments for the treatment of all kinds of material of investigation and enquiry. In the earlier part of the seventeenth century, works of importance, however long and recondite, were written in Latin, not merely from the

love of masterful pedantry, but for the absolutely practical
reason that Latin was the international language of well
educated people.[1] A typical instance was Bacon, with his
Novum Organum and *De Augmentis Scientiarum*, the latter of
which was an expansion of the treatise in English named *The
Advancement of Learning*. The publication of books in both
Latin and English thus marks a transition stage in the movement from Latin to English, as the medium for communication. But it will be remembered that Copernicus, Gilbert,
Harvey, Newton, announced their scientific discoveries in
Latin, not because they were profound classical students, but
because Latin was the common language of scientific writers at
home and abroad, as it was the ordinary language both for
speech and writing between scholars, scientific people, professional men and diplomatists. The erudite Savile was Latin
secretary to queen Elizabeth. In 1644, the title of the office
was changed to "Secretary for Foreign Tongues to the Joint
Committee for the two Kingdoms," and, as already stated, it
was under this designation that John Milton assumed the post
in 1649. Though this is a sign of the coming change, when the
French ascendency in Charles II's reign was to lead, eventually,
to the substitution of that language in the sphere of diplomacy,
it is not to be supposed that the change was a *tour de force*. It
had been silently prepared for in the close *rapprochement* of
England with French protestants and in the inter-relations
already described. Yet, in 1659, John Pell, on a mission in
Germany, spoke Latin to a burgomaster "who told me he had
given over speaking in Latin these 50 years," and answered in
High Dutch. Edward Leigh, in his *Advice on Travel* (*c.* 1660),
still requires gentlemen to be well equipped in conversational
Latin. Academically, the ideal of Latin-speaking was well
preserved. Brinsley, in his *Ludus Literarius*, 1612, expects
school lessons in grammar to be conducted by questions and
answers in the Latin language. Disputations and orations
were in this language, not only in universities but, also, in
grammar schools. Casaubon conversed in Latin with James I
and with the bishops; university plays were often in Latin; and
sermons had to be in the same tongue for degrees in divinity.

[1] In 1635, Sir Francis Kynaston published a translation into Latin of Chaucer's
Troilus and Criseyde, for the use of foreign readers.

In 1635, Cornelius Burgess preached in Latin to his fellow puritan ministers in London. In fact, Latin occupied very much the position that mathematics now assumes on the modern side of a public school, in relation to physical science studies. It provided the necessary equipment for other studies, and the school curriculum was framed with a view to relieving the university from its teaching. The curriculum consisted of *Pueriles Confabulatiunculae* (children's Latin talk), colloquies, catechisms in Latin and Greek, systematic grammar, translation and re-translation, and the whole round of vocabularies, the making of Latins, letter-writing (on the model of Cicero's *Epistulae*, proceeding to those of modern writers—Politian, Erasmus, Ascham, Manutius, Lipsius—and the composition, concurrently, of original epistles), themes, with full equipment of adages, apophthegmata, *flores*, phrase-books; then making verses, and, finally, the glory of sixth form work, producing and declaiming original orations. Thus, the school discipline in Latin was never more complete than in the first half of the seventeenth century. For, in all the above divisions of work, a bewildering collection of text-books had accumulated, and the foreign apparatus of Latin study was more prominent in English schools than the text-books written by Englishmen. Nothing, perhaps, better illustrates the progress of Latin studies than the increase in size, exactness and comprehensiveness, of Latin dictionaries, say from that of Elyot's *Dictionary* in 1538 to Holyoke's posthumous monster *Dictionary* of 1676, or, indeed, from the first edition of Francis Holyoke in 1617 to the final form given to it by his son in 1676.

If the output of critical scholarship in Latin by English scholars in this period be relatively small, it is accounted for by the fact that excellent editions of Latin classical writers had already been provided in foreign editions, as, for instance, in the Elzevir texts. What was accomplished was, therefore, rather in the way of selection and compilation from the research work of foreign Goliaths of scholarship.

The highest Latin scholarship was centred in its practical use in writing, as, for instance, in the works of Ussher, Gataker and Selden. As showing a fluent control over rhythm, metre and style, English writers made a high bid for excellence, in the persons of such Latin poets as Owen, Barclay, Dempster, Milton, May and Cowley.[1]

If Latin, then, was a necessity, Greek, also, was a pressing accomplishment, for a large constituency besides the professor and scholar. Nor were Greek experts so few as is often supposed. In *The Authorised Version* of the Bible (1607–11), adequate scholarship in Greek was available in Thomas Ravis, George Abbot, James Montague, Thomson, Savile, Perin, Harmar, William Barlow, Hutchinson, Spencer, Fenton, Rabbett, Sanderson, Dakins. Of the other translators employed on the Old Testament *Apocrypha*, John Duport, Downes and Bois were of still greater renown for their knowledge of Greek. J. Bass Mullinger remarks on the low state of Greek in English universities in the latter part of the sixteenth century. He names Whitaker, Dering, Gabriel Harvey, Aylmer, as almost alone proving that Greek at Cambridge was "not extinct." It was otherwise in the period 1600–60. Andrew Downes, professor of Greek in Cambridge from 1585 to 1625, published lectures on Lysias: *De Caede Eratosthenis* (1593) and on Demosthenes: *De Pace* (1621). Francis Hicks, a gentleman of Worcestershire, made Greek his study and recreation, and published a translation into Latin, with notes, of select dialogues of Lucian, 1634. John Price, one of the greatest scholars of the period, professor of Greek at Pisa, showed great learning in his commentaries on the New Testament, illustrated by references to Greek and Latin Fathers (1646–7). In 1636, Gerard Langbaine published his notes on Longinus. In 1637, John Harmar, regius professor of Greek at Oxford, issued his etymological Greek lexicon. In 1652, Thomas Gataker produced his *Marcus Antoninus*, Greek text, with Latin translation and commentary. Finally, in 1661, Joseph Caryl, Thomas Cockayne, Ralph Venning, William Dell, Matthew Barker, William Adderley, Matthew Mead, Henry Jersey, all nonconformist ministers, jointly published a Greek-English dictionary of all the words in the New Testament.

This list is only representative of the types of works in

---

[1] See the account of John Barclay's *Argenis* and *Euphormionis Satyricon* (*ante*, Vol. IV, pp. 291, 292 ff.). The anonymous prose *Nova Solyma* (1648), with its remarkable scheme of education, deserves mention.

Greek. But we must take into account the undoubtedly deep knowledge of Greek possessed by Gataker (who had been taught by Bois), overshadowed as it is by his Hebrew and other oriental studies; by Ussher with his expert knowledge of Greek geography, astronomy and other Greek material for chronology, his treatise on the origin of the Greek *Septuagint* and the editing of two ancient Greek versions of the *Book of Esther;* by Selden, the great dictator of English learning, in his *Marmora Arundeliana*, 1628, in which he was helped by Patrick Young and Richard James; by John Hales and the Cambridge Platonists; by John Milton; by Philemon Holland[1] and the other translators.

Besides grammar text-books and annotations on Greek authors, there is evidence of ready knowledge of Greek in all kinds of writers, and indications of a not uncommon erudition. Jeremiah Whitaker, of Oakham free school, read all the epistles in the Greek Testament twice every fortnight. John Conant, regius professor of divinity in Oxford, often disputed publicly in Greek in the schools. In the period 1648–59, the disputations at Oxford were often in Greek. Henry Stubbe, in 1651, wrote, in *Horae Subsecivae*, translations into Greek from Randolph and Crashaw. But the readiest in this art was James Duport, who wrote Greek hexameters on the death of the vice-master of Trinity college, Cambridge. He rendered into Homeric verse *The Book of Job* (1637) and *Proverbs, Ecclesiastes* and *The Song of Solomon* (1646), and won high recognition by these feats.

From this brief review, it is evident, especially as to the years immediately preceding 1660, that the attraction in Greek studies is drawing towards Biblical literature; and Hebrew is becoming a necessary learned language. From the time of the new Elizabethan and Stewart foundations of grammar schools, the three "holy" languages—Latin, Greek and Hebrew— had been the aim of protestant workers in education, not only for providing antagonists capable of meeting Catholic opponents in disputation, orally and in books, but, also, for com·

---

[1] Although Philemon Holland cannot be regarded as a scholar in the same sense as Salmasius in *Plinianae Exercitationes* (1629), his translation of Pliny justifies the attribution to him of considerable Latin learning. Holland's translation of Plutarch's *Moralia* (1603) and the *Cyropaedia* of Xenophon (1632) show his knowledge of Greek.

ing "nearer" to the primitive times of the Christian era.   Boys
in school were to learn their catechism in a Greek text, read the
New Testament in Greek, learn, if might be, to speak in Greek.
The aim of school and university, in their Greek studies, was,
in the long run, theological.   Theological study required, in
addition to Latin, a knowledge of the Greek language; if
possible, of Hebrew also; and Busby, at Westminster, tried
the daring experiment of adding oriental languages (Arabic
particularly).   For *The Authorised Version* of the Old Testament (with the *Apocrypha*), thirty-two Hebrew scholars were
chosen.   These included that "second Mithridates" in learning, bishop Lancelot Andrewes; Adrian Saravia, who was
the teacher of the still more learned oriental scholar Nicholas
Fuller; Lively, for thirty years regius professor of Hebrew at
Cambridge; Chaderton, the famous master of Emmanuel
college, Cambridge; Spalding, from whom Gataker learned
the rudiments of Hebrew; John Rainolds of Oxford, the redoubtable controversialist; Holland, of the same university,
"mighty in the Scriptures"; Kilby, rector of Lincoln college;
Miles Smith, of whom Wood says that he had Hebrew "at
his fingers' ends," and to whom Chaldee, Syriac and Arabic
were "almost as familiar as his native tongue"; Samuel Ward,
who was the constant correspondent of Ussher in Biblical and
oriental criticism; John Bois, who was at least as learned in
Greek as in Hebrew; and that "eminent light" in all learning,
bishop Bilson, the great theologian, and a reviewer of the
whole translation.   Cambridge and Oxford were thus fully
represented, and the needs of a great joint work of learning were
readily and adequately met by the supply of scholars.

Whilst *The Authorised Version* of the Bible itself marked an
era, the progress of oriental learning was carried to far greater
heights in the succeeding half century.   William Bedell read
the Greek Fathers and historians in Greek, attained "no mean
skill" in the Syriac, Arabic, Chaldee and Hebrew tongues,
wrote (as already mentioned) an English grammar for Italians
to read English divinity, and produced the Old Testament in
Irish when he became bishop of Kilmore and Ardagh.   James
Ussher, archbishop of Armagh, investigated, by inductive and
comparative methods, a basis of universal chronology.   With
indefatigable zeal, he worked on the antiquities of Irish history,

collected and collated oriental MSS., was permeated with patristic knowledge and did much original critical work in editions of several of the early Fathers—Polycarp and Ignatius and St. Barnabas. He was a voluminous correspondent with all great researchers into antiquity—classical, hebraistic, early Christian and oriental. In short, he was one of the very greatest of English scholars. Thomas Gataker, puritan rector of Rotherhithe, wrote his *Cinnus, sive Adversaria Miscellanea* and learned commentaries on books of the Old Testament, and established for himself as high a reputation for oriental scholarship abroad as in England. John Selden, in his *De Dis Syris* (in Latin), 1617, investigated the history of the idol deities mentioned in the Old Testament, and made his work a comprehensive enquiry into both Syrian and other heathen theologies. Joseph Mede, an encyclopaedic scholar in mathematics, physics, botany, anatomy and astrology, was, also, a profound "Hebrician," and added to the store of scholarship in Egyptology and in the origin of Semitic religions. Brian Walton's great polyglot Bible, in progress from 1652 to 1657, must rank as the highest peak of English co-operative scholarship in a period which was remarkable both in its wealth of eruditional effort and in the significance of its concentration of deepest learning on the Bible centre. This stupendous polyglot Bible uses altogether nine different languages, Greek, Hebrew, Samaritan, Chaldee, Syriac, Arabic, Ethiopic, Persian, Latin, though no part of the Bible is given in more than six or less than three languages simultaneously. In addition to texts, there is a vast body of apparatus, *e.g.* treatises on weights and measures, geographical charts, chronological tables and prolegomena, Chaldee Targums; and one of the six folios consists of various readings and critical remains. Brian Walton, the editor, afterwards bishop of Chester, published an introduction to oriental languages, but was by no means the most learned scholar assisting in the polyglot. Among the collaborators were Ussher and Selden, already mentioned; John Lightfoot, the greatest Hebrew scholar of that age; Abraham Wheelock, first lecturer in Arabic combined with (Anglo-)Saxon at Cambridge, and an acknowledged scholar in Persian; Samuel Clarke, architypographus of Oxford university, "inferior only to Pococke in Eastern learning."

Finally must be mentioned Meric Casaubon, son of Isaac
Casaubon, who published classical commentaries on Marcus
Antoninus (1643), and Epictetus (1659), and had written in
1650 a commentary on the Hebrew and (Anglo-)Saxon languages. Curious as the combination of Old English and Hebrew may seem, it marks the two new directions of English
research in the period, the joy of the discovery that Britain, too,
had antiquities and an ancient church history. From various
sources, the conviction gathered strength that there were
more ancient civilisations than Greece, which threw light on the
classics and on Jewish history. The supply of Hebrew grammars, even of English production, was adequate; and, in 1646,
Edward Leigh's *Critica Sacra* was published, the best Hebrew
lexicon which had yet been produced in England. In 1644, an
ordinance of the Lords and Commons, "after advice had with
the Assembly of Divines," required, amongst other qualifications of candidates for the ministry, "that trial be made of
skill in the Original Tongues by reading the Hebrew and Greek
Testaments and rendering some portions of them into Latin."

Sixteenth century classical studies had provided huge
quarries from which the seventeenth century dug out further
materials; but, with their instruments sharpened and improved
by practice, scholars proceeded to undertake pioneering operations on a wider scale. The pedagogical maxim of "turn all
knowledge to use" was now more sedulously followed. The
knowledge of Hebrew and oriental languages developed with
amazing rapidity, even as scientific studies advanced by leaps
and bounds, after Bacon's summons to make good the deficiencies of past ages in the world of knowledge. In both cases,
however, this splendid progress was due to the incessant and
life-long toil of classical humanists and grammarians in perfecting methods of enquiry and research, in firing the imagination with re-constituted empires and literatures and in
framing standards of evidence. The intellectual recovery of
Roman and Greek literature and antiquities had shown the way
for discoveries in ancient life and institutions, and had taught
men how to treat, for purposes of illustration and comparison,
the civilisations of Hebrew and the other oriental peoples,
our own Old English antiquities and those of ancient Ireland.
The investigation of those languages, literatures and institu-

tions made necessary an enquiry into ancient times, and scholarly methods were required for this. In this respect, scholars like Gataker, Selden, Wheelock and Ussher obey the traditions of Budaeus, Casaubon and Scaliger, though in other directions, and often *non passibus aequis*. But, in the case of English scholars of this period, there is this difference—the scholarly aim in all directions was subservient to the religious interest.

In the universities, theology[1] was the chief subject, and, as J. Bass Mullinger says, with few exceptions, secured the attention of all those "who contended for intellectual distinction, for popularity and for the prizes of high office and social influence." The colleges of the university, whether of medieval or of later foundation, were theological in their intention. The seven liberal arts still remained as a survival, the *quadrivium* of arithmetic, geometry, music and astronomy finding a centre in Gresham college, London, with gentlemen and, especially, physicians, as students. The *trivium* subjects of rhetoric and grammar were at least started at school, and were developed, together with logic, at the university; and the dialectical method was the acknowledged traditional and current discipline of academic training, whether in law, physic, or theology. Often, the student in law or physic took a keen interest in theology. Accordingly, theology had full sway in the universities, and, as students left the university, their knowledge of Greek and Hebrew became contributory to the great divinity stream. Venn has shown that, in 1630, one out of 3600 of the male population of England and Wales proceeded to Oxford or Cambridge as against one in 9000 to-day, and the influence of academic traditions may be judged by the fact that, in the admissions to one college (Gonville and Caius) in Cambridge, in ten years, as many as forty schools are to be found named in the county of Norfolk. Grammar schools (public and private) were particularly numerous in this period, and managed to cast a Scriptural and theological colour around ordinary instruction. Never was there in the

---

[1] Even in mathematics, which might be expected to be detached from theological associations, the *odium theologicum* found vent. Sir Charles Scarborough was a student of mathematics at Caius college, Cambridge. The head of that college saw him reading Clavius upon Euclid, observed *è Societate Jesu* on the title, and said: "By all means, leave off this author, and read protestant mathematical books."

annals of the English church a more eloquent, pious and erudite band of Anglican theologians than at this time.[1] In fact, Selden tells us of his own time: "All confess there never was a more learned Clergy." The university, however, in the time of the commonwealth, was held by some puritans to be a needless, and, indeed, harmful, training-ground. Milton, himself a university man, was disgusted with university methods and curricula. He saw no need for the training of ministers in disputations, to confute papists, involving the reading of Fathers and councils, "immense volumes and of vast charges." A minister's library could be adequately furnished for £60, though "some shame not to value a needful library at £600." A minister can receive his education at any "private house," instead of at the university. "Else to how little purpose," he goes on, "are all those piles of sermons, bodies and marrows of divinity besides all other sciences, in our English tongue; many of the same books which in Latin they read in the university?[2]" Already, the private teaching of men like Gataker, raising "schools of the prophets," had begun, and, after the act of Uniformity, was to grow and prosper until, in the eighteenth century, it provided an education, which Milton had seen to be possible, better than the universities in their decadent state could afford.

Milton's anti-university view, held, he suggests, by the "first reformers of our religion," was the accepted commonplace, for the most part, of the various sectaries into which puritanism had been broken up in the commonwealth. The Calvinistic theocracy could be traced in the Word of God as revealed in the Bible, and all other knowledge was needless. The two parties of the learned supporters of patristic studies— those who felt the necessity of a scholarly background for Scripture teachings, and those who held all knowledge outside of the Word of God as "trash"—represented the whole body of the nation (with the exception of those who held that the true interpretation of the Bible was a direct inspiration from God apart from any human learning) and were united in requiring verbal knowledge of the Bible text, even if they looked for elucidation and commentary on the doctrines derived from it.

[1] See *ante*, Chap. VI.
[1] *Likeliest Means to Remove Hirelings out of the Church*, 1659.

Large portions of the Scriptures were known by heart, not only by ministers, but, also, by the laity, and even by children, who were also well drilled in Foxe's *Book of Martyrs* and other histories of persecutions. Whilst French Huguenot children were trained, Spartanlike, to look forward to dying for the faith, English children, from the earliest age, were disciplined in prayer, in reading books of devotion and in the close knowledge of Bible histories and Bible doctrine. Preachers, like Joshua Hoyle, sometimes were occupied for fifteen years in expounding straight through the whole of the Bible, taking a verse at a time. Hoyle, indeed, started again, and went on for another ten years in the same course. Again, Arthur Hildesham, in 1635, in the puritan concentrative manner, gave 152 lectures on *Psalm* li. Anthony Burgess, in 1656, delivered 145 expository sermons on the seventeenth chapter of *St. John*, and wrote an expository commentary on the first chapter of 2 *Corinthians*, filling a folio of 657 pages. Gataker's *Annotations on the Bible* (1659) occupied a folio volume; but that is small in bulk in comparison with some other performances. Jeremiah Burroughs filled four volumes in a commentary which failed to finish 13 chapters of *Hosea*. William Greenhill required nearly 3000 quarto pages for *Ezekiel*, whilst, for *Job*, Caryl was not content with less than 4690 folio pages. Theodore Haak, in 1657, published, in two folio volumes, a translation of the *Dutch Annotations* on the Bible, an outcome of the synod of Dort, in 1618, but this large work includes a translation of the Bible. The *English Annotations*, in two folio volumes, represents the best English exegetical work of the period, including amongst its writers Ley, William Gouge, Meric Casaubon, Francis Taylor and, once more, the encyclopaedic scholar, Thomas Gataker. As a work of systematic compilation, English effort in this direction was crowned by Matthew Poole's *Synopsis Criticorum Bibliorum* (in Latin), in five folio volumes, taking in its survey all available criticisms and annotations hitherto produced. Poole was at work on this gigantic task 1660–76.[1] By means of compendia, abridgments, epitomes of all kinds, Scripture

[1] A Latin commentary, still larger though not so laboured, *Critici Sacri*, was published in London in 1660, in nine folio volumes. The latter contains 9679, and Poole's *Synopsis* 5109, double-columned pages.

histories, geographies, concordances, expository lectures and sermons, the vast accretion of Scripture learning was disseminated throughout the land by the 10,000 clergy, not to count leaders of sectaries and voluntary preachers.

Collections of systematic divinity in "marrows," "bodies" and "sums" were extremely numerous and supplemented Scripture knowledge in all directions. On the subject of church government, innumerable treatises were written, but none approached in solid intellectual power Hooker's *Ecclesiastical Polity*, of the Elizabethan period, or Richard Field's *Of the Church* (finished 1610). In doctrinal exposition, bishop Pearson's *Exposition of the Creed* (1659) must be regarded as a masterpiece of the period.

Some of the characteristics of the time, emerging from the whole of these manifestations of learning in patristic, classical, oriental and Biblical culture must be briefly noted. The medieval conception of the authority of Aristotle and scholasticism was shattered. It was transferred in all its ingrained strength and with infinitely increased brooding awe to the Bible. Science, even, could not yet make effective claim to detachment and self-contained aims. But Bacon's view of *antiquitas saeculi juventus mundi* was elaborated in a learned work (1627) by George Hakewill, a vindication of the superior culture and progress of the modern, as against the ancient, world. A spirit of optimism favoured both literary and scientific research, for the age realised its control over the methods and instruments of enquiry. The Greeks and Romans could not retain the absolute allegiance even of scholars, for, after all, they were heathens, and the new light shed on the Bible, and the grand vision of a theocracy on earth, made attractive to the whole nation, learned and unlearned, a willingness to pay the price of knowledge, within the restricted sphere of Biblical studies. Hence, we notice psychologically, there were developed enormous industry in learning, endurance in listening to preachers and teachers, tenacious memory and the power of visualising and concentrating the thoughts on Bible heroes, Bible stories, Bible language and Bible aspirations. Scripture students were indefatigable workers. Bishop Morton was at his studies before four o'clock in the morning, even after he was 80 years of age. Matthew

Poole rose at three or four o'clock, ate a raw egg at eight or nine, another at twelve and continued his studies till late in the afternoon. Sir Matthew Hale, for many years, studied sixteen hours a day. For several years John Owen did not allow himself more than four hours' sleep. Feats of memory are as remarkable for their frequency as for their comprehensiveness, and were practised from early childhood in the repeating of sermons, in the learning of Latin grammar and in almost every academic discipline. Moreover, the number of references to memory testifies to the conscious cultivation of the art. The exercise of visualisation of the Old Testament histories was heightened by stories of martyrs; and the family tradition and household culture that made these events "real as life" in puritan homes supplied the mental basis for justifying doctrine and precept. In short, the scholarship and learning of this period, by their direct bearing upon the Bible, permeated and transfigured the national life in a rare degree, giving it, in spite of all its excesses and deficiencies, a strenuousness, sobriety, and, on the whole, a sincerity, probably never so largely sustained, by book learning, in any age, and rarely in any country. And yet, of the highest and purest scholarship, it is true, as Mark Pattison says, in reference to Casaubon:

To search antiquity with a polemical object is destructive of that equilibrium of the reason, the imagination and the taste, that even temper of philosophical calm, that singleness of purpose, which are required in order that a past time may mirror itself on the mind in true outline and proportions.[1]

[1] *Isaac Casaubon*, p. 466.

CHAPTER XIV

English Grammar Schools

I T was but slowly, and long after the reformation had been carried into effect in England, that the transition from the scholastic to the humanistic theory of education began to be perceptible among the grammar schools of the country. An endeavour has, indeed, been made in recent years to show that the tendencies at work during the reign of Edward VI were essentially reactionary, and that nothing of much importance resulted from the liberal and enlightened policy of Somerset. Such a theory, however, is very far from being borne out by the evidence, which proves that, not only were important new foundations established under his auspices, and subsequently, by Northumberland, but that the views which found expression in their organisation and discipline were virtually identical with those which afterwards obtained under Elizabeth. The great queen, although holding the memory of Somerset in aversion, had always cherished a sisterly regard for the youthful monarch, whose remarkable precocity of intellect, love of learning and strong religious convictions (harmonising, to a great extent, with her own) had commanded the admiration and respect alike of scholars and of politicians during his lifetime. The influences that predominated during the reign of Mary, on the other hand, had been reactionary, and became yet more so under the joint rule of the queen and her consort. But, so soon as Elizabeth found herself "supreme governor" of the church, the Edwardian policy in relation to education was, forthwith, adopted by her as her own—much as the *Prayer Book* of 1552 was again prescribed, with but slight alterations, for use in the English ritual; and it is to be borne in mind that Burghley had been the personal friend of Somerset, under whom he served as an officer of the crown. Accordingly, it is in the reforms advocated during the reign of Edward, that the subsequent designs of our most discerning legislators are rightly to be regarded as taking their initiative, however much they might be baffled or delayed, for a time, by the selfish aims of courtiers intent on little else save their personal enrichment and that of their families and dependants. In the rapacity of those who should have been foremost in setting an example of self-abnegation, the young king and his adviser encountered, indeed, a resistance which they were but very partially able to overcome.

The latest researches in the history of our public schools exhibit Winchester and Eton, the two most ancient of their number, as designed to enjoy peculiar advantages and an exceptional independence, while, at the same time, occupying the position of training institutions in relation to centres of more advanced education—the former to New college, Oxford, the latter to King's college, Cambridge.[1] As Winchester college had now been in existence somewhat more, and Eton college but a little less, than two centuries, it becomes interesting to compare the progress of the one with the other,[2] and that of both, in turn, with the development of other great public schools which were subsequently founded—that is to say, with St. Paul's, Christ's Hospital and Harrow, with Westminster and Merchant Taylors', with Shrewsbury and Rugby: all of which, with the exception of the first-named, represent the original design of Edward VI, as carried into effect after Somerset's death by Northumberland and, subsequently, by Mary and Elizabeth.

Winchester, the most ancient and conservative of all, was still governed mainly by the statutes of William of Wykeham. It had been distinctly menaced with dissolution by the Chantries act of 1547; but the actual result of the royal injunctions was little more, in the direction of reform, than to make the Latin or English version optional in the study of the text of the New Testament, although prescribing the use of the vernacular by the scholars at grace and at their devotions. The school

---

[1] See *ante*, Vol. II, pp. 405, 406.

[2] The features of resemblance and of direct imitation between Winchester and Eton have already been referred to in Vol. II, Chap. xv.

continued to be recruited mainly from the diocese of Winchester and from the midland counties; it had educated Chicheley, Chandler (afterwards dean of Hereford), Warham and Grocyn; its loyalty never swerved. When King Edward visited the city in 1552, commoners and scholars had alike composed congratulatory verses; they did the same when the marriage of Mary and Philip was celebrated in their ancient cathedral; and, again, when Elizabeth visited the college in 1570. But, in 1560, the college petitioned successfully, along with Eton, to be allowed the use of the *Latin Prayer Book;* while the number and importance of its converts to Rome, in the latter part of the century, was a symptom that could not be disregarded. During James's reign, more than one visitation, together with a series of injunctions issued by archbishop Bancroft, clearly indicate abuses, both in management and discipline, which betray the fact that the financial administration by the master and fellows was conceived on principles not a whit more disinterested than those of the commissioners of Edward VI. Eton, on the other hand, now begins to enter on a career of marked improvement, after a series of depressing experiences. It had seen the lilies tremble on the college shield, and ultimately disappear, altogether, from the shield of the foundation at Cambridge. But the wise supervision exercised by Waynflete, as provost, continued to operate after his promotion to the see of Winchester, and was continued, with equal ability, by his successor, William Westbury, promoted from the headmastership. It is scarcely an exaggeration, indeed, to assert that the rule of the latter, which extended over a whole generation, was the salvation of the college, for it was by Westbury's courage and tact that the designs of Edward IV—to whom, far more justly than to the sixth of the name, the epithet of "despoiler" might have been applied—were ultimately frustrated. Had the fourth Edward been able to accomplish his purpose, the entire foundation of Eton college would have become merged in that of the dean and chapter at Windsor, and the name of Henry VI would have disappeared as that of a founder.[1] As it was, the progress of the college was materially checked, for many years after; and, not until about the time that the college on the banks of

[1] See Maxwell Lyte, *Hist. of Eton College*, chap. IV.

the Cam was beginning to acquire new lustre by the completion of its noble chapel, did something of a like prestige begin
to gather round the college on the banks of the Isis. The
revenues of Eton, however, continued to decline; although, in
1536, along with Winchester, it succeeded in obtaining ex-
emption from payment of tithes; and it was only with the accession of Edward VI that any appreciable change for the
better took place. The interest shown by that monarch in
Eton affairs is probably attributable, in part, to the fact that
Richard Cox, who had preceded Udall in the headmastership
(1528–34), was both the young king's tutor and almoner;
while the increase in the number of oppidans, noticeable after
the dissolution of the monasteries, may be explained by the
fact that they brought with them (although contrary to the
founder's designs) a certain augmentation of their teachers'
scanty incomes. In the first year of Edward's reign, the college
acquired certain advowsons and estates which had before been
held by the suppressed orders.[1] Cox's successor, Udall—
described by Walter Haddon as the "best schoolmaster and
the greatest beater" of his time—can hardly be said to have
raised the reputation either of the Winchester where he had
been educated or of the college which he was called upon to
rule, although he so far outlived the obloquy which he encountered as to die master of the school at Westminster. But
the precarious condition of affairs throughout the country,
which menaced every institution and every office, is also to be
recognised in the fact that the headmastership of Eton was
held by no less than twenty-one individuals during the sixteenth century. The function of the provost was to exercise a
general superintendence over the financial administration and
also to ensure a due performance of the duties attaching to
each subordinate office—not excepting that of the headmaster himself. The appointment of Henry Savile to the
provostship was wrung from the queen only by his own repeated solicitations, and, moreover, it was a direct infringe-
ment of the college statute, which enjoined that a candidate
should be in holy orders, and vested the election itself in the
provost and fellows of King's; but, notwithstanding, the royal
intervention proved eminently beneficial in the sequel, and

[1] Lipscombe, G., *Hist. and Ant. of the County of Buckingham*, IV., 474.

Savile's claims were indisputable. He had travelled much; he was a savant and a collector of manuscripts; and it was chiefly through the influence of Burghley (no undiscerning patron) that, some ten years before, he had been promoted to the wardenship of Merton college—an office which he continued to hold, in conjunction with the provostship, down to the day of his death. His fine presence, great powers of work and genuine attainments eminently fitted him, indeed, for the discharge of official duties, and, although not free from the reproach of excessive eagerness in the accumulation of wealth, it might be urged in extenuation that he showed almost equal readiness to part with it again, in promoting worthy objects. On succeeding to office, he made it one of his first cares to restore and augment the library, the fabric of which, at that time, was in a ruinous condition, while the collection itself had remained very much what it was at the death of Edward VI. As a master, however, Savile inspired awe rather than affection; with the King's men, he was distinctly unpopular, owing to his obvious partiality for promising "aliens." The oft-cited story, preserved by John Aubrey, recording his antipathy against "wits," is hardly to be taken seriously, and was probably little more than a sarcasm, designed to convey his majestic contempt for those artifices wherewith the ingenious schoolboy, from time immemorial, has sought to produce upon a master the impression of a painful studiousness which has no actual existence.[1] The men whom he promoted to fellowships at Merton—to name only Henry Cuffe, afterwards regius professor of Greek, Francis Mason (author of *Vindex Ecclesiae Anglicanae*), Edward Reynolds and John Earle, afterwards bishops of Norwich and Worcester respectively—together with his discerning patronage of the then struggling study of mathematics in Merton, certainly suggest something more than a stolid preference for mere plodding industry over original power and special aptitudes.

In the meantime, not a few of the newly founded grammar

---

[1] The sense in which the term "wit" is used by Aubrey (*Lives*, II, ii, 525) differs, probably, from that in which it is employed by Hacket (see *post*, p. 378), who belonged to an earlier generation, and it may be questioned whether Savile himself used the word. It was not until after the restoration that it came to denote ingenuity of contrivance rather than intellectual capacity.

schools, as they saw the endowments intended for their benefit intercepted by the despoiler, must have heard with envy how Winchester and Eton had escaped a like fate comparatively intact. Of this, Sedbergh affords a noteworthy illustration. Roger Lupton, a native of the town, and afterwards provost of Eton, had already founded there, in 1528, a chantry, "to pray for his sowle and kepe a free schole." As, however, he saw his foundation menaced with destruction, and, at the same time, noted the advantages which had resulted from the affiliation of the above colleges to New and King's respectively, he resolved on the institution of a grammar school (on the site of his chantry) which should stand in similar relation to St. John's college, Cambridge. Among those who had enriched themselves from the spoils of the dissolved monasteries was Sir Anthony Denny, an old "Pauline," and also a member of St. John's; and, possibly, it was some misgiving with respect to the sources of much of his acquired wealth that led him, in his later years, to contemplate an act of reparation and establish Sedbergh school on a firm foundation. St. John's still preserves the letter (1549), composed by Roger Ascham, in which the college authorities thank the knight for his services, and, after observing that Sedbergh has always sent up excellent scholars, represent themselves as still by no means free from anxiety with regard to its fate. It was not, indeed, until after Lupton and Sir Anthony had both been dead, the former eleven years, the latter about two, that, in February, 1551, the royal grant was issued for the establishment of a free grammar school, to which St. John's college was to nominate the master on condition that it appropriated two fellowships and eight scholarships for "scollers of Sedberg"[1]— an item of evidence which serves to show that, side by side with the process of confiscation which went on during the reign of Edward, there were other forces in operation, some of which, at least, served not only to stay the hand of the despoiler, but, also, to call into existence a succession of new foundations. That the main impulse in connection with this latter movement proceeded from the young king himself hardly admits of reasonable doubt. In the language of Freeman, "it was the one act" in Edward's reign "in which the public good was at

[1] Baker's *Hist. of St. John's College* (ed. Mayor), 1, 374.

all thought of," and the king, "*of his own act*, applied a part
of the revenues of the suppressed colleges and chantries to the
foundation of that great system of grammar schools which
bear his name." The preamble of the royal charter given to
the school at Louth (the town where the Lincolnshire rising in
1534 first broke out), in the fifth year of his reign, may be
cited as an illustration of the convictions by which Edward,
throughout, was actuated:

"We have," says this document, "always coveted, with a most
exceeding, vehement, and ardent desire, that good literature and
discipline might be diffused and propagated throughout all parts
of our Kingdom, as wherein the best government and administration of affairs consists; and therefore, with no small earnestness,
have we been intent on the liberal institution of Youth, that it may
be brought up to science, in places of our Kingdom most proper
and suitable for such functions, it being, as it were, *the foundation and growth of our Commonwealth.*" [1]

In some cases, indeed, as, for example, at Bedford and at
Morpeth (both 1552) and at St. Albans (1553), the initiative
proceeded from the mayor and burgesses of the community.
In others, a like design was carried into effect only through
private benevolence, as at Whitchurch (1550) and at Leeds
(1552); while, in not a few cases, the endowment was altogether inadequate and eventually died out, and the school
with it. But, after due allowance for such deductions, it
remains undeniable that, in this, the twentieth century, the
foundations at Bath, Birmingham, Bradford, Bury St. Edmund's, Chelmsford, Crediton, Grantham, Lichfield, Ludlow
(in Shropshire), Norwich, Sherborne, Skipton, Tonbridge,
Wisbech, are to be seen as not merely existing, but, for the
most part, flourishing, institutions, standing in direct connection with the universities, and dignified by the names of a long
succession of distinguished men whom, in the course of the
three centuries and a half that have elapsed since their creation
or re-endowment by the youthful Edward, they have educated
within their walls. The endeavour that has been made to represent Edward himself as a mere tool in the hands of his ministers, and the numerous endowments that still bear his name as

[1] Carlisle, N., *Endowed Grammar Schools*, I, 822.

having been so largely absorbed by the cupidity of his courtiers as altogether to nullify their legitimate application, is, indeed, substantially rebutted by the above enumeration.

During the reign of Mary, there followed a marked diminution in the number of new foundations; but the grammar schools at Oundle (1556), Repton (1557) and Brentwood (1557) received their charters, these being the most noteworthy examples, and the two latter having been endowed by private benefactors. Soon after the accession of Elizabeth, however, the movement acquired fresh force under the influence of Burghley and archbishop Parker, and upwards of one hundred and thirty free grammar schools trace back their beginning to her reign. With the accession of James, his able minister Salisbury might plausibly have urged, amid the financial disorder with which he had to contend, that, so much having recently been done, the further endowment of new centres might be left to a more convenient season. This course, however, the evidence shows, neither he nor his successor was inclined to pursue; and, although the monarch himself had no more notion of economy than Edward, and his reign lasted only half as long as that of his immediate predecessor, the number of schools founded during the period was, proportionably, greater. But, inasmuch as, in the southern and eastern counties, the want had already, to a great extent, been supplied, it was chiefly in the west, the midlands and the north, that the new foundations rose, and these, again, for the most part, where neither monastery nor chantry had previously existed—although at Repton it had been the design of the founder, Sir John Port, to found a chantry school.

In the meantime, in the capital itself there had risen up those great schools which, alike in their conception and administration, presented a singular contrast to the exclusiveness and immobility of Eton and Winchester. Erasmus had given it as his opinion that there was no better guardian of such institutions than the married citizen, the *cives conjugati*, a point with respect to which his varied experience of seats of learning, both abroad and in England, certainly entitled him to be heard, and a view to which subsequent history lends considerable support. The civic founder assumed, indeed, in relation to education, an attitude in singular contrast to that

of the courtly despoiler. "Like as a father pitieth his children," so the wealthy merchants of London, roused, it may be, in
the first instance, to a sense of their duty by appeals from
divines and philanthropists, proved equal to a great occasion,
and gave liberally of their substance to the institution and
maintenance of those historic foundations which have entitled
the memories of John Colet, Sir Thomas White and Thomas
Sutton, to take rank with those of the noblest benefactors of
their country. The school founded (1509) by dean Colet, with
William Lily for its master, still used the *Aeditio*, or accidence,
compiled by the former and the Latin *Syntax* of the latter[1]
(both in 1509 and in English), as well as the less elementary
Syntax written by Lily in Latin (1513), compilations which
may, indeed, be regarded as the original of all the sixteenth
and seventeenth century Latin grammars in use in the schools
of England; while Nowell's *Catechism*, either in its longer or its
abbreviated form—the choice between the Latin and the
English version being left to the discretion of the master—
may be said to have been the corresponding manual of religious instruction for nearly the same period, its use, in one
form or the other, being made imperative on all schoolmasters
by the canons issued under Bancroft's auspices in 1604.
Meanwhile, St. Paul's school had continued to prosper until
it became the pride and admiration of London. Its catholicity
—its doors being open "to the children of all nations and
countries indifferently"—the discernment manifest in every
detail alike of its curriculum and of its discipline, together
with the sound sense and scientific insight which had guided
the construction and arrangement of its new buildings, had
won for the school an almost unrivalled reputation, which was
further enhanced when Richard Mulcaster[2] was appointed to
the office of highmaster. His successor, Alexander Gill the
elder, numbered John Milton among his pupils, and deserves
mention here as one who, in his *Logonomia Anglica*, showed
that he was well read in the poets of his day.

Under the same auspices, and with the same governors,

---

[1] For an account of these two manuals, see Foster Watson's *English Grammar
Schools to* 1660, chap. xv. See, also, *ante*, Vol. III, pp. 485–489, as to the
curriculum in English schools.

[2] As to Mulcaster, see *ante*, Vol. III, pp. 494, 495.

had been founded (1541) the Mercers' school, which rose on the site of the ancient hospital of St. Thomas of Accon, one of the once famous order of the Knights Hospitallers. The house of that order had been closed in 1538; but, three years later, it was opened as a free grammar school, and already reckoned Colet, Sir Thomas Gresham and Davenant (afterwards bishop of Salisbury) among its *alumni;* while, to quote the language of Carlisle, it subsequently "vied, both in number and eminence with the greatest schools in London and in the disputations of scholars on festival days."[1]

At Westminster, the existence of the school might be traced back to the fourteenth century, the roll of the treasury of Queen Eleanor's manors recording, in the year 1386–7, a payment to the master of grammar and 22 boys; but Henry VIII first established it on a definite basis. During the reign of Elizabeth, the school had been brought into direct relation with Trinity college, Cambridge; and, in 1575, Gabriel Goodman, dean of Westminster, had succeeded in introducing some novel provisions in the regulations laid down by his predecessor, among them that relating to the admission of scholars, whereby it was now enacted that no boy should be admitted under the age of eight or allowed to stay after eighteen—limitations rendered necessary by the fact that parents would sometimes send their children when scarcely over five. Gabriel Goodman, notable as having been a member of three Cambridge colleges in succession, and a benefactor of the university, was, throughout his life, an active promoter of education and learning. In his capacity of dean, he may, indeed, seem somewhat dwarfed in comparison with his two successors—bishop Andrewes, and the last of the ecclesiastical lord chancellors, John Williams. But, both the latter had some cause to be grateful to their predecessor for his thoughtful bequest of that pleasant college retreat at Chiswick, where the elms which he had planted afforded to subsequent generations grateful shade in summer and "a retiring place" from infection when the plague visited the capital. Of Andrewes, Hacket tells us that he never walked to Chiswick for his recreation "without a brace of the young fry; and, in that way-faring leisure

[1] *Endowed Grammar Schools,* II, 42.

had a singular dexterity to fill those narrow vessels with a funnel"; while, at the college itself, he often

sent for the uppermost scholars to his lodgings at night, and kept them with him from eight till eleven, unfolding to them the best rudiments of the Greek tongue, and the elements of the Hebrew Grammar, and all this he did to boys without any compulsion of correction; nay, I never heard him utter so much as a word of austerity among us.

Of Williams himself, his biographer tells us that

he was assiduous in the school, and miss'd not sometimes every week, if he were resident in the College, both to dictate lectures to the several classes, and to take account of them. The choicest *wits* had never such encouragement for praise, and reward.[1]

Under Williams's successor Laud, further regulations were introduced, among which the most noteworthy was that whereby

the best scholars in the seventh forme were appointed as Tutors to reade and expound places of Homer, Virgil, Horace, and Euripides, etc. . . . at those times . . . wherein the scholars were in the schole, in expectation of the Master.[2]

The Merchant Taylors' school, founded in 1561, was a no less conspicuous example of civic liberality and generosity of spirit than was St. Paul's—its statutes, indeed, being little more than a transcript of those given by Colet to the earlier foundation, and its scholars, in like manner, being admissible from "all nations and countries." Within five years of the time when the school was first opened, on a site between Cannon street and the Thames, it had already acquired additional importance by the fact that Sir Thomas White, a member of the company's court, having recently founded the college of St. John the Baptist at Oxford, proceeded, on drawing up certain additional statutes for the society, to enact that forty-

---

[1] Hacket, *Life of Williams*, I, 45.

[2] See the account of the daily routine of a Westminster schoolboy's life (*c.* 1610–20), printed, from a transcript preserved in the State Paper office, in G. F. Russell Barker's *Memoir of Richard Busby* (1895), pp. 77–82. The transcript is said to be in the handwriting of Laud, who was a prebendary of Westminster from 1621 to 1628.

three scholarships on the foundation should be restricted to scholars from Merchant Taylors', such scholars to be "assigned and named by continual succession," while, at the same time, he retained the nominations in his own hands. This measure—suggested, obviously, by the example of the founders of Winchester and Eton—was at once productive of a considerable increase in the numbers. In certain additional statutes for his college, the founder had also directed that, in elections to scholarships, poverty should weigh in favour of a candidate, and "Tobie Matthew," the president of St. John's, had, consequently, sought to evade the obligation to elect forty-three scholars entirely from a school in which a lower class element was, at first, undoubtedly large. He grounded his defence on the plea that the college itself was depressed by straitened resources. Fortunately, however, sundry bequests for the specified purpose of aiding poor students afterwards fell in, and served, to some extent, to alleviate the pressure while the institution of examinations, to be held three times in the course of the year, did much to raise the school in public estimation; and the company itself, assembled in court, was able to declare that Merchant Taylors' was "a schoole for liberty most free, being open expressly for poore men's children, as well of all nations as for the merchaunt tailors themselves."[1] In 1607, a banquet, honoured by the presence of the king, when prince Charles was admitted a freeman of the company and Ben Jonson composed an interlude for the occasion, seems to have ushered in a period of growing prosperity, which lasted unbroken until the destruction of the school buildings in the great fire of 1666. It was not all parents, however, who could contemplate with equanimity the prospect of their offspring being educated along with those of the poor; and when, within a few years after the above banquet, Thomas Farnaby, a former postmaster of Merton college, well acquainted with the educational system of the Jesuits, opened a school in Goldsmiths' alley, it was soon sufficiently obvious that he had ministered to a genuine want. He had boarders as well as day scholars; his class-rooms formed an imposing structure and his whole premises were palatial; his ushers were well drilled in their special work. His numbers, consequently, soon rose

[1] Staunton, *Great Schools of England* (ed. 1869), p. 177.

to three hundred, of whom the great majority were the sons of titled families.[1] He was himself an excellent classical scholar with a European reputation. At the royal request, he compiled a new Latin grammar avowedly designed to supersede the labours of Lily, and also brought out, in 1612, an annotated text of Juvenal and Persius which went through numerous editions, and was followed by other classical authors. It was about the same time, that John Brinsley, at Ashby-de-la-Zouch, propounded, in his *Ludus Literarius,* a new mode of translation, and invested the teaching of grammar with unprecedented importance by his elaboration of method.[2] His austere, though not harsh, discipline inspired parents with more than usual confidence; but, unfortunately, his puritan sympathies brought his flourishing school under the episcopal ban, and he was fain to retire to London.

The majority of the grammar schools throughout the country continued to recruit their numbers from a certain definite area, represented by the parish or the county in which they had been founded, according to the conditions prescribed in their respective charters. Generally speaking, the *free school*— by which we must understand "a school in which learning is given without pay"[3] — was open to the sons of all freemen within the specified limits. A *public school,* on the other hand, was open to the whole kingdom,[4] and, in some cases, to scholars of other nationalities, and thus, almost necessarily, involved

[1] See *Autobiography* of Sir John Bramston, the younger (himself one of Farnaby's pupils), *Camden Soc. Pub.* (1845), p. 101.

[2] Foster Watson, in his *English Grammar Schools* (pp. 262–7), has supplied us with a detailed comparison of Brinsley's method with that of Roger Ascham.

[3] "It has been denied that this was the meaning of 'free (grammar) school,' *Lat. libera schola grammaticalis,* as the official designation of many schools founded under Edward VI," but see Murray's *Dictionary, s.v.* "Free," § 32 b, for the evidence in favour of the affirmative. We have also to bear in mind how largely, in the sixteenth and seventeenth centuries, teachers, even at the universities, taught *gratis,* and, more especially, the Jesuits. A passage cited by Leach, A. F., in his *English Schools at the Reformation,* p. 82, shows clearly, however, the sense in which the term was accepted in the year 1548, a chantry priest being there described as licensed "to kepe a gramer scoole *half-free,* that ys to saye, taking of scolers lerning gramer 8*d.* the quarter, and of others lerning to rede 4*d.* the quarter," that is to say, receiving payment of only a *moiety.*

[4] See *Letter from Samuel Butler, D.D., to Henry Brougham, Esq., M.P.,* 1821, in which the writer, himself master of Shrewsbury, assumes the correctness of the above definition. Printed in Baker's *History of St. John's College* (ed. Mayor), II, 933–4.

payment, at least for maintenance or board. Of the gradual change of the former into the latter, the foundation of John Lyon, a yeoman of Harrow, affords a remarkable illustration. In the year 1571, he had procured a charter for a free grammar school in the village of Harrow-upon-the-Hill, at which children of the village were to receive gratuitous instruction. In 1590, having duly endowed the same, he appointed six governors and created four exhibitions, two at Oxford and two at Cambridge, of the value of five pounds each. But it was not until the middle of the seventeenth century that this modest beginning expanded into a project for attracting the sons of well-to-do parents to a centre which, by virtue of its healthiness, proximity to the capital and excellent system of instruction, offered an unprecedented combination of advantages; while its unrestricted extension was facilitated by the full discretion originally conferred on the governors to modify the statutes as they thought fit.

The free school founded at Rugby, in 1567, by Laurence Sheriff, "citizen and grocer of London," remained, for a long time, in like manner, comparatively obscure, being much hampered by the founder's revocation of a money grant, and deriving, for many years, but a slender revenue from that "Conduit Close," on the outskirts of London, which afterwards developed into an El Dorado.

The annals of Shrewsbury present us with a complete contrast. Endowed by Edward VI, at the joint petition of the burgesses of the town and the gentlemen of the county, its charter remained in abeyance throughout the reign of Mary; and it first rose into repute under the rule of Thomas Ashton, fellow of St. John's college, Cambridge, in the reign of Elizabeth. Ashton was himself entrusted with the compilation of the statutes, wherein it was enjoined that, in all admissions, the "godliest, poorest, and best learned" should be preferred. Shrewsbury, moreover, had the whole of Shropshire at its back, and the first register of admissions (1562), containing two hundred and eighty-nine names, among them sons of knights and esquires, showed the proportion of "strangers" to "townsmen" to be unusually large. In 1564, Philip Sidney and Fulke Greville were admitted on the same day; and, under John Meighen, a layman, who filled the office of headmaster more than half a century (1583–1635), the numbers rose rapidly, so that Camden, in 1586, could venture to declare that Shrewsbury was "the best filled school of all England." The relations maintained by Shrewsbury school with St. John's college help us to follow its subsequent history; and, from the correspondence that went on between the two foundations, we learn that the fortunes of the school, in the reign of James I, passed through a period of decline: so much so, indeed, that, in 1627, the bailiffs report that the masters are resigning, "to the generall grief of the Towne," and that the school is "in very great decay."

Of the five schools which rose within the city walls of the capital, none appealed more strongly to civic sympathy than that of Christ's Hospital, especially designed for "young fatherless children," who were to be admitted to receive both maintenance and education in the ancient buildings which had formerly given shelter to the suppressed community of the Grey Friars. The foundation, along with the other royal hospitals, had been marked out for endowment both by Henry VIII and by his son, and it was only eleven days before the death of the latter that the young king signed the charter whereby the governors were to be allowed to receive land in mortmain or to acquire it to the value of "foure thousand marks by the yeare." But, to quote the words of its historian, "Christ's Hospital owed its start, as it has owed its steady continuance in well-doing, to the generosity of the citizens of London";[1] and the pressing needs of the poorer London population may be discerned in the fact, that all that was requisite for admission was a certificate, that "the child was above four years of age and born in wedlock," and that its father was a freeman. Unfortunately, there had been no definite apportionment of the original endowment among the different hospitals, and, amid the conflicting claims of these institutions, those of the school were passed over. Had it not been for the liberality of its own governors, indeed, the new foundation would, probably, have been either dissolved, or compelled to send adrift a large proportion of the four hundred children to which, towards the close of the sixteenth century, it gave shelter and instruction. At the critical

[1] Annals of Christ's Hospital (ed. 1908), p. 31.

juncture, however, permanent relief was afforded by dame Ramsey (widow of a former lord mayor), through whose munificence the school came into possession of estates then producing four hundred pounds a year, together with a fund for the maintenance of four scholars at the university, as well as the advowsons of five livings. In the time of William Camden, the historian—himself an *alumnus* of the school, and, subsequently, headmaster (1593) of Westminster school—the numbers had reached six hundred.

In the fabric which had been the house of another suppressed religious order, the same that traced back its origin to the Grande Chartreuse in southern France, Charterhouse began its existence in 1611. Its founder, Thomas Sutton, a native of Lincoln, was a successful government official, whose views had been enlarged by travel, who was conversant with several modern languages and who had also gained considerable military experience as an officer in the regular forces under Elizabeth. But his chief aim, throughout life, was the acquisition of wealth; and, at the age of fifty, he further augmented what was already a large fortune by marriage with a wealthy widow. His wife, however, bore him no children; and, having settled in London, he formed the resolve of devoting his vast means (he was supposed to be the wealthiest commoner in England) to the foundation of a hospital and free school within the precincts of an ancient mansion, which, since the dissolution of the Carthusian order, had been the residence of successive members of the nobility, and was now purchased by Sutton from Thomas, earl of Suffolk, for £13,000. The premises of Howard house, as it had before been designated, included, not only "divers courts, a wilderness, orchards, walks and gardens," but, also, certain "mesuages" adjoining, and, consequently, afforded ample accommodation for both hospital and school. The orders relating to the latter—first promulgated in 1627—are noteworthy as marking a distinctive advance in the conception of the public school. It was required, with respect to each of the forty scholars on the foundation, that he should come "sufficiently provided with good apparel," that he should be of "modest and mannerly behaviour," "be orderly and seasonably dieted, cleanly and wholesomely lodged." None was to be admitted under the age of ten or above fourteen. The masters were not only enjoined to be "moderate in correction," but, also, "to *observe the nature and ingeny* [sic] *of their scholars* and instruct them accordingly." Latin prayers and collects were to usher in, and to end, the studies of each day; while the upper form were to be provided with Greek Testaments for their use in chapel.

Other foundations, standing in close connection with the capital, were those of St. Saviour's in Southwark (1562) and St. Olave's (1570), both of which represented the voluntary principle, as originating in the spontaneous action of the inhabitants and being designed for the free education of sons of parishioners exclusively. That of Stratford-le-Bow (1617) was founded for the parishes of Stratford, Bow and Bromley-St.-Leonard, by Sir John Jolles, to afford instruction in "grammar and Latin." "Alleyn's College of God's Gift in Dulwich" (1619), instituted along with certain almshouses, was opened with a formal ceremony, at which lord chancellor Bacon presided. Few similar foundations, however, have offered a more melancholy example of the frustration of the designs of the founder. It was not until 1858 that the existing college was established by act of parliament, and put in possession of ample revenues which, for more than two centuries, had been misappropriated.

We may here mention that, within the period covered by the present chapter, was born in Southwark, near by London Bridge, John Harvard (1607), who, after graduating at Cambridge, where he was a member of Emmanuel college, set sail for New England, and left half his estate in endowment of a school or college devoted to "the education of the English and Indian youth of this country in knowledge and godlynes," a school which has developed into the Cambridge of the New world.

With the advance of the seventeenth century, and the growing influence of puritanism, the position and relations of provincial grammar schools became, for a time, considerably modified. Hitherto, the close connection with the universities of most of those which possessed any endowment—the necessary result of their scholars being eligible to scholarships or exhibitions at one or other of the colleges, while the master was generally a graduate of Oxford or of Cambridge—had led to the education they imparted being strictly classical in character and modelled on the requirements of a university curriculum. In Rutland, for example, the statutes and ordinances given by Robert Johnson (archdeacon of Leicester, 1599–1625), for the free grammar schools which he founded at Oakham and Uppingham, and drawn up in the first year of the reign of Charles I, were strictly on the traditional lines—the twenty-four governors being required to be chiefly "parsons," including the bishop, dean and archdeacon of the diocese, a "knight, esquire, or gentleman" being only occasionally admissible; the master was to be a "master of arts, and diligent in his place, painful in the educating of children in good learning and religion, such as can make a Greek and Latin verse,"—the usher "a godly, learned, and discreet man, one that can make true Latin, both in prose and verse," and bound "not to disgrace the Schoolmaster or animate the scholars in undutifulness towards him." Such were the conditions prescribed even by one who was the close friend of Laurence Chaderton, master of Emmanuel college, Cambridge (under whom that society assumed its especially puritan character), and who sent his son, Abraham Johnson, to be educated there, with the express sanction of the founder, Sir Walter Mildmay. In fact, the influence of the local clergy, in the earlier part of the century, made it difficult for a founder, desirous of introducing any innovations with respect either to subjects taught or methods of instruction, to open a school, that claimed to be preparatory to the universities, with reasonable prospect of success.

In the course of another ten years, however, the ascendency gained by presbyterians and independents, first in the Westminster assembly and, subsequently, in parliament, began to operate, eventually culminating in the expulsion of the Anglican clergy from both Oxford and Cambridge; and, however much such a revolution in the character and composition of those bodies might be deprecated, it could hardly be maintained that their condition during the reigns of James I and his son was on a level with the requirements of the times. In each, the course of studies was too narrow, the discipline lax and the cost of living, for the ordinary student, holding neither scholarship nor exhibition, a serious obstacle. Among puritans and members of the church of England alike, accordingly, those parents who attached importance to the religious element in the education of their sons, and who could afford to retain the services of a private tutor, often preferred to keep them at home; but, if unable to do this, they would send them to a "private grammar school," where Latin, Greek and, sometimes, Hebrew, would be taught, although rather with reference to Scriptural studies than the acquirement of a classical knowledge of those languages. With families of the upper class, again, it was a common practice for the eldest son, as soon as he reached the age when he would otherwise have gone to the university, to be sent to travel abroad with his tutor; and, with that experience, the period of tutelage was supposed to reach its consummation. At the larger public schools, however, it now became not uncommon for pupils to remain until they had reached the age of nineteen, or even twenty—at Eton and Westminster this was especially the case—and the maintenance of discipline became somewhat more complicated. It is with reference to such conditions as these that John Locke, who, educated at Westminster under Busby and, afterwards, as senior student and lecturer at Christ Church, Oxford, had had ample opportunities for forming an opinion, summed up the comparative advantages of home and public school education in the following words:

Being abroad [*i.e.* at a public school], 't is true, will make your son bolder and better able to bustle and shift among boys of his own age; and the emulation of school fellows often puts life and industry into young lads. But till you can find a school, wherein it is possible for the master to look after the manners of his scholars, and can show as great effects of his care of forming their minds to virtue, and their carriage to good breeding, as of forming their tongues to the learned languages, you must confess that you have a strange value for words, when, preferring the languages of the ancient Greeks and Romans to that which made 'em such brave men,—you think it worth while to hazard your son's innocence and virtue for a little Greek and Latin.[1]

In other words, it was the aim of John Locke to place the emphasis on education rather than on instruction; and,

[1] Locke, *Thoughts concerning Education* (ed. Quick, R. H.), p. 46.

throughout the period with which we are concerned, there appears to have been a desire on the part of founders to give the schoolmaster a somewhat larger discretion. At Ashford in Kent, it is true, Sir Norton Knatchbull and his nephew, although both of them distinguished as scholars and patrons of learning, had retained the limitation of the school which the former had founded (1632), allowing it to remain as that of "a free school for the instruction of children of the inhabitants in Latin and Greek"; but, at Audlem in Cheshire, founded by two citizens of London some ten years later, their design is described as being the free instruction of the youth of the parish, "in such authors of the *English*, Latin, and Greek tongues as are usually read in such schools"; while Robert Lever, in 1641, founded his school at Bolton-le-Moors in Lancashire, for like instruction, not only in grammar and classical learning, but, also, "in writing, arithmetic, geography, navigation, mathematics, and modern languages." Other founders preferred to use less definite terms; and, in Huntingdonshire, the new school at Ramsey (recently redeemed from the fenland) was, by mutual agreement (1656), designated as "for the education of the youth in the best ways of religion and learning"—for which a precedent had been set at Kidderminster, where, in 1634 (long prior to the association of the school with Worcester college, Oxford), the words used were, "in good literature and learning"; while, at Bradford, incorporated in 1662, we find "for the better bringing up of children and youth in grammar and other good learning and literature."

Generally speaking, the profession of a schoolmaster, at this period, was only too truly described by a high authority, namely, archdeacon Plume (fellow of Christ's college, Cambridge, and founder of the Plumian professorship in that university), as being "in most places" "so slightly provided for, that it was undertaken out of necessity, and only as a step to other preferment";[1] while, in 1654, we find the preacher of the funeral sermon for Thomas Comber, master of Trinity college in the same university, describing him, when an usher at Horsham, as "not like those now a days who make their scholars to hate the Muses by presenting them in the shapes of

---

[1] Account of Hacket, prefixed to his *Century of Sermons*, by Thomas Plume, D.D. (1675), p. iv.

fiends and furies."[1] This severity, not to say brutality, in enforcing discipline, appears to have increased, rather than diminished, subsequently to the restoration, and Plume insists on the superiority, in this respect, of the schools attached to "cathedral and collegiate churches" over other grammar schools throughout the country, where, he goes on to say,

schoolmasters are of late years so fanciful, inducing new methods and compendiums of teaching which tend to nothing but loss of time and ignorance.[2]

[1] *Sermon at the Funerall of Dr. Comber*, by R[obert] B[oreman], B.D. (1654), p. 4.

[2] Account of Hacket (*u.s.*), p. xix.

CHAPTER XV

The Beginnings of English Journalism

IN its origin, journalism was not the child of the printing press. The germ of it is to be found in the circular letters sent round after Agincourt and other medieval battles; and the profession of a writer of "letters of news" or "of intelligence" dates from the establishment of regular postal services.

Long before this, however, statesmen had found it necessary to have a constant supply of news. In the days of queen Elizabeth, Robert Devereux, earl of Essex, founded a staff of clerks in order to provide himself with news. His establishment for this purpose vied with that of the government itself. His clerks, Anthony Bacon, Sir Henry Wotton, Cuffe, Reynolds and Temple, so plentifully supplied him with intelligence that they were one of the sources of his power. But these were not journalists writing for the public; they were simply retainers of a great noble, members of a class of whom the cultured and intelligent John Chamberlain, correspondent of James I's Ambassador, Dudley Carleton, is the chief. Chamberlain's letters are numerous, and give graphic pictures of life in London at the court of James I.[1]

A long time elapsed before English journalism could call the printing press to its aid. The royal prerogative in the circulation of news, the vexatious licensing system, the regulations of the Star chamber, together with the religious strife of the times, all combined to prevent the publication of

---

[1] As to "intelligencers," cf. *ante*, Chap. VIII.

any sort of periodical until 1620, and all journals of domestic news until 1641, when the great rebellion was about to begin.

[Printing] hath been a pestilent midwife to those accursed brats, Error in the Church and Sedition in the State. Nor indeed, if a man may dare to speak it, are the governors themselves wholly blameless for such inconveniences. For Printing being ever accounted among the Regalia of every government, as well as coining etc., it should be looked on with such a jealous and strict eye, there should be such a circumspect care of prevention, and such painful pursuance of misdemeanours as would be required against the most dangerous crimes.[1]

Thus wrote a pamphleteer, in defence of Oliver Cromwell during the great press persecution of 1653, and the statement may be taken as fairly representing the mind of all parties throughout the seventeenth century.

The first traces of journalism in the printing press were in the broadside ballads about battles and tragical events of the day. To these were soon added isolated pamphlets usually termed *Relations* of news; but pamphlets of this nature, describing domestic events, were rare before 1640. In the meantime, periodical pamphlets had sprung into existence on the continent; and these constituted the bulk of the sources from which the English *Relations* were taken. English periodicals can now definitely be stated to have first been printed at Amsterdam, in 1620, as the enterprise of Dutch printers. They appeared as a result of the expulsion from Bohemia of James I's son-in-law, the elector palatine, and so-called 'Winter (*i.e.* Twelfth night's) king.' The first Englishman to publish them was Thomas Archer, of Pope's Head Alley, Cornhill, in 1621. Archer was soon imprisoned, and was succeeded in the same year by Nicholas Bourne.[2] These early prints and the pamphlets which succeeded them were

---

[1] *Sedition Scourg'd, or a View of that Rascally and Venemous Paper entituled; a charge of High Treason exhibited against Oliver Cromwell, Esq., etc.,* printed 20 October, 1653, and probably written by John Hall.

[2] ' The First English Newspaper ' in *The Nineteenth Century and After*, March, 1914. Very few of these early papers exist, and none of those printed by Archer in 1621 has yet been discovered.

not at first numbered and never at any time had a regular running title. This last device, properly characterised as a "catchword," did not come into being until the year 1642, when it was occasioned by competition. Other stationers, of whom Nathaniel Butter was chief, joined Archer and Bourne as publishers, and, in 1625, Archer alone appears to have published a periodical in competition with Butter and Bourne. He made the first attempt at a "catchword" on the title of his periodical by styling himself (not the pamphlet) "Mercurius Britannicus" —evidently modelling himself in this on "Mercurius Gallobelgicus." The headings of these pamphlets usually varied according to their themes; but they were generally spoken of as the *Coranto* or "current" of news—that is, a "relation" which ran on, instead of being confined to one pamphlet. Sometimes, another Italian word, *Novella*, was also applied to the *Relations*. For example, Joseph Mead wrote to a friend on 8 November, 1623, "I send you to-day besides the Corranto, a double novella to the ordinary intelligence"—the *Relation*, in that case, being the story of the fall of a building in which a number of Catholics were listening to a sermon. Nevertheless, all *Corantos* dealt exclusively with foreign news, down to the year 1641.

These *Corantos* were the subject of much ridicule, particularly at the hands of Ben Jonson. Indeed, so strong a vein of personal animosity towards captain Francis Gainsford, who, probably, wrote the earlier *Corantos*, and towards Chamberlain, his probable protector, is to be noticed in Jonson's masques and in his *Staple of Newes*, that it may be surmised that, at some time or other, Jonson's conduct in the wars in the Low Countries had been unfavourably described by Gainsford. Be that as it may, the ill repute which Jonson contrived to fasten upon the profession of the author of a newsbook survived, and survived unjustly, for many years.

On 17 October, 1632, the Star chamber finally prohibited the printing of all *Gazettes* and news from foreign parts, "as well Butter and Bournes as others," and, thenceforward, until 20 December, 1638, no *Corantos* appeared. On the last date, Butter and Bourne, by royal letters patent, were granted the monopoly of printing foreign news: "they paying yearly

towards the repair of St. Pauls the sum of £10." No. 1 of
the new "newsbook" was dated the same day, with the title
*An abstract of some speciall forreigne occurrences brought down
to the weekly newes of the 20 of December.* Anthony à Wood
tells us that William Watts of Caius college, who was also
an Oxford doctor of divinity, wrote more than 40 of these
newsbooks, "containing the occurrences done in the wars
between the King of Sweden and the Germans." There was
a total absence of considered editorial comment in these newsbooks, nothing but bare translations being permitted. The
preface to the first number is a very good example of the terminology in use:

> The Currantiers to the Readers. Gentle Reader. This in-
> telligencer, the Curranto, having been long silenced and now per-
> mitted by authority to speake again, presents you here at first
> with such things as passed some months since; not because we
> conceive that they are absolutely Novels unto you; but first, be-
> cause there is fraud in generalities, we thought fit to acquaint
> you with each particular: and, secondly, that by these ante-
> cedents you may better understand the consequents which we
> shall now publish weekly as heretofore.

Difficulties with the licenser soon followed; the *Corantos*
were again suppressed, reappeared and, finally, vanished altogether among the shoals of pamphlets pouring from the press
in 1641 and 1642. With the passing of the *Coranto*, came the
"newsbook" or *Diurnall* of domestic news.

In abolishing the Star chamber (5 July, 1641), the last thing
which the Long Parliament had in view was to grant liberty
to the press. Preparations for a censorship were at once
taken in hand, the delay until June, 1643 in carrying them into
effect being occasioned solely by the struggle with the king.
In November, 1641, parliament encroached upon the royal
prerogative by permitting *Diurnalls* of its proceedings (to
which other news was added) to be published under the *imprimatur* of its clerks. There was but one post a week from
London at this time, on Tuesday, and the result of the permission was that, in a week or two, as many as fifteen *Diurnalls*,
undistinguishable save by their contents and (occasionally)
by the printers' or booksellers' names attached, appeared

every Monday, to the ruin of the scriveners, who had been in the habit of sending out letters of news every week. Copyright (at the time not supposed to exist at common law) had been endangered by the abolition of the Star chamber's licensers; and, if we bear in mind the scurrility which had previously characterised political and religious pamphleteers and broadside writers, it is not surprising to find that the crowd of counterfeit *Diurnalls* and even more numerous *Relations* were dishonest productions. Throughout the year 1642, both Houses were extremely busy in punishing writers and printers, particularly of *Relations;* a process only terminated in 1643 by the appointment of a licenser—Henry Walley, clerk to the company of stationers—recognition of the "catchword" or newspaper title, protection of copyright and the wholesale stamping out of the forging, counterfeiting and, occasionally, blasphemous writers of *Relations*. Henceforward, journalists were a recognised body, their periodicals became easily distinguishable and the *Relations* accompanying them can be marked off and identified.

Of the vast, unique and practically complete Thomason collection[1] of tracts of the times, extending over the period from 1641 to 1660, at least one third consists of newsbooks, and, when to this are added the *Relations* and other tracts allied to the newsbooks, more than one half the total collection of over 22,000 pieces is to be ascribed directly or indirectly to journalists of the day and to their associates.

To identify the writers and describe their work critically is, to a great extent, the task of the student of history rather than that of the student of literature; for it is in their political and religious significance that the greatest interest lies. Nevertheless, all the main features of the modern newspaper were attained for a time; the work of the descriptive reporter, the war correspondent and considered editorial comment continually cropped up in the most unexpected manner, and, occasionally, from the most unexpected persons. These newsbooks were usually sold at a penny (about four times the value of our modern penny) and, when there was any repression of

[1] A catalogue of this, in chronological order (each piece having been dated by Thomason on the day he purchased it) was printed in 1908. The dates are nearly always the days of publication and have been accepted in the text.

their number or their news, they were largely supplemented by the uncensored letters of news posted with them. Quantities of these newsletters are to be found among the Clarke papers at Worcester college, Oxford. At their best, the newsbooks, as they were called, consisted of two sheets, *i.e.* 16 pages quarto, and, whatever their size, were invariably called "books." A sheet was a pamphlet and nothing else. Throughout the Stationers' registers, the term "table" is uniformly used for a "broadside": "news-sheet" and "newspaper" were never used.

The first of the patriarchs of English journalism—the man who first wrote purely English news—was Samuel Pecke, a scrivener with a little stall in Westminster hall. A presbyterian enemy, while attacking his moral character, admits that he "did at first labour for the best intelligence." Since he did not excite much animosity in his opponents, the remark may be taken to be correct. Even Sheppard says that Pecke tried to be impartial. His *Diurnall Occurrences* of 1641 and 1642, printed first for William Cook and, afterwards, for John Okes, Francis Leach and Francis Coles, were soon followed by *A Perfect Diurnall*. Previous to June, 1643, there were many counterfeits of this journal, which lasted to October, 1649, and was followed by another *Perfect Diurnall*. This last began in December, 1649 and ended in 1655, and, at first, Pecke was only "sub-author" of it. His career then ended, and nothing more is known of him. Other periodicals written by him are *A Continuation of Certain Speciall and Remarkable Passages*, published by Leach and Coles in 1642, and, again, in 1644-5; and a *Mercurius Candidus* in 1647. He was twice imprisoned by parliament; once in 1642, for some error in his intelligence, and, again, in 1646, for publishing the Scots papers.

Pecke was a somewhat illiterate writer, and, in his reply to Cleiveland's *Character of a London Diurnall*, quotes Hebrew under the impression that he is citing Greek. Except that he was the first in the field, and that his news is more reliable than that of others, there is very little to be said of his work; none of the later developments, such as the leading article, advertisements and so forth, originated with him.

Sir John Berkenhead began his *Mercurius Aulicus* at Oxford in January, 1643, and the appearance of this, the only royalist periodical for some years, with its contemptuous ridicule of the dishonest and illiterate parliamentary press, was an important factor in deciding the two Houses to set on foot their wholly beneficial licensing regulations in June. Sir John Denham's *Western Wonder* has recorded the untruthful manner in which Hopton's victorious hunting of Chudleigh from Launceston was described in the *Relations*, and how an ambuscade on Sourton down, on 25 April, 1643, was magnified into a special intervention of the Almighty by fire from heaven:

> Do you not know not a fortnight ago
> How they bragg'd of a Western Wonder
> When a hundred and ten slew five thousand men
> With the help of lightning and thunder?
>
> There Hopton was slain again and again
> Or else my author did lye
> With a new Thanksgiving for the dead who are living
> To God and His servant Chidleigh.

A few months later, *Mercurius Aulicus* was secretly reprinted in London. The Oxford and the London edition do not invariably contain the same matter; but, apart from this, and from a difference in size of the two editions (the Oxford one being the smaller), there is little to mark one from the other.

As a general rule, it may be stated that this periodical, throughout the year 1643, and, indeed, until the royal fortunes turned, is trustworthy, and markedly superior in every way to all its opponents. Mockery was one of Berkenhead's most effective weapons against his enemies; but (as will be shown) he was not long to remain unopposed in the exercise of this weapon.

Mercurius Aulicus ended in September, 1645; it was succeeded in the same year by *Mercurius Academicus*, which lasted until 1646; and, until the autumn of 1647, these were the only royalist periodicals which appeared. It will thus be seen that, save chiefly in the years 1647 to 1650, there was practically no royalist press at all. Sir John Berkenhead was, also, the writer of the royalist *Mercurius Bellicus*, which appeared for a short time in 1647 and, again, in 1648. He became licenser of all books under the royal prerogative at the restoration, before the passing of the licensing act of 1662, but, except as licenser and friend of Henry Muddiman, the privileged journalist of the restoration, he had nothing further to do with journalism.

In spite of the vast number of titles of journals which appeared between 1643 and the second and final suppression of the press by Cromwell in 1655, the journalists of the rebellion were but a small band.

John Dillingham, a tailor living in Whitefriars, was the writer of *The Parliament Scout*, and, for a time, leader of the parliamentary press. He was a presbyterian, opposed to independency and, unfortunately for him, unorthodox in his views. This, together with an attack on the parliament's general in a leading article, was the cause of his newsbook being suppressed in January, 1645. He was permitted to continue writing *The Moderate Intelligencer* in the same year (chiefly concerned with foreign news) until the first suppression of the newsbooks in October, 1649; but he then drops out of view and no more is known of him.

Dillingham was so disgusted with his own side that he dared to put in his newsbook, in 1648, the sentence *Dieu nous donne les Parlyaments briefe, Rois de vie longue*. He was a bitter enemy of Laud. A presbyterian critic wrote of him that he had

a snip at all men that stand firm to the covenant. The man is so pragmaticall, that he thinks he can teach the Parliament how to order state affairs, the Ministry how to frame their prayers and begin their sermons. . . . He would be thought not only a deep politician, and divine, but a mathematician too [*i.e.* an astrologer]. . . . God send us a speedy conclusion of Peace, that we may have no further use of an army. And that the Moderate Intelligencer may return to his trade, which I fear he hath almost forgotten.[1]

As a matter of fact, Dillingham got into trouble because of his leading articles, of which species of journalism he was one of the first originators. In being persecuted, he was not singular; the author of *Mercurius Civicus* (May, 1643–December, 1646) and *The Kingdomes Weekly Intelligencer* (January, 1643–October, 1649) shared the like fate. *Mercurius Civicus*

[1] *The copy of a Letter written from Northampton*, 6 February, 1646.

was suppressed for its too outspoken loyalty to its king. The writer of these periodicals is known only by his initials R. C. He was a strong presbyterian, a soldier and the journalist of Sir William Waller. In Denham's *Second Western Wonder* (concerning the battle of Roundway down), *Mercurius Civicus* is the "book" referred to, lady Waller the preaching lady and the "Conqueror" Sir William Waller himself.

> When out came the book which the newsmonger took
> From the preaching ladies letter
> Where in the first place, stood the Conqueror's face
> Which made it show much the better
>
> But now without lying, you may paint him flying
> At Bristol they say you may find him
> Great William the Con, so fast he did run
> That he left half his name behind him.

Mercurius Civicus was the first illustrated journal, and usually appeared with some political or military leader's portrait on its title-page. The woodcuts were nearly as bad as the rimes which sometimes accompanied them. R. C. also wrote *The Weekly Intelligencer of the Commonwealth* from 23 July, 1650 to 25 September, 1655, reviving it in 1659 (May to December). Sheppard says that R. C. was a scholar, and poor, owing to his loyalty and to his presbyterian views. William Ingler, who is but a name, wrote *Certaine Informations* in 1643 and 1644. Henry Walley, the licenser, another strong presbyterian, was the writer of *The True Informer* (1643-5) and *Heads of Chiefe Passages in Parliament* (continued as *The Kingdomes Weekly Account of Heads*) and other items, in 1648.

George Smith began his *Scotish Dove* in 1643. This was a periodical remarkable for its fanatical opposition to any observance of the Christian festivals, particularly Christmas day. Smith preached so many sermons on the subject in his journal that his periodical is almost valueless for intelligence; and, at the last, in 1646, it was suppressed by parliament and ordered to be burnt by the hangman for insulting the French. Smith modified his presbyterianism in later years and became a somewhat hypocritical advocate of Cromwell and his policy;

his change of sides, however, does not seem to have benefited him.

John Rushworth superseded Walley as licenser on 11 April, 1644, and wrote *The London Post*, which appeared from 6 August, 1644 to 4 March, 1645, and, again, from 31 December, 1646 to February, 1647. The sources of his *Collections* are thus indicated.

At the end of August, 1643, captain Thomas Audley appeared with his *Mercurius Britanicus* as an openly scurrilous opponent of *Mercurius Aulicus*. The two soon fell into a tiresome and continuous wrangle which few, nowadays, will care to follow. Audley was but a carpet knight, did not go to the wars and, when Rushworth obtained leave to appoint a deputy licenser in September, 1644, acted as licenser in his stead. He was succeeded in his "author's" chair of *Mercurius Britanicus* by Marchamont Nedham, who carried his scurrility to such an extent that, in the number for 4 August, 1645, he published a *Hue and Cry* after the king, couched in offensive terms. For this, Audley, his licenser, was imprisoned and forbidden to license again, and Rushworth's clerk Mabbott was installed in his place. Nedham's scurrility, nevertheless, continued to increase, and, on 18 May, 1646, he reached the climax, even attempting to make mischief between the two Houses. He was sent to prison and was only released on condition of not writing any more pamphlets. *Britanicus* thus came to an end. Audley wrote *Mercurius Diutinus* (not *Britanicus*) at the end of the year.

Daniel Border, another scrivener, and an anabaptist, was the writer of *A Weekly Accompt* (1643); *The Weekly Account* (1643-7); *The Perfect Weekly Account* (1647—a counterfeit of the true journal of the same name); *The Kingdoms Weekly Post* (1648); *The Kingdoms Faithfull Scout* (1649); *England's Moderate Messenger* (1649); *The Impartial Scout* (1650); and, probably, other periodicals later. Walker was his enemy, and his intelligence was defective; Sheppard calls his principal newsbook the *Scout* an Augean stable. Simeon Ashe and William Goode, the earl of Manchester's chaplains, were the writers of *Intelligence* from his army in 1644. Durant Hotham, son of Sir John Hotham and translator of the writings of Jacob Boehme, wrote *The Spie* in 1644 (30 January–25 June).

Richard Little was probably the author of *Mercurius Academicus*, Bruno Ryves wrote *Mercurius Rusticus* (a solitary counterfeit, dated 26 October, 1643, was issued by the poet Wither) and Daniel Featly probably wrote *Britanicus Vapulans* and *Mercurius Urbanus*. All these last were ephemeral.

In 1647, Henry Walker, the red-haired ironmonger nicknamed "Judas" by the royalists, first began to sign his periodicals as a journalist, writing under the pseudonym (an anagram of his real name, "Luke Harruney." Walker's output of books and pamphlets as politician, as journalist, as religious reformer, as Cromwell's preacher, as the apostle of Drogheda and Dunbar and, it must be added, as forger and literary pirate, exceeds in number that of any other writer between 1647 and 1655; not only was the historical significance of some of them of great importance, but his relations with Cromwell were so intimate, that any estimate of the protector's character and career which fails to take into account his connection with Henry Walker must be called incomplete. George Fox, the quaker, in his *Journal*, has summed up Walker's character. Charged by Walker with immorality and sorcery, Fox has recorded in his diary that Walker was "Olivers priest," always about him and a "liar," a "forger of lies."

These statements were strictly accurate. Walker began his literary career in 1641 by being imprisoned by the House of Lords for writing two libels in verse entitled, respectively, *The Wren and the Finch* and *The Prelates Pride*. In consequence of this, he fraudulently printed the name of William Prynne as writer to his next libel— *A Terrible outcry against the loytering exalted Prelats*. The forgery did not pass undiscovered; and, on 20 December, 1641, he was for the second time sent to prison—on this occasion, by the House of Commons.

The title of his pamphlet, *To your tents O Israel*, which he threw into the king's coach—into the king's face—the day after Charles's unsuccessful attempt to arrest the five members, is better known. This sent his printer, Thomas Paine, to prison,[1] while Walker himself was put in the pillory, and he then

---

[1] Paine received a gratuity of £20 for this from the council of state on 19 September, 1650. See *Calendar of State Papers Domestic*.

vanished altogether from the public eye, taking service in the army. When he reappeared as "Luke Harruney," writer of *Perfect Occurrences of Every Dayes Journall*, it was in succession to John Saltmarsh the army preacher, to whose memory, after his death at the end of the same year, he paid the tribute of a pamphlet of forged prophecies.[1] Another forgery, in 1647, was *The bloudy Almanac* for 1648, by John Booker, with an illustration of the king kneeling at the bar of the House of Commons on the title-page.[2] Yet one more fraud was perpetrated by him on 3 February, 1648, entitled *Severall Speeches at a Conference concerning the power of Parliament to proceed against the King for misgovernment*—a theft and adaptation of the *Conference about the Next Succession to the Crown of England* attributed to father Robert Persons, the Jesuit, to which Verstegan may have contributed. A much bulkier and more pretentious volume, a translation of Hubert Languet's *Vindiciae contra Tyrannos*, was issued from the press by Walker on 1 March, 1648; but it may be doubted whether he was the actual translator.[3] When king Charles interceded for him with parliament in 1642, stipulating that he was not to suffer either in life or limb, Walker addressed his sovereign in terms of the most extravagant praise, calling heaven to witness that he would lay down his life for him, and eulogising his piety and goodness. If all this be borne in mind and compared with Walker's *The King's Last Farewell to the World* (30 January, 1649), and his *History of the Life Reigne and Death of the late King Charles collected out of Choyce Record*, begun as a supplement to his newsbook in 1652,[4] and evidently suppressed by the licenser on account of its shameful statements, it will be manifest that Oliver's "priest" was also a hypocrite.

After the death of the king, Walker became the principal journalist of the day, was given living after living and was

---

[1] A farcically silly pamphlet generally ascribed to Saltmarsh, printed by Ibbitson. See *Mercurius Melancholicus*, 1–8 January, 1648, p. 112.

[2] December 1647, *The bloudy Almanac for the present jubilee*. By Mr. John Booker. Printed by John Clowes. See *Mercurius Melancholicus*, 18–25 December, 1647, p. 98, and Martin Parker's *When the King shall Enjoy his Own Again* (second edition).

[3] William Walker, of Darnal, Sheffield, secretary to major-general Lambert, was Henry Walker's brother (Add. MSS. 21, 424, f. 203). The translation has erroneously been attributed to him. See Gatty, A., *Hallamshire*, p. 424.

[4] In *Severall Proceedings*, no. 143, 17–24 June, 1652.

made a preacher at Somerset house. To such a reputation did he attain, that the man whose Hebrew anagrams in his *Perfect Occurrences* were the laughing stock of London was appointed Hebrew lecturer in Sir Balthazar Gerbier's academy and delivered "four orations in exposition of the Hebrew . . . upon the first days work of the Creation of the World."[1] Nedham, at the same time, applied for the post of lecturer in rhetoric but failed to obtain it.[2] Walker was the "loving and affectionate friend" of Cromwell's other and better known chaplain Hugh Peters. This religious teacher was colonel of a regiment of foot at the taking of Drogheda on 12 September, 1649;[3] and a letter from him, which Walker received on 28 September, 1649 and at once took to the House of Commons, was the first authoritative news published of Cromwell's proceedings at Drogheda.

This letter explicitly said "none spared," and, notwithstanding the fact that the garrison consisted of only 2552 all told,[4] put the total slain (exclusive of Cromwell's men) at 3552. Walker could not be prosecuted for making this disclosure, as the letter had been read in the House, so he was prosecuted for publishing his newsbook on the same day without a licence.[5] In addition to this, the extreme step was taken by the council of state of suppressing the whole licensed press in order to prevent further disclosures. For the seven weekly licensed newsbooks in existence on 28 September, two weekly official journals were substituted, of which the first numbers appeared on Tuesdays, 2 and 9 October respectively.

---

[1] *Severall Proceedings*, Dec. (sic) 4-11 January, 1650, p 195.

[2] *The Second Character of Mercurius Politicus*. By Cleiveland, 23 October, 1650.

[3] "Master Hugh Peters, who is now to fight with the sword as well as the word is made a Collonel of foote" (*The Kingdomes Weekly Intelligencer*, 2-9 October, 1649). "The business of Mr. Peters regiment referred to the Irish Committee," etc., etc. (*Calendar of State Papers Domestic*, 19 October, 1649). "Your father Peters is a Collonell and governor of Milford Haven," Emanuel Downing to J. Winthrop, 29 February, 1650 (*Collections of the Massachusetts Historical Society*, 4th series, vol. VI, p. 76).

[4] Gilbert's *Contemp. Hist. of Affairs in Ireland*, vol. II, p. 496.

[5] *Perfect Occurrences*, 21-28 September, 1649, has a postscript stating that it was unlicensed. A memorandum was made by Frost on the fly-leaf of an order book of the proceedings to be taken against Walker. This appears calendared on p. 16 of the *Calendar of State Papers Domestic* for 1650, is undated and is separated by fourteen blank pages from the entries with which it is wrongly calendared.

Of these periodicals, the first, *A Briefe Relation*, was written by the council of state's own secretary Walter Frost, ex-manciple of Emmanuel college. Frost, on the 21st, had been authorised to write a newsbook on Thursdays, but now had to hurry his projected journal and publish it on Tuesday, 2 October, three days earlier. To hide its real character, he marked the second and succeeding numbers "*Licensed* by Gualter Frost Esquire, etc." The second official periodical was *Severall Proceedings in Parliament* written by the clerk to the parliament, Henry Scobell, and started in such haste that it, also, at first came out on Tuesday.

A new licenser, the secretary of the army, had been appointed by the act of 20 September, 1649. This was Richard Hatter, and he had licensed the newsbooks for the week beginning Monday, 1 October. The council of state, therefore, wrote, on 2 October, to alderman Sir John Wollaston, that they "did not know" Hatter to be secretary, and gave him instructions to fine the writers and printers. Irritated at this denial of his office, Hatter continued to license for another week; and, thus, further details of the massacres leaked out. "None spared" referred to the inhabitants, and not to the garrison of the town;[1] there was treachery in obtaining the garrison's surrender;[2] and 1000 people had been butchered in St. Peter's church, the remark being added that mass had been said there on the previous Sunday—a reason which presupposes the fact that women and children would flee thither when in danger of death.[3] Finally, a royalist journalist published letters from Dublin detailing the steps taken by Cromwell to suppress the news, giving details of torture and mutilation and showing that the carnage had lasted for several days.[4] Cromwell's despatches bear every trace of having been framed in order to accord with just so much of the facts as might leak

---

[1] The comment on these two words of *The Kingdomes Weekly Intelligencer*, 25 September–2 October, p. 1518, renders this clear. See, also, p. 1513.

[2] *The Perfect Diurnall*, 1–8 October, p. 2695, glossed this over as "persuasion." Compare with this, Walker's other unlicensed pamphlet *Two letters from Liverpool*, published on 22 September (wrongly dated 11 September in the Thomason catalogue) with its reference to "quarter offered but would not be accepted of."

[3] *The Moderate Intelligencer*, 27 September–4 October.

[4] *Mercurius Elencticus*, 8–15 October.

out; but, in doing this, he failed to reckon with his chaplains, Peters and Walker.

Later in the year, Walker became sub-author of *Severall Proceedings*, and, in the following year, it was entirely abandoned to him. John Rushworth began an official *Perfect Diurnall of the Armies* at the end of December, 1649 and Pecke became sub-author of this. Both periodicals existed until the final suppression of the press in September, 1655.

When Cromwell returned from Ireland, in June, 1650, licensed periodicals were once more suffered to appear.

Other periodicals written by Henry Walker were *Mercurius Morbicus*, 1647; *A Declaration collected out of the journals of both Houses of Parliament*, 1648; *Packets of Letters* (printed by Ibbitson), 1648; *Heads of a Diarie*, 1648; *Tuesdaies Journall*, 1649; and he also wrote the *Collections of Notes at the King's Tryall*, printed by Ibbitson.

When Cromwell took all power into his hands, Walker was held in great honour, became pastor of a "gathered church" at St. Martin's Vintry (the "three cranes' church" as he called it), published a catechism, a volume of "spiritual experiences of beleevers," hymns and a treatise entitled "*Τραγήματα*" *Sweetmeats*, remarkable for the folly of its contents and its blasphemous dedication to Cromwell. Most of his publications were anonymous, but are immediately to be recognised either by his reference to himself and to his church, or by his style and his publisher Ibbitson's name, for Ibbitson rarely published any other author's writings.

At the return of the Rump in May, 1659, all Cromwell's officials were dismissed, including Nedham; and its council of state destroyed the protector's monument, the crown, etc., in the abbey.[1] In order to stir up opposition to the new rulers, Walker, thereupon, published a description of Cromwell's sayings upon his deathbed,[2] in which he not only vilified the quakers once more but, also, attacked the Rump. Though

---

[1] *The Weekly Post*, 31 May–7 June, 1659, *A brief View*, etc., by Younger, W., 2 August, 1660.

[2] *A collection of passages . . . by one who was groom of his chamber*. The pamphlet was entered in the Stationers' register by Ibbitson on 7 June, 1659, Carlyle attributed this tract to Charles Harvey, Lingard to Underwood. See the derisive description of Walker and the pamphlet at the end of *Mercurius Democritus* for 7–14 June, 1659.

he obtained no support, he seems to have been imprisoned for writing this tract,[1] which was carefully shunned by all writers of the seventeenth century, but accepted by Carlyle in the nineteenth. It contains a typically untruthful version of a prayer by Cromwell.[2]

The crown and coping stone of this man's baseness was his last book, published in August, 1660, a religious eulogy of Charles II, entitled *Serious Observations lately made touching his Majesty* and literally bristling with texts; the hypocrisy of its writer is evident if it be compared with his earlier broadsides concerning Charles II. *The Mad Designe* (6 November, 1651) and *The true manner of the crowning of Charles the Second King of Scotland together with a description of his life and a clear view of his court and Counsel* (1 January, 1651). What became of Walker after this no one knows.

The royalist press of 1647–50, carried on in spite of every effort to suppress it, calls for a few words. Cleiveland seems to have been the moving spirit of the numerous ephemeral *Mercuries* which appeared in 1648 and 1649; Samuel Sheppard undoubtedly undertook the largest part of the work, and was the originator of *Mercurius Pragmaticus*. Both roundhead (presbyterian) and royalist joined in the racy and scurrilous denunciation of the independents and regicides. Pride the swineherd (who could neither read nor write), Joyce the tailor, Rolfe and Hewson the shoemakers, Scot the minotaur, Marten and his mistresses, Cromwell with his red nose and the rest of the revolutionaries, all afforded a rich field for ribaldry and, above all, there was Walker, with whom the *Mercuries* teem. *Mercurius Melancholicus*, written by Martin Parker the ballad writer, is full of Walker; and so is the counterfeit of this periodical which was written by major-general Massey's chaplain John Hackluyt.

To Sheppard may be attributed a share in the writing of *Mercurius Elencticus*, when its real author, Sir George Wharton, was in prison. *Mercurius Elencticus* is full of biographies of the rebels, none of which have ever been disproved and

---

[1] *Calendar of State Papers Domestic*, 1659–60, p. 47.

[2] The true version, as heard by major-general Butler, is in Neal's *History of the Puritans* and in a contemporary copy of Butler's MS. at Lambeth palace. If this be compared with Walker's version, and the attack on the Rump on p. 21 of his pamphlet, the object of his alterations is manifest.

large numbers of which can be corroborated from other sources.

Other periodicals by Sheppard were *Mercurius Dogmaticus* (1648) and *The Royall Diurnall* (1648). In 1651, he issued *Mercurius Pragmaticus Reviv'd*, continuing it as *Elencticus* and (both titles being disallowed) wound it up as *Mercurius Scommaticus*. In 1652, he wrote another *Pragmaticus*, a *Phreneticus* and a *Mercurius Mastix*—the last an amusing and valuable skit on the journalism of his day. His pamphlet, *The Weepers*, also contains most indispensable information about the writers of newsbooks.

John Hall, poet and pamphleteer, was hired by Lilly the astrologer to attack Wharton in 1648 and wrote the *Mercurius Brittanicus* and *Mercurius Censorius* of that year in defence of the parliament.

A certain John Harris, better known as "Sirrahniho" and "Oxford Jack" (he is throughout easily identified by the latter nickname), who had been a printer to the army and terminated his career as major John Harris, hanged for forgery at the restoration, was the author of the *Mercurius Militaris* and *Anti Mercurius* of 1648. Though he was Cromwell's spy, yet the antipathy he ever displayed towards Cromwell (both in his original petition in the *State Papers* and in his newsbooks) is very curious.

Gilbert Mabbott, son of a Nottingham cobbler and Rushworth's clerk, was a leveller, and was removed from his post as licenser for this in 1649. He was the writer of *The Moderate* and of a scurrilous *Mercurius Britannicus* in 1649. He pretended to hold views in favour of the freedom of the press in 1649, when he found that he was to be removed, but he was restored to his post in 1653.

John Crouch the printer first appears on the scene in 1647 as the writer of occasional counterfeits of *Mercurius Melancholicus* and *Pragmaticus*. In 1649 and 1650, he wrote the vulgar, scurrilous and occasionally amusing *Man in the Moon*, spending some time in the Gatehouse prison in consequence. Between the years 1652 and 1655, he wrote the licensed periodicals known as *Mercurius Democritus*, *Fumigosus* and so forth, which were indecent and obscene throughout. Some numbers, duly licensed and authorised by Cromwell's licenser,

Mabbott, during the years 1653 and 1654, contain songs comparable to the most indecent verse of Rochester himself.

When Cromwell turned out the Rump in 1653, a printer called John Streater, a captain and quartermaster-general of the Irish army, circulated a paper of "queries" among his brother officers; for this, Cromwell dismissed him from the army as "unfit," and Streater underwent a lengthy and illegal imprisonment, at the expiration of which he issued two remarkable periodicals, entitled, respectively, *Observations, Historical Political and Philosophical, upon Aristotle's first book of Political Government, together with a narrative of State affairs* (no. 1, 4 April, 1654) and *A Politick Commentary on the life of Caius July Caesar* with *Perfect and Impartial Intelligence* (no. 1, 23 May, 1654). These, in some sort, were an anticipation of *Killing no Murder*, and it is odd that they should have been unnoticed in modern times. Streater's account of his troubles is to be found in his *Secret Reasons of State* (23 May, 1659). The Rump gave him a regiment in 1659, and, though he was arrested in 1661, the licensing act of 1662 honoured his stand for freedom of parliament by expressly exempting him by name from all its provisions. He was a prosperous printer (chiefly of law books) for the rest of his life, and died in 1687.

Cromwell's last journalist was Marchamont Nedham, who, unlike Walker, was an educated man, a graduate of All Souls, Oxford. But he possessed neither honour, religion, morals nor definite political convictions. He wrote anything for anybody and lived simply for money. He shall never be mentioned "but to his everlasting shame and infamy," wrote Cleiveland; yet, at the time when this was said, Nedham had not touched his lowest depths. In 1648 (probably not before this time, nor after February, 1649), he wrote the royalist *Mercurius Pragmaticus*, taking it out of the hands of Samuel Sheppard, and adopting the same tiresome trailing one which he had used in his roundhead journal *Britanicus*. After his imprisonment, in 1649, he was willing to write pamphlets for the regicides, was rewarded by a pension of £100 a year and, on 13 June, 1650, started the first permanent official journal, *Mercurius Politicus*. Cromwell left for Scotland at the end of the month, after a sermon by Henry Walker, and

Nedham then inserted so scandalous a series of articles on the Scots in *Politicus* that, at last, Cleiveland came forward (on 14 August, 1650) with a *Character of Mercurius Politicus*, a furious and merciless exposure, in which he described Nedham's wit as having

scandalized both sexes, disobliged three parties, reproached our whole nation, and not only ours but all others having declared himself as the disgrace so to be the public enemy of mankind . . . our lay spalatto, a three piled apostate, a renegade more notorious than any in Sally or Algier;

adding, in conclusion:

Yet it is not fit that we should be at the mercy of a Tavern, and the drunkenness of an arbitary Pen. Must we be subjected to his two sheets of "High Court of Justice?" We are content to serve, but it mads us to be reproached, and by such a one as him; for there is no such torment to a Christian as to be tyrannized over by a Renegade. . . . So insatiable is his appetite of speaking ill that there is no person so intimate to him, or so deserving; nothing so secret or religious which he abuseth not to that purpose; so that he is neither to be tolerated in Society nor policy, neither in Conversation nor a State; but, rather, as a public parricide, to be thrown into the sea in a sack, with a cock, and ape, and a serpent, the right emblems of his politic triplicity.

On this, Nedham's articles were stopped, and it is probable that he was removed from his authorship, and John Hall, the other paid writer, installed, for a time, in his stead.[1]

Beginning with 26 September, 1650, and ending with 12 August, 1652, *Politicus* contained a series of leading articles advocating republican institutions, with studied moderation. Their style is good, and they occasionally quote Thomas May's *Lucan*. There were one or two reprints of parts of them in pamphlet form, and, on 29 June, 1656, Thomas Brewster (Vane and Marten's publisher) reprinted the articles which were published between 16 October, 1651 and 12 August, 1652, condensed into a book under the title *The Excellencie of a*

---

[1] Wood intimates that Nedham left off writing *Politicus* soon after the start. *The Hue and Cry after those rambling protonotaries of the times, Mercurius Elencticus, Britanicus, Melancholicus and Aulicus* (7 Feb., 1651) contains a personal description of the writer of *Politicus* which can only apply to Hall.

Free State, by way of an attack upon Cromwell, as, at the time, trying to stamp all semblance of a free state into the dust. The book was also prefaced by an attack upon Howell, who had urged Cromwell to take all power into his hands. It has quite absurdly been attributed to Nedham, at that time Cromwell's paid spy as well as journalist and the very last man likely to attack him. According to Sheppard's *The Weepers*, published on 13 September, 1652, *Politicus*, at that time, was written by someone in authority (the reference is clearly to these articles) and some member of the council of state, possibly Marten, must have been the writer of them. Milton licensed *Politicus* for a portion of the time, from January, 1651 to January, 1652 (the fact is not to the credit of the author of *Areopagitica*); but the supposition that he may have had a hand in the composition of the articles may, on internal evidence, at once be dismissed.

When Cromwell finally suppressed the licensed press in September, 1655, Nedham began a second official periodical, *The Publick Intelligencer*, published on Mondays. Other periodicals written by him before this were *Mercurius Pragmaticus*, 1652 (probably not more than one number), in opposition to Sheppard's *Pragmaticus*, *Mercurius Britannicus*, 1652 (the first five numbers only), *Mercurius Poeticus*, 1654, and *The Observator*, 1654.

With the exception of his own advertising periodical *The Publick Adviser* of 1657, Nedham had no competitor until the Rump was restored in 1659. He then lost his pension, and his two periodicals were handed over to John Canne, the anabaptist printer and preacher, on 13 May, 1659. Nothing dismayed, Nedham changed sides once more, wrote a book for the Rump entitled *Interest will not lie*, levelled against the restoration of Charles II, and recovered his periodicals on 16 August, 1659. General Monck's council of state "prohibited him" altogether in April, 1660, and he then fled to Holland, but, having obtained his pardon under the great seal, returned in September, 1660.[1] He afterwards practised medicine and died in 1678, but succeeded in writing pamphlets for Charles II before his death.

A periodical in French was issued throughout the wars.

---

[1] *The Man in the Moon*, 1 October, 1660.

This was *Le Mercure Anglois*, apparently written by John Cotgrave, under Dillingham's influence, from 17 June, 1644 to 14 December, 1648. A second periodical, entitled *Nouvelles Ordinaires de Londres*, was started in 1650, and lasted to the restoration, being revived again in 1663 by Henry Muddiman and Thomas Henshaw of Kensington. There is a good collection in the Bibliothèque Nationale, Paris.

One phenomenon to be noticed in all the pamphlets of the great rebellion is the fact that, though the writers, in many cases, were drawn from the most uneducated classes, their style continually improves. Correct English and spelling are as conspicuously present in Pecke's and Walker's latest periodicals as they are markedly absent in the earlier years. For this, the correctors of the press were responsible. Many a poor clergyman ejected from his living must have earned his bread in this way. In the case of Pecke's periodicals, the career of the corrector of the press of Mrs. Griffin, publisher of Pecke's last *Perfect Diurnall*, is well known, owing to his having been thrown into prison for treason in 1660. He was Cromwell's "son-in-law," Thomas Philpot[1] of Snow hill, and his examination after his arrest shows that he had been very well educated.[2] He began life as a scholar of Christ Church near St. Bartholomew's hospital, and, after this, became a king's scholar at Westminster school. Then he went to Trinity college, Cambridge, for about eight years, proceeding M.A. From 1641, he was schoolmaster at Sutton Vallamore, Kent, for four years. After this, he became corrector of the printing presses of John Haviland and Mrs. Griffin, of Richard Bishop and widow Raworth, and, at the restoration, was employed by Robert White and Edward Mottershead. Philpot, therefore, was responsible for the neat appearance and correct language of Pecke's later pamphlets.

At the end of April, 1659, the Rump parliament had permitted licensed newsbooks to be revived; but when, thanks to general Monck, it resumed its sittings for the second time in

---

[1] He signs himself "your son-in-law" to his printed petition to Cromwell presented 9 October, 1654. He is identified in *Mercurius Aulicus*, no. 1, 13–20 March, 1654. Nos. 54 ff., 143 and 147 Tanner MSS. at Oxford are by Thomas Philpot.

[2] *Calendar of State Papers Domestic, Chas. II*, vol. XXIV, no. 105 (Calendar of 1660–1, p. 427).

1659, in December, its council of state—of which Thomas Scot was the head—decided to suppress all outside "newsbooks."[1] Two journalists only were allowed to publish news twice a week. One was Nedham, with his *Publick Intelligencer* and *Mercurius Politicus*, and the other was one Oliver Williams, Scot's *protégé*, with his *Occurrences from Foreign parts* and *An Exact Accompt*, published on Tuesdays and Fridays. From a postscript to the *Occurrences* for 8–15 November, 1659, it appears that John Canne was then writing his periodicals for Williams, though he did not do so before this date.

Oliver Williams was the holder of the unexpired term of a patent for an advertising or registration office granted to captain Robert Innes many years previously by Charles I. On the strength of this, he had tried to prohibit Nedham's *Publick Adviser* in 1657, and, after the restoration, asserted that it conferred upon him the sole right to publish newsbooks. This was a falsehood. When Nedham fled the kingdom, he at once seized the opportunity and issued a new *Politicus* and *Publick Intelligencer*, as well as other periodicals, marking them "published by authority." It is very probable that his advertising offices and newsbooks masked some conspiracy, but the end came when he attacked the duly authorised journalist, Henry Muddiman, and drew attention to his own claims; for his periodicals were then (in July, 1660) suppressed. But, when the Rump authorised Nedham and Williams to print news, Clarges, general Monck's brother-in-law and agent in London, also obtained permission to have a third bi-weekly published under his direction, selecting as his writer a young schoolmaster educated at St. John's college, Cambridge, called Henry Muddiman, who had never written for the press before. As the son of a Strand tradesman, he must have been well known, both to Clarges (a Strand apothecary) and to his sister Mrs. Monck (widow of a Strand tradesman). The general, if the Rump had only known it, was about to have someone to see that his manifestoes were truthfully put before the nation. One has only to compare Nedham's and Williams's periodicals with those of Monck's journalist to see that this was necessary.[2]

---

[1] See Thomason's notes on his tracts, E 1013 (2) and (23).

[2] The confidence placed by Monck in him is shown by the following title-pages:

(11 April, 1660) *The Remonstrance and Address of the Armies of England,*

On Monday, 26 December, 1659, the new journalist issued his first newsbook, *The Parliamentary Intelligencer* (afterwards the *Kingdom's Intelligencer*), with the ominous motto on the title-page, *Nunquam sera est ad bonos mores via;* and, on the following Thursday week, the first number of his other weekly "book," *Mercurius Publicus*, appeared. Thus, he was in opposition to Nedham from the start.

A few days later, Pepys made Muddiman's acquaintance and went with him to the Rota club, where he paid eighteen-pence to become a member. The club met at a coffee-house called the Turk's head, which was kept by one Miles, in Palace yard, "where you take water," as Audrey remarks, and which was frequented by a number of "ingeniose gents," who discussed Harrington's idea of yearly balloting out a third of the House of Commons in so skilful a manner that the arguments in the parliament house "were but flatt" to it. Pepys found that his new acquaintance had a very poor opinion of the Rump, "though he wrote news-books for them," and recorded his impression that he was a "good scholar, and an arch rogue" for speaking "basely" of the Rump. Needless to add, he was soon to be undeceived as to the nature of the parliament for which the new journalist was writing.

Thus began the career of the most famous of all the seventeenth century journalists; one whose principal "paper"— *The London Gazette*—is with us still. That he has been forgotten is due to the fact that he made few private, and no public, enemies; for he was not a controversialist, and, throughout his life, devoted himself to what, after all, is the principal part of a journalist's duty—the collection of news. He had an assistant, a Scot named Giles Dury, who, if his wife's name, "Turgis," in his marriage licence in 1649, is a misread-

---

Scotland and Ireland to the Lord General Monck. Presented to his Excellency the 9th of April 1660. St. James's April 9, 1660. Ordered by his Excellency the L. Gen. Monck. That the Remonstrance and Address of the officers of the Army presented this day to his Excellency be forthwith printed and published by Mr. Henry Muddiman. William Clarke Secretary. London Printed by John Macock.

(28 May, 1660) His Majesty's letter to His Excellency the Lord General Monck. To be communicated to the officers of the Army. Brought to his Excellency from his Majesties Court at the Hague by Sir Thomas Clarges. Rochester. 24 May, 1660. I do appoint Mr. Henry Muddiman to cause this letter to be forthwith printed and published. George Monck. Printed by John Macock.

ing for Clarges, must have been a relation of Sir Thomas Clarges. Anthony à Wood tells us that Dury soon "gave over"; thus, in a few months' time, when Nedham and Williams had successively been repressed, Muddiman was sole journalist of the three kingdoms.

This was not his only reward, for the important privilege of free postage was also given to him. Thus, anyone was at liberty to write to him, post free, to tell him what was going on in any part of the kingdoms, he also having the right to send letters in return without charge. He, therefore, opened his first editorial office at the Seven Stars in the Strand, near the New Exchange (the site of Coutts's old bank), and attached himself to the office of secretary of state Nicholas, afterwards of lord Arlington, whither, after a time, the bulk of his letters were addressed, either to himself or, by his own direction, to Sir Joseph Williamson, then under-secretary and, after a time, his censor. A correspondence of this kind, of course, was of very great importance to a government anxious to know what was going on in different parts of the realm, and it largely accounts for the great bulk of the restoration state papers. The fact that parliament, in June, 1660, prohibited printed reports of its proceedings and never removed the embargo until the end of the century, made his letters of news much in request, and, in this way, that which might have been thought the least important and the least lucrative part of his work really assumed the greatest consequence. So, when Sir Roger L'Estrange's open request for the sole privilege of writing the "newsbooks" succeeded, at the end of 1663, Muddiman was but little injured and does not at all seem to have resented his supersession.

A more dangerous enemy than L'Estrange was Sir Joseph Williamson, for whom Muddiman started the *Gazette* at the end of 1665 and crushed out L'Estrange; finally, when Williamson tried to deprive him of his newsletter correspondence, Muddiman started another periodical—the official *The Current Intelligence* (of 1666)—under protection of Monck's cousin, another secretary of state, Sir William Morice. Thus, Williamson was brought to terms. He had to carry on a newsletter correspondence himself after this, in order to feed the *Gazette;* but his duties prevented his giving his personal attention either to the *Gazette* or to his newsletters; and, while the former lapsed into a moribund condition, the latter did not pay. The newsletters of the man whom he had attempted to oust became a household word throughout the kingdom.

These newsletters, closely written by clerks (from dictation) on a single sheet, the size and shape of modern foolscap, headed "Whitehall," to show their privilege, beginning "Sir," and without any signature, misspelt, the writing cramped and crabbed to a degree, but literally crammed with parliamentary and court news, are easily distinguishable from the rarer productions of less successful writers. They were sent post free twice a week, or oftener, for £5 a year and, from the lists of correspondents at the Record office, as well as from numerous references to Muddiman in the various reports of the Historical Manuscripts commission, it is evident that no personage of consequence could afford to dispense with them. A vast number of them still exist; one collection contains a complete series for twenty-two years. They have never yet been systematically calendared and published.

Anthony à Wood continually visited Short's coffee-house in Cat street, Oxford, in order to read "Muddiman's letter" and was in the habit of paying two shillings "quarteridge" for them when they were done with. Roger North, in the life of his brother, shows that they were held in much the same esteem at Cambridge.

Once or twice, Muddiman got into trouble. In 1676, the king was much annoyed at a statement made in a newsletter found in a coffee-house, to the effect that a fleet was to sail against Algiers under Sir John Narborough and that the duke of Monmouth was to be one of his captains. The letter was at once suspected to be Muddiman's. Pepys got a copy of it for Williamson, and Muddiman was examined before the council, the king stating that he would not suffer either Muddiman or any other person to divulge anything agitated in council "till he thought fit to declare it." When the matter was enquired into, the writer was proved to have been Williamson's own head clerk, and he had to dismiss him. The following year, Muddiman was arrested for "writing confidently that the Spaniards intended war against England," but nothing seems to have come of it. Wood also records in his diary that, in 1686, in the days of James II, Street, judge of assize at Oxford, spoke in his charge to the grand jury against newsletters, particularly Muddiman's, and, after noting that they "came not to Oxon afterwards," adds, "other trite and lying letters came."[1]   But, as he was on the popular side and opposed to James II, his letters were soon back again.   His *Gazette* may be said to have been the first printed newspaper, for it at once gained the title of a "paper" as being a departure from the ancient pamphlet form and no longer a "book." It was only "half a sheet in folio" and clearly designed to be sent with his letters.   The word "newes-paper" was not long in being coined as a result, and, from analogy with this, was at last obtained the word "newsletter."

The career of Sir Roger L'Estrange, who supplanted Henry Muddiman for about two years, would (like that of Henry Walker) require a volume to do it justice, if his surveyorship of the press were taken into account.   Nevertheless, his *rôle* as journalist was brief, uneventful and unimportant.   His two periodicals *The Intelligencer* and *The News* (31 August, 1663 to 29 January, 1666) were only half the size of his predecessor's publications and, in 1664, were paged and numbered together as one periodical.   This was a device to make them pay.   L'Estrange was a better pamphleteer than journalist; his *Observator*, issued in later years, consisted of nothing but comment without news.   When Muddiman put an end to L'Estrange's journals with the *Gazette* in 1665, L'Estrange, by the king's orders, was pensioned off with £100 a year charged on the *Gazette*, his future services as surveyor of the press being paid for, in like manner, by £200 a year out of the secret service money.

Of the immense journalistic output which Cromwell had suppressed, the net results at the end of the reign of Charles II were: first, the official recognition of the necessity to gratify the public desire for news, shown in the continuance of the *Gazette* as a permanent institution; and, secondly, the striking manner in which newsletters were permitted, unfettered and uncensored, for the benefit of the upper classes, to supply the defects of the official print.   No longer ridiculed, newsletters

[1] Jeffreys took the extreme step of suppressing coffee-houses that "dealt in newsletters."   *Ellis correspondence*, by A. Ellis, 11, p. 243.

at last obtained a place in public esteem which had never been obtained by newsbooks. That, before the end of the century, the liberty of the press should begin and the modern newspaper follow, was but a logical corollary to this.

at last obtained a place in public esteem which had never been attained by newsbooks. Thus, before the end of the century, the liberty of the press should begin and the modern news-paper follow, was but a logical corollary to this.

CHAPTER XVI

The Advent of Modern Thought in Popular Literature

THE WITCH CONTROVERSY. PAMPHLETEERS

THE enlightenment of the renascence had never penetrated the deeper recesses of the popular mind. The social, religious and economic revolutions of Tudor times; the fermentation of city life under Elizabeth and James; the growth of national consciousness; the discoveries of travellers and men of science; above all, the popularisation of biblical and classical literature, had added enormously to the interests and imagination of the ordinary man, without transforming his sentiments, convictions and ideals. His mental vision was crowded with new and engrossing objects, but his outlook remained medieval. It was the task of the Jacobean and Caroline generations to effect a mental reformation. Had the age been a time of political peace and social calm, the first half of the seventeenth century would have proved to be one of the most interesting epochs in English literature. In an atmosphere of learning and discussion, humanists of the period would have adjusted their heritage of old-time beliefs and as-pirations to the maturer, more tolerant wisdom of Erasmus, More, Wier, Bullein, Montaigne, Scot, Ralegh, Shakespeare, Earle and Bacon. All that was best in the Middle Ages would have expanded into modern thought, and a second, more spiritual renascence would have inspired a series of master-pieces, such as the work of Vergil and Molière, in which the past and present join hands. As it was, though knowledge continued to increase, the thoughts and emotions of the people were diverted by class hatred, religious controversy and the political crisis. The consciousness of fellowship. essential to intellectual progress, had died out. Thus, humanists, instead of broadening and redirecting the tendencies of popular thought, either relapsed into scepticism, as in the instances of Robert Burton and Sir Thomas Browne, or let loose their augmented volume of learning and sentiment into the old, narrow channels. Whenever an age fails to find new interests, intellectual intemperance results. And, just as, at an earlier date, social writers lost touch with ideas and squandered their originality on experiments in style,[1] so, now, the more learned divines and physicians devoted their scholarship and research to the barren mysteries of demonology.

In order to understand the witch controversy of the seventeenth century, it is necessary to remember that primitive people had always cherished a veneration for the "wise woman,"[2] probably a relic of the mother-worship of the premigratory period, and that her broom, ladle and goat may, possibly, be regarded as symbols of her domestic power. She was supplanted by the new polytheism of warrior spirits; and, when they gave way, in their turn, to Christianity, some of the dispossessed deities became saints, while others went to join this earlier deity in the traditions and folk-lore of the people. As western Christendom became familiar with the teaching of the Greek church and with eastern religions—at first by the researches of theologians and then through the Saracenic wars in Spain and the crusades—these rites and superstitions were gradually coloured with rabbinical conceptions of the devil's hierarchy and with the Neoplatonic doctrine of demons and intermediary powers. Despite the rationalism of Jean de Meung and Roger Bacon,[3] patristic conceptions of demonology were codified and systematised in the Middle Ages. Such superstitions as the incubus and succubus, the

[1] See *ante*, Vol. IV., Chap. xvi.

[2] Karl Pearson: see essays on "Woman as Witch," "Ashiepattle," "Kindred Group-marriage" in vol. II of *Chances of Death*, 1897.

[3] *Roman de la Rose*, pt. II, c. 1280. *Epistola fratris Rogerii Baconis de secretis operibus artis et natura et de nullitate magiae, c.* 1250 (ptd. *Theatrum Chimicum,* Nürnberg, 1732).

transmutation of men into beasts, the power to fly by night were then, definitely, incorporated in medieval theological conceptions. From the twelfth or thirteenth century onwards, new feelings of horror and loathing began to be associated with this entanglement of traditions. Not only was the underworld of disinherited deities regarded as a rival by the Church, and, therefore, credited with the infamies which are usually attributed to heretics,[1] but as men struggled towards a higher level of civilisation, they instinctively accused these pariahs of all that they were endeavouring to eliminate from their own daily lives. The calamities and controversies of the fifteenth and sixteenth centuries only added to men's sense of danger and misery and inspired a yet more pessimistic school of demonologists, led by Jacquier, Institoris and Sprenger. By the time we reach the seventeenth century, the imaginary realm of spirits, ghosts, gnomes, fairies, demons, prophets and conjurors—now stigmatised as the implacable enemies of mankind—became allegorical or symbolic of all that was degraded, perverted, revolting or terrible. The devil, from being a denizen of lonely or impassable places, had now grown to be the monarch of innumerable hosts. As the fifteenth and sixteenth centuries had been disgraced in the eyes of the priesthood by blasphemous parodies, so, now, the diabolical empire was believed to be a monstrous imitation of the kingdom of heaven, with disgusting travesties of church ritual. The fiend's one object was to seduce mortals from the worship of God, and as, from early Christian times, both monkish doctrinaires and secular humourists had depicted women as loose, malevolent or ridiculous, so, now, it was with this sex rather than with men that he found his easiest victims and most willing allies. This predilection stimulated the dreams of diseased imagination. The witch or "wise woman" was looked upon as the devil's chosen handmaiden. The most elaborate pornography grew up around this supposed union, and the witches' sabbath or Walpurgis night—a relic of mother-worship, at which licence abounded—was conceived to be a kind of devil's mass, at which debauchery ran riot.[2] Other

---

[1] See, especially, the bull of Gregory IX, 13 June, 1233.
[2] See Jules Baissac, *Les Grands Jours de la Sorcellerie*, 1890, chap. VI. See, also, chap. VII in *Illustrierte Sittengeschichte*, by Fuchs, E., 1909.

obsessions came to be connected with the witch horror. From prehistoric times certain animals had been regarded as spirits of evil. Recollections of these legends blended with the fear of noisome and poisonous animals, and led men to believe that such creatures were auxiliaries of Black Magic. Human deformity abounded in medieval slums, and people still believed in monsters half man and half beast. And, as witches were hideous hags, men attributed to these old women the birth of abortions such as Hedelin, [1] Stengesius [2] and Paré [3] described and the people themselves read of in broadsides.

From prehistoric times, men had been, and were still, accustomed to regard the trivial enterprises and interests of bucolic life as under the influence of witches. Such things as the growth of crops, the fall of rain, the churning of milk, the disappearance of household utensils and the birth of children, came within their province, but, now that all the mystery of evil and suffering had gathered round these beings, strange and appalling diseases were believed to come from their power. Epilepsy, somnambulism, St. Vitus's dance, hysteria and hypnotism were attributed to venefical agency. They could slowly murder human beings by sympathetic magic or change them into animals. Nay, more, with the help of the devil, they could call back the dead, or some semblance of the dead, to aid them to win ascendency over human beings.

It will hence be readily understood that, at the opening of our period, the belief in witchcraft had grown to be more than an antiquated superstition. It represented the Gothic obscenity, grotesqueness, profanity, madness, cruelty and paganism, which progress had branded as accursed but could not eradicate from the imaginations of men. Had an age of moral reflectiveness succeeded to the creative energy of Elizabeth's reign, the Jacobean and Caroline generations would have turned the light of the new learning on their own minds and formed a higher conception of divine power and human dignity. But the heat of controversy rendered introspection impossible, and humanists were too busy refuting each other's political

---

[1] *Des Satyres, Brutes, Monstres et Demons. De leur Nature et Adoration*, par Francois Hedelin, 1627. (Hedelin is better known as the Abbé d'Aubignac.)

[2] *De Monstris et Monstrosis*, 1647 (?).

[3] *Deux livres de chirurgie*, 1573. Eng. trans. by Johnson, T., 1649.

and religious errors to cultivate high seriousness of thought. Thus, those who felt that all was not well with the world, and who were not inspired by any movement towards a more cultured and spiritual interpretation of life, returned to examine the old allegory of human imperfection and defencelessness, finding in the books of the past and the disorder of the present only too much to justify a belief in witchcraft.

To begin with, as progress had not been universal, those who could not move with the times tended to cling to old beliefs from instinctive distrust of what was new; while others, dismayed at the collapse of faith and tradition, were ready to believe anything which represented humanity as corrupt and afflicted. The Faust legend was still a parable of the age. Many who viewed with horror the careers of John Dee, Edward Kelly, Simon Forman, Dr. Lambe, William Lilly and Elias Ashmole, were not prepared to deny that witches and magicians bartered their souls in the insane desire to pass the limits divinely placed to knowledge and power. Again, the renascence had accustomed men to intenser and more versatile habits of thought; inventions were more ingenious, thinkers were more subtle. Consequently, those who were still convinced of original sin, would attribute to the devil the heightened intelligence and duplicity of man, rather than deny his existence.

Now that the thoughts of men were turned in this direction, they continued, like their predecessors from St. Augustine downwards, to discover authority for superstitions in their most revered sources of knowledge. Neoplatonism was used to corroborate the doctrine of spirits and angels, and, besides, to deny that the world was full of demons was to be a Sadducee. Moreover, positive proofs of devilry and magic could be deduced from holy writ. The serpent in the garden of Eden, Pharaoh's conjurors, the afflictions of Job, Balaam and his ass, the witch of Endor, the "voice of the charmer," the transmutation of Nebuchadnezzar, the Gadarene swine, "the lunatic boy," and Simon Magus were understood in the light of seventeenth-century demonology. Classical lore, which carried hardly less weight than Scripture, could be as easily interpreted. The incubus and succubus were discerned in the union of gods and goddesses with mortals. The belief in witch-begotten monsters was confirmed by tales of the Minotaur, lamiae, empusae, lemures and satyrs.[1] If Circe could turn men into swine, Neptune and Aeolus raise storms, Juno travel through the air, Apollo strike down with disease, Venus become invisible, why should not more modern magicians? They learnt from Apuleius that men could be changed into animals; from Horace and Lucan that witches practised abominable rites in secret, and from Tacitus, Suetonius and Ovid that spells, incantations and sympathetic magic could be used to destroy the life of a fellow creature.

For many, and, in some cases, subconscious, motives, men wished to believe in witchcraft; and, since the intellect generally follows the emotions, the age found more reasons for believing the propositions formulated by Molitoris,[2] and for literally discharging the mistranslated mandate, "Thou shalt not suffer a witch (*Mekasshepha*) to live," than for believing the arguments of Agrippa, Erasmus, Wier, Reuchlin, the authors of *Epistolae Obscurorum Virorum*, and Scot.[3] Puritanism, with its gloom, its intolerance and its sense of spiritual conflict, has been held largely responsible for the persecution that now arose. But the causes lay deeper than any sectarian movement and actuated men of different creeds, who might otherwise have advanced the culture of their age. Holland, in a tedious dialogue,[4] proved the existence of witches from the Bible, and established the likelihood of their lust for blood by quoting the sacrifice of Iphigenia and the cruelties of Nero and Maxentius. He claimed that they should be put to death, even if unconvicted of magic, as being renegades and perverters. With soulless resignation, he recognised in them God's chosen sign of the world's sins, especially papistry, and His scourge wherewith to plague apostates. Passing over Nashe's brilliant and erratic protest[5] against superstition,

---

[1] Cf. Walter Mapes, *De nugis curialium*, c. 1180, in which Satan admits that Ceres, Priapus, naiads, fauns, dryads, satyrs, Bacchus and Pan have been changed into devils.

[2] See *Dialogus de Pythonicis Mulieribus*, 1489.

[3] For the recrudescence of the witch panic in Tudor times, see *ante*, Vol. III, Chap. v, pp. 126 ff.; for the part played by Erasmus see, especially, *Colloquia Familiaria*; for Reuchlin, *De verbo mirifico*, 1494; for Wier, *De Praestigiis demonum*, 1564.

[4] *A Treatise against Witchcraft*, 1590.

[5] *The Terrors of the Night, or a Discourse of Apparitions*, 1594; see *ante*, Vol. IV, chap. XVI, pp. 372-373.

which squandered flashes of cultured ridicule on the unessential question of dreams and probably never reached serious controversialists, we find George Gifford returning[1] to the discussion in 1593. His new production, *Dialogues of Witches and Witchcraft*, is an important sign of the times. It treats of rustic superstitions, and, in a spirit of simple, broad-minded Christianity, he maintains, as Wier had already asserted, that witches and sorcerers have no diabolical power; that blight, the sickness of cattle and human ailments are the work of heaven alone and should be atoned for only by prayer and fasting. The treatise has many touches of character drawing, and this interest in human nature, combined with a sense of God's omnipotence, might well have led the author in the steps of Reginald Scot. But the growing pessimism of the age had turned Gifford's gaze from what is good in life. He still finds truth in the scholastic doctrine that the devil is a watchful diplomatist who takes possession of some malevolent old hag at a time when men are disturbed by calamity, causing her to claim the authorship of what has really been sent from heaven. He argues that the fiend, thanks to his superhuman knowledge, forecasts the future and then inspires "wise men" to make a show of causing what the devil has merely foreseen. In either case, these impostors consent to intercourse with the devil, are decoys to lure men from the worship of God and, therefore, should be put to death.[2]

In 1603, king James, who had taken a prominent part in the trial of Geilis Duncan and her associates, caused his *Daemonologie* to be printed and published in England. This dialogue, despite the jejuneness and insipidity which characterise all the literary efforts of that royal pedant, is a remarkable work. Like other witch treatises at the opening of the century, it still retains a critical and scholarly attitude towards the subject. James realises, as Burkard had done, that werewolves are the creation of a disordered fantasy, and that nightmares (popularly explained as a sensation of diabolical contact) are some reaction of the "humours" of the imagination.

---

[1] He had already produced *Discourse of the Subtle Practices of Devilles*, 1587.

[2] Hobbes held nearly the same view; arguing that witches should be punished although they have no real power, because they *think they have*, and *purpose* to do mischief. See *Leviathan*, p. 7, ed. 1651.

He agrees with St. Augustine that the apparent miracles of the devil are merely deceptions practised on the senses, and, though he naturally believes in demons and spirits, yet he follows the same authority and Roger Bacon[1] in asserting that the infernal world is thoroughly under the dominion of God. But James was a true child of his age. In an epoch of heightened competition and bitter feuds, he prefers to believe that people invoke infernal aid from lust for riches or revenge, rather than to attribute all witchcraft to the influence of melancholy.[2] When convinced of the probability of a league between devil and man, all the king's theological erudition is manipulated into proofs of this theory. The book is a manual, not discussing the question from an individual point of view, but recapitulating and enforcing the thories of previous demonologists, with a wealth of authoritative quotations dear to this learned age. Thus, despite unnecessary digressions into the realm of philology and scholasticism, the doctrine is presented with a realism and fulness of detail[3] which always carry conviction, and every reader found his own superstition recorded and stamped with the seal of royal approval. This powerful manifesto ended with the ill-fated recommendation that death should be inflicted on the evidence of children or even of fellow criminals (as in trials for treason) or after the water test and discovery of the devil's mark.[4]

The next few treatises on witchcraft add but little to the theories of Gifford and king James. William Perkins, in his *Discoverie of the damned Art of Witch craft* (1608), is, perhaps, the most typical. Perkins is oppressed with the spectacle of human error: he sees that men have the instinct to worship some god and that, in hours of great danger or superhuman effort, they turn for help to some higher power. But the true God has placed a limit to the knowledge and power of men, and many ambitious mortals are blind to these restrictions and endeavour to pass the goal of ordinance. When an author had taken this condemnatory view of men's struggle for knowledge

---

[1] *De Civitate Dei*, I. 18, c. 18, and *De Secretis Operibus Artis*, c. I, II.

[2] Bk. II, especially chap. II.   [3] Bk. II, chaps. II, IV, V, VI.

[4] For explanation of water test, see p. 425. The devil's mark was any part of the body which, after contact with the devil, lost sensation. Such local anaesthesia is a recognised symptom of hysteria.

and power, he could hardly refuse to believe that the devil was ready to help them. So he follows the authority and example of king James, describing Satan's well-organised kingdom and the illusory signs and wonders he works for those in his service. But, though he follows his predecessors by demanding the sentence of death against those convicted, he is one of the first to discountenance[1] the old-fashioned tests by hot iron, water or scratching, and to urge the necessity of carefully sifting circumstantial evidence.

Perkins's protest marks the beginning of a new phase in this discussion. So far back as 1576, seventeen or eighteen persons had been condemned for witchcraft at St. Osyth, and three more at Malden in 1579.[2] After parliament had followed their monarch's *Daemonologie* with a law condemning all witches to death, a series of official inquisitions, held especially in Lancashire, Essex and Yorkshire, brought to light innumerable cases of women, and sometimes of men, who confessed to a secret union with the devil. The seducer had access to them in all conceivable shapes, from a loathsome animal to a handsome man, leaving some point of contact on their bodies insensible to pain, and assigning to each a posse of attendant imps, who sucked their blood through teat-like orifices in the skin. Thanks to this intercourse, witches gained power to plague the persons and properties of their enemies. Modern psychology has recognised in these hallucinations the symptoms of different kinds of insanity and perversion,[3] and, of course, many confessions were wrung by torture from accused women in the hope of pardon or at least of respite from their anguish. But, in the seventeenth century, with its

---

[1] Chap. VI, "The Application of the Doctrine of Witchcraft to our Times."

[2] See the pamphlet of that year with a title eminently illustrative of this movement, *Detection of Damnable Drifts, practized by 3 Witches, arraigned at Chelmsforde in Essex . . . Set Forth to discover the Ambushementes of Sathan, Whereby He Would Surprise us, lulled in securitie and heardened with contempt of God's vengeance threatened for our offences.*

[3] See Freimark, *Occultismus und Sexualität*, 1909; Laurent-Nagour, *Occultismus und Liebe*, 1903; Lehmann, *Aberglaube*, 2nd ed. 1908; Delasseux, *Les Incubes et les Succubes*, 1897; Brevannes, *L'Orgie Satanique*, 1904; Paul Moreau, *Des Aberrations du Sens Génésique*, 4th ed. 1887; K. H. Ulrichs, *Incubus, Urningsliebe und Blutgier*, 1869. See also, papers by Freud, Jung, Ferenczi and Ernest Jones in *The American Journal of Psychology*, April, 1910.

ignorance of nervous diseases, tracts[1] disseminating these accounts appealed to the people's half suppressed sense of horror and love of impurity and created a profound impression. Writers now began to discuss the judicial aspects of witchcraft; but, however critical might be their attitude to methods of conviction, they never questioned the reality of the crime. Thus, John Cotta, a physician, who had insight enough to expose the frauds of quack doctors,[2] displays all the enlightenment of his age in *The Triall of Witchcraft, showing the true and righte method of discovery* (1616), but cannot dissuade himself from believing in magic and sorcery. He begins by declaring the subject to be beyond human knowledge and approachable only through conjecture and inference. By this devious method, he deduces that evil spirits exist, quoting the usual testimony from sacred and classical history; but his common sense prompts him to warn his readers that those suspected of witchcraft are often mere impostors or unconsenting agents in working the devil's miracles. He even employs his erudition to expose the fallacy of the water test.[3] But the many current reports of witchery lead him to agree with Reginald Scot that magic must have been at work when diseases produce unaccountable symptoms or defy accredited remedies.[4] And he maintains that the testimony of reliable witnesses or the detection of occult practices are enough to bring a witch to the bar. Edward Fairfax, translator of Tasso, and author of *Godfrey of Bulloigne*, succumbed to the prevailing panic. In an admirable piece of narrative prose,[5] he ascribes the mental disorders of his children to witchcraft, though the hallucinations and seizures are mainly due, in the case of younger children, to infantile hysteria and, of the elder girl, to suppressed eroticism. Nor could Richard Bernard, though a lucid and scholarly thinker, resist the conclusion of

---

[1] See bibliography and *A Collection of Rare and Curious Tracts relating to Witch craft*, 1838. For reprint of Thomas Potts's account of the famous trial of the Lancashire witches, 1613, see *Chetham Soc.*, vol. VI, 1835.

[2] *Discovery of . . . Ignorant Practicers of Physice*, 1612.

[3] The water test consisted in plunging the suspected person into a pond; if really a witch, who had renounced her baptism, the water would refuse to take her in and she would float. See chap. XVI.

[4] See chap. X.

[5] *A Discourse of Witch-craft as it was acted in the family of Mr. Edw. Fairfax . . . in* 1621.

many confessions and condemnations. In his *Guide to Grand Jury Men* (1627), he restates the arguments of the demonologists, from Sprenger to Cotta, and elaborates them with all the thoroughness of conviction. And yet Bernard is fully conscious of a vast error due to incredulity and inexperience. In the *First Booke*, he quotes the Bible to prove how much of supposed witchcraft is either mental disease or mere self-deception; and, towards the end of his work, he declares that the rumours of magic are often "the vain conceits of the addle-headed, or of silly fooles or of prattling gossips or of superstitiously fearful; or of fansieful melancholicks or of discomposed and crased wits."

Thus, though Bernard had all the knowledge and penetration necessary to refute these superstitions, he was too closely in touch with his age to see differently from his fellows. The evil had, indeed, reached its climax. Just as the anarchy of the reformation[1] had made men feel that all the army of Satan was let loose among them, so, now, in the time of civil war and hatred, each faction imputed such diabolic criminality to its opponents that the devil's presence was expected everywhere. The vampires and jackals of society began to trade on this obsession. Not only were such lying pamphlets published as *A Most certain true and strange discovery of a witch being overtaken as she was standing on a small plank board and as sailing it over the river of Newbury*, 1643, but "gulgropers," "falconers," "ranck-riders" and "ring-fallers" found that witch-hunting was more profitable than coney-catching, with the added luxury of abiding by the law. Children, who had always figured largely in the felony of the age, made a profession of feigning the symptoms of the bewitched. Such juvenile perjurers as the "Boy of Bilson" and the "Boy of Battlesdon" foamed at the mouth and fell into trances in the presence of certain old women.[2] Matthew Hopkins, a monster of impudence and iniquity, actually styled himself the "Witch-finder General" and manipulated the panic of his

---

[1] See Vol. III, Chap. v, pp. 124–125.

[2] See *Wonderful News from the North*, 1650; these and other reports of witch trials have been collected and discussed by Wallace Notenstein in *History of English Witchcraft from 1558 to 1718*, published by the American Historical Association, 1911.

age so successfully that parliament commissioned him to perform a circuit for the detection of witches, paying twenty shillings for each conviction. Again, literature, for want of wider scope, came under this contagion. Hopkins produced in 1647 *The Discovery of Witches; in answer to severall Queries;* a catechism in which he explains the symptoms of witchery and his methods of investigation. Yet this manifesto is less fantastic than some books thick with academic learning. Among the rest, John Stearne's *A Confirmation and Discovery of Witch-Craft* (1648) is unique. Though written in a spirit of impartial enquiry, the treatise contains perhaps the most bizarre collection of witch confessions in the world.

If intellectual progress can be compared to a journey, the Caroline age represents that stage in which pilgrims, having lost the track amid dangers and difficulties, turn backwards and search frantically for it along the earlier parts of the route. In this retrogression, the study of witchcraft led thinkers to investigate other forms of magic and occultism which might quietly have passed out of memory, especially astrology and alchemy.

From prehistoric times, it had been natural for man to regard all he sees and hears as connected with or like to himself. This sense of sympathy with creation had been developed by the thinkers of different countries till, in Pythagorism, it reached the doctrine of the "harmony of the spheres." Aristotle had taken a hint from this theory, in explaining the human body to be an aggregate of parts, so closely correlated that no unit could be affected without disturbing the rest. Later, the Stoics, imbued with eastern cosmic theories, had applied this physiological conception to the world as a whole. As in the human microcosm, so in the universal macrocosm, there was a constant play of interaction among the component parts. When this creed had been established, it was inevitable that the stars, with their mysterious motions and strange persistent brightness, should be considered to have a special influence over events on earth, and men believed that the course of mundane affairs could be predicted by studying these heavenly manifestations. Thus, "judicial astrology" came to be recognised as one of the seven liberal arts. Throughout the

Middle Ages and renascence it was occasionally banned, on
the authority of St. Augustine, as heresy against the doctrine
of free-will,[1] but would have been quietly abandoned in favour
of astronomy, if men had not either clung to it for want of
confidence in the new culture of their age or else attacked it as
being a snare of the devil.   In 1601, John Chamber produced
A Treatise against judicial Astrologie.   He begins his treatise
with a wearisome array of theological quotations and interpretations, as was inevitable in attacking what Aristotle was
considered to have taught and Abraham was supposed to have
practised.   He does not deny that astrology may contain the
truth, but he realises that men have not knowledge enough to
find it.   On the one hand, the influence of the stars cannot
be calculated, because many exist about which we know
nothing; and, on the other hand, we cannot discern the critical
moments of life at which the horoscope should be taken.   Such
events as being born or falling sick are astrologically unimportant; they are merely results; the causes, which really
prove the turning points in life, are too obscure to be timed.[2]
Yet this scholar, who studied astronomy and understood causation, supports Sprenger's contention[3] that, if astrologers
sometimes prophesy truly, it is because they are witches and
in league with the devil.   Sir Christopher Heydon answered this
book with an elaborate treatise[4] in which we still meet the
picturesque fantasies of the Middle Ages, asking Chamber
whether it is likely that the stars "onely bespangle Heaven
like vaine ornaments" while "the basest weede under his
feete" has medical power.   But, in less than ten years,
Chamber's friend George Carleton, bishop of Chichester,
composed, and ultimately printed in 1624, *ΑΣΤΡΟΛΟΓΟ-
MANIA: the madness of astrologers*, a voluminous rejoinder,
which condemns astrology as being no part of mathematics

---

[1] *E.g.* John of Salisbury declared astrology to be the beginning of idolatry,
Pico della Mirandola and Savonarola rejected the superstition, and Erasmus ridiculed it in *Encomium Moriae.*
[2] Chap. VI.   [3] *Malleus Malef.* pt. I, Q. XVI.
[4] *A Defense of Judiciall Astrologie in answer to a treatise lately published by M.
John Chamber*, 1603.   Among the Saville MSS. at the Bodleian is Chamber's
answer: *A Confutation of astrological Demonology in the Devil's School.*   The
dedication is dated 2 February, 1603 /4.   Apparently it was never published.
See *D. of N. B.*

or natural philosophy "because it proceedeth not by demonstration from certaine known Principles." But, though Carleton exacts a scientific basis for any system of speculation worthy of credence, yet he, too, is haunted by fear of the foul fiend. This excessive desire to know the future is not merely human folly; it is inspired by the devil.

Since medieval philosophers had learnt to regard creation as an aggregate of parts which influence one another, like the organs of a single body, their aim had always been to discover the innate sympathies and antipathies of things. When they had gained control over these tendencies, alchemists hoped to be able to remodel nature; especially by producing gold and silver out of inferior metals. These aspirations had not been definitely disproved, and now began to influence religious idealists, who could find only schism and controversy in the worship of the church. Dissatisfied with what they held to be the sensuous materialism of Roman worship, these purists declared themselves Lutherans, but, instinctively in love with pantheism and the mysteries of intuitive knowledge, they became disciples of Paracelsus and convinced themselves that they had found out the secret of all knowledge in a system of magic which penetrated the interior constitution of things. Yearning vaguely for a more spiritual conception of life, they professed to be engaged in the alchemical reconstruction of the world, by curing disease and creating precious metals. Their love of mysticism was gratified by uniting all such enthusiasts into a secret society to carry out the *magnum opus* under the symbol of the Rosy Cross.

Whether Rosicrucianism be of prehistoric antiquity[1] or not, it reached England from Germany at the beginning of the seventeenth century. The mystery surrounding this brotherhood and the strange symbolism of their doctrine provoked much misrepresentation, but, as most errors vaguely represent some intellectual movement, so Rosicrucianism, though retrograde and chimerical, is a recognition of the immaterial world and an assertion of man's supremacy over it. With this germ of progress, the fraternity did not lack apologists among men who could find no saner scope for their spiritual longings. Robert Fludd mournfully reviews the ineffectiveness and con-

[1] See Waite, A. E., *The Real History of the Rosicrucians*, 1887.

fusion of modern science, calling on his contemporaries to turn again and study the occult meanings of ancient philosophy. John Heydon sought to discover the secret of healing in the forces of nature, and has left a description of the Rosicrucian kingdom copied from the renascence Utopians and almost suggestive of *Erewhon*. Thomas Vaughan, though disclaiming all connection with the brotherhood, was yet imbued with the same spirit. For him, the coming of Elias meant the advent of the heavenly alchemist who should transform the universe into the pure gold of the spiritual city of God. For a while, these doctrines helped to disseminate a purer, nobler conception, both of God and man, and thus played a part in the change which came over the nation in the sixties. But such a sect could end, eventually, only in teaching self-justification and substituting what is vague and allegorical for practical Christianity. Like the witch terror, astrology and other relics of the Middle Ages, hermetic and cabalistic sciences were destined to be discredited—though not effaced—in the spiritual and intellectual revolution which they contributed, in some measure, to bring about.

This revolution, the advent of modern thought, took place as soon as the people had cultivated the habit of looking at a question from more than one point of view. The Baconians and a few of the Theophrastians[1] had acquired this impartiality and reflective scepticism from the study of the classics or of Montaigne; but the people were already absorbed in a controversy which appealed to their medieval instinct of unquestioning self-sacrifice in a cause. At an earlier epoch, this obstinacy and prejudice would have been a permanent obstacle to intellectual progress. Fortunately, the seventeenth century was not only an age of factions; it was an age which kept a diary. Every outburst of folly or hatred was printed on the impulse of the moment and scattered through the streets. Aggregates of people are proverbially irresponsible; but, in this case, the national conscience was gradually confronted with an incriminating record which with other influences shamed the people into a united effort towards progress.

The history of this mental awakening is the history of the broadside. Ever since Tudor times, the people had been ac-

[1] *E.g.* Earle and Stephens.

customed to see their thoughts and feelings reflected in penny
flysheets.[1] But, despite its universality of range and immense
popularity,[2] this fugitive literature was still an undeveloped
genre. The effusions which caught the passing attention of
'prentices, housewives and tradesmen, at street corners and
in city squares, were addressed to narrow, preoccupied in-
telligences and could never rise to the level of literature. But
London was swarming with young men[3] of wealth or birth who,
as an outcome of feudalism, believed that only the king had a
right to rule and that gentlemen should be above every profession except that of fighting for him. These "Hotspurres of
the Time," as a puritan writer calls them, amid the disorder and
dissipation of London life, claimed an interest in the literature
of the moment. Even the scapegoat of the *Gull's Horne-
booke*[4] was fashionable enough to compose poems and criticise
plays. But, though these "roaring boys," "hectors" and
"cavaliers" cultivated the clinches and conceits then in vogue,
much as they did extravagance of dress, they found that the
recognised vehicles of preciousness, such as character sketches
and epigrams, were too restricted, and, at the same time, too
laboured a field, to suit their full-blooded, though desultory,
attention to the arts. They required a genre which would
give full vent to their recklessness and animal spirits, and
they found this mode of expression partly in jest-books, but
much more in street ballads, which breathed the very essence
of old London and, almost imperceptibly, had blended with
their revels through the city.

Thus began the first stage in the development of the street
ballad. Cavaliers brought into it their dare-devil joviality
and carelessness and the wider interests of their active lives.
At the same time, the simplicity of ballad metre, adapted to a
catch melody, and the break between each stanza, precluded
complexity of thought or accumulations of periphrases. Old
types of humour[5] still survive, such as mock testaments and
burlesque laudations; but they take the form of rollicking
songs made up of ingenious conceits. Permanent comic char-

[1] *Ante*, Vol. III, Chap. v, p. 107. [2] *Ante*, Vol. IV, Chap. xvi, pp. 414–415.
[3] *Ante*, Vol. IV, p. 405.   [4] *Ante*, Vol. IV, p. 406.
[5] For discussion of these types see *ante*, Vol. III, Chap. v, pp. 95–106, and
bibliography, pp. 548–556.

acters like the miller, the tinker or the beggar reappear in the shape of lyricised monologues.[1] Drinking songs are plentiful, as in olden times. But, though we still find coarse merriment over red noses and claret-coloured complexions, though Walter Mapes's humorous touches of ancient and ecclesiastical lore are quite discarded, and wine—generally in opposition to plebeian beer—is frankly prized for its generous heat and exhilaration, yet the cavaliers also sing of it as the spur to heroic action and a solace in trouble or captivity. Besides wine, these songs discuss women. Some recount lawless and ungallant adventures reminiscent of the *Fabliaux* and jest-books; others remain frankly goliardic in their cynical invective against marriage or in their satire on female vanity, lust and caprice; some others are pervaded by the grossest sensuality. Yet, even here, the new influence is easily recognisable. Many of these effusions are full of the courtier's cult of the fair sex, which, though fulsome and extravagant, was introducing new words and expressions into the language. Even the common paramour is sometimes encircled by a halo of poetic phraseology which hides her baseness, while other poems, in the new atmosphere of action, breathe a manly independence and contempt of uxorious servitude. But the elevation of the popular song is most noticeable when it treats, in clear, simple verse, the more serious subjects which these cavaliers understood only too well, such as the power of money, the injustice of fortune or the tyranny of the sword.

Thus, the metres and diction of popular catch-pennies had risen to the level of educated and experienced men. By the third decade of the seventeenth century, these fugitive fly-sheets had also been called upon to serve the purpose of the political rancour and indignation which retarded intellectual progress and plunged England into civil war. Once again, the pamphleteers and ballad-mongers of the time had recourse to old forms of literature to convey their sarcasm and innuendo. For instance, one lampoon on Buckingham's expedition to France, with the refrain "The cleane contrary way," is copied from the *Cujus contrarium verum est* of medie-

---

[1] For the development of "scoundrel verse," see Chandler, F. W., *The Literature of Roguery*. vol. I, chap. III, sect. IV.

val satire,[1] and two more, in imitation of Lucian or Dekker,[2]
are dialogues between Charon and the murdered duke. Another pamphlet, travestying the title of a newspaper as *Mercurius Diabolicus or Hell's Intelligencer*, shows us the devil, in
answer to a citizen's question, recounting the pressure of work
in hell since parliament came into power; and, in 1660, when
that body dissolved itself and a general desire for the restoration of the king was felt, a ballad *News from Hell or the
Relation of a Vision*, represents the devil's amazement and
incredulity that England, lately "His sweet darling dear," was
now proving false to her allegiance to hell. Others, such as
Heraclitus' Dream (1642), representing the shepherd (*i.e.* the
church) shorn by his sheep, are copied from medieval dream-
visions.

The monologue was further developed and reached a high
level of satire in such pieces as *Truth Flatters Not* (1647), in
which, after pope, priest and prelate have betrayed their
worldly ambition and duplicity, each in a soliloquy, Truth
censures them all in a closing speech. Or, in *Three Speeches*
(1642), satirising the narrowness and self-satisfied philistinism
of the commercial class, as exemplified by "Master Warden's"
political oration to his fellows; his wife's comments on the discourse to her friends and the chambermaid's views on affairs
in general and especially on papistry. The old dramatic
broadside is still found in *A coffin for King Charles; a Crowne
for Cromwell; a Pit for the People* (1649).

Other forms of popular literature were at once adapted to
the factious feelings of the people. In *Mercurius Melancholicus, or Newes from Westminster* (1647), the old idea of "a
dozen arrant fooles and knaves" is still preserved. Mock
testaments were used by both parties as at the time of the reformation,[3] much like the more modern "burning in effigy,"
to vilify not only persons but causes. In the new spirit of the
times, they became more like allegories than mere lampoons.
For instance, *A True Inventory of the goods and chattels of Super-*

---

[1] *Ante*, Vol. II, Chap. XVI, p. 438.

[2] The idea of a visit to hell is almost continuous in literature since Homeric
times, and had been used by Jacobean writers, especially by Dekker, T., in
Newes from Hell, 1606; see *ante*, Vol. IV, Chap. XVI, pp. 403, 404 and bibliography
under Dekker, T., p. 597.

[3] Cf. *The Wyll of the Devyll, ante*, Vol. III, Chap. V, p. 97.

stition (1642) tells how Superstition, of the parish of Blind
Devotion in the county of Corrupt Doctrine and in the kingdom of Idolatry, bequeaths his goods and chattels.   Puritans,
especially familists, constantly resorted to their Bible to heap
obloquy on the worldliness and licence of the cavaliers.   In
the *Dammee*[1] *Cavaliers Warning piece* (1643), they construed
Obadiah's tirade against the Idumeans into a censure of the
royalist party; *The Debauched Cavalier, or the English Mid-
ianite* (1642) is an attempt to discover, in the lives of king
Charles and his supporters, the enormities with which Israel's
enemy was credited: *The Downefall of Dagon* (1643) is the
demolition of the cross in Cheapside.   The dialogue had, for
centuries, been a familiar form of discussion and satire, so now,
many puritan pamphlets are modelled on the catechism.
Some are serious booklets, such as *The Souldiers Catechism*
(1644), in which a Christian's right to take up arms in defence
of religious and civil freedom and his duty as a true warrior
are taught by question and answer.   But there still lingered
among the people the medieval tendency to travesty sacred
formulas, and this love of parody led pamphleteers to vent their
irony in mock catechisms as well as in mock testaments.
The most abject self-incriminations are put into their opponents' mouths.[2]   A subtler and more mordant irony pervades *The City Dames Petition in the behalfe of the long afflicted,
but well affected cavaliers* (1647).   Certain wives of London
tradesmen sign a letter begging the king and parliament to stop
the war.   The document explains that the good women—
true descendants of the Wife of Bath, Maid Emlyn and Jill
of Brainford—who mind their husbands' shops, sorely miss not
only the custom, but, also, the courtship of those gallant ex-
quisites whose breath was "as sweet as amber" and whose
essences made the dames' establishments as "fragrant as the
spring's first flowers."   The royalist party met their opponents
with the same weapons.   They refuted puritan calumny

---

[1] As the puritan strictly excluded oaths from his conversation, the cava'ier
cultivated them.   His "Damn" was almost proverbial and is the theme of the
vindictive ballad *A total Rout, or a brief discovery of a Pack of Knaves and Drabs*
(1653).
[2] *Cavaliers' Catechisme, or the Reformed Protestant catechising the anti-christian
Papist*, 1643.

and asserted their faith in the divine right of kings by such manifestoes as *The Cavaliers Catechisme and confession of his faith* (1646), while they vented their scorn and hatred of the parliament by representing it at prayer for release from its own imputed sins in *The Parliaments Letanie* (1647). Even amid the bitterness of defeat, the cavalier gaiety lives in these litanies; in one of them,[1] supplications to avoid such afflictions as usurers, parliamentary government and Oliver Cromwell are offered up in rollicking verses suggestive of a drinking song.

Controversialists tended to ridicule their antagonists under some typical name or character. Thus, we find the presbyterian party frequently attacked under the name of Jack Presbyter or Sir John Presbyter, just as, when the republican party rallied at the time of the Rump, their opponents alluded to them by their own battle-cry "The Cause."[2] But, more often, the Londoner's interest in notorieties, which had already, in less troublous times, made household words of such characters as Hobson and Tarlton,[3] now created a demand for allusions to individuals. Thus, satirists were led to cultivate the heart of personal caricature and ridicule which was soon to become the chief excellence of political songs. There are sarcasms on prince Rupert's dog, Oliver Cromwell's nose[4] and Ireton's effeminate chin. But many pamphleteers still utilised the decasyllabic couplet, which Hall and Marston had established as the recognised vehicle of personal invective. These satirists improved on the confused and obscure diction of their models, but they cramped themselves in a style too staid and monotonous for the whimsical vein of the true lampoonist. They were more successful in the formal epigrams and elegies which appeared in multitudes, especially to lament the death of Essex in 1646, of Charles in 1648 and of Gloucester[5] in 1660.

---

[1] *The Cavaliers Letanie lately composed by a well willer to his Majesty's person and all his most Loyall Subjects*, 1648.

[2] *E.g.* Prynne's *The Republican and others spurious good Old Cause briefly and truely anatomised*, 1659.

[3] See *ante*, Vol. IV, Chap. XVI, p. 411.

[4] *E. g. A Case for Nol Cromwells Nose and the Cure of Tim Fairfax's Gout*, 1648, and *The Blazing-Star, or, Nolls Nose Newly Revived and taken out of his Tomb*. By Collonel Baker, 1660. [5] See *Catalogue of the Thomason Tracts*, 1908, B.M.

As the civil war was, in some respects, a struggle between systems and institutions, many pamphleteers cared less about individuals than classes, and resorted to character sketches as the handiest weapon for type satire. The Theophrastians[1] had taught succeeding generations how to create a lifelike word-picture out of all that was ridiculous or objectionable in any social type. When mutual opposition made the puritan more rigidly correct and the cavalier more aggressively self-assertive, there were endless opportunities for crisp, concentrated portraiture. And yet, only a few sketches, such as the versified *A Puritane set forth in his lively colours . . . with the Character of an Holy Sister* (1642) or the trenchant study *The Drunkard's Character* (1646) or T. Forde's collection of clear-cut portraits entitled *Times anatomised* (1647) or John Wilson's picture of purity and single-heartedness, *A New Anatomie or character of a Christian, or a Roundhead* (1645), preserved the statuesque outline of the genre. In the heat of political conflict, men cannot detach their minds from episodes and side issues; they need to argue over isolated questions, and, thus, the bulk of political character sketches digress into particulars till many of them become little else than manifestoes or "queries." John Cleiveland, who begins his portraits with Overburian flashes of wit and fantasy, soon forgets himself and his subject in bitter criticisms of his opponents, in one character sketch[2] exclaiming: "But I have not Inke enough to cure all the Tetters and Ring-worms of the State." So completely is the style absorbed in the heat and the haste of civil feud, that some so-called "characters" merely retain the title, presumably because of its popularity.

These many types of literature were employed by pamphleteers because the spirit of conflict was still that of the sixteenth century. In the Middle Ages and at the renascence, controversy appealed to men's passions rather than to their intellect. The issues were generally so simple that combatants had not any need to argue deeply; but the cause lay so near their hearts that they could not keep from obloquy. Hence, they invented a whole literature of vituperation, so that the same insults could be repeated again and again in new ways.

[1] *Ante*, Vol. IV, Chap. XVI, pp. 383, 391.
[2] *The Character of a London Diurnall*, 1644.

The seventeenth century inherited this armoury of invective and also their ancestors' single-hearted eagerness to use it. Yet a large proportion of broadsides have no peculiarity of form or style and, so far as genre is concerned, remain street ballads. After this reversion to simplicity comes the beginning of a great change. Even before the king's standard was raised, there were a number of level-headed democrats like the author of *The present estate of Christendome* (1642), who takes a statesmanlike view of the unrest pervading Europe and suggests practical remedies for each country including his own. But, when hostilities had once broken out, the sentiments of the common people also became more complex. A national controversy was an interchange of assertions; but, for the average man, the civil war was a game of chess,[1] in which not only his opinions but his sympathies, ideals and, perhaps, life and property, were the pawns. Hence, while some pamphleteers were irrevocably committed to the support of one faction, others found their partisanship distracted by all manner of calculations, conjectures and conflicting emotions, and their broadsides became reviews of the situation.[2] Parodies, epigrams, testaments and portraits were not of any service to such commentators. While *Corantos*, *Mercuries* and *Diurnalls* were developing into newspapers, they wrote their leading articles—for such is the character of these ballads —in the form of street verse, because the people, from force of habit, still looked to this type for an expression of their own opinions. But their work, nevertheless, is new in spirit.

The comments and arguments of these broadsides are not original or profound; but they show that a large proportion of the people had become reflective. Not only ballads, but pamphlets and tracts now adopt a more thoughtful tone and we enter on the third stage in the development of flysheet literature. When bloodshed had begun, the ordinary citizen also realised that civil war was far worse than the victory of either party, and tracts began to appear such as *England's*

---

[1] *The Game of Chesse, a metaphoricall Discourse showing the present estate of This Kingdome* (1643).

[2] See many of the pieces in *Rump: or an exact collection of the choycest Poems and Songs relating to the Late Times. By the most Eminent Wits, from anno* 1639 *to anno* 1661. 1662. Facsimile rpt. n.d.

*Miserie, if not prevented by the speedie remedie of a happy union
between His Majestie and His Parliament* (1642). Or, again,
the leaders in the struggle were bitterly and unjustly satirised
for preventing peace in *Mr. Hampden's Speech occasioned upon
the Londoner's Petition for Peace* (1642) or in *The Sense of the
House* (1643), which put into the mouths of orators selfish and
inept reasons for continuing the war. R. W., who had already
upheld the parliamentarian cause in several pamphlets, now
brought the wisdom and experience of antiquity to bear on
the question of actual fighting. In *The Character of Warre*
(1643), he discusses its justification but observes "that none
delight in the sound of the warlike Drums or in the Alarmes of
Warr; but onely they who never tasted the bitternesse thereof." The author of a weird fantasy entitled *A Winter Dreame*
(1649), describes in rhythmic and harmonious prose how he
seemed to visit the different countries of Europe distracted by
war, ending with England, the most stricken of all. Protests
are also heard on behalf of the simpler joys of peace, but none
set forth this new spirit of common humanity more effectively
than *The Virgins Complaint for the Losse of their sweethearts
occasioned by these present wars* (1643). From the strenuous
days of Elizabeth, the great personalities of history had
appealed to men's imagination; and now, in the excitement
of war, people found themselves even more in sympathy with
bygone days. *The Penitent Traytor* (1647), representing the
confession of a Devonshire gentleman condemned for treason
against Henry III, is only one of many ballads which brought
the past into touch with the emotions of the present. But
the middle classes were now beginning to think, and to turn
to history for guidance in perplexity.[1] Thus, even at the
outset of the struggle, they welcomed such pamphlets as
*Some wiser than Some; or A Display of the Times past and
present, with some probable conjecture of the times to come* (1643).
A growing spirit of protest against excess runs all through this
period of anarchy. In 1641, the jangle of conflicting creeds
was exposed in *A Discovery of 29 Sects here in London*, and,
again, in 1646, by Thomas Edwards's *Gangraena*. But, among
other such censures, none illustrates better the new temper of

[1] Cf. *Morall Discourses and Essayes* by T. C., 1655. See, also, *Expedients for
Publique Peace*, 1660.

the times than H. B.'s *The Craftsmans Craft, or the Wiles of the Discoverer* (1649), which revolts not against the number of sects but against the spirit of calumny in which they carried on their controversies. As the fortune of war varied from week to week, the evil effect of mendacious and inflammatory news-sheets became only too evident. The maker of broadsides had been an object of censure since Elizabethan times, and, just before the outbreak of the war, an act suppressing unlicensed printers was made the occasion for a malicious dialogue on this needy brood.[1] In 1642, a Theophrastian character sketch describes the ballad-monger's fiery nose and wretched drunken rimes, full of libels and lying rumours.[2] There is a mellower spirit in *The Great Assizes holden in Parnassus*, at which the scholars of the renascence acting as judges, the great English poets (including Drayton, Shakespeare and Massinger) as jury, with Ben Jonson as keeper of the "Trophonian Denne" and John Taylor as crier of the court, arraign these new-fledged periodicals for perverting the truth, defiling literature, seducing readers from more serious books and disseminating poisonous doctrines. The proceedings are narrated in smooth decasyllabic verse, with many sly touches of humour.

With all its errors and excesses, the great rebellion was, for many men, a crusade against the vices of feudalism. Reforming zeal was in the air, and, during the civil war and the protectorate, earnest men were busy investigating social and administrative abuses which had not been direct issues of the struggle. Controversies which seem to arise in puritan bigotry, disclose a thoughtfulness and sanity quite foreign to Elizabethan exposures. The hatred of elaborate dress, which began with the fanaticism of the Adamites, gradually changed into a respect for the dignity of the human form. Broadsides ridiculed fashions because they were incongruous, and John Bulwer, in his *Anthropometamorphosis* (1653), collected all the stories, ancient and modern, of savages' adornments and mutilations, to show how men disgrace what was made in

---

[1] *The Downfall of temporizing poets, unlicensed printers, upstart booksellers, trotting Mercuries and bawling Hawkers*, 1641.

[2] *A True description of the Pot-Companion Poet, Who is the Founder of all the Base and libelous Pamphlets lately spread abroad.*

God's image. A hatred of gluttony runs through the paper war waged against Christmas celebrations. Puritan distrust of women had started again the time-honoured controversy as to feminine character; but now the dispute broadened into moral councils on love or marriage and is free from pruriency. The most revolting coarseness is still found, but only in diatribes against prostitution. The greater number of pamphlets merely ridicule the inconstancy, vanity or caprice of women. Many are cast into the form of dialogues and epistles. And, although humourists, in this age of constitutional anomalies, found piquancy in picturing female parliaments and commonwealths in which women assert their independence, the satire has lost the venom of the preceding age.

Other pamphleteers turned their attention to abuses in the administration of justice. The system of imprisonment for debt had already been attacked as early as 1618 by Mynshul's curious *Characters of a Prison;*[1] and, in 1622, the remarkable *A Petition to the King's most Excellent Majestie* had urged the injustice of imprisoning a man because of his financial losses and the folly of depriving the state of serviceable citizens, besides eloquently describing the mental anguish and moral degradation of gaol life. These evils became tenfold more apparent during the disasters and disorganisation of the civil war. One writer[2] tells how the minor officials of the court gain access to the ear of the judge and use their influence to further their own ends; another[3] describes the mercenary character of lawyers and their devices for delaying judgment, thereby filling their own pockets; another[4] protests against the tyranny and exaction of gaolers. The turns of fortune, in these insecure times, had brought many law-abiding and educated men to prison, who beguiled their weariness and sorrow by writing. Thus, quite a literature of gaol-birds sprang up, one of the best productions being Sir Francis Wortley's spirited ballad[5] on the incarcerated royalists in 1647. When the protectorate was

---

[1] *Ante,* Vol. IV, Chap. XVI, p. 400.

[2] *The Courts of Justice Corrected and Amended, or The Corrupt Lawyer Untrust, Lash'd and quasht,* 1642.

[3] *A Looking glasse for all proud, ambitious, covetous and corrupt Lawyers,* 1646.

[4] *Liberty vindicated against slavery,* 1646.

[5] *A Loyall Song, of the Royall Feast kept by the Prisoners in the Towre* . . . (On the occasion of a present of two brace of bucks from the king).

established, men hoped that peace would leave the government leisure to rectify these and other abuses. Pamphlets and flysheets on legal and prison reform now became even more numerous; and, though these writers have neither the style nor the vigour of earlier times, they nearly all show a sense of human rights and a practical insight into the far-reaching effects of social evils, very different from the narrow violence of Jacobean and Caroline pamphleteers. Everywhere, the people seemed to feel the need of reconciliation and fellowship. In 1647, *The Cavaliers' Diurnall written by Adventure* replaced real news or invective by playful sarcasm and literary trifling, suggestive of the Addisonian circle. Even in *A Relation of the Ten grand, infamous Traytors, who for their murder and detestable villany against our late soveraigne Lord King Charles the First* (1660), the horror of regicide is almost lost sight of in the cultivation of style.

Tolerance, reasonableness and sympathy were by no means strangers to English literature; they had graced the works of scholars and courtiers; they had shed their charm over the drama. But it was not till the end of the civil war that the middle classes, as a whole, began to outgrow medieval habits of thought and expression and to cultivate modern "civilitie." As we have seen, this advance was partly due to reaction of sentiment, but, even more, to a certain change in the people's mode of life. The citizens of old London were gregarious, and, as the civil war had been a conflict of opinions no less than of arms, they had developed the necessity for discussion. Being careful both of their health and of their purse, they did not like to meet in taverns, but began to frequent coffee-houses, because a cup of the newly-imported Turkish beverage cost only one penny and was supposed to cure minor ailments.[1] As early as 1659, Miles's coffee-house in Palace yard was the meeting place of James Harrington's club, the "Rota," a debating society for the discussion of political problems.[2]

[1] See *A Cup of Coffee, or Coffee in its Colours*, 1663, and *A Brief Description of the Excellent Virtues of that sober and wholesome drink called Coffee and its Incomparable effects in preventing or curing most diseases incident to Humane Bodies*, 1674.

[2] See *The Rota: or the Model of a Free State, or Equal Commonwealth; once proposed and debated in brief and to be again more at large proposed to and debated by a free and open society of ingenious Gentlemen*. And *The Censure of the Rota upon*

By 1662, the Latine coffee-house, near the stocks, was the resort of doctors and scholars, and we learn from the amusing verses of *News from the Coffee-house* (1667), that, in some places, the conversation turned on city fashions and foibles as well as on affairs of state. In 1675, the author of *The Coffee-houses Vindicated* expresses the true power of these resorts, when he asks

> Now whither shall a person, wearied with hard study, or the laborious turmoils of a tedious day, repair to refresh himself? or where can young gentlemen, or shop-keepers, more innocently and advantageously spend an hour or two in the evening, than at a coffee-house? . . . To read men is acknowledged more useful than books; but where is there a better library for that study, generally than here; among such a variety of humours, all expressing themselves on divers subjects according to their respective abilities?

Thus, the middle classes had at last found a field in which it was possible to realise Montaigne's and Cornwallis's[1] ideal of observing human nature, and a literature at once sprang up to satisfy this new-born curiosity in the humours of coffee-house life. *The Character of a Coffee-house* (1673) brilliantly describes, in true Overburian style, the amateur politicians grouped round some self-constituted authority and introduces a scathing portrait of the "Town-wit," the descendant of Dekker's Gull, who interrupts citizens' discussions with his obscenity and profane language; and, in 1677, a volume of conversational anecdotes collected at these rendezvous was published by Roger L'Estrange.[2] As the coffee-houses had a mixed *clientèle* in which republican equality was the order of the day,[3] the consequent freedom of conversation and unrestrained display of personality offered a new field for the writer of dialogues. This genre had already become, in the hands of such writers as Gifford, king James, Walton and especially Nicholas Breton, a recognised means of conveying ideas to the people, and their followers began by choosing

---

Mr. Milton's Book entitled The Ready and Easy Way to establish a Free Commonwealth. Both in 1660.

[1] *Ante*, Vol. IV, Chap. XVI, p. 393.

[2] *Coffee-house Jests. By the author of The Oxford Jests* [i. e. W. Hickes].

[3] See *Rules and Orders of the Coffee-house*, attached to *A Brief Description*, 1674

coffee-houses merely to give an attractive background to the discussions. *The Coffee Scuffle* (1662), caricaturing a learned argument between a domineering pedant and a man of the world, shows that literary burlesque could at length find more subtle and refined material than in the days of *Barnabees Journal* and *Moriomachia*, while two other pamphlets[1] turn an essay on popery into a lifelike discussion between a voluble captain and a supercilious young lawyer who meet at one of these houses. In these and other productions of like nature, the arguers begin to be more important than the argument. The street, the tavern and the home had for centuries displayed the boorishness or brutality of men; but the coffee-house revealed oddities of thought and manner far more interesting to the modern observer. These quaint ideas and touches of eccentricity were only to be brought out in conversation, and so the dialogue gradually became a study of character culminating in some of Addison's charming sketches.

This friendly interest in the peculiarities of character increased the abhorrence with which men viewed the revilings[2] of the age of the civil war. The age was bent on mutual respect and consideration. So they turned to the study of letter writing to cultivate a more suave spirit of intercourse. Davies[3] describes "the gentler art" as "the cement of all society, the foundation and Superstructure of all Friendship and conversation." It is true that epistolary correspondence had been recognised as a literary type since the renascence had brought men into touch with Cicero, Seneca and Guevara, and that, as early as 1586, Angell Day had produced a manual of letter writing,[4] while other writers, including Nicholas Breton[5] and Joseph Hall,[6] had appealed in this form to the public; but, then, the art was being cultivated as a literary experiment. The new generation were more interested in courtesy and the

---

[1] *A Coffee-House Dialogue*, 1679, and *A Continuation of the Coffee-House Dialogue*, 1680.

[2] See J. Pettus's prefatory letter to *Lovedays Letters Domestic and Forreine*, edited by his brother in 1659.

[3] Dedic. to Boswell, G., in *Letters of Affaires, Love and Courtship. Written to Several persons of Honour and Quality: By . . . Monsieur de Voiture*, 1657.

[4] *English Secretary.*

[5] *A Poste with a Packet of Mad Letters*, 1603.

[6] *Six Decads of Epistles*, 1607–10.

expression of mutual respect.   For them, letter writing was a civilising influence.   So they looked for their models, not among the ancients, but at the French court, where a period of peace and concentrated government had developed a more refined and intellectual ideal of social life.   Thus, writers who might, thirty years earlier, have revived and adapted ancient styles of literature, now edited and translated the letters of Balzac, de la Serre and Voiture, or cast their tractates into an epistolary form in which the courtesies of this type of literature were scrupulously observed, as in *Metamorphosis Anglorum* (1660), addressed to Don Lewis de Haro.   The taste for novels of chivalry[1] had never quite died out and now became again fashionable, because the society of the restoration found in the French romances that art of sentimental courtship which had again become the ideal of refinement and high breeding. W. Browne translated Gomberville's *Polexandre* in 1647, and other translators followed him with the romances of La Calprenède and Madeleine de Scudéry.   Paraphrases were followed by imitations.   Roger Boyle published *Parthenissa* in 1654, Sir George Mackenzie wrote *Aretina* in 1661, John Crowne produced his solitary romance *Pandion and Amphigenia* in 1665; and, although these compositions are interminably long and loosely constructed, the reader could learn therein how to turn a compliment, express his passion, write a love letter and interpret the sentiments of his heart after the style of the Hôtel de Rambouillet.   More practical civilisers collected anecdotes and apophthegms which might help to teach good manners.   The cult of "ana," like that of the epistolary art, was of ancient origin,[2] and had flourished through the Middle Ages and the renascence.[3]   But, again, new tendencies led men away from antiquity.   Though compilers of such miscellanies are particularly liable to draw on familiar material,[4] the present generation preferred anecdotes of king Charles I,

---

[1] See Raleigh, W., *The English Novel*, 5th ed., 1903, chap. IV, from which these facts are taken.

[2] See Wolf, J. C., Intro. to *Casauboniana*, 1710.

[3] *E. g.* Gregory the Great's *Liber Dialogorum* (reminiscences of St. Benedict and his companions, sixth to seventh centuries), *Lutheri Colloquia Mensalia*, 1566, *Melanchthoniana*, 1562.

[4] *E. g. Witty Apophthegms . . . by Francis Lord Bacon* are current witticisms of antiquity derived originally from Cicero, Suetonius and Plutarch.

the marquis of Worcester or Sir Thomas More, which culminate in some courtly phrase or witty but suave rejoinder; and Selden's *Table Talk*, which Richard Milward probably compiled soon after his death,[1] would be welcomed because of its tolerance, moderation and breadth of view.

Now that men had reached this new stage of progress, the Baconian essay began to lose its value. There were still a few followers of the old school who, like Thomas Manley,[2] sought distraction from war and politics by compiling maxims and meditations out of their desultory reading. But the enthusiasm for discovering lessons of self-education in the classics now flagged because the charm of novelty was gone, and the humanists of the protectorate were too full of the work of reconstruction to centre their reflections on themselves. Thus, the essay gradually ceased to be an intellectual diary and showed signs of becoming an organ for propagating ideas. An exiled royalist with the intention "to sport away the tedious houres with the dalliance of my pen" described his experiences abroad in *The Character of Spain* and *The Character of Italy* (both in 1660). But the two sketches expand into veritable treatises with their invectives against Jesuits, papistry, alchemy and the gunpowder plot, varied by observations on history and sociology.

Men were dissatisfied with their state of culture, because they had begun to realise its possibilities. The conviction was steadily growing that scholars, as Waterhouse declared in *An Humble Apologie for Learning and Learned Men* (1653), were "the Horsmen and Chariots of any Nation"; not an academic caste, but civilisers. For this reason, they were willing to criticise that system of half-scholastic education which had nourished the witch controversy and left many other perplexities unsolved. As early as 1646, John Hall, in *Horae Vacivae*, declared that ancient philosophers should only be studied because they stimulate discussion on modern topics. In 1653, John Webster[3] examined all the established branches

---

[1] Selden died in 1654; *Table Talk*, though not published till 1689, is dedicated to "Mr. Justice Hales," *i.e.* Sir Matthew Hales, who ceased to be judge of the Common Pleas in 1658. See ed. by Singer, S. W., *Library of Old Authors*, 1890.

[2] *Temporis Angustiae*, 1649.

[3] *Academiarum Examen, or the Examination of Academies*, 1653.

of learning and declared that conservatism was keeping knowledge from shedding any light on life and its mysteries. In 1657, a writer on education, who signs himself "J. B. Gent," superseded Milton's and Peacham's treatises with the remarkable *Heroick Education*. The author gives the death-blow to formalism, by insisting that each pupil has a peculiar individuality and, therefore, requires a special training. The average lad of gentle birth is an obscure maze of cross-tendencies which he has not yet learnt to control, and the tutor's first duty is to make an intimate study of his character. His pupil is led towards good or evil by some enjoyment incidental to its pursuit, and the teacher, by closely watching his appetites, maladies, dreams and "colour" will be able to find out what particular pleasure appeals to his instincts. Mental training must be equally unfettered by tradition. The students of the renascence had aimed at accumulating vast stores of erudition under the control of a quick memory. But the youth of the restoration must, also, cultivate "commonsense," that is, wisdom to digest and apply his learning. Nor must his intellectual individuality be fettered by imitating another's style, "for discourse and writing being images of the soul, every one expresses his thoughts differently according to his own genius." Now that the age had realised the necessity for mutual respect and forbearance, the student must acquire tact and address no less than knowledge and, above all, the knack of adapting himself to other people's moods and tastes which is the true art of conversation.[1]

Humanists were not content with putting knowledge to new uses. Now that a settled government gave them leisure to catch the spirit of continental philosophy, writers began, even in popular productions, to criticise the sources of knowledge itself. Meric Casaubon brought out *A Treatise concerning Enthusiasm* (1665) in which he argues from history and literature that inspiration, whether in rhetoric, poetry or the actor's craft, and ecstasy, whether in divination, worship or contemplation, are no supernatural gift but merely the working of nature and subject to illusion. The author of *Be Merry and Wise, or a Seasonable Word to the Nation* (1660) caught the spirit of his time when he exhorted his readers to

[1] Part II, chap. VII.

break away from the phrase-making of the Caroline generation and devote themselves in earnest to the work of reconstruction, asking "can anything be more Ridiculous then to stand Formalizing, in a case where tis impossible to be too early or too zealous?" Joseph Glanvill, in *The Vanity of Dogmatizing* (1661), reminded men how hypothetical and conjectural all knowledge was, how unreliable is the evidence of our own senses, and how completely fantasy and inclination dominate our convictions. In these and such like books the influence of Van Helmont and Descartes is evident and still more that of Agrippa, whose *De Vanitate Scientiarum*, though partly a burlesque, was reprinted, translated and often quoted because it insisted that the culture of the renascence was not all it pretended to be.

Thus, the civil war had given new life to English thought, first by solving the social and political controversies which had diverted humanists from better things; then, by exposing, in all their primitive repulsiveness, the fanaticism and bigotry which, for half a century, had withstood progress; then, by introducing the habit of discussion and reflection among the people as a whole, filling them with the desire for peace, order and mutual tolerance. The time for a creative genius had not yet come, but it was an age of criticism and revision, and we have seen how the middle classes were beginning, on the one hand to cultivate consideration for the individual and on the other hand to examine dogmas and traditions in the light of humanity and common-sense. It still remains to show how all these tendencies led thinkers to continue the vexed discussion on sorcery and occultism, and, without the aid of fresh material, to put a new construction on the data which had served Sprenger, Bodin, Gifford, James, Perkins and Cotta.

Astrology had already been condemned by Chamber and Carleton; but the belief in predictions became so widespread during the hazards of the war that, when Lilly prophesied a more than usually terrible series of disasters, to follow the eclipse of 1652, John Evelyn tells us that the common folk would not "worke nor stir out of their houses so ridiculously were they abus'd by knavish and ignorant stargazers." But the same year saw an excellent piece of sarcasm on this prophecy, entitled *Strange Predictions*, and John Gaule, who had once been a believer in the superstition, brought out a voluminous refutation,[1] in which he attributes the success of astrology to its votaries' eagerness to be deceived and reminds his readers that, even if a constellation could affect a new-born babe, the child's training, home-life and social position will soon supersede such influences.

Other attacks on stargazing followed, but it was the horrors and iniquities of the witch persecution which chiefly claimed the attention of humanists. Robert Filmer employed the critical common-sense of his generation to attack Perkins's book in *An advertisement to the Jury-men of England* (1653), pointing out that compacts between the devil and old women, even if mentioned in the Bible, were hardly a matter for serious consideration, since the witch can always escape from her obligation by repentance and is, at the worst, only an accessory in any deed and, therefore, should not be punished before the principal. Thomas Ady, in *A Candle in the Dark* (1656), discussed the subject with the same practical logic but with a wider knowledge of the world. Like Harman, Chettle, Greene, Nashe, Dekker and Rowlands, he was familiar with the jugglers, diviners, ventriloquists and conjurers who still infested England, and he argues that such as these were the so-called witches and magicians whom Saul persecuted and *Deuteronomy* condemned to death. Fifty years before, Gifford had silenced the plea for clemency by arguing that witches desire diabolical power and, therefore, should die. But the present age was too engrossed in the practical problems of this world to succumb to such unreasoning fear of the devil, and Ady deems it sufficient refutation to expose the witchfinder's methods of conviction.

Although both Filmer and Ady begin their treatises with the inevitable discussion on Biblical authority, their work is important because, like their forerunner Reginald Scot, they brought the kindly wisdom of daily life into this academic controversy. In this respect, they prepared the way for John Wagstaffe. His book, *The Question of Witchcraft debated* (1669), makes full use of his predecessors' appeals to common-sense, but he goes beyond them by also appealing to secular

[1] Πῦς-μαντια *The Mag-astro-mancer or the Magicall-Astrologicall-Diviner Posed and Puzzled,* 1652.

scholarship and erudition. He sketches the history of religious persecution, and argues that, from the days of Maxentius and Theodosius onwards, the church has endeavoured to suppress heresy, solely in order to extend its own temporal sovereignty.

Meanwhile, demonology was not in need of apologists. R. T., in *The Opinion of Witchcraft Vindicated* (1670), attempted to counteract the effect of Wagstaffe's book by reminding his readers, as many demonologists had done, that the devil is a servant of God, employed on his errands, nor have we any right to deny his existence because we cannot explain to ourselves how he acts. Glanvill followed the same line of argument in *Philosophical Considerations touching Witches and Witchcraft* (1666). Meric Casaubon, in *Of Credulity and Incredulity* (1668) discusses many wonders which the enlightenment of his age had now proved to be natural phenomena. But he is alarmed at the spread of rationalism and too deeply imbued with reverence for the Bible to question any doctrines which were supposed to emanate from that source. So he condemns as atheists and uneducated all those who denied a league between the devil and men, and dwells on the enormous volume of testimony, ancient and modern, literary and judicial, in proof of sorcery. And yet it is manifest that these scholars were pleading a lost cause. Men believed in witchcraft so long as its horror, grotesqueness and defilement fascinated their imagination. The earlier demonologists had quoted Scripture and the classics to the full, but their conviction really rested on the prurient or ghastly anecdotes with which this superstition abounded. The spell of mystery and horror still exercised its power over the vulgar, and broadsides continued to report cases of bewitchment; but the age had learnt to criticise its own ideas and educated apologists already showed a degree of sensibility and intellectual refinement quite inconsistent with these beliefs. The superstitition still seemed to thrive because it had not yet been confronted with the purer, keener outlook of the restoration.

This was the work of John Webster. His book *The Displaying of supposed Witchcraft* (1677) does not contribute any new material to the controversy; in fact, he admits himself that the demonographers had already been "quashed and silenced" by Wier, Tandler, Scot, Ady and Wagstaffe. But, while

reproducing their arguments, whether based on theology or
common-sense, he did more than they all, by bringing the
controversy into an atmosphere in which the superstition
could not live: the atmosphere of confidence in nature and
reverence for an immaterial God.   Now that Hakewill, Harvey,
Newton and Locke were teaching men to investigate and not
fear the mysteries of life, Webster insists that all evidence in
support of sorcery should be subjected to the same scientific
scrutiny.   Besides, what need was there to suspect the handi-
work of the devil in any miracle, when "Mr. Boyl" was able
to "manifest the great and wonderful virtues that God hath
endowed stones, minerals, plants and roots withal," when
Van Helmont had already proved that metals have even greater
healing power and Paracelsus had ascribed this power to God.
Now that natural laws were being discovered, Webster represents this God, not according to the old anthropomorphic ideas,
but as a transcendental spirit, who rules men through their
thoughts and wills.   Satan is merely one of the means of communication.   Hence, if there is a league between the devil
and a witch, it is "internal, mental and spiritual"; the league
which always exists between a malefactor and the spirit of
evil.   For Webster is the first to point out—what many of his
contemporaries must have felt—that the current theory of
witchcraft was utterly unworthy of the modern conception of
human nature.   Neurasthenics, whose imaginations have been
infected with stories of ghosts and goblins, may conceive
themselves to be the victims of all kinds of malpractices and
diseases.   But the devil only enslaves men by "their corrupt
wills and dispositions."

Webster's book by no means drove out superstition.   The
belief in necromancy, sortilege and magic exists at the present
time in cities as well as in rural districts and will always be
found wherever the great emotions of life[1] are wrought to a
higher pitch than the intellect.   But *The Displaying of supposed Witchcraft* marks the time when this error definitely
lost its hold on men's lower passions and on the sense of human
degradation.   The period of witch persecutions has universally
been regarded as the darkest blot on English civilisation and it
produced a literature no less dreary.   Witch treatises, with a

[1] Cf. Benson, R. H., *The Necromancers*, 1910.

few exceptions, are voluminous, rambling and ill-constructed
dissertations in which patristic dogmas and scholastic arguments are endlessly reiterated.   And yet one is almost tempted
to regard this controversy, together with the civil war pamphlets and the puritan tirades, as an inevitable phase in the
evolution of English modern thought.   Movements like the
renascence, which appeal chiefly to courtiers and scholars,
who, after all, are only the surface of a nation, can well be
inspired from foreign sources.   But when a whole people change
their attitude of mind, the impulse must come from within.
We have seen how social and political influences drove popular
writers to the most extravagant thoughts and utterances,
thereby creating an atmosphere in which great works cannot
thrive.   But, at the same time, it must be remembered that,
if informal literature ran to excess, it became, in this way,
a self-exposure, and startled the whole nation into an effort
towards higher civilisation.